All About the
GREYHOUND

All About the
GREYHOUND

ANNE ROLINS

RINGPRESS

New revised edition published by
Ringpress Books, 1991
By arrangement with Weldon Publishing
Sydney, Australia

First published 1982
Revised U.K. edition 1986
2nd revised U.K. edition 1988
3rd revised U.K. edition 1991
© Copyright 1982 Anne Rolins

ISBN 0 948955 12 0

All rights reserved
Typeset in Australia by Savage Type Pty Ltd, Brisbane
Printed in Singapore by Kyodo Printing Co (S'pore) Pte Ltd

Ringpress Books Ltd, Spirella House, Bridge Road,
Letchworth, Herts SG6 4ET
Tel: 0462 674177

CONTENTS

ACKNOWLEDGMENTS

The information included in this book is derived from a wide selection of text books, lecture notes, veterinary reports, research material, and from practical experience.

I am grateful to the following authors for providing information and articles: Mr Stefan Brasch for 'Complete Dry Foods'; Mr Noel Banks for 'Mechanics of Reproduction' and 'A Pearl of Great Price' from the *Australian Greyhound Stud Book* Vol. 24 1974–75; Mr Barry Ward for 'Problems Confronting the Introduction of AI into Australia' (previously printed in the *Victorian Greyhound Weekly*); and to the W. B. Saunders Company, Philadelphia and London, for permission to use *Dorland's Illustrated Medical Dictionary* — 24th edition, as a reference for the glossary. In addition, many individuals have offered constructive criticism and counsel.

The preparation of this book was assisted by the exchange of ideas and by discussion with those involved in the greyhound industry. To those people I am indebted for their helpfulness, viewpoints, and suggestions.

I would like to acknowledge my debt to Mr P. J. Thackeray, Product Manager of Pfizer-Agricare Pty Ltd, for making available to me detailed photographs of worm species and relevant literature.

My thanks to those who granted permission for reproduction of photographs and to those who supplied photographs for the book: Mr E. J. Monk, Group Publicity Manager of the G.R.A. Property Trust Limited (England), for the fine selection of photographs and accompanying information; the Gabba Greyhound Racing Club; the Melbourne Greyhound Racing Association; the Sandown Greyhound Racing Club; Mr R. Fraser, Racing Manager, Wembley Stadium Limited; the New South Wales Coursing Association Limited; Mr J. M. Fitzpatrick, Comdt., Secretary of the Irish Coursing Club; Mr Bill Bracht, author of *Greyhounds and Mechanical Lure Racing*; Mr W. Atkins; Mr J. Coleman; Mr B. Ward; Mr F. Schock; Mr A. Quinn; The *News*, Adelaide; Ariel Photographers, Victoria; Airviews Limited, Manchester Airport; and the *South Australian Greyhound Trainer.*

I am grateful also to Mr L. J. Corbett and Dr John Kohnke, B.V.Sc., R.D.A. of Medical Research Pty Ltd, for their valued assistance and the selection of notes made available.

A special word of thanks to Neil Rolins, my husband, for his viewpoints and assistance in the preparation of this book; Mrs L. P. Reed, in particular, and Miss G. Lohinsky, for their assistance with typing; and Mr R. L. Reed for his general guidance.

INTRODUCTION

It is the purpose of this book to provide a framework for knowledge in the owning, training, and breeding of greyhounds. This knowledge must be supplemented with a great deal of personal judgement. To many, this very reliance on personal ability renders greyhound racing a very rewarding business. One must implement organised knowledge and apply it in the light of realities to gain a desired result. Those who diagnose 'by the book' or attempt to train a greyhound by memorisation of principles are almost certain to overlook practical realities. Virtually all areas of knowledge have tremendous expanses of the unknown. The need for a clear concept of greyhound training and for a framework of related principles has been recognised for years. Use established guide lines to help solve problems without engaging in laborious research or risky trial and error.

Every effort has been made to avoid giving an impression that there is an established procedure by which perfect results can be obtained. This has been done to help foster a critical attitude on the part of the reader and to create an awareness that there are still many questions left unanswered. The knowledge presented in this book should render you more able to deal with problems that may confront you, to know when to seek the assistance of an expert, to be more able to define the greyhound's requirements, and to judge and utilise solutions. This, I believe, is a large part of what it takes to become a successful greyhound owner, trainer, or breeder.

In owning and training a racing greyhound the effect of a poor decision on the owner's or trainer's part is swift and sure. A hare pursued by a greyhound takes the wrong turn only once and likewise in greyhound training the cost of error may be high. In the world of greyhound racing poor decisions mean loss of competitive advantage and the measure of a trainer's worth lies in the quality of his decisions. It is of paramount importance to gather the facts and analyse them, to seek solutions, and to develop the solution that seems most likely to be successful. It seems to me that you can sometimes learn a good deal about a subject if you find out first what it is not. Then, after you have found out what it is not, you can understand more clearly what it is.

1

THE ORIGIN OF THE GREYHOUND

The Celtic greyhound, we are led to believe, is the earliest ancestor of what the antiquarian courser calls the 'long dogs'. The greyhound of early days stands at the head of a small class of *Canes celeres*, of which this individual seems to have been specially selected by the Celts for their sporting practices, and to the culture of which they must have directed a great deal of attention before they could have even laid the foundation for the vast change it was yet necessary to bring about, before they could rank with those alluded to by Arrian's translator when he observes: 'No *Canis venaticus* can be enrolled here who runs otherwise than on sight of his game — it is his characteristic property'. Flavius Arrianus, a Greek historian and philosopher with the pen-name of Arrian, was born in the year A.D. 96 and he composed the first known treatise on an individual genus of dog; he refers to it as the Celtic Hound.

The very designation of this dog has occasioned almost as much research as his origin, for the translator of Arrian says, 'The term "greyhound" has confounded English etymologists as much as that of "vertagus" has puzzled Latin commentators. It is variously spelt by our English writers: as "grehounde" by Juliana Berners, "a grehounde sholde be heeded lyke a snake"; "greihounde' by Chaucer, "greihoundes he hadde as swift as foul of flight". Lord Berners writes "grayhounde"; Junius, "graihound"; Gesner, "grewhound"; Harrington, "grewnd". The terms "grewhound", "grewnd", "graihound", "grayhound", "canis graecus", and "graius" all indicate a supposed connection with Greece. "Grew" is often used for "Greek" by Douglas and Lindsay.' Nevertheless, the translator of Arrian did not believe the genuine Celtic hound was known to ancient Greece, which opinion is in great measure confirmed by the silence of

The Celtic greyhound

Xenophon on the subject, who wrote so expressly on venation (hunting) generally. Other investigators would rather seek the origin of the English name in the predominant colour of the dog — grey, gray, grai, grei. The theory that 'grey' means 'dog' and 'hundr' means 'hunter' (greyhundr) supports the argument that the prefix is completely unrelated to the colour of the dog. The *International Encyclopedia of Dogs* puts forward the theory that the 'grey' is debased from 'gaze', which is descriptive of a dog which pursues its game by sight.

Mr Thacker, a courser of no mean celebrity, advocates in his work on coursing (vol. i, p. 74): 'In the succession of the ages, as this species of dog was distributed over different parts of the globe, where different languages prevailed, he was known by different names, characteristic of his manner of pursuing his game, and descriptive of his shape and qualities, as long-dog, field-dog, griphound, grighound (Anglo-Saxon derivation), grehound, and so forth.'

I more readily yield to the opinion of the learned Dr Caius, a sixteenth-century writer and physician to Queen Elizabeth, in his work *De Canibus Britannicus*: 'A gre quoque grehund apud nostros invenit nomen: quod praecipui gradus inter canis: gre enim apud nostros gradum denotat.' (The greyhound with us derives his name from gre, because he holds the chief rank among dogs, gre with us denoting rank.)

Obaldeston, a sporting author of respectability, supposed that 'It was the degree of superiority in this over all other dogs which, by suffering a curtailment, left him a grey hound.'

The early history of the greyhound has been supposed by many to point to Greece as the country in which he originated; others, with whom I agree, make him of Celtic origin. 'The greihounde of King Cranthlynth's dayes,' says Holinshed, 'was not fetched so far as out of Grecia, but rather bred in Scotland.' However, the translator of Arrian does not believe that either the English, Scottish, or Irish greyhounds are indigenous to Great Britain but rather that 'all our insular sorts originally sprang from the Celtic vertagus; the probability of which is supported by the history of the distribution to the Celts themselves, and the name under which the dogs were sent by Flavian to his brother Symmachus at Rome. May we not therefore conclude, the Irish and Scotch greyhounds to have been primarily derived from the Celtic

stock, accompanying these emigrants of Celtic Europe to Ireland, and thence to Scotland, in one or other of which territories they received the name of *Canes scotici*, from the English emigrants of Celtica who accompanied them? And may not the English greyhound, improved in speed by careful management and judicious breeding, as his master increased in civilisation and became more reclaimed, be derived through such intermediate links, from the same parent source?' The view here taken is certainly in perfect accordance with history and is also borne out by analogical facts.

The importance of the origin of the greyhound is great to the zealous patrons of the sport, to admirers, and to those who are interested in the origin of this elegant animal. One obstacle in the way of investigating the history of this dog has arisen from the different appellations given to it in accordance with the fancy of the natives in different parts of the country, of Irish wolf-dog, Irish greyhound, Highland deerhound, and Scotch greyhound. Mr Scrope, in his *Art of Deer Stalking*, has introduced some observations on the origin of the greyhound: 'Amongst the oldest Scotch authorities are some sculptured stones in the churchyard of Meigle, a village of Perthshire. These stones represent in relief the figures of several dogs, which bear so strong a resemblance to the Highland deerhound as to leave no doubt that they are intended to represent this species. The date of this sculpture is considered by antiquaries, and in particular by Chalmers, to have been previous to the introduction of Christianity, and as early at least as the ninth century.' The opinion of this intelligent author on the origin of the greyhound is very much in unison with my own opinion and also with that of authorities. The progressive improvement of this dog from the Celtic origin through the grades of Irish and Scotch strong greyhound to the elegant courser or long dog, seen in its highest form at our coursing meetings and in mechanical lure racing, closely tallies with conclusions formed and stated by investigators in years gone by.

The true *Canis leporarius*, or greyhound, was not cultivated as a distinct breed in Greece until after the time of the elder Xenophon. It is true, authorities of no mean note appear to have encouraged a belief in an earlier existence. Solomon, in his *Proverbs* (ch. xxx. v. 30) is thought to allude distinctly to the greyhound 'as one of the three things which go well', the lion and the he-goat making up the trio. However, authorities incline to the opinion of the learned Bochart, in his *Praefat. Ad Lictorem*, that the horse was much more probably the subject referred to.

'The earliest notices of the greyhound, it is probable, are those met with in the *Metamorphoses* of Ovid, i. 533, vii. 781, and in the *Poem on Hunting* of Gratius the Faliscan.' The work of Ovid (43 B.C. to A.D. 18), *Metamorphoses* (Transfigurations), is a poem of fifteen books and 12 000 lines related in approximate chronological order from the creation of the world to his own day. 'Slight mention of the canis gallicus and his coursings, is also to be found in the writings of Martial, Julius Pollux, and Oppian, as well as in the *Cynegeticon* of Nemesian, which appeared towards the close of the third century, where the form of the greyhound and the arts of breeding, rearing, and feeding of this dog are treated on somewhat at large'. 'The French,' says Turberville, 'use their greyhounds only to set back sets, or recoytes for deare, wolfe, foxe, or such like, whereas we here in England do make great account of such pastime, as is to be seen in coursing with greyhounds at deare, hare, foxe, or such like, even of themselves, when there are neyther hounds hunting nor other meane to help them.'

Coursing, according to our present conception of the term, with the true *Canis leporarius*, is seldom ever mentioned in their cynegetical works. The writings of Jacques du Fouilloux and Jean de Clamorgan, it is true, make mention of the greyhound, but it is employed only in chasing the wolf, fox, deer, and similar prey. A species of French coursing is noted by Turberville, and was probably derived from an ancient Celtic practice, which was to try for a hare while the company was standing apart with greyhounds, which were thus ready as the hare broke cover, on being slipped, to spring on it.

The greyhound cannot be considered as an original animal without upsetting our faith in

Super Rory, 1972 World Record Holder — 525 yards in 28·62 seconds

the uniformity of nature's proceedings. This breed is, without doubt, of great antiquity, but originated from sundry modifications effected by various means. As man diversified his own predacious habits, as well to gratify his love of change as his love of gain, so he attempted to apply his human powers judiciously over the animal frame, as we have seen in so many instances, and in none more than in the dog. Without doubt, man implemented his powers to his own purpose, as either fancy or necessity directed. Selections were made from those dogs which exhibited sufficient lightness of frame to enable them to compete with the deer, wild goat, fox, jackal, hare, etc., by coursing in sight, instead of employing numbers in a more lengthy pursuit by scent. Such an origin we may attribute to the first greyhound types, and I have mentioned how increased slenderness of form might be acquired, but attention is drawn to the fact that it was ultimately at the expense of the scenting powers. This change was not effected immediately; its gradations were consequently not marked, nor has history recorded the physical phenomena associated with it in order of their occurrence. Additional information has enabled moderns, by analogical reasoning, and by such faint gleams as penetrated the almost obscure early records, to satisfy themselves that the greyhound form is the effect of cultivation. There are, in fact, few alterations in size, figure, and the outer coverings of animals which man cannot vary at his bidding. Nothing in the frame is fixed but the number and general connection of the bones.

The Italian greyhound owes much of its diminished bulk to climatic influence, as well as to the judicious selection of parents, and to long-continued in-breeding, which appears to diminish the progeny. Scotland, on the contrary, a more northerly locality, has long been celebrated for its greyhounds which are large and wiry-coated. These are probably a genus of the early Celtic greyhounds, which, yielding to the influences of a colder climate than that from which they came, became coated with thick, wiry hair. In Ireland, where the climate was milder, the coat, although not altogether smooth, was less crisp and wiry. In both localities, there being at that period boars, wolves, and bears, powerful dogs were required. In England, these wild beasts were exterminated earlier and consequently the same type of dog was not kept there but by breeding was made finer in coat

and more slender in form. When the larger wild beasts afforded by the country disappeared, the greyhound was less required for his strength and more for his speed. He was bred somewhat finer and was much employed in fox coursing which, around 1901, was a favourite diversion. As the hare gradually became a prominent object of pursuit, the form of the greyhound became more slender so that speed might be increased.

The credit for having selectively bred the greyhound to increase his speed goes to the Arabs, who delighted in blood sport and the thrill of the chase. The greyhound figured prominently in the sport of these mounted people. The ability of the greyhound as a hunter for sport directed his future with the wealthy classes and he became their status symbol. An old Welsh proverb reads: 'You may know a gentleman by his horse, his hawk, and his greyhound'. From the eleventh to the fourteenth century the Laws provided that the greyhound be exclusively a dog of royalty and nobility and very much a symbol of class. Henry VIII declared that no nobleman's education was complete unless he was skilled in the art of raising and training greyhounds for coursing. Canute enacted a law in 1016 that 'no meane person may keep any greyhounds.' The value of the greyhound was in excess of that of a serf and the penalty for causing the death of a greyhound was the same as that for murder.

That the smooth-haired greyhound was held in great esteem through the ages is confirmed by the desire to eliminate the wiry, rough-coated hound by crossing with the smooth-coated hounds introduced in various parts of the world. During the middle of the eighteenth century Lord Orford, an eminent patron of coursing, directed his powers to the promotion and improvement of the sport; he particularly had in mind the improvement of the form and quality of the greyhound. Initially he crossed the greyhound with the lurcher, hoping to gain an accession of attention and teachableness. Secondly, he crossed the greyhound with the Italian greyhound in an attempt to increase the delicacy of the skin, lightness of the frame, and speed of motion. Lastly, by crossing with the bulldog, he reckoned on gaining a small ear, finely tapered tail, sleek coat, tremendous courage, and savage determination to kill. He continued this cross for seven generations, succeeded in the production of these favourable points, and ultimately possessed 'the best greyhounds ever known'. In addition, and also for the first time, the brindle-coated greyhound, which is now commonplace, appeared. From Lord Orford's bitch, Czarina, came the greatest coursing stock in Britain. The *Sportsman's Guide* says of Czarina: 'She won 47 matches without ever being beat.' In her thirteenth year she was put to Jupiter (belonging to Lord Orford) and included in this first litter was a dog called Claret. Claret's mating with a bitch belonging to Major Topham of the Wold Cottage, Yorkshire, produced three of the best greyhounds ever seen before or since—Snowball, Major, and Sylvia. All three won every match for which they ran. Snowball was a beautiful jet-black, while Major and Sylvia were brindled. 'Snowball won 10 large pieces of silver plate, and upwards of 40 matches, having never refused a challenge, though many of the most famous dogs in Great Britain were brought to run against him; and at length he challenged the whole world, but found no one to accept it.' Snowball stood at stud for a fee of 3 guineas per service. Sir Walter Scott immortalised the memory of this famous greyhound:

'T'was when fleet Snowball's head was
   waxen grey,
A luckless lev'ret met him on his way:
Who knows not Snowball? He whose raced
   renowned
Is still victorious on each coursing ground;
Swaffham, Newmarket, and the Roman
   camp,
Have seen them victors o'er each meaner
   stamp.
In vain the youngling sought with doubling
   wile
The hedge, the hill, the thicket, or the stile;

Experience sage the lack of speed supplied,
And in the gap he sought, the victim died.'

King Cob was another dog possessing the bulldog blood and he was the first dog whose services were made available to the public. King Cob bloodlines produced the famous Master McGrath, who won the English Waterloo Cup in 1868, 1869, and 1871. Master McGrath was owned by Lord Lurgan, who had much success with the dog as a puppy in Ireland. In 1868, when Lord Lurgan took Master McGrath to England for the Waterloo Cup, he was completely unknown over there. Master McGrath defeated the favourite, Brigade, and went on to win the final and become a public hero. In 1869 he repeated his triumph. In 1870 he was beaten by Lady Lyons. Master McGrath immortalised himself in 1871, when he won the Waterloo Cup for the third time, after which he was commanded to appear before Queen Victoria at Windsor Castle. The dog never again appeared in public and died of a heart disease two years later, having won thirty-six out of thirty-seven courses and stake money totalling £1750. In 1882, when Lord Lurgan died, a coursing critic who wrote under the pen-name of Sirius said that Lord Lurgan left behind 'a name which will continue imperishable in the modern annals of the leash, and the triumph of his renowned greyhound, Master McGrath, probably the most extraordinary performer ever slipped to a hare —and the most distinguished, too, since while Lord-in-Waiting, Lord Lurgan was commanded by the Queen to introduce Master McGrath at Court—will live in song and story so long as the sport shall continue to flourish.'

2
THE HISTORY OF COURSING

The term, coursing, is understood to denote a branch of hunting in which the dogs employed pursue their game by sight only, in contra-distinction to stag and fox hunting in which the scent of the chased animals enables the pursuers eventually to run them down. It is evident, therefore that the dogs employed in coursing must have sufficient speed to keep their fleetest game in view. The animals coursed by the ancients were of varying types, such as the wild ass, the stag, the mountain goat, the wolf, the jackal, the boar, the fox, and the hare, and consequently dogs of very different degrees of power, size, and hardiness were required. All of the dogs employed, however, had one common property—that of hunting by the scent the pursued animals left behind. The true coursing dogs, which hunt merely by sight, would have been useless in those times, because the abund-ance of wild beasts would have distracted the attention of unscenting dogs and dis-sighted them. Although the scenting dogs employed were of only moderate speed, they were able to rest by night and so suspend the chase, again pursuing their prey with certainty when morning came.

Coursing, like other sports, has its advocates and its enemies. It is not fit that we should all favour the same pursuit, but it is proper that we should not underrate the amusements followed by others. Many characters are zealous in the practice of coursing, yet it is difficult to open the eyes of many who as zealously pursue other sports, 'to the halo which brightens the feats of the long dogs'. This extract from Arrian exhibits the favourable character of coursing: 'For coursers, such at least as are true sportsmen, do not take their dogs out for the sake of catching a hare, but for the contest and sport of coursing, and are glad if the hare meets with an escape: if she fly to any thin brake for concealment, though they may see her trembling, and in the utmost distress, they will call off their dogs, and more

particularly so when they have run well. Often indeed, when following a course on horseback, have I come up to the hare as soon as caught, and myself saved her life: and then, having taken away my dog and fastened him up, allowed her to escape. And if I have arrived too late to save her, I have struck my head with sorrow, that the dogs had killed so good an antagonist.'

Among the innumerable lovers of coursing, Mr Barnard, of the Coursing Club of Malton, stood conspicuous. The *Stud Book*, for a time kept by Mr Goodlake, originated with Mr Barnard, a learned and accomplished gentleman. The *Greyhound Stud Book* was established in England in 1882.

The antiquity of the sport of coursing is great, and its notoriety has accompanied it to the present time. The concurrent testimonies of writers of great reputation have left us in possession of the opinions and practices of the coursing amateurs of many ages. The history of coursing is much indebted to a translation of Arrian by a scholar who preferred to conceal his name and was known only as a 'Graduate in Medicine'. The interesting and authentic infor-mation on the rise and progress of coursing which is presented in the work of this scholar is unrivalled in any other single work. To this man we are under great obligation for 'a cup of cups should be awarded to him whose pen has run a course which almost defies competition'.

The practice of coursing had attained a syste-matic form and was accurately described by Arrian, a Greek historian and philosopher born in the year A.D. 96, and whose celebrity as an author gained him the honourable title of 'the younger Xenophon'. The coursing of several animals with fleet dogs was practised before the time of Hadrian, and the Antonini. Nevertheless, it is conjectured with much probability, from the silence of the elder Xenophon concerning the subject, that hare coursing with the true

The Duke of Edinburgh and his greyhound, Playfield Leader, who races for the National Playing Field Charity *(Courtesy of G.R.A. Property Trust Limited)*

greyhound was not known or practised until after his time.

After the time of Arrian, history is almost barren on the subject of coursing as a sport. It is true that Gratian, the Faliscan, left an imperfect sketch on the subject, and Ovid also, in his *Metamorphoses*, describes a single-handed course, of which the translator of Arrian observes: 'as it is the first attempt of the kind by any classic author, so it is unrivalled in the accuracy of its technical phraseology and the beauty of its poetry'. The sports of the leash were noted by Martial, Julius Pollux, and Oppian, the celebrated Greek poet. Spelman informs us that during the time of Charlemagne

the court had officers of the greyhound kennel, who superintended the coursing practices. Nevertheless, many centuries passed by without any acknowledged manuscripts on the subject making an appearance, and there are only occasional allusions to the greyhound and his high repute as characterising the rank of his possessor.

About the middle of the fourteenth century Gaston Phoebus produced a composition, entitled *Des Deduitz de la Chasse de Bestes Sauvaiges et des Oyseaux de Proye*, which was followed in the latter part of that century by a composition of Edmund Duke of York, the fifth son of Edward III, entitled *The Mayster of*

Game. This work accurately described the dogs of the chase generally, but the greyhound was particularly referred to. 'With copius general descriptions of our ancient field sports, and animals obnoxious to the chase, *The Mayster of Game* unites specific delineations of the shape of each variety of *Canis venaticus*, employed by British sportsmen of past days, with occasional references to the chase practices of foreign countries.' Coursing is slightly touched on in the *Noble Art of Venerie* by Turberville and in the *Jewel for Gentrie* by Gascoigne, both of which appeared in the early part of the sixteenth century. Gervase Markham in his *Countrey Contentments* and *Countrey Farm* fully described the history and practice of coursing.

Lord Oxford founded the first coursing club, the Swaffham Club in Norfolk, in 1776. Membership was limited to twenty-six, the number of letters in the alphabet, the letter which each member chose being the initial of his dog's name. It was also necessary for each member to assume a colour.

The Ashdown Park Club was established by Lord Craven in 1780. The early prizes were silver collars, which were continued until the death of Lord Craven in 1792, when annual cups were substituted for collars.

The Malton Coursing Club, established in 1781, was limited to twenty members and a meeting was held twice in the season. Initially, silver cups were the prize contended for, next a goblet, and then a 50-guinea cup, which was run off in a class of sixteen dogs.

Louth Coursing Club originated in 1806, commencing with two annual meetings and then one meeting only took place on the third Monday in November.

The Newmarket Club met twice, instead of three times during the season, as formerly in the favourable months for the sport, of November and February. Both were open meetings which extended over three or four days. It was usual to slip a dog only once in a day—a practice induced primarily by the severity of the course.

Deptford Inn Coursing Club was established in 1819, and has always held a high rank in the coursing annals. The extreme care in preserving the game made the hares plentiful and the coursing ground was fine.

In 1825 the Altcar Club was formed by the Earl of Sefton and Viscount Molyneux. On the first day of the meeting the members congregated at the Waterloo Hotel, Liverpool, and eleven years later the proprietor, William Lynn, inaugurated an eight-dog stake which he called the Waterloo Cup. The English Waterloo Cup (established in 1836) is the premier coursing classic in the world. It is contested on the estate of Lord Sefton at Altcar and among the sixty-four dogs are entries from all parts of Scotland, England, and Ireland. The Cup is contested at the end of February or the beginning of March. The thirty-two dogs defeated in the first round contest the Waterloo Purse. Only those holding nominations are permitted to enter a dog for the Waterloo Cup and the greyhound must be registered with the National Coursing Club, which came into existence in 1858 as a result of the fact that by then the meeting had gained worldwide fame and the need for an organised body of national repute was apparent. In 1881 the N.C.C. decided that after 15 July 1883 all greyhounds contesting meetings in the British Isles should be registered with the club. A certificate was supplied by the N.C.C. at a fee of 5 shillings for naming a greyhound and entering it in the *Stud Book*. The certificate was signed by the breeder who was required to previously register the litter at a fee of 5 shillings. The markings of the greyhound were carefully noted. In 1894 the N.C.C. ruled that all litters were to be registered within two months of the date of whelping. Consequently, a complete record of every pedigree greyhound is kept.

The Irish Coursing Club was formed in 1916 when it was proposed that it should break away from the N.C.C., which had previously controlled coursing meetings in Ireland. T. Morris was elected as secretary of the I.C.C. on 13 September 1915.

As to the judging, points are awarded for six varying skills:
1. Speed. One to three points are awarded depending on the degree of superiority exhibited.
2. Go-by. Two or three points are awarded in cases where a dog begins a course a length behind his opponent, passes him, and gains a length lead.
3. The turn. One point is awarded when the hare is brought round at not less than a right angle from his former line.
4. The Wrench. Half a point is awarded when the hare is turned from her line at less than a right angle.
5. The Kill. Two points or less are awarded, depending on the skill displayed.

6. The Trip. One point is awarded where the hare is flung off her legs but nevertheless escapes.

The greyhound which earns the maximum number of points is the winner. The programme for small, one-day events is usually made up of eight or sixteen-dog stakes, while thirty-two and sixty-four-dog stakes are contested at national events extending over two or three days.

There are few counties in England that cannot boast of a coursing club. There are many clubs in Scotland, and they are on the increase in Ireland. Open meetings have been established everywhere both for produce stakes, for which puppies are entered at the conclusion of the previous season, and for stakes, for which dogs of all ages are entered the day prior to the running. The stewards of coursing meetings advertise under whose rules the meetings will be conducted, a practice which has eliminated difficulties.

Coursing rules are very important, both to the practice of the sport and to the harmony which should exist between members of coursing clubs. Coursing was extremely popular during the reign of Queen Elizabeth I, who personally patronised it and further increased its celebrity by bringing about a more complete organisation of the sport by means of a system of laws and regulations. The Duke of Norfolk, himself a zealous courser, compiled these regulations so judiciously that, with very few minor alterations, they have continued to guide the coursing practices of the present day. The Duke of Norfolk's coursing rules were amended by Mr Thacker and are considered to be very judiciously framed. Many coursing meetings were guided by them and they eventually superseded all others. The new laws of coursing were drawn up and agreed upon at a meeting of noblemen and members of established clubs in England and Scotland, held at the Thatched House Tavern in St James Street on Saturday, 3 June 1838; the Earl of Stradbroke was chairman. These laws were intended to be the basis of a uniform code of laws for general adoption in all coursing societies. No two courses being exactly alike, it was wondered whether the new rules would be satisfactory. It was decided that the appointment of a judge who enjoyed public confidence was the best means of affording general satisfaction.

The early English and Irish settlers introduced the first greyhounds to America. In 1878 the sport of live-hare coursing began in Kansas and, a short time afterwards, in other mid-western States. In 1896, at Abilene, the National Coursing Association of America was established. This was the controlling body of all coursing in the mid-western U.S.A. The American Waterloo Cup, Waterloo Purse, and Waterloo Plate commenced in 1886 and are classic coursing events which have continued to the present day.

On 28 April 1770 the first greyhound was landed in Australia at Botany Bay. One bitch and one dog were among the 'baggage' of botanist Joseph Banks, who sailed from England with Captain James Cook aboard the *Endeavour*. Authorities have presumed that Banks, a lover of fresh game, was totally aware of the hunting ability of the greyhound. Governor Phillip brought greyhounds with him when he and the first immigrants came to colonise Australia in 1778. The greyhound was presumably instrumental in supplying fresh game for the pioneers. Because the main game was wallaby and kangaroo, the greyhound became known as the 'kangaroo dog'.

The first coursing meeting planned by a group of sportsmen took place at Naracoorte in South Australia in 1867. The wallaby was used as a lure. The Naracoorte Coursing Club was officially established in 1868. The first Waterloo Cup of 1868 was a sixteen-dog stake which was won by Jason, owned by Henry Jones, a hardworking cattleman who became very prosperous on account of the huge prices paid by miners for his cattle when the Victorian Gold Rush commenced. Sir James Fergusson, the governor, attended the 1870 Waterloo Cup meeting at Naracoorte. Naracoorte became the principal coursing centre of the colony and people came from far and wide to attend the meetings.

In 1873 the first public coursing meeting was held at Sunbury by the Victorian Coursing Club. Live hares imported from England were used as lures. Generally speaking, the grounds used in early Victorian days were very different from the smooth downs of the English countryside. Many English authorities were of the opinion that the hare had a definite advantage, owing to the conditions of the ground. In Australia, meetings were conducted under conditions which would call for postponement in England. Many good dogs were eliminated, seriously maimed, or even killed as a consequence of coursing over flint-hard ground under appalling conditions. On some occasions the dogs were so cold that they could hardly move as they coursed amid the rain, hail, and snow, and on other occasions they would suffer from sunstroke or die from sheer exhaustion. It took an exceptional dog to score a kill, as shown by the fact that in 1879 no kills were recorded in the final of the Waterloo Cup, Waterloo Plate, or Waterloo Purse. Many dogs ran themselves to death behind the hardy, game Australian hares. In some of the rough country it was stated that the odds were 1000 to 1 on the hare escaping.

The first public coursing meeting using live hares was held on W. J. Clarke's Sunbury estate in Victoria in 1873. It was the first meeting in Australia to be conducted under National Coursing rules. Sir George Bowen, the Governor of Victoria, was the club's patron. Mr Clarke was the president of a committee composed of members of Parliament, doctors, lawyers, merchants, and squatters. The National Coursing Club of Victoria adopted the rules of the National Coursing Club of England and the first official judge at the Sunbury meeting was Mr R. Tattersall. He was succeeded by Mr Warwick. In 1875, Mr F. Gardner was brought out from England to replace Mr Warwick, at a fee of £300 plus £50 towards his expenses for the season. Mr Gardner was described as 'one of the youngest and the best of our judges'.

The treatment of judges by coursers was atrocious and the insults and abuse eventually caused the V.C.C. to allow the choice of the judge to be by election by the owners of nominated dogs. There had been many disgraceful exhibitions of bad temper and there was a complete lack of the true sporting spirit among the coursers.

Coursing generally, and in particular the Waterloo Cup, became extremely popular in Victoria, as shown by the tremendous increase in prize money for the Waterloo Cup—in 1873 the winner received £130 pounds; £250 in 1874; £500 in 1875. By 1875 numerous clubs had been formed throughout Victoria at places such as Ballarat, Ararat, Kilmore, Melton, Kyneton, Maryborough, Wyndham, Beaufort, Stawell, Echuca, and Carisbrook, to name a few.

The first public coursing meeting in New South Wales was held at Bathurst in 1876. Mr Gardner was the founder of the New South Wales Coursing Club. There was extreme jealousy between Victoria and New South Wales, and this only served to cause the introduction of coursing to New South Wales to be

Influential Australian sire, Benjamin John (Take A Bow–Rebel Wayne), winner of 1969 Australian Cup and Hobart Thousand. Take A Bow won 1962 Australian Cup *(Courtesy of South Australian Greyhound Trainer)*

received with all the more enthusiasm. Mr Edward Lee was President of the New South Wales Coursing Club and it was at Leeholme, the home of the Lee family, that the club held its meetings for the first five years. Sir Hercules Robinson, the Governor, became Patron of the New South Wales Coursing Club. By May 1876 Mr A. H. Gardner had become secretary and he proved to be the most energetic and conscientious force behind the club, so much so that he became known as 'the father of coursing in New South Wales'.

Because of some of the under-handed machinations of coursers in Victoria, the New South Wales club saw fit to require nominators for the Bathurst meeting to supply the name, colour, and pedigree of their entries and also to disclose whether the dog had ever raced under another name.

The first New South Wales Waterloo Cup

was conducted at Woodstock Estate, at Rooty Hill, in 1881. This site was founded because it was close to Sydney, Bathurst being too great a distance from the metropolitan area. Walter Lamb pioneered open coursing in the Sydney metropolitan area, an extremely costly operation. Mr Lamb directed all his efforts toward the establishment of coursing for the benefit of the public. He had workmen clear and fence 485 hectares of land at Woodstock Estate, the entire estate comprising 2000 hectares. The denseness of the forest at the perimeter of the fences affords evidence of the work accomplished in the preparation of this enclosure. Mr Lamb also had 10-hectare breeding paddocks set aside to house hares which he brought from Melbourne. No expense was spared and Mr Lamb did everything in his power to render coursing popular.

Queensland held its first organised coursing meeting at Warwick in September 1901. Since the organisers had not found a wealthy patron to direct efforts towards importing hares and fencing paddocks, they used wallabies as lures. The first Queensland Waterloo Cup was held at Pittsworth in 1901.

New Zealand held its first Waterloo Cup in 1878.

On 1 November 1937, the Australian and New Zealand Greyhound Association was inaugurated to control the swiftly growing sport. The Australian Register of Names of Greyhounds was begun in 1939, and 1940 saw the publication of the first edition of the *Australian Greyhound Stud Book*.

The Tasmanian Coursing Club held its first organised coursing meeting at Quamby Estate, Hagley, near Launceston, in 1878. The Tasmanian Waterloo Cup was conducted at Quamby Estate, which remained the principal site of open coursing in Tasmania.

Coursing became the fastest growing sport in the colonies and ranked third only to racing and cricket.

Mr Lamb was responsible for the establishment of the first Plumpton in Australia. 'Plumpton' was the name of a small town in Essex, England, where coursers came up with the revolutionary idea of restricting the size of the competition paddock by fencing it in and so conducting 'artificial coursing' in an enclosure. The hares were trained to become familiar with the artificial escape hatches which served the dual purpose of retaining them for future courses and protecting the greyhounds from overexertion. Spectators could now view the entire course from one locality, the supply of hares was assured, and the courses became of reasonably constant length. The Plumpton was well supported.

In Australia, Mr Lamb followed along the lines of Mr Case's original enclosure at Plumpton which was fabricated in 1862 on Case's farm, later purchased by a public company for £60 000. Rooty Hill Woodstock estate was the site of Mr Lamb's Plumpton. A Plumpton was later established by the V.C.C. at Sunbury estate. From then on, at greyhound sales or auctions it was disclosed whether a dog would be best suited for 'open' or 'enclosed' coursing meetings. Greyhounds were bred more for speed, as this was the major requirement for enclosed coursing. A great deal of attention was directed toward breeding.

Plumpton, being the first human-devised control of coursing, was a change of paramount importance, as it eventually led to the introduction of mechanical lure racing as we know it today. The decline of coursing in English-speaking countries is primarily attributable to the introduction of mechanical lure racing, which gained overwhelming popularity. Today, live-hare coursing in Australia is conducted only in South Australia, while in England, Swaffham and Altcar are the only clubs still in existence. In the U.S.A. it is conducted on a limited scale in Kansas and Texas.

3

MECHANICAL LURE RACING

AUSTRALIA

Mechanical lure racing in Australia was pioneered by an American, 'Judge' Frederick Swindell, who arrived in Australia early in 1927. He incorporated a company, The Greyhound Coursing Association, and obtained a lease from the New South Wales Trotting Club, permitting the construction of a mechanical lure circuit on the inside of the trotting track at Epping Racecourse at Glebe, which is now known as Harold Park.

The first registered meeting was conducted on Saturday, 28 May 1927, with betting by bookmakers being a feature. Meetings commenced at a second track at Shepherds Bush, Mascot, in November 1927. December 1927 saw a change of government, which prohibited betting after 6 p.m., and when the tracks altered to afternoon racing, betting on mechanical lure racing was made illegal. Following a further change of government in New South Wales, a bill was passed in 1931 which legalised mechanical lure racing at night with accompanying betting. The Bill permitted two licences within a 64-kilometre radius of the Sydney G.P.O., but a licence was issued only to the Harold Park track. This incident led to a Royal Commission on Greyhound Racing which retracted proprietory control of the sport and a licence was granted to the New South Wales Trotting Club to hold non-proprietory race meetings at Harold Park; approximately twenty years elapsing before the licence was returned to greyhound interests. The licence for the Mascot track was not renewed because the company was going into liquidation.

In 1934 the New South Wales National Coursing Association formulated a code of racing rules which was very much opposed to the code of rules of the Trotting Club. It was eventually accepted that the N.C.A. would be the controlling body in the sport because it held the Register.

A licence for mechanical lure racing at Wentworth Park, which is government owned, was granted to the New South Wales N.C.A. in 1939.

The New South Wales Greyhound Breeders Owners and Trainers Association (G.B.O.T.A.) was formed in 1939 and, following the legalisation of night trotting with betting, the greyhound racing licence for Harold Park was handed over to the G.B.O.T.A., this body renting the facilities for greyhound racing from the Trotting Club.

As a consequence of army activities at Wentworth Park during the second World War, the N.C.A. conducted its meetings at Harold Park. Following the war, Wentworth Park, which initially started with an outside lure, was converted to an inside lure on 26 December 1948, the race distances being 580 yards (530 metres) and 790 yards (722 metres). In 1948 the loam surface of the Harold Park track was converted to grass, the race distances being 500 yards (457 metres) and 800 yards (732 metres).

I have put forward New South Wales as an example of the manner in which greyhound racing is controlled in Australia, and although there are some variations from State to State, the general principles are common to greyhound racing throughout Australia.

The New South Wales Government, by an Act of Parliament (Gaming and Betting Act, 1912) has established laws which control the licencing of greyhound tracks, etc., and has in fact established a Greyhound Racing Control Board which has its offices at 18 Bridge Street, Lidcombe, and its policies are implemented by a full-time staff. The G.R.C.B. has the authority to control and regulate greyhound racing in accordance with the Act. Each club must be registered with the Board before it is permitted to race. The actual promotion of racing is in the hands of forty-three individual clubs which hold licences to conduct greyhound racing in New South Wales. Subject to them complying with the rules and the conditions of the licence, they may promote greyhound racing as they see fit.

All pure-bred greyhounds are registered with the N.C.A. and are therefore eligible to race or to be used for breeding purposes; the owner of any greyhound would not necessarily be registered with the G.R.C.B. until he wished to name the greyhound and then race the greyhound. The N.C.A. registers the animal and is the sole registrar of greyhounds in New South Wales according to the Gaming and Betting Act No. 25, 1912 which advises in detail the manner by which the G.R.C.B. is comprised and re-elected.

A publication entitled 'Club Rules for Greyhound Racing approved by the Greyhound Racing Control Board of New South Wales' advises of the rules under which all registered persons and clubs are bound. In addition to these rules which related to clubs, there are also Board Rules governing the control and regulations of greyhound racing in New South Wales.

The following is a list of the controlling bodies for greyhound racing in each state of Australia.

South Australian Dog Racing
Control Board   (08) 51 2337
Aston House, 17 Leigh Street,   (08) 211 8084
   Adelaide, South Australia 5000
National Coursing Association of Victoria (03) 26 4519
Racing Industry Centre, Third Floor,   (03) 26 1662
   1 Queen's Road, Melbourne, Vic. 3004
Greyhound Racing Control Board of Victoria
As above
National Coursing Club of Tasmania   (003) 31 2857
PO Box 399, Launceston, Tasmania 7250
Greyhound Racing Control Board of
Western Australia   (09) 325 7588
MVIT Building, Fifth Floor,   (09) 325 7737
   255 Adelaide Terrace, Perth,
   Western Australia 6000   (09) 325 7736
Greyhound Racing Control Board
of Queensland   (07) 391 7822
PO Box 179, East Brisbane, Queensland 4169
Darwin Greyhound Racing Association
PO Box 39645 Winnellie,
   Northern Territory 5789
Greyhound Racing Control Board of
New South Wales   (02) 646 3933
PO Box 138, Lidcombe,
   New South Wales 2141
New South Wales National Coursing
Association   (02) 819 7664
PO Box 30, Rozelle,   (02) 819 7622
   New South Wales 2039   (02) 819 7592
                                                       (02) 819 7373

AMERICA

The mechanical lure was first demonstrated by Owen Patrick Smith at Hot Springs, South Dakota, in 1905. The first successful meeting was conducted at Salt Lake City, Utah, in 1906, following which other tracks opened at Tuscon, Arizona, in 1909, and at Houston, Texas, in 1912. Smith and Sawyer unsuccessfully introduced mechanical lure racing at Emeryville, California, in 1919. In 1921, daytime racing was introduced in Chicago, Illinois, but protests from employers against absenteeism and from supporters of horse racing, led to the introduction of night racing. Smith's company presented greyhound racing as a subservant to horse racing in Hialeah, Florida, and the first Miami Greyhound Derby was contested in March 1922. Since 1925, when night racing commenced, greyhound racing has flourished as an exciting spectator sport and gambling medium. Many tracks were established in rapid succession — St Petersburg Kennel Club in 1925, Biscayne Club in 1925, Sanford-Orlando Kennel Club in 1927, and West Flagler Kennel Club in 1930. The West Flagler Kennel Club track is situated near Miami International Airport. It has a loam surface and races are conducted over 550 yards (503 metres), 647 yards (592 metres), and 770 yards (704 metres). Flagler's International Classic is the world's richest greyhound race and consists of seven preliminary races leading up to the final.

All greyhound tracks in U.S.A. are privately owned and are registered as either kennel clubs or greyhound parks conducted as proprietary business ventures. Public educating establishments do not exist, although there are places available where trainers may educate their dogs. These places are comprised of a small and a large circular track and a straight track, all of which have loam surfaces.

A kennel must have at least twice the number of dogs in work than it has contracted to race in order to ensure that it can meet its contract requirements in the event of injury to dogs. The racing seasons for each track are allocated by the Florida State Racing Commission, some tracks being unsuitable in winter.

Generally speaking, mechanical lure racing in the U.S.A. comes under the control of State Racing Commissions and public interest is of paramount importance, supervision extremely rigorous, and penalties severe. State Racing Commission officials have access to the records of track licencees and it is their obligation to report laxity or negligence on the part of the tracks to the Commission. Representatives appointed by the Commission possess the power to grant or revoke licences and also have access to all sections of the track. Greyhounds are maintained in the custody of Commission officials two hours prior to the race program and they are then locked in kennels until being paraded before the race. After the race they are returned to their owners. Frequent testing is undertaken to guard against attempts to stimulate or depress greyhounds. Following kennelling the dogs are under the control of the track and are handled by employees of the kennel club. Thirty minutes prior to the commencement of each race the dogs are transferred to kennel handlers who parade the dogs in an enclosure and no handler has prior knowledge of which dog he will handle or what race he will be involved in.

There is a 20-minute interval between races, during which the dogs are paraded for public inspection. Generally speaking, the dogs stand behind the boxes for 10 minutes prior to being boxed to ensure that the public has ample time to back them. All betting is conducted through the totalisator, a unit being $2.00, and there are no course bookmakers. Dogs remain in the boxes for three minutes before the lure is started, at which moment the track lights are switched on full and other course lighting is dimmed.

Prize money paid each week is approximately four per cent of the turnover for the week and is calculated in accordance with the grade of the race. Approximately fifty per cent is allotted to the winner; thirty-five per cent to second; ten per cent to third; and five per cent to fourth. Average prize money is not as high as at Wentworth Park and Harold Park in New South Wales, Australia.

Mechanical lure racing is conducted on thirty-four tracks located in the following states.

Arizona	5	Massachusetts	3
Arkansas	1	Montana	1
Colorado	4	Oregon	1
Florida	17	South Dakota	2

All tracks in the U.S.A. have a sand/loam surface, because seasonal meetings are conducted at least six times a week, generally with a twelve-race program. Race times are not thought to be as important as we in Australia consider them to be, because the tracks vary daily in accordance with watering and general

conditions. The lure is on an extended arm and comprises one or two rabbits and is at least 60 centimetres above the ground. Two electric motors power the carriage and each motor is capable of driving the carriage at the required speed in the event that one motor should fail. This type of lure is known as the Aldritt bunny, the electric power being supplied from a power rail and an earth rail beneath the carriage rails.

The majority of tracks in the U.S.A. conduct eight-dog races, but in Denver, Colorado, Portland and Oregon, there are nine runners in each race. The racing colours are as follows.

Trap 1.   Red with a white numeral
Trap 2.   Blue with a white numeral
Trap 3.   White with a red numeral
Trap 4.   Green with a white numeral
Trap 5.   Black with a red numeral
Trap 6.   Yellow with a blue numeral
Trap 7.   Green with a white and red numeral
Trap 8.   Black and yellow vertical strips with a white numeral
Trap 9.   Purple with a white 'X'

The muzzle, not the dog's nose, determines the finish at the line.

In the U.S.A. all greyhounds are classified at the commencement of each season, in accordance with their race record and schooling races, into eight varying grades—AA, A, B, C, D, E, F, and G. The race cards exhibit the grade of each race contested and indicate the position in each race. Some tracks have made their own modifications, but it is accepted practice that a greyhound graduates one grade when he wins his first race. If the dog runs worse than third on two consecutive occasions or worse than second three times in succession, he is down-graded. If the dog wins two consecutive races he is maintained in his grade for a minimum of three additional races.

American clubs are loath to waste good betting time allowing feature race winners to be exhibited to the public, although their presentations are spectacular. Any big race final is listed as the last race so that betting is not curtailed and the club is not deprived of the all-important dollar. The mighty dollar, however, does provide the American public with breathtaking amenities at all tracks, and these are far superior to anything in Australia. There are no struggling owners in America, because the system renders it impossible for them to exist and, generally speaking, owners are wealthy people who have made their money in some other field and have gone in for greyhound racing as a hobby or tax deduction.

The West Flagler Kennel Club, established in 1930 and capable of accommodating 17 000 spectators, is referred to as 'Fabulous Flagler' because of its magnificent amenities and spectacular presentations, in addition to the fact that the richest greyhound race in the world is conducted there. The Biscayne track, established in 1926, boasts an ultra-modern track with a loam surface of 495 yards (452 metres) and two straights of 117 yards (107 metres) and turns each of approximately 130 yards (119 metres) in periphery. The majority of races are conducted over distances of 605 and 862 yards (553 and 788 metres) but occasionally sprint races are contested over 330 and 550 yards (301 and 503 metres) in which instances the lure starts from in front of the starting boxes instead of coming from behind the boxes. The track is 6 metres wide. The photo-finish film is marked so that every dog's time and distance from the winner is known. The ever-increasing appeal of the sport has made greyhound racing one of the major sporting spectacles of the U.S.A.

MEXICO

While Flagler is America's number one track, the Juarez track in Mexico is perhaps the most beautiful in North America. The Juarez Greyhound Club is situated about 8 kilometres over the border from El Paso, Texas, and was established in 1964. The track has a loam surface and affords interference-free racing over distances of 550, 680, and 770 yards (503, 622, and 704 metres). Juarez is both a horse-racing and a greyhound-racing track. The dog track is on the outside and where it crosses the horse track it is equipped with a unique system which allows the dog track to swing to the inside when the horses are racing, from January to March; the outside rail acts as the inside rail for the horse track and is repositioned for the dog racing at night. The spectacular building with its imposing architecture is completely enclosed, with glass on the track side; it has airconditioning, bars, restaurants, closed-circuit television, refined decoration, and totalisator and dining facilities. A golf course and artificial lake are located within the track grounds. There are no shadows on the track and no posts to obstruct the view of spectators. Mercury oxide lighting has obviated the need for overhead lights. Com-

prehensive race books are available in English and Mexican. A minimum of one hurdle race is conducted at each meeting and a total of twelve races are run on a program. The track has an inside lure and the mode of racing conforms to the standard American procedure. The greyhounds under contract are kennelled and trained on the club grounds and only twelve kennels have contracts with the club. Prize money is low as a result of the poor economy. All dogs are from American kennels, because the breeding and ownership of greyhounds is discouraged in Mexico. All betting is conducted through the totalisator, and from the money wagered seventy-six per cent is returned to the punters, four per cent goes to the government, and twenty per cent to the track from which three per cent is allocated as prize money. Of this three per cent, sixty per cent goes to the winner, thirty per cent to second, and ten per cent to third-place getters.

The Caliente track, located at Tijuana, is also a combined horse racing and greyhound racing track. The same organisation owns both of the Mexican greyhound clubs, proprietary racing for profit being conducted by the track owners. The clubs permit wagering on the major tracks throughout America and Mexico via bookmakers.

BRITAIN

Mechanical lure racing was first conducted in Britain at the Welsh Harp, Hendon, in 1876. A race between two greyhounds pursuing a dummy hare was one of the spectacles at a sporting show, the event being conducted on a 400 yard (365 metre) straight grass track. The artificial hare was mounted on an apparatus which ran in a groove extending the entire length of the track. The apparatus was moved along by a windlass. The first race implementing the mechanical lure was won by Charming Nell, owned by Edward Dent, breeder of the famous Fullerton. This new sport was soon forgotten, perhaps because it was conducted over a straight course and did not compare with the excitement and interest of coursing. In fact, the majority of coursing enthusiasts regarded it as something of a joke.

The shrewd minds of the American entertainment industry visualised the enormous potential of night racing as a lavish spectacle, with all the colour and excitement of show business, as an entertainment in its own right. The sport

Ballinska Band (Lively Band–Certral), equalled Glen Rock's track record of 29·16 seconds in 1977 after missing the start, stamping him as one of the finest English Derby winners of the past decade *(Courtesy of G.R.A. Property Trust Limited)*

Westmead Champ (Westmead County–Hacksaw), 1976 St Leger and Gold Collar classics winner and 1976 Joint Greyhound of the Year with Mutt's Silver *(Courtesy of G.R.A. Property Trust Limited)*

Mutt's Silver (The Grand Silver–Simple Pride). 1976 Spiller's English Derby winner and 1976 Joint Greyhound of the Year with Westmead Champ *(Courtesy of G.R.A. Property Trust Limited)*

attained tremendous popularity in Florida and its success prompted promotion of the sport in other states.

Interested parties in England were attracted to this new sport and they approached Major L. Lyne Dixon who, along with Charles Munn (an American), Sir William Gentle, and Brigadier-General Critchley, pooled some capital, in addition to obtaining a bank loan, and formed The Greyhound Racing Association Limited, which had its headquarters at Manchester. It was agreed to fabricate a track on Sir William Gentle's land at Belle Vue, Manchester. The track was constructed according to the specifications of Owen Patrick Smith's track at Hialeah, Miami, and it was hoped that the leading coursing clubs would support the new sport and supply dogs to participate at the meeting. As a consequence of lack of support, the Association was forced to purchase dogs in order to fulfil requirements for the meeting. On 24 July 1926, the first meeting was conducted before a crowd of 1700. The programme comprised six races – three races over 440 yards (402 metres), two over 550 yards (503 metres),

and a hurdle race over 440 yards (402 metres). The first greyhound race in Britain was won by a dog named Mistley. Attendances increased markedly and, by October 1926, the average size of the crowd at the meetings had reached 11 000. In April 1927 a track was opened at Liverpool, in June a track was opened at White City, London, and later that year tracks were opened at Wembley and Harringay. Total attendance at all tracks for 1927 was estimated at in excess of 5 million and by 1932 the attendances had exceeded 20 million. The sport enjoyed much popularity, primarily because spectators could gather round the oval circuit, with the dogs always remaining in view. Today there are in excess of 100 tracks in Britain, the principle track being Wimbledon, London.

With the tremendous popularity of the sport came many problems, such as the use of ringers and dope, and numerous other malpractices that blackened the reputation of the sport. The resourcefulness of those in search of easy money was beyond the wildest imagination. Prior to the race menthol crystals were administered to dogs and consequently, after a smart beginning, the dogs would gradually have their wind cut, giving the impression that they had broken down. Stones, chewing gum, and rubber bands were some of the items placed between a dog's toes to render sufficient discomfort to slow down the dog several lengths, thus making the animal eligible for lower-grade events. Beauty specialists were employed to dye and/or remove specific hairs from the coat of ring-ins. A wide range of drugs was utilised and baits were thrown into kennels. Even some of the officials were involved in dishonest practices and there was clearly a need for an authoritative controlling body. In 1928 The National Greyhound Racing Society and the National Greyhound Racing Club were formed with a view to protecting public interest, eliminating malpractices, and promoting the sport. The National Greyhound Racing Society of Great Britain Limited, a federation of companies owning racecourses licenced by The National Greyhound Racing Club, acted through a body of public stewards with no financial involvement in the management of greyhound racing. The National Greyhound Racing Club was responsible for the general conduct of racing and, in 1928, it fabricated a code of rules which are basically those in force today.

In 1972 The National Greyhound Racing Society and The National Greyhound Racing Club were replaced by the The National Greyhound Racing Club Limited which is composed of the following:

1. General Committee
The General Committee controls club finances, appoints senior officials, and receives annual reports from the Racing, Policy, and Liaison Committees, and oversees general policy.

2. Racing Committee
The Racing Committee is a racing control body exercising complete supervision of racing matters at all licenced tracks.

3. Policy Committee
The Policy Committee is a negotiating body with the Goverment, bookmakers, the Press, television, etc. This committee exercises authority in all non-racing business matters.

4. Liaison Committee
The Liaison Committee is a body whose business is to submit recommendations from other parties, such as the owners, trainers, and breeders, to the Racing and Policy Committees, and to handle problems affecting the sport.

There are in excess of sixty tracks operating independently of the National Greyhound Racing Club Limited, some of which are on a par with the major NGRC tracks both in the level of security and in public amenities. The major difference is that greyhounds at independent tracks do not run in their stud book names. In the early days individual ownership was eliminated at some NGRC tracks because the tight closed kennel system provided that all greyhounds in the kennels were the property of the track. The idea of buying greyhounds and leasing them to the track patrons who were responsible for them met with much popularity because it maintained the right of individual ownership.

Some tracks still own many of the greyhounds but nowadays most are owned by individuals, companies or by syndicates. Because the closed kennel system was viewed as an exclusive instrument of authority, major modifications were applied and a C Licence system was introduced to allow the training of greyhounds in family ownership.

The success of this system led to the dispersed or contract system under which a private trainer agrees to provide racing greyhounds for a track. The trainer was under contract to the track to supply a specific number of dogs for each meeting. To allow an individual to own and train his own greyhound, owner-trainer and permit licences have been introduced. A permit licence holder can keep his dog at home and still race at an NGRC approved permit track even though his kennelling facilities may not reach the high standard required for the private, professional trainers or owner-trainers.

White City Stadium was constructed for the 1908 Olympic Games and received its name from the brightness of the building. The track became the mecca of the greyhound racing world since the opening night on 20 June 1927, when Charlie Cranston won the first race before a crowd of 100 000 enthusiasts. The Greyhound Derby was contested for the first time at White City in 1927 over 500 yards (457m) and the event was won by Entry Badge, owned by Edwin Baxter. In 1928 the event was contested over 525 yards (480m) as this distance had been accepted as standard by the majority of tracks. Later it was extended to 500m.

Derby Results 1927–1987 (not run 1941–1944)

Year	Winner	Time (seconds)	
1927	Entry Badge	29·01	(500 yards/457 metres)
1928	Boher Ash	30·48	(525 yards/480 metres)
1929	Mick The Miller	29·96	
1930	Mick The Miller	30·24	
1931	Seldom Led	30·04	
1932	Wild Woolley	29·72	
1933	Future Cutlet	29·80	
1934	Davesland	29·81	
1935	Greta Ranee	30·18	
1936	Fine Jubilee	29·48	
1937	Wattle Bark	29·26	(National record, hand-timed)
1938	Lone Keel	29·62	
1939	Highland Rum	29·35	
1940	G. R. Archduke	29·66	(Record–Run at Harringay Stadium)
1945	Ballyhennessy Seal	29·56	
1946	Monday's News	29·24	(Final record)
1947	Trev's Perfection	28·95	(Final record)
1948	Priceless Border	28·78	(Final record)
1949	Narrogar Ann	28·95	
1950	Ballymác Ball	28·72	(Final record)
1951	Ballylanigan Tanist	28·62	(Final record)
1952	Endless Gossip	28·50	(Final record)
1953	Daw's Dancer	29·20	(Photo time)
1954	Paul's Fun	28·84	
1955	Rushton Mac	28·97	
1956	Dunmore King	29·22	
1957	Ford Spartan	28·84	
1958	Pigalle Wonder	28·65	(Photo-timing record, Derby Final)
1959	Mile Bush Pride	28·76	
1960	Duleek Dandy	29·15	
1961	Palm's Printer	28·84	
1962	The Grand Canal	29·09	
1963	Lucky Boy Boy	29·00	
1964	Hack Up Chieftain	28·92	
1965	Chittering Clapton	28·82	
1966	Faithful Hope	28·52	(Photo-timing record, Derby Final)

Above: White City Stadium, England *(Courtesy of G.R.A. Property Trust Limited). Below:* White City Stadium on Derby-Final night *(Courtesy of G.R.A. Property Trust Limited)*

1967	Tric-Trac	29·00	
1968	Camira Flash	28·89	
1969	Sand Star	28·76	
1970	John Silver	29·01	
1971	Dolores Rocket	28·74	
1972	Patricia's Hope	28·55	
1973	Patricia's Hope	28·66	
1974	Jimson	29·76	
1975	Tartan Khan	29·57	
1976	Mutts Silver	29·38	
1977	Balliniska Band	29·16	(Equalled 500 metre White City track record held by Glen Rock)
1978	Lacca Champion	29·52	
1979	Sarah's Bunny	29·53	
1980	Indian Joe	29·68	
1981	Parkdown Jet	29·57	
1982	Lauries Panther	29·60	
1983	I'm Slippy	29·40	
1984	Whisper Wishes	29·43	
1985	Pagan Swallow	29·04	
1986	Tico	28·69	(480 metres) Wimbledon
1987	Signal Spark	28·83	
1988	Hit The Lid	28·53	
1989	Lartigue Note	28·79	
1990	Slippy Blue	28·70	

White City closed in September 1984 and left a big void for greyhound racing fans in Britain. The Derby was switched to Wimbledon and is now raced over a new distance of 480 metres. First prize was increased to £40,000 in 1990, when Druids Johno, owned by HRH Prince Edward, was the beaten favourite. Other than the English Derby, principal events include the Oaks (transferred from Harringay following the track's closure in 1987 to Wimbledon) for bitches and the Grand National, a hurdles event over 474 metres moved to Birmingham Hall Green following the closure of White City. Sherry's Prince established himself as a truly great hurdler when he won his third Grand National in 1972 after winning all his heats, as on the two previous occasions.

On 19 May 1928 the first race was contested at Wimbledon and was won by J. H. Baker's World of Roses II. The Laurels is contested at Wimbledon over a distance of 460 metres. It is interesting to note the number of occasions that the Laurels has been won by the same dog, generally in successive years. The first dual winner was Ballyhennessy Sandhills in 1937 and 1938. Ballymac Ball was successful in 1949 and 1950. Duet Leader won in 1955 and 1956 (winning in both years from trap one). In 1966 Conna Court became the fourth dual winner. Endless Gossip was the first greyhound to break 28·00 seconds for the event, with the time of 27·96 seconds in 1952. In 1932 Beef Cutlet won the Laurels in 28·47 seconds, a then world record for the 500-yard (457-metre) course. Wimbledon has taken over from White City as the headquarters of greyhound racing and holds numerous open race competitions, including the Puppy Derby, and the Oaks, contested by dogs and bitches over 15 months but which are classed as puppies until

Wembley Stadium, England. The track has a grass surface, straights of 91·5 metres and the circumference is 435 metres incorporating four bends. Type of hare — outside McGee. Race distances — 490, 655, and 845 metres *(Courtesy of Wembley Stadium Limited)*

the end of the year following that of their birth. Castledown Tiptoes was the only greyhound to win both events in the same year and was afterwards sold for £3000.

Greyhound racing commenced at Wembley Stadium on 10 December 1927. Wembley offers refinement combined with entertainment and racing of the highest standard. The main event in the Wembley calendar is the stayers' classic, the St Leger, contested over 655 metres, the first to win this event being the great bitch, Burletta. Wembley was the first track from which a greyhound meeting was broadcast, this being on Easter Monday, 1940, when Junior Classic won the final of the Spring Cup.

A recession seriously affected greyhound racing in the 1960s and the 1970s and the number of tracks has sharply reduced.

West Ham track was mourned by many. It had the longest straights in Britain and also had wide sweeping bends. It hosted the Cesarewitch, contested over 600 yards (548 metres). Many outstanding greyhounds figure among its winners, including the legendary Mick The

Miller in 1930, Future Cutlet in 1931 and 1932 and Brilliant Bob whose 30·80 seconds was the fastest time clocked when the race was contested over 600 yards (548 metres).

On West Ham's closure the race was switched to Manchester Belle Vue where it became a marathon event and is contested over 815 metres. Clapton was another East London track to close. It was the only track with a central hare and it was the home of the Scurry Gold Cup. Clapton was the fourth London track to open, the first meeting being held on 7 April 1928. Brave Enough was the first dog to break the 24·00 seconds barrier. In 1933 Creamery Border clocked 23·31 seconds, establishing a new track and national record, winning the final by 16 lengths. Gorey Airways won the Scurry Cup twice in 1959 and 1960. The competition was moved to Slough on Clapton's closure and Brighton trainer George Curtis' charge Yankee Express became the first greyhound to win a classic three times in succession when he won the event in 1982, 1983, 1984.

The 1980s have been a traumatic time for

the sport as the prime sites occupied by greyhound racing stadia have become increasingly under threat from developers. White City's closure has been followed by the closure of Slough in March 1987, and Harringay, considered by many as the best running surface in the country, closed in September the same year. Over the same period a number of provincial tracks have also succumbed to the pressure from developers. But on the plus side, a couple of new tracks have opened at Swaffham and Canterbury and the sport is enjoying something of a renaissance nationwide with bigger crowds and higher tote takings being reported at most major tracks. The emphasis is now on providing improved facilities such as restaurants and incorporating other leisure activities at the stadia, to make them financially viable.

The surge of popularity for greyhound racing can also be attributed to the crowd-pulling power of two remarkable greyhounds. Scurlogue Champ, marathon superstar and winner of the 1985 Cesarewitch and 1985 and 1986 BBC TV Trophy, became a household name because of his famous late, late run. The dog who was trained by Ken Peckham, would come from last, sometimes as much as 12 lengths adrift, to win race after race. It was said that he was the only greyhound that knew where the finishing line was!

Ballyregan Bob, trained by George Curtis, first got the nation behind him when he broke the U.K. record of 21 consecutive wins. But then Curtis and owner Cliff Kevern decided the dog should attempt the world record of 31 consecutive wins, held by the American greyhound Joe Dump. There followed a thrilling story of success and anguish as the brilliant six bend stayer struggled to overcome injury in his bid for the record. On a memorable night in December 1986 watched by a crowd of 10,000 at his home track Brighton and millions of TV viewers, Ballyregan Bob stormed to victory recording 32 consecutive wins. The next day he was headline news in all the national newspapers and greyhound racing received a tremendous boost.

Following the closure of Slough, Catford has become the new home for the Scurry Gold Cup and is now run over 385 metres.

The Cobb Marathon over 810 yards (740 metres) was held at Catford for many years and was later replaced by the Boxing Day marathon over 888 metres. Castledown Prince won the first Cobb Marathon in 1942 in 49·69 seconds. The Gold Collar Classic, once 440 yards (402 metres) and now 555 metres is contested here, the first winner being Wild Woolley in 1933. In 1947 Trev's Perfection won the Gold Collar and set a record by also winning the English, Scottish and Welsh Derby in the same year, a feat equalled only by Mile Bush Pride and Patricia's Hope.

Walthamstow is located on the eastern side of London and is the City's most successful track. It opened in 1933 and its facilities have been updated in recent years. It now boasts several restaurants, a night club and a children's playground. Most of the facilities are under cover.

The major event staged at the track is The Grand Prix contested over 480 metres. The competition was given classic status in 1971.

IRELAND
Mechanical lure racing commenced in Ireland in May 1927 at Celtic Park, Belfast, the Irish Coursing Club, formed in 1916, being the controlling body. Today the Republic of Ireland has eighteen tracks, the main track being Shelbourne Park Greyhound Stadium, Dublin. The Irish Greyhound Board (Bord na gCon) was constituted in 1958 and is the controlling body.

Tracks in Ireland always used to have grass surfaces but now the majority have grass straights and sanded bends. Six dogs compete, the racing colours being as follows:
Trap 1. Red with a white numeral
Trap 2. Blue with a white numeral
Trap 3. White with a black numeral
Trap 4. Black with a white numeral
Trap 5. Orange with a white numeral
Trap 6. White and black horizontal stripes with a white numeral

Shelbourne Park is perhaps the centre of track racing in Eire and was the first track to open south of the border, on 14 May 1927. The modernised track is the scene of greyhound sales conducted by Shelbourne Park Sales Pty Ltd during the year, the sales generally being held once a week and occupying two entire days. The marked increase in the prices paid for greyhounds is exhibited by comparing prices received from the auction sales. In 1942 total sales figures were £16 644 and in 1944 £92 000. In 1946 figures reached nearly £150 000. By 1970 sales had reached £300 000 per annum.

From 1970 the Irish Derby was referred to as Carroll's Irish Derby because the Dublin cigarette manufacturers, P. J. Carroll & Co. Ltd, have sponsored the event. In 1970 the winner received £5000. In 1973 this was increased to £10 000; 1975 saw the winner's prize increased to £11 000; and 1976 saw the winner's prize further increased to £15 500. In 1977 the winner received £17 500. The 1985 Carroll's Irish Derby total prize fund was in excess of £50 000. In 1988 Kerry Group took over sponsorship and the prize fund is now £65 000 with £30 000 going to the winner.

The fastest time recorded in a Derby heat or final was clocked by Ashmore Merry — 28·74 seconds in the 1976 semi-finals. Spanish Battle-ship, owned by 'Chub' O'Connor and trained by Tom Lynch, won the Irish Derby in three consecutive years, 1953, 1954, and 1955. Only four bitches have won the premier Irish Classic, namely Monologue in 1933, Muinessa in 1937, Brave Damsel in 1941, and Catsrock Daisy in 1972. The shortest winning margin was a short head, when Linda's Champion won in 1977 and the longest winning margin was six lengths when Perrys Apple won in 1960.

The Cork track was purchased by the Bord na gCon in April 1969 to prevent it falling into the hands of land speculators.

The Laurels, a classic event inaugurated in 1944, was allotted to this track and was first won by Robeen Printer in the time of 28·98 seconds. Spanish Chestnut won the Laurel

Irish Derby Winners 1932–1987

Year	Winner	Time (seconds)	Track
1932	Guideless Joe	30·36	Shelbourne Park
1933	Monologue	30·52	Shelbourne Park
1934	Frisco Hobo	30·45	Harolds Cross
1935	Roving Yank	30·18	Shelbourne Park
1936	Minstrel Rover	30·48	Harolds Cross
1937	Muinessa	30·83	Shelbourne Park
1938	Abbeylara	30·09	Harolds Cross
1939	Marching Thro Georgia	30·05	Limerick
1940	Tanist	29·82	Shelbourne Park
1941	Brave Damsel	30·64	Shelbourne Park
1942	Uacterlainn	30·22	Cork
1943	Famous Knight	30·26	Harolds Cross
1944	Clonbonny Bridge	30·53	Shelbourne Park
1945	Lilac Luck	30·12	Harolds Cross
1946	Steve	30·20	Shelbourne Park
1947	Daring Flash	30·04	Harolds Cross
1948	Western Post	29·90	Shelbourne Park
1949	Spanish Lad	29·87	Harolds Cross
1950	Crossmolina Rambler	29·70	Shelbourne Park
1951	Carmodys Tanist	29·64	Harolds Cross
1952	Rough Waters	29·95	Shelbourne Park
1953	Spanish Battleship	28·78	Harolds Cross
1954	Spanish Battleship	29·64	Shelbourne Park
1955	Spanish Battleship	29·53	Harolds Cross
1956	Keep Moving	29·18	Shelbourne Park
1957	Hopeful Cutlet	29·60	Harolds Cross
1958	Colonel Perry	29·79	Shelbourne Park
1959	Sir Frederick	29·30	Harolds Cross
1960	Perrys Apple	29·55	Shelbourne Park
1961	Chieftains Guest	29·45	Harolds Cross
1962	Shanes Legacy	29·58	Shelbourne Park
1963	Drumahiskey Venture	29·60	Harolds Cross
1964	Wonder Valley	29·30	Shelbourne Park
1965	Ballyowen Chief	29·42	Harolds Cross
1966	Always Proud	29·44	Shelbourne Park

1967	Russian Gun	29·44	Harolds Cross
1968	Yellow Printer	29·11	Shelbourne Park
1969	Own Pride	29·20	Harolds Cross
1970	Monalee Pride	29·28	Shelbourne Park
1971	Sole Aim	29·12	Shelbourne Park
1972	Catsrock Daisy	29·20	Shelbourne Park
1973	Bashful Man	28·82	Shelbourne Park
1974	Lively Band	29·11	Shelbourne Park
1975	Shifting Shadow	29·35	Shelbourne Park
1976	Tain Mor	29·35	Shelbourne Park
1977	Linda's Champion	29·53	Shelbourne Park
1978	Pampered Rover	29·23	Shelbourne Park
1979	Penny County	29·28	Shelbourne Park
1980	Suir Miller	29·18	Shelbourne Park
1981	Bold Work	29·32	Shelbourne Park
1982	Cooladine Super	29·15	Shelbourne Park
1983	Belvedere Bran	29·65	Shelbourne Park
1984	Dipmac	29·15	Shelbourne Park
1985	Tubbercurry Lad	29·14	Shelbourne Park
1986	Kyle Jack	30·41	Shelbourne Park*
1987	Rathgallen Tady	30·49	Shelbourne Park
1988	Make History	30·26	Shelbourne Park
1989	Manorville Magic	30·53	Shelbourne Park
1990	The Other Toss	30·14	Shelbourne Park

twice in 1949 and 1950, and his son, Spanish Battleship, won in 1955. In 1961 the distance over which the Laurels is contested was altered from 500 yards (457 metres) to 525 yards (480 metres) and this distance has been retained. In 1971 Ivy Hall Flash clocked 29·15 seconds and in a heat he set a new track record of 29·10 seconds. Greyhound racing has grown markedly in popularity since the Cork track commenced greyhound racing on 13 June 1936.

The Irish Grand National hurdle event, a classic event over 525 yards (480 metres), has been transferred from Thurles to Shelbourne Park, but the former track still retains the Tipperary Cup, a 525 yards (480 metres) open flat event.

The Irish Cesarewitch, an open 600 yards (548 metres) classic event is contested at Navan and is worth £4000 to the winner.

Harolds Cross is situated in Dublin and is a picturesque and well-laid-out track. Harolds Cross opened one year after Shelbourne Park. The first Grand National was contested at Harolds Cross in 1932. The Puppy Derby is contested at Harolds Cross and was originally conducted over 500 yards but is now run over 525 yards (480 metres). In 1944 automatic starting boxes were introduced to replace the hand-operated traps. The first prize for the Burmah Castrol Puppy Derby is £7,000. The

Irish Greyhound Oaks over 525 yards is worth £12,000 to the winner.

Tom Hussey, Minister of State for Agriculture, performed the official opening of the new stand at Harolds Cross on 15 December 1978. The new development includes a glass-enclosed, heated grandstand, incorporating seating, restaurant, tote and bar facilities, and a very modern lighting system. The original stand was erected approximately fifty years before.

The Bord na gCon purchased the Harolds Cross track in January 1971 at a cost of £309 790 and since that time a considerable amount of money has been spent on improving the facilities at this major Dublin track.

The Harolds Cross track initially commenced racing on 10 April 1928. The six-race programme included one hurdle race and commenced at 8 p.m. The opening race, the Ulster Plate (for bitches only), was won by M. J. Mulhall's Dragues, which began from box six at the odds of 5:4.

The admission charges for the opening night were as follows: Grandstand 5s, Ladies 2s 6d, Special Enclosure 2s, Popular Enclosure 1s. The race card was sold for a cost of sixpence. The original directors of the Dublin Greyhound and Sports Association Limited were J. B. Frazer (chairman), Ed Teehan (vice-

The distance changed from 525 yards to 550 yards (503 metres) in 1986.

chairman), J. J. Flood, J. G. McEntagart, B. Hamilton, and J. J. Fagan. Six of these directors also acted as stewards for the Harolds Cross track.

Clonmel is the headquarters for the Irish Coursing Club and was one of the first tracks to open. Hurdle racing is a feature of the meetings here and flat races are conducted over 330 yards (302 metres) and 525 yards (480 metres). In 1939 the National Sapling Stakes was inaugurated, Sporting Fancy winning the event. In 1944 the title was altered to the National Puppy Stake and the event is now known as the National Breeders Produce Stakes.

Racing is conducted at Limerick on Monday, Thursday and Saturday nights and attracts star-studded fields of greyhounds over its courses of 300 and 525 yards (277 and 480 metres). Limerick staged the 1978 Irish St Leger, a classic event over 550 yards (503 metres) for seventy-two greyhounds. The total purse is in excess of £15 000.

Racing at Mullingar Greyhound Track is conducted over 325 and 525 yards courses on Tuesdays and Saturdays. The town of Mullingar has become famous for the progeny of its great sire, Castledown Lad. Managha Boy held the track record here for many years when he recorded the time of 30·28 seconds in 1938.

SPAIN

Greyhound racing in Spain is very well organised. The official controlling body of sports in Spain is the Consejo Superior de Deporte (Supreme Sports Council), which in turn delegates authority to various subsidiary authorities. The official controlling authority for greyhound racing, both on the track and for coursing, is the Federacion Espanola Galguera (Spanish Greyhound Federation). Until the Spanish Greyhound Federation was constituted in December 1939, it had been impossible for any organised board to control greyhound racing and obtain unity. This was a consequence of the fact that, although the Club Deportivo Galguero Espanol (Spanish Greyhound Sporting Club) was the official controlling authority of greyhound racing in Spain since 1930, the political unrest in the country at that period did nothing to contribute to the reorganisation that this Club was endeavouring to bring about.

Ruled by the Spanish Greyhound Federation, many regional federations exist in all the Spanish provinces where greyhound racing is practised. There are ten tracks throughout Spain affiliated to the federation. Two in Madrid, four in Barcelona, one in Valencia, one in Palma de Mallorca and two in Las Palmas de Gran Canaria (Canary Islands). The premier international track competitions are conducted in Barcelona and Madrid. Meetings are conducted daily, but there are also matinée meetings on Sundays and on public holidays. All tracks have a sand surface and are systematically operated with electro-mechanical apparatus. Betting is controlled electronically.

Classic competitions are conducted annually, both in coursing and track racing, by the Spanish Greyhound Federation and there are general rules in addition to the established rules. Only those greyhounds which are not imported and are registered in the Libro Federativo de la F.E.G. (Registration Book of the S.G.F.) may enter; but in the classic events such as puppy trials (puppies up to 24 months), three trials annually, track, regional, Spanish national, league, feminine, and Count of Lerida championships, the notification of the mating of the dam and whelping of the pup must be registered in the books of the Federation. Only pups of 14 months or over may enter all competitions.

In addition to the previously mentioned classics, other trials exist, such as the Spring, Summer, Autumn, and Winter Premium Stakes, each of which is contested in two versions — one for imported dogs and one for national dogs. There are also various other local competitions among which the following are of note:

Premio Internacional de Madrid (International Premium of Madrid),
Premio Internacional de Barcelona (International Premium of Barcelona),
Trofeo Marques de la Floroda (Marquis of Florida Trophy),
Copa Good Year (Good Year Cup), and
Derby Galguero Espanol (Spanish Greyhound Derby).

Notable trials are the Regional Championship, the Spanish Nationals, and the Spanish Greyhound Derby. The Spanish National, with four dogs running from each track, is usually conducted at a different track each year with the object of promoting and affording opportunity to each of the tracks, as well as to the owners, trainers, and spectators. The Spanish

Greyhound Derby, the most important of the competitions, has acquired international standing, with countries such as England, Ireland, U.S.A., and Mexico participating. In recent years the Derby has been held alternately between the Madrid track, Madrileno, and the Barcelona track, Meridiana. Imported greyhounds are not permitted to enter for the classic events, since these are only for those dogs which are whelped and bred in Spain. However, there are many open races and international competitions conducted throughout the year, where imported dogs may enter, and they are generally superior to the national dogs. With such a low standard of breeding, and taking into consideration that approximately 1500 greyhounds are required to run daily, Spain finds it necessary to import many dogs from Ireland annually, for which reason one frequently finds that the greyhounds imported are not of the standard that one would wish.

Racing is categorised on all Spanish tracks into first, second, third, fourth, and fifth categories. The first category is subdivided into A and B, A covering champions only. Nuevo Campo Espana, officially opened on 10 March 1935, was one of the first tracks established in Spain. It is a sand track with an inside perimeter of 348·2 metres, straights of 78·5 metres and bends of 95·6 metres. As in the rest of Spain, there is a Regional Federation in Las Palmas which is controlled by the Spanish Greyhound Federation. The best times registered as valid track records at Nuevo Campo Espana track are as follows: Stylish Fly over 425 metres, 26·20 seconds on 30 November 1975; Rainy Weather over 600 metres, 38·20 seconds on 25 December 1974.

The first race of the day usually commences at 6.30 p.m.; morning meetings commence at 11 a.m. There are six or seven participants in each race, although normally six. Prior to entering the kennels, where the dogs remain until they are taken to the starting boxes, the greyhounds are exercised, inspected by the stewards, and paraded in front of the spectators. In Nuevo Campo Espana there are a total of twenty races per week-night with seventeen on Sundays and public holidays; the distances vary between 275, 425, and 600 metres, the standard being 425 metres. The most important competition conducted at Las Palmas is the Copa Good Year (Good Year Cup) contested over a distance of 600 metres and this competition awards large cash prizes in addition to several valuable trophies. Greyhounds from Ireland, from several national Spanish tracks, as well as the best from the local track, participate. The Good Year Cup was created in memory of the great dog Good Year who, with his incredible performances, created an enormous following for greyhound racing in Las Palmas. Good Year was owned by D. Tomas Naranjo Suarez and had originated from the London tracks and met the conditions necessary for becoming a Derby dog. Good Year's performances in the handicap races attracted large numbers of spectators to the track and he never had a serious opponent. Situated 30 yards (27 metres) behind the starting line of the First Category, he caught up with the other runners before they reached the first bend and generally completed the race several lengths in front of the nearest competitor. Good Year has sired many famous greyhounds, the most notable being Intrepido, Perla, and Pinta. The Las Palmas Greyhound Federation has provided many Spanish champions. The Good Year races and the acquisition of seven national titles by dogs from the local track, have afforded prestige to greyhound racing in the Canary Islands.

There is no entry fee for races in Spain. Not only placed dogs are awarded prizes, but also every participating greyhound receives a prize in order to assist with the maintenance cost of running a greyhound. The ambition of many greyhound owners is to win a trophy.

The 1978 Spanish Derby at Canodromo Meridiana, Barcelona, was won by the locally owned and trained Ballinderry May (Leaders Champion–Shanghai Lough). Although none of the Irish team reached the final it was still a triumph for Irish breeding. In an exciting final Ballinderry May beat Tucksy by a short head in the time of 30·60 seconds (450 metres). Another Irish-bred dog, Tis Time, finished half a length away, third. The Consolation Derby was won by the Irish-bred May Amber (Heathermore King–Amber Choice) in the time of 30·70. This bitch is owned by Pepe Ordonez, a celebrated bull fighter and a frequent visitor to Ireland. Ballinderry May was bred by Pat and Gina Sullivan, Kilsheelan, Co., Tipperary; the Consolation Derby winner, Kay Amber, was bred by Sean McNamara, Derrindasse, Duagh, Listowel, Co., Kerry.

4

THE FORM OF THE GREYHOUND

The cultivated greyhound exhibits a model of elegance and a combination of symmetrical proportions probably unrivalled by any other animal but the racehorse.

The perfection of the mechanism for speedy progression is apparent throughout his structure. Whether we regard his organs separately or conjunctively, they are admirably adapted for vast powers of locomotion: we cannot view him without being surprised at the great alterations which can be effected in the animal frame by culture; for the greyhound form, coupled with the peculiarities which attach thereto, could hardly have originated in nature. The peculiarities I refer to are the compensations which nature always exacts on all forced improvements. In the greyhound this compensation for the increased speed brought about by artificial means, consists in deteriorated powers of scent, and the abstraction of a portion of general intelligence. Regarding the most admired and approved form of greyhound, the ancients and the moderns are in agreement as to all essential points.

THE HEAD

The head of the greyhound is strikingly beautiful. Arrian observes: 'It should be light, but whether the nose be hooked or flat he appears indifferent about: but the nostrils should be wide, and not blunt, in their termination.' Xenophon greatly disapproves of hook-nosed greyhounds of any kind: also the 'Mayster of Game' would have for his 'greihounde a longe hede and some deleymakyd in the manare of a luce, a good large mouthe and good sesours the on agein the other, so that nether jawes passe not him above, ne that thei above pass not hem by nether.' Markham also observes that the greyhound head should be 'fine, long and lean, with a sharp nose, rush grown from the eyes downwards'. Cultivation has here exemplified its powers in a surprising manner, by a con-

siderable fining and elongation of the entire head, but while this was taking place, and the greyhound was consequently becoming more capable of not only overtaking its prey, but also of seizing it, the animals to be seized were to some extent compensated. A balance was struck between extra powers given and former ones, which were either completely taken away or very much modified. In consequence of the attenuating and lengthening of the head of the greyhound, the internal cavities became necessarily contracted and the frontal sinuses were thereby greatly diminished, and with their decrease of surface, the scenting powers likewise decreased. The cranial cavities also diminished and with that a lessened volume of brain ensued which proved unfavourable to a full development of some organic functions and also of those higher traits of what may be called intellectuality.

With regard to the ears, Arrian says: 'Let them be large and soft, so as to appear from their size and softness as if broken.' But he has no objection to their standing erect, provided that they are neither small nor stiff. The translator of Arrian aptly remarks: 'The modern courser prefers the small ear, as do all others of our countrymen, we believe, from Markham, who recommends "a sharp ear, close and falling".'

From these ancient authorities, covering a period of approximately 600 years, we may conclude that a long, lean head with strong, level jaws and a sharp, close-falling ear is a distinctive and desirable feature of the breed.

THE EYES

'The eyes of the greyhound,' Arrian says, 'should be large, up-raised, clear, and so strikingly bright as to flash with fire.' He notes black as a commendable colour of eye. Xenophon condemns grey-eyed hounds. Oppian, however, is not averse to light-eyed dogs, but on the contrary prefers

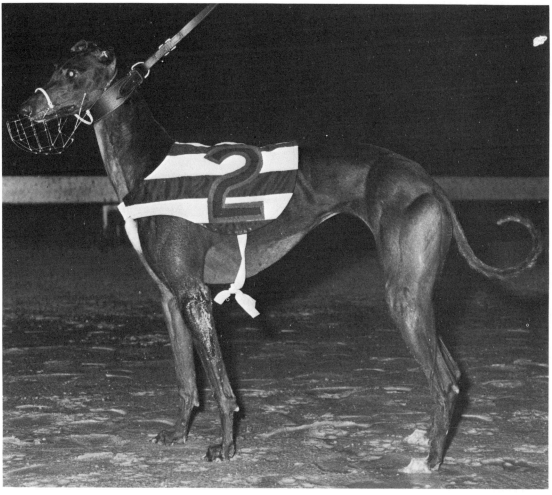

The perfection of the mechanism for speedy progression is apparent throughout the structure of the cultivated greyhound (Photo — Anne's Record) *(By permission of W. Atkins)*

these eyes above all others. Edmund de Langely, a son of Edward III and a Master of Hounds and Hawks to Henry IV, would have them black. Markham would have 'a full clear eye with long eyelids' and had not satisfied himself as to a preferable colour. The general consensus of opinion is that if the eye be full, round, clear, and good, it matters not what is its colour.

THE NECK

The form of greyhound's neck is aptly described by Arrian. 'It should be long, round, and flexible, so that, if you forcibly draw the dogs backwards by their collars, it may seem to be broken, from its flexibility and softness.' A long head and neck are particularly important in coursing to enable the greyhound to lift his hare without

extreme stooping of his body, which might bring him down with injurious force, as one may have observed where the head and neck have been short. Wynkyn de Worde, who wrote in 1496 on coursing, observes: 'A greyhounde should be heeded lyke a snake, and neckyd lyke a drake.' De Langely would have 'the neke grete and long, bowed as a swanne's neke'. Matheson says: 'The neck should be long and muscular and beautifully symmetrical and with not the slightest suggestion of flabbiness.'

All authorities agree that the neck should be long, strong, flexible, and elegantly arched. There have been many instances of top-class greyhounds, notably on the track, who possess course, thick heads and short, bull necks, and although far from being desirable, it is to be preferred to the thin, weak neck.

39

THE CHEST AND SHOULDERS

Arrian asserts that broad chests are to be preferred to such as are narrow; he would also have the shoulders stand wide apart and loose and free from each other, as without that they lose much ground in turning, and the looser they are just behind the shoulders the better for that purpose and without any disadvantage to their speed in straight running, but rather to the contrary. The front aspect of the chest should be sufficiently broad to offer ample attachment to the motive muscles of the limbs.

A deep chest is a most essential point in a greyhound. In proportion to the depth of chest is the abdominal contraction; thus the deepest chested greyhounds (when in good condition) usually have the smallest bellies and consequently no interruption is offered to the under stretchings of the hind legs beyond the forelegs. Neither is there then any injurious stomachic pressure on the diaphragm or midriff, nor any unnecessary abdominal load to carry.

A large, barrelled dog should be avoided, but a directly flat-sided dog is to be more studiously avoided. The last two or three ribs should be well arched out, for it is to their inner surface that the curtain of the midriff is attached, which circumscribes the lungs on its pectoral surface, and the stomach on its abdominal disc; consequently its greater extent of surface is equally favourable to both respiration and digestion.

In the greyhound, hare, and horse, the scapula presents a broad surface for the attachment of a large mass of muscle. In each of these animals it is obliquely placed, and on the degree of obliquity of its attachment depends the extent of its operation forward and backward. Consequently, broad, deep, obliquely placed shoulders always bespeak a great extent of stride in the fore limbs.

THE FORELEGS

The forelegs are more important organs in the greyhound than many imagine. It is necessary that the forelegs be good, well set on at the shoulder, not out-elbowed, bony and straight, and well set on at the feet. Many greyhounds have long, straight forelegs but are deficient in muscular substance in the upper part of the foreleg or forearm and/or have an ill-furnished true arm (the part between the point of the shoulder and the elbow). Unless the bone of the true arm is long, the stride will be contracted; and unless its muscular masses are large and firm, its reaches will not be repeated either in quickness or force.

The forearm (the portion of the leg between the elbow and the knee) should be long, straight, and muscular. To what extent length of forearm contributes to the speed of a greyhound when galloping, can be seen by considering that, if at each stroke of his gallop only 1 centimetre is gained, the accumulation over a long distance may decidedly turn the scales in favour of the dog who is so formed. Furthermore, as the portion of the forelegs below the knees acts primarily as a spring to prevent concussion (it plays this role only when receiving the hind parts thrown upon it when it does nothing towards increasing the length of the stride), consequently the advantage of a long forearm, especially when assisted by a very low placing of the knee, must be apparent.

THE FEET

Matheson observes: 'The feet should be the shape of those of a cat, the bones should be thick and strong with no lumpiness, the claws should be thick and strong, the pads should be very elastic and cushion-like with a hard surface, the heel pad should fit tightly into the toe pads . . .' Markham would have 'a fine, round, full cat's foot, with strong cleyes and tough soles'.

The cat-like foot conveys an adequate idea of the form which is desirable for the foot of the greyhound, for although the canine claws are not retractile like those of a cat, the arched phalanges and the under padding of the foot of the cat present much of the form which is recognised as both a support and an assistant in progression. The splayed foot detracts from the speed of the dog and is more prone to injury.

THE BACK

In the *Countrey Farm* Markham says: 'A long, broad, and square beame back, with high, round fillets, deep, swine-sided, with hollow bended ribs' is desirable. Length is to be more desired than the figure of the short dog. Mr Thacker justly observes: 'It is the strength of the back which is brought into requisition in particular in running over hilly ground; and here may be said to rest the distinction between long or short backs, supposing both to be good and strong; the more lengthy the back, and proportionately strong, the more he is calculated to beat the shorter-backed dog on the flat; but on hilly

Dolores Rocket (Newdown Heather–Come On Dolores), bred, owned, and trained by H. White, ranks as one of the greatest bitches to grace the British racing scene

ground, one with a shorter back will have an advantage. The longer backed ones cannot buckle and unbuckle so quickly as the shorter ones; this quickness on hilly ground, as compared with flat ground, is more requisite than length of stride; besides which, the shorter dog has more power to raise himself up to mount the hill than the longer one; to bring his hind legs forward, the extreme ends of both fore and hind quarters act as a lever against his middle, in the inverse ratio to a lever lifting a weight by a long purchase, and the longer the lever the greater the purchase against him; consequently, the longer the back the longer the lever against his other powers called upon to resist it.' (Vol. ii, p. 92)

Without doubt, length of back is favourable to quick turning. A short-backed dog may possess equal speed to a long-backed one, but the long-backed dog has the advantage in track racing in that he is able to turn and recover himself on his legs, if checked, in less time than

a short-backed one. Also, in coursing, a short-backed dog may fling himself at the hare with equal speed as a long-backed one, but the long-backed dog will turn and recover himself more quickly.

Generally speaking, long backs are to be favoured, provided such a back is united to strong loins and wide-spreading thighs. A certain flexibility in the back, which admits of its being brought into a curve, is desirable; and the longer the back, the greater will be the curvilinear direction. Whether the back be long or short, the curve is formed in one effort.

THE HIND QUARTERS

The hind quarters should exhibit strength by their extent across and their firmness. Progression is accelerated in the greyhound by the propulsory efforts of the muscles of the hind quarters. The thighs and loins should be large and exhibit very powerful muscular markings so that when the dog is viewed from behind they should appear to cover the side long view of the body.

The hock, also, to be good, must be wide and, like the knee, should be as low placed on the limb as possible because on the extent of the angles formed between these several portions of the hind limbs, depends the extent of the space passed over at each bound.

THE COAT

With few exceptions, the texture of the coat of the greyhound of the present day is very soft and fine. However, rough-coated dogs may still be encountered.

In 1835 A. Graham's rough-coated brindle dog, Gilbertfield, won the Glasgow Gold Cup, contested by ninety-one dogs. The following season, Goth, a son of Gilbertfield, won the Clubs of Scotland Gold Cup, contested by eighty-seven dogs. The continued success of descendants of Gilbertfield showed that winning blood may be transmitted in a rough line. The rough-coated dogs bred by A. Graham were of such merit that roughness of coat has ceased to bar dogs from clubs and meetings since then.

It is thought that among the early races, fawn colour predominated; but at present it is no more common than any other colour. The brindled dog has been slighted as exhibiting the bull-dog cross of Lord Orford but nevertheless there have been many excellent brindled dogs. Arrian was totally indifferent to colour, as was his eminent translator. The preferences for certain colours are 'as fickle and fanciful as versatility and want of due experience could make them'. Oppian would have red, russet, or fawn greyhounds. De Langely favoured the 'rede falow with a black moselle'. The 'Suffolk Sportsman' on this subject remarks: 'I insist upon whole colours, save the throat or the breast. Black, red, fallow, dun, mouse-colour, blue, and the pure white; all with coats short, smooth, and soft as a mole's. The party colour I cannot allow, or the brindled.'

The colour of the coat of the greyhound is with some an important factor, but I am in agreement with the many others who adopt the old adage that 'a good dog, like a good horse, cannot be of a bad colour'. There is no virtue in colour and no positive dependence can be placed on colour. It may be indicative of particular lines of ancestry to which certain puppies in a litter take, but it is no guide as to selecting a winner.

THE TAIL

The tail, without doubt, has something to do with progression, as we may judge by its sweeping gyrations when the dog is galloping, but most notably it is seen in action in turning. The greyhound's tail assists generally in his propulsory efforts, and more particularly in his turnings and wrenchings. It is the general opinion of breeders that the tail be of considerable length. However, there are both reasons and facts to prove that the greyhound's tail is not necessary to his predatory exertions. There is no doubt that the tail acts as a kind of rudder, but the length of the tail does not appear to be of great consequence for there have been many good greyhounds grace our tracks which have exhibited only mere stumps of tails.

LENGTH, HEIGHT, AND WEIGHT

The length, height, and weight of greyhounds differ considerably. It is the opinion of many authorities that length more than height is essential to speed. There are many instances of small dogs winning from large dogs, but with equally good proportions, length, height, and substance. Sir William Clayton, on this subject, says: 'I may, perhaps, in the opinion of some sportsmen, entertain an erroneous idea, but I cannot subscribe to that of a small greyhound being equal to one of a larger size. The medium is, in fact, the height to be desired, and I consider the superiority to be decided on mathematical principles. A given length must cover a given space of ground, and the short small greyhound must necessarily make more strokes than a larger one to cover the same space of ground, and, consequently, must be sooner fatigued. The great overgrown dog I equally exclude, for the bulk there counteracts itself, and the extreme length cannot recover itself to repeat the stroke, so that the ground covered by the length is then lost by failure in the repetition of the stroke.' (*Treatise on Greyhounds*, p. 13.)

THE CHOICE OF A GREYHOUND

Of the sporting qualities of the greyhound, speed, determination, stamina, and track sense are most essential. Condition is equally important, but it must be considered as much a sporting quality of the trainer whose judgement brings his greyhounds into that state, as of the dogs who are objects of it. Speed is dependent largely on conformation in addition to nervous influence, physical factors, and the overall condition of the dog which results from judicious dieting, training, etc.

Every greyhound inherits, to a greater or lesser degree, the characteristics of its ancestors. Some may inherit brilliant boxing ability, some gain superior early pace, and others brilliant sustained pace over a long distance. Others inherit the tendency to interfere or stop chasing once the lead is taken from them. Bone quality is an inherent factor which renders some more liable to break bones than others. The factor which is most difficult to evolve is the will to win. Breeding alone is no guarantee of ability, but it perhaps helps in choosing between several greyhounds of similar ability. The breeding of a dog is a serious consideration.

Many authorities prefer bitches rather than dogs. Arrian says: 'The greyhound bitch is fleeter than the dog, but the dog has more bottom than the bitch; and because he can run through the whole year, is a much more valuable acquisition: and as good bitches abound, but it is no easy thing to meet with a thorough good dog, the latter is on this account more precious: and again, it is fortunate if bitches preserve their speed to the fifth year, whereas dogs retain theirs even to the tenth' (p. 151). Markham says: 'It is an old received opinion that the greyhound bitch will beat the dog.'

From my studies and observations it would appear that, in the same number, there are fewer bad bitches than bad dogs, and that a top-class dog is superior to a top-class bitch. Generally speaking, the top-class greyhounds are not necessary perfect specimens, but they are so evenly balanced that no outstanding defect is exhibited in their conformation. With very few exceptions, the top-class greyhound embraces symmetry, elegance, balance, condition, and freedom from all forms of coarseness. We could not believe for a moment that a coarse bushy tail, a rough coat, over- or under-shot jaws, or a coarse thick head could affect the speed of a greyhound, but I am in agreement with the many authorities who are of the opinion that these signs exhibit a lack of quality and are signs of degeneracy.

5

THE SKIN

'There is no magician's mantle to compare with the skin in its diverse rolls of waterproof, overcoat, sunshade, suit of armour, and refrigerator, sensitive to the touch of a feather, to temperature, and to pain, withstanding the wear and tear of the years and executing its own running repairs.'

This vital organ of the body reflects the health of the animal and even reveals such conditions as dehydration, internal disease, disease of the skin structure itself, and infestation by internal and external parasites. A healthy skin is of prime importance and should have a soft, pliable, springy feel to it, accompanied by a soft, glistening coat of hair. If the skin is dry, with no spring to it, and does not rapidly return to its normal presence when pinched or twisted with the hand, or is harsh with accompanying dandruff, this usually indicates some degree of ill health.

The tissues of the body are bathed in a fluid medium and the waterproof nature of the skin retains the fluid. Untreated burns involving one-third of the total skin area may rapidly prove fatal due to the loss of fluid, the proportion of fluid to the red blood cells falling to such a degree that the blood cannot function.

The skin consists of two layers, the epidermis and the dermis. The epidermis is a many-layered pavement of squamous epithelial cells devoid of blood vessels and nourished by a plexus of capillaries situated in the upper part of the dermis. Although the epidermis can be divided morphologically into four various layers—the horny, granular, prickle cell, and basal layers— each level in the skin represents a stage in the life of the epidermal cell.

The columnar cells of the basal or germinal layer give rise, by cell division, to the prickle cells. These polygonal cells are intimately connected by protoplasmic fibrils, or prickles, to their neighbours. As new cells are formed beneath them the prickle cells move upwards to the surface. As they approach the surface they take on their primary function of producing the protective material, keratin.

The physico-chemical changes which take place in the cells prior to keratinisation, produce the granular layer. Finally, the epidermal cells die, lose their nuclei, and form the protective keratin of the horny layer of the skin.

Injury or removal of the superficial layers of the epidermis increases the rate of mitoses in the basal layer and the gaps are repaired. Friction and the wearing away of the horny layer results in greater production of keratin and an increased thickness. The pads of the dog's feet are a good example of this. Also situated in the basal layer of the epidermis are the melanoblasts, or pigment producing cells. The dermis is composed of bundles of collagen fibres which serve as a framework and support for the blood vessels, nerves, lymphatics, sweat glands and hair follicles.

The keratin of the epidermis is kept supple by the secretions of the sweat and sebaceous glands and fat produced by the epidermal cells. Generally speaking, dogs have very few sweat glands over their skin area and therefore rely on the numerous sweat glands in the pads of their feet and the respiratory system to dissipate the majority of heat. In the male, the hairless scrotum also aids in this regard. By dissipation of sweat from these areas and by the regulation of blood flow in its vessels, the skin plays an important part in temperature control—indeed loss of heat occurs almost entirely from these areas.

The sweat glands, which are situated deep in the dermis, are formed of a coiled tube of cubical epithelium which leads via the sweat duct to open on the surface of the skin through spiral clefts between the epidermal cells. The sweat glands are under the control of the central nervous system and can be stimulated to secrete by the need for the animal to lose heat, or by fear.

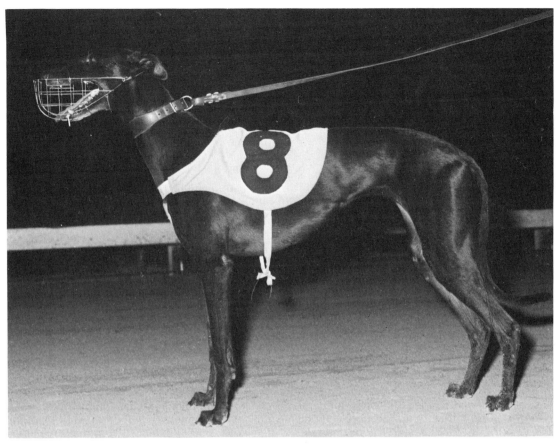

Above: Ascapella Miss, a 30-kg black bitch by Chariot Charm out of Fullock, set the 704-metre track record at the Gabba track in September 1974 *(By permission of W. Atkins). Below:* The Gabba track, Queensland, Australia, has a grass surface and races are conducted over 420, 558, and 704 metres *(Courtesy of the Gabba Greyhound Racing Club)*

The sebaceous glands are wedged in the angle between the hair and the arrector pili muscle, the contraction of which expresses into the follicle the oily sebum. They are composed of specialised epidermal cells which form the sebum by the degeneration of their own cell substance in a comparable way to keratin formation by the normal epidermal cell. Sebum production is not under nervous control but is dependent on the size and mitotic activity of the sebaceous cells which are themselves influenced by the pituitary and sex hormones.

Hair and nails are specially modified keratin structures, both being formed by invaginations of the epidermis. Hairs are dead keratinised cells firmly cemented together which protrude from the hair follicles, tubes of epidermis sunk obliquely in the dermis, and grow from the dilated end or bulb. The general covering of hair on the body of the dog is designed mainly for protection and to aid in the regulation of body temperature. In cold weather, the hair grows more thickly thus trapping more air among its fibres and consequently helping to keep the animal warm. In hot weather, the dog sheds these extra hairs and less air is trapped, allowing a greater amount of heat to escape into the atmosphere. The skin is thickest and the hair is most dense over the neck, back region, and sides of the dog than it is on the under surfaces. These areas are regarded as the most vulnerable regions in a fight. The arrector pili, strands of smooth muscle which are capable of raising the hair erect by their contraction, are numerous in these regions. This explains why, when a dog 'gets his bristles up', the hair is seen to stand upright along the region of the back. The hair around the toenails is designed to deflect dirt and these hairs should never be clipped.

A nail is a hardened, flat, resilient structure resting on the nail bed which, formed by the germinal layers of the skin above a vascular dermis, confers the pink tint of the nail. Joggling a nail between the finger and the thumb reveals the extent of the nail root, buried under the nail fold. The nail grows from its root at the nail matrix.

The skin is richly supplied by sensory nerves and by sympathetic fibres to the vessels, arrector pili muscles and sweat glands. From a deep plexus in the dermis branches they run to a superficial dermal plexus. Each single fibre divides into many ramifications, all of these for one nerve fibre apparently terminating in the same way, either as a free ending or in a specialised encapsulated ending. That the skin represents a mosaic of 'areas' for pain, pressure, and temperature may be readily appreciated by drawing a pencil lightly across the back of the hand and immediately the feeling from specific areas is peculiarly cold. However, the structures and functions subserving these sensations are not definitely known as yet. Sensations are probably not all simple because each has time, space, and intensity aspects, and many are compound, e.g., wetness elicited by cold and pressure, oiliness by warmth, stickiness by variable and moving pressure.

The daily grooming of greyhounds, with a soft glove and/or brush, is necessary in order to maintain a healthy skin and coat. This helps remove dirt and external parasites as well as stimulate the blood flow of the skin by its massaging effect.

It is inadvisable to bath with shampoo or hydrobath a dog more than once a week as too frequent bathing will dry the natural oils from the skin and hair. Specially prepared dog shampoos should be used to bath your greyhound, as they have very sensitive skin which may often react rapidly to the use of harsh chemicals. If the skin does become dry and scaly, the dog may be wiped with a clean rag sprinkled with castor oil to assist in replacing the essential oils of the skin. Another good method is to feed a teaspoonful of cod liver oil twice a week.

Before we consider diseases of the skin, a brief description of the general terms used in describing different types of skin lesion may perhaps be useful.

Macule, (Latin: macula), a discoloured spot on the skin that is not elevated above the surface; an area distinguishable by colour or otherwise from its surroundings.

Papule, (Latin: papula), a small circumscribed, solid elevation of the skin.

Vesicle, (Latin: vesicula), a small blister; a small, circumscribed elevation of the epidermis, containing a serous fluid.

Bulla, (Latin: bulla), a large blister or cutaneous vesicle filled with serous fluid.

Pustule, (Latin: pustula), a vesicle filled with pus instead of serous fluid.

Wheal, a slightly elevated area on the body surface which is redder or paler than the surrounding skin; it is often attended with severe itching, and often disappears quickly.

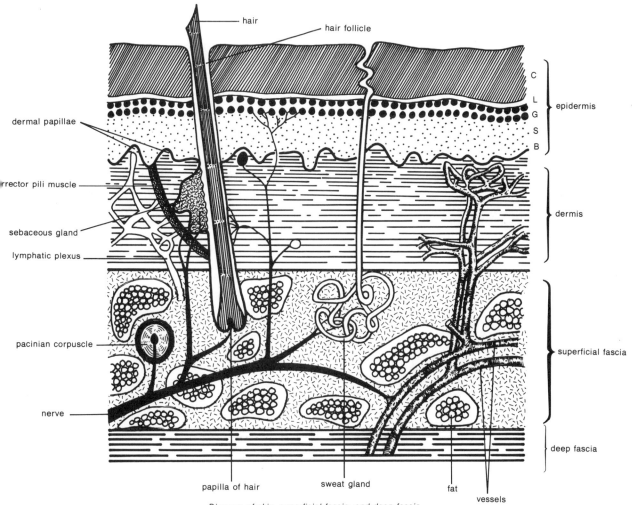

Diagram of skin, superficial fascia, and deep fascia
C, L, G, S, B—strata corneum, lucidum, granulosum, spinosum
and basal layer, respectively.

Scale, (French: écale—shell, husk), a thin compacted, plate-like structure, as of epithelial cells, on the surface of the body, or shed from its skin.

Weeping, arises when there is marked exudation of serum from the skin, usually as a result of acute inflammatory reactions.

Crust or scab, (Latin: crusta), a formed outer layer, especially an outer layer of solid matter formed by the drying of a bodily exudate or secretion. A scab is the crust of a superficial sore.

Many other terms are also used in describing skin diseases, but these are generally self explanatory.

GENERAL PRINCIPLES OF TREATMENT

In addition to the specific treatments used in diseases of the skin there are certain general principles which are applicable to the majority of skin lesions.

1. Remove the cause, if possible

Cease using any drug which may be responsible for the skin eruption, remove any offending articles either in the diet or in contact with the skin, or eradicate any parasite.

2. External applications

These play an important role in the treatment of skin diseases and the following are in common use:

a. *Powders* Powders may consist of one powder or a mixture of powders and are of use on moist areas to dry the skin. They are also beneficial in preventing friction on the skin.

b. *Lotions* These are widely used, particularly

47

for weeping lesions, and are best applied by dabbing them on with lint. Lotions generally contain substances of a cooling nature and are usually aqueous solutions or suspensions in which spirit is occasionally embodied for its cooling effect.

c. *Liniments* Liniments are usually applied to the skin by means of friction, most of them having a counter-irritant effect. Thus camphor is an important constituent of most liniments. Liniments frequently have an oily basis, as this facilitates friction and thus increases their rubefacient power.

d. *Ointments* An ointment consists of a base such as yellow or white soft paraffin, wool fat, or lard, in which the medicament is uniformly dispersed. It may or may not be intended for absorption into the skin, and therefore a base is chosen with this in mind. The paraffin bases are not so readily absorbed as the natural fats and waxes such as lard and wool fat. It must be borne in mind that the absorption of the active ingredient may be retarded by the use of unsatisfactory bases. To overcome this there is a tendency to use the emulsion bases. Ointments are preferred for the more chronic scaling lesions.

e. *Creams* Creams are preparations made with emulgents. These are generally smeared on the skin or applied with gauze.

f. *Pastes* This term is used to designate a preparation which is of thicker consistency than an ointment. This harder consistency usually being due to the addition to the greasy base of some solid ingredient such as starch. Pastes are frequently used when a drying, absorbent preparation is required.

When ointments and pastes are applied, the removal of the previous application should be effected by swabbing with cotton wool soaked in oil. These preparations should be thickly applied and as little occlusive dressing as possible used.

g. *Poultices* A poultice is a pasty mass which is applied hot to the part and is composed of bases which will retain the heat for a considerable time. Poultices are very valuable counter-irritants and often contain antiseptic substances.

3. Cold, heat, and radiation

Cold, usually in the form of carbon dioxide 'snow', is used in the removal of warts and naevi. Heat, often in the form of a cautery, is also used to remove warts and naevi. Ultraviolet light may also prove beneficial in the treatment of some diseases of the skin.

4. Antibiotics

It is believed that antibiotics act mainly by interfering with bacterial metabolism. For example, it has been suggested that penicillin acts by upsetting the metabolism of the ribonucleic acid present in the cell walls of growing gram-positive bacteria and this prevents the absorption of glutamic acid and lysine which they require for their existence. Gram-negative bacteria can synthesise these substances and are consequently not affected in this way by penicillin. Any improvement due to the use of an antibiotic will be apparent fairly quickly and if there is no response within two or three days some other agent should be used. Some of the antibiotics, notably penicillin, also possess a bactericidal action against certain bacteria at the time of mitotic division.

It is generally agreed that antibiotics should be reserved for serious cases of specific infective conditions and preferably where the organism has been proved to be sensitive to the antibiotic to be used.

5. Steroids

Steroids are available in the form of sprays, creams, and ointments for the treatment of local areas of eczema, sensitivity dermatitis, and pruritis.

DISEASES OF THE SKIN

The skin, together with its underlying tissues, comprises an elastic body which is able to withstand a considerable degree of stress, friction, and pressure of various types without harm, provided its inherent property of resilience is not impaired.

Callus

Mechanical stimulation of the skin to produce overgrowth of the stratum corneum, or horny layer of the skin, is commonplace. Callosities may form where areas are exposed to undue pressure and/or friction or as a result of the dog lying on hard surfaces such as wood or concrete. This callus formation is mainly seen on the hocks and elbows of the dog as hard, hairless areas. Fluid may accumulate beneath the skin in the area of the callosity, particularly on the

Above: Sandown track, Victoria, Australia, has a sand surface and races are conducted over 513 and 718 metres. *(Courtesy of Aerial Photographers.) Below:* Olympic Park track, Victoria, Australia, has a sand surface, straights of 70 metres, and a circumference of 440 metres incorporating four bends. Race distances—511, 732 metres. *(Courtesy of Melbourne Greyhound Racing Association)*

elbows, and give rise to an unsightly bursa. The hair on the muscles of the hind quarters may also be rubbed off over a period of time.

Treatment merely involves supplying the dog with soft bedding such as straw, blankets, compound rubbers, or shredded newspaper. It is important to see that the dog does not chew or swallow the bedding.

The transition of a callus from the physiological to the pathological state is gradual and, although one can readily draw a distinction, the dividing line where one finishes and the other begins is impossible to define.

1. *Physiological callus*

The proper function of the epidermis is to form cells and for them to pass to the surface and cornify. The rate at which they grow is determined by the work the skin has to do and thus the bulkage of cells deposited in a callus is the result of a normal process, i.e., a functional increase in response to the necessity for affording protection to a part subject to the work. A callus, therefore, is basically a natural or physiological process, it is a condition pertaining to normal health and cannot be described as a diseased condition. Callus is a type of compensative hypertrophy, i.e., the extra growth compensates in response to increased functional activity and the increased production of keratin is merely an extension of the normal process of cornification.

A callus is essentially an adaptive process, i.e., it is an attempt on the part of the tissue to accommodate itself to a special variety of stress beyond the normal skin requirements. The hardness and thickness of the horny mass is due to:

a. The cells increasing both in quantity and rate of growth.
b. The normal dispersal of loosened cells ceasing.
c. The heavy deposit of keratin, which comprises of close mesh, forming a hard, uniting network.

2. *Pathological callus*

A pathological condition is an abnormal one, the cells undergoing changes as a result of the abnormal conditions acting on them. Increased functional activity arises from the attempt on the part of the body to resist demands which would be of an injurious nature. Fundamentally, therefore, the difference between physiological and pathological callus is that the first is a healthy response to work, whereas the latter is a response to conditions likely to be unfavourable to normal cell life, i.e., trauma or injury. There is a functional disturbance, the pathological process being largely a defensive and reparative one.

Pathology of a corn

The pathological process which occurs when a corn is formed is identical with that of a callus, except that there is an additional stage when the portion subject to most pressure becomes compressed into a concentrated core. It is this core formation which differentiates a corn from a callus. The pressure causes the core to be forced upon the dermis and this reduces the size of the underlying papillae and, if the pressure is of adequate intensity, the papillae in the area will undergo a process of atrophy and eventual obliteration. The stimulating nature of the intermittency of blood supply causes those papillae which are able to maintain their full development to undergo hypertrophy. Hence, sectionally, a corn generally has atrophied papillae below the core and hypertrophied ones at its periphery. The pain is caused by pressure on the nerve endings.

Chronic corns, particularly those on the pads of the dog's feet, may be subject to a fixation to deeper structures. This attachment will be noticed if the area is pinched up with the fingers, all the tissues between the fingers rising except the corn. This binding down of the base of the corn is due to the additional fibrous tissue deposited as a result of the chronic inflammation.

Treatment of corns and callus

In the painless removal of corns and callus it is desirable that only a scalpel or suitable instrument be used which can be manipulated with ease and be maintained in first-grade order. Instruments which are so crudely shaped that they are difficult to handle can seldom be used without causing some degree of pain.

The operator ultimately adopts his own method for the removal of corns and callus which may be:

1. By the process of minute paring away of the hardened tissue (minute section).
2. By paring and ultimately removing any central points of corn that may remain (partial section).
3. By accurately separating the hard skin from the normal skin by the use of forceps and a

dissection along the line of demarcation (entire section).

The majority of operators prefer the first two methods, the last being used only when a nucleus is very concentrated and penetrating deeply into the underlying tissues. It is usually held that it is far easier to render the operation painless by the minute and partial section methods than it is by the use of entire dissection. Painlessness is secured by keeping the tissues as steady as possible during manipulation of the scalpel. By so doing, the operator prevents the tissues being dragged upon, not only by the pressure of the blade but also by the pulling of the corneous mass upon the adjacent tissues. The index finger and the thumb are usually employed to stretch and apply tension to the tissues against the action of the blade, moving the fingers so as to gain the maximum stretch in whatever direction the blade is moving.

Success in ascertaining the depth of cut depends to no small degree on a keen sense of colour. Corns and callus are usually of a dusky-yellow colour unless soggy with sweat from the dog's pads, when they will often appear whitish. The pink tinge from vascularity becomes more apparent the nearer one gets to the papillae, when the operation requires greater care. Until experience is gained it would be wise to refrain from using those drugs which tend to obscure the natural colouration. With experience, the alteration in colour that would occur from the use of such drugs as salicylic acid or iodine would not give rise to any great problem, but with the inexperienced operator it is almost certain to lead to too deep an incision. Until one is experienced it is not easy to judge the depth of a corn when it is embedded in a mass of callus, particularly when the callus is dark in colour and of long standing. To operate straight through a callus to enucleate a corn is a bad technique and is sure to cause a good deal of pain. By removing the callus first, the amount of actual dissection of the nucleus is reduced to a minimum.

For the sake of convenience the action of drugs which exert an influence on corns and callus may be classified as follows:

1. Exfoliants or keratolytics

These are drugs which have the capacity to disintegrate keratinous tissue. Salicylic acid probably has the most therapeutic value as an exfoliant and it acts by disintegrating the superficial layers of the skin, the cells of which become swollen and opaque, the swelling relieving the pain by lifting the crust of hardened squames from the lower epidermal layers. By so doing, pressure is relieved from the nerve endings and the congested vascular supply is not so confined. The acid varies in its action according to its concentration, mode of application, and the length of time it remains in contact with the tissues. There is no absolute rule as to what precise strength should be applied, for it is a matter of judgement as to how much can be tolerated short of producing injury to deeper tissues. Another factor due much consideration is the depth of subcutaneous tissue underlying the corn.

2. Astringents

Corneous growth can be controlled to a certain extent by the restricting or tightening effect which an astringent substance has on the tissues. By this means the growth rate of the epidermis can be retarded by the coagulation of the protein content of the reproductive cells or of the intercellular fluid which feeds them. Of the many drugs capable of producing an astringent action, few are suitable for the purpose of influencing corn formation, the one generally employed being silver nitrate. Silver nitrate has the great advantage of being self-limiting and therefore easily controlled in its depth of action. The coagulum produced has a tightening effect on the vessels of the skin and consequently relieves the congestive pressure below the corneous crust. Fluid pressure on the nerve endings is lessened and pain alleviated.

On the pads of the feet the corneous growth may be stimulated by sweat production. Silver nitrate has a distinctly beneficial action by constricting the orifices of the glands and so stopping the infiltration of sweat and reducing the rate of growth of cells producing the corn or callus. The application of silver nitrate after operating causes considerable contraction in the bulk of the corn, the moist nature of the swollen keratinous layers ceases, and subsequent operating is facilitated.

Silver nitrate has a burning action if over-applied and an overdose may produce deep action before the self-limiting nature of the coagulum can act as a barrier to its further action. The chemical burn produced may be extremely painful. Dosage must be carefully regulated and kept within the limits of astringency. Superficial astringency of adequate value commences in the region of a ten per cent concentration which may be applied in either water or spirit. A fairly energetic action is obtained by using twenty-five per cent concentration, while at fifty per cent it usually burns the tissues. The ten per cent concentration is of value if the tissues bleed during removal of a corn, as at this strength it also possesses a certain degree of styptic value which causes little discomfort.

If pain from the action of silver nitrate is excessive, its action may be neutralised by a saturated solution of common salt.

3. *Emollients*

Emollients are of value as softening agents; the more pliable the post-operative corn cavity can be made, the lower will be the liability to rapid reformation of the corn. By modification of the violence of pressure and friction as they fall on part greasy and oily substances diminish the growth rate of hard skin. If one interposes a slippery substance between the ground and the pad the irritation arising from friction and pressure is reduced considerably. By persistence, fibrous tissue can be softened and normal skin-elasticity restored. In the presence of the numerous sweat glands on the pads of the dog's feet the skin's absorbent powers are greatly increased and softening ointment is able to penetrate more readily.

Generally, a combination of absorbable and non-absorbable greasy agents is employed, the basic idea being that the absorbable substance will penetrate deeply and soften the tissues, while the non-absorbable substance will maintain its body mass external to the skin for sufficient time to act mechanically as a slippery body. Various proportions of hydrous lanolin and soft paraffin, stiffened with hard paraffin, represents one combination. Other substances in common use include anhydrous lanolin, soft soap, cold cream, and castor oil.

All emollient substances should incorporate antiseptic value. The use of iodine ointment as a routine type of emollient is beneficial as it is not only antiseptic but also mildly counter-irritant in action. This facilitates the flow of tissue fluids and so relieves pain and congestion.

4. *Analgesics*

There are a few drugs which may be employed specifically for their ability to lessen pain. Phenol and pyrogallol, although used mainly for their pain reducing qualities, also possess additional advantages. Phenol has a softening value and pyrogallol possesses astringent action. Phenol acts directly on the peripheral nerve endings and consequently diminishes sensitivity. Although it is a valuable drug, it must be used with great care, the main risk being not so much in its strength as in its continuity of action.

Phenol may be applied to a corn, before or after an operation, to deaden pain. Its action is quick and effective.

Pyrogallol acts by its ability to absorb oxygen from the tissues, its analgesic action being partly attributed to the fact that it penetrates via the superficial vessels and thus lessens fluid pressure within the capillaries which relieves irritation of the cutaneous nerves.

Both phenol and pyrogallol may be relied upon to soothe and constrict the part.

Benzocaine has a beneficial action on certain types of painful corns and may be applied in ointment form. Its analgesic action is aided by the softening effect of the hydrous lanolin, the usual vehicle employed.

Mange

Mange is of two types, sarcoptic or demodectic, both being caused by small mites and both being contagious to other dogs. The mite inhabits the hair follicles and deeper layers of the skin. A veterinarian should be consulted in either case as a programmed approach to treatment is generally indicated if a cure is to be effected. Diagnosis is made by the use of skin scrapings.

1. *Sarcoptic mange*

Sarcoptic mange is not as common as demodectic mange and is somewhat easier to cure. This type of mange presents as inflamed areas devoid of hair and predominantly appears on the face, legs, and abdomen, accompanied by small pustules, particularly around the ears. The mite causes severe irritation of the skin and the dog may scratch the affected areas until the skin bleeds.

Treatment involves bathing the dog every two or three days in an insecticidal dog wash such as 'Malawash' and applying, when the dog has dried off, a soothing cream to the affected areas twice daily. A common treatment is with benzyl benzoate emulsion which is applied all over the animal from the neck downward, the animal first having been bathed and all the lesions thoroughly scrubbed to lay open the burrows. Benzyl benzoate emulsion dries in about 10 minutes. A second application is often made the following day.

It is of paramount importance that the dog's

kennel and its contents and the normal area of habitation be thoroughly disinfected to prevent re-infection. Care should be taken to see the dog does not drink the solution in which he has been bathed or lick the preparation which has been applied to his skin, as these preparations are poisonous. If the mange is widespread it may be advisable to clip the hair prior to treatment.

2. *Demodectic mange (follicular mange)*

In this case the mite inhabits the bulb of the hair follicle and consequently the application of preparations to the skin serves little purpose. There are a number of treatments available, but veterinary advice should be sought at the first sign of demodectic mange. This type of mange presents as irritated areas around the eyes, mouth, or other areas of the body. The hair becomes thin, dry, and scaly, with bald patches of varying size often following. The condition must be cleared before the animal is permitted to race.

Investigation has revealed that in demodectic mange the mite also inhabits the spleen, liver, kidneys, lymph nodes, and muscles of the tongue of the affected dogs.

There may be a hereditary tendency toward this terrible complaint. There is no guarantee of success in the treatment of this type of mange and it may involve several months of treatment or even enter the category of incurable disease and involve the entire body area of the animal. If the complaint is known to be of hereditary origin or if it reaches the incurable stage, it is perhaps best to put the dog down rather than to subject the animal to severe, prolonged treatment which obviously will have little chance of success.

Many methods of treatment and preparations which prove successful in the treatment of sarcoptic mange may only be of value in treating demodectic mange if the condition is not hereditary and if it is in the very early stages.

Tetmosol, arsenical, and iodine preparations have been implemented, together with injections, which have resulted in varying degrees of success but, generally speaking, there is little chance of a cure once the disease has gained a hold.

If adequate attention is directed to the cleanliness of the dog, his living area, items used for grooming purposes, and to feeding utensils and proper nourishment, then it is extremely unlikely that these complaints will be contracted.

Bacterial infections

The skin of the dog is normally colonised by an innumerable flora of organisms which reside in crypts, hair follicles, sebaceous glands, and their ducts. Their number and distribution vary with climate, age, hygiene, and from one site to another. This resident flora is only temporarily reduced by bathing or application of antiseptics. In addition, there is a transient flora largely confined to the more exposed areas and which includes potential pathogens. The healthy canine skin disinfects itself, destroying certain bacteria with unsaturated fatty acids contained in sebum, and others by desiccation so that this transient flora is only able to establish itself for a few hours and is easily got rid of by washing the dog with a suitable soap and water. In a contaminated environment, transient pathogens may acquire temporary resident status. If the skin remains healthy, such a state may be shortlived but, if a breach of continuity of the skin occurs, or if the defence mechanism is impaired by skin disease, active infection of the skin may take place.

Furunculosis (boils)

Once the skin has become colonised by pathogenic staphylococci, friction appears to be one of the precipitating causes of boils. The majority of boils encountered in greyhounds appear on the face, head and neck.

Once a boil is established on the skin, many traditional methods of treatment seem only to spread the infection. The application of kaolin poultices macerating and warming the surrounding skin, or occlusion beneath adhesive plaster producing a poultice of pus. It is therefore hardly surprising that one boil is frequently followed by others. Skin damaged by eczema or dermatitis has a far greater susceptibility to invasion by staphylococci, and furunculosis is a common complication of these cases. The skin disease may not be obvious and it is important to remember that hidden patches of eczema and lesions caused by pruritis ani (intense itching of the anal region) or pruritis vulvae (intense itching of the external genitals of the female) may be the point of origin of infection.

Treatment is aimed at preventing the surface spread of infection. Adhesive plaster should be avoided as a dressing and if some cover is necessary gauze and bandage are preferable. Penicillin usually clears the condition. Attention should be given to the diet and general health.

Acne

Acne is a skin disease which may be associated with a puppy attaining the second set of teeth, the complaint being comparable with the acne of human adolescents. The face, nose, and cheeks of the dog are the sites usually affected. Acne is more frequent in dogs with scurf. In some cases the diet may aggravate the condition, especially if it is high in carbohydrate content. Climatic factors also influence the course and extent of the lesions. Exposure to the sun and wind increases desquamation of the exposed skin and diminishes the hyperkeratosis of the hair follicles.

The typical lesions are red papules and pustules. In severe cases with much pustule formation scars may develop with consequential permanent damage. Old dogs have been known to contract pimples between their toes or boils in that region.

Thorough cleansing of the affected area is necessary and it is also essential to express as many of the pimples as possible. The resultant cavities may be cleansed with boracic lotion. Treatment will involve doses of penicillin. The accompanying irritation of this complaint will probably induce the dog to rub his face on objects within his living area, thus making the condition worse.

Ringworm

This extremely contagiouis fungal infection may affect dogs, cats, and humans. Microsporon canis may be derived from cats, dogs, or infected humans, and is seen as an irregular, bald area dotted with distorted, broken stumps of hair with accompanying erythema, scanty pustules, and scaling. These lesions heal in the centre, thus giving the characteristic ringed or circular outline from which the disease takes its name.

Examination of a hair stump in a potash preparation reveals it to be packed with spores and examination under Wood's light produces a turquoise fluorescence of each infected hair. If Wood's light is not available, infected stumps can be revealed by dabbing the suspected area with an ether-soaked swab; as the ether evaporates, the affected stumps retain a frost and can be easily distinguished.

Griseofulvin therapy is generally successful. Whitfield's Ointment is another preparation which is available for treatment of this com-

plaint. Every care should be taken to keep the affected area as dry as possible, and brushes, bedding, etc., should be thoroughly disinfected. It is also necessary to guard against reinfection from wet floors. One should wear rubber gloves when treating the infected animal and disinfect the gloves in a strong solution of Condy's Crystals and then oxalic acid before removing them.

Eczema

This term is used to describe several varieties of skin condition which possess a number of common features. The exact cause, or causes, of eczema are imperfectly understood; why it should develop in some animals from contact with certain substances is unknown and it would seem that there must be some internal factor present which renders eczematous animals very sensitive to mild irritants. In support of this theory is the fact that certain forms of eczema are associated with allergic diseases like asthma and hayfever. In a great many cases eczema can be attributed to external irritants such as soaps, chemicals, plants, foodstuffs, etc.

The various types of eczema have different individual features, but the lesions have the following common characteristics:
1. The lesion usually appears as a reddening, or erythema, of the skin.
2. Vesicles are superimposed on the erythema.
3. Weeping generally occurs due to serum exuding from the vesicles, and crusts may also form.
4. The condition usually becomes chronic with the development of thickened, pigmented skin and scaly lesions.
5. The lesions usually itch.

To determine the cause of eczema it is advisable to have the veterinarian take a skin scraping in order to determine the nature of the agent responsible. It is essential to remove any irritant which may possibly be the cause of the eczema. The animal's resistance must be built up and any septic focus or disease must be treated.

Local treatment is important and the preparation applied varies according to the stage of the eczema. In the acute weeping stage a lotion, such as calamine lotion, is used and applied on gauze or lint and as little covering as possible is applied. Sedatives may be added to the lotion to allay the itching. In the less acute stage an oily liniment is preferred. Pastes, such as zinc paste with the addition of tar, or crude coal tar itself, are useful applications.

In all cases of eczema, soap and water usually aggravate the condition and are forbidden. In severe cases of eczema which do not respond to other measures, hydrocortisone ointment applied locally often has dramatic results. This has the great advantage of not causing any of the side effects seen when hydrocortisone and allied drugs are administered systemically. Unfortunately following cessation of treatment, the condition may relapse in some cases.

Fly dermatitis
Dermatitis due to flies is common in the summer, particularly if one's kennels are in the vicinity of horse stables. The use of fly repellents and ointments is necessary. The tips of the animal's ears may become so badly affected as to drip blood and are then open to infection. Flies spread disease in the following way:
1. By depositing their own excrement on food.
2. By drowning in liquids—the faecal matter from their contaminated feet and wings dissolving in the liquid.
3. By vomiting the germ-laden contents of their stomachs in order to dissolve foodstuffs on which they land, since flies can only take in food in liquids.
4. By getting animal faecal matter on their feet and then landing on their next meal, thus depositing germ-laden matter from their feet on the area.

Sprays, creams and repellent sticks are readily available for the prevention and treatment of fly dermatitis. These preparations may be used daily or as necessary to obtain the desired control. Care must be taken to avoid getting the preparation in the animal's eyes or mouth.

Flea-bite Itch
This condition arises from flea infestation. The female flea lays her eggs not only on the body of the dog but also in small crevices in the dog's living quarters. The flea bites a minute hole in the host's body through which it sucks blood. Following feeding, the flea leaves a bloody smear and faecal matter on the surface of the skin which can be observed and felt in the animal's coat as tiny dark sand-like grains.

Defestation of both the dog and the kennel must take place together to prevent re-infestation. The dog should not be permitted to lick his coat. Employ a safe, effective powder and apply it all over the coat, including the head, ears, and under the tail. Rub it in well. After 1 or 2 hours the coat should be brushed to remove the dead matter. Flea infested bedding should be burned.

Warts
A wart is a highly vascular, benign growth which involves not only the epidermis but also the dermis. Warts may form on any part of the dog's body and exhibit peculiarities in shape in various situations. Thus, they may be present as a simple cauliflower-like growth, as single thread-like projections, or as irregular masses of flat-topped lesions. On the pads of the feet warts appear as flattened growths due to their compression under weight-bearing. Warts appearing in this area are generally very painful and necessitate immediate treatment. In some cases maximum pain occurs during pressure, but in other instances the dog may not be particularly conscious of pain until the foot is relieved from pressure, when there is a great resurgence of blood into the growth, causing a throbbing sensation. On the other hand, the dog may be quite untroubled by the existence of the wart. Where there is no serious obstruction to the protrusion of the growth, warts are found to be covered with rough, thickened epidermis which is often fissured and cauliflower-like in appearance.

The aetiology of warts is still subject to considerable discussion. The weight of evidence is clearly toward the virus theory. The infective nature of these growths was first demonstrated by Variot in 1893; he demonstrated that warts were auto-inocuable and transmissable. The long incubation period following experimental inoculation tends to support this theory of virus infection. The prolonged incubation period of virus diseases is well known and is considerably in excess of most bacterial infections. In some instances the incubation period of experimentally produced warts extended up to nearly 20 months. Roxburgh, in 1944, brought to our notice that all types of wart arise from the same virus.

Although warts may be found on dogs of any age, they are most common in the young. Trainers may be familiar with the frequency with which warts occur when there has been every opportunity for contagion, as, e.g., after visits to the track where the virus may gain entry through the pads of the dog's feet or through a small cut or graze. For the same reason warts are common in boarding and rearing establishments.

Evidence has been revealed, in recent investigations on viruses, regarding the tendency which some varieties have to remain latent and non-pathogenic in the living cell. There is a possibility that this may be the case with the wart and that irritations of many types may act as stimulants to induce activity in the virus and cause proliferation of the cells. Traumatic irritation has been acknowledged as playing a part in the formation of warts. Irritation from a protruding toenail is often observed as a precursor of warts. It will be similarly noted how frequently they are to be seen in situations where a part has been subjected to pinching or friction. It has been suggested by Whitfield that, although warts may be highly infective in nature, they may also develop traumatically, the growth being the product of dilatation of the capillaries arising from injury to the cutaneous vessels.

The essential difference between the hypertrophy associated with a corn and that of a wart is that with the corn it is purely the extension of a normal process of cell growth and degeneration, whereas with the wart the growth process is in itself abnormal and cell degeneration is delayed. Warts are encapsulated with a bed of fibrous tissue and the skin striae will be seen to be pushed apart and absent within the capsule, whereas in a corn the skin striae are continuous through the corn proper.

Treatment of warts

Warts on the plantar surface of the pads must, in general, be treated far more vigorously than those in other locations. No one method of treatment can be held to be 100 per cent effective in all cases. Results obtained are no doubt proportionate to the skill of the operator rather than to any specific virtue inherent in the agent applied. In the majority of cases the operator should be a veterinarian. Thorough eradication of the growth usually affords complete immunity for life, but unsuccessful treatment apparently makes the wart more resistant to subsequent treatment.

1. *Chemical cautery*

The main consideration is that the chemical cautery should be rapid in action and penetrating, without inducing more pain than is necessary. It is important to note that it is of little value to persist in the use of a particular drug when the tissues do not appear to respond to its use.

Great care is needed to protect the surrounding healthy tissue. This may be done by encircling the growth with a generous ring of vaseline. An efficient technique for ointments and crystals is to apply over the area of the growth a piece of adhesive plaster in which a hole has been cut to expose the wart, the hole being the exact size of the wart and care being exercised to see that the plaster adheres firmly to the skin. A piece of adhesive felt of suitable thickness, in which a similar hole has been cut, is then applied and the cavity thus formed acts as a receptacle for ointments and or crystals and, by preventing pressure on the growth, allows the wart to protrude, thus facilitating removal. A piece of adhesive plaster is strapped across the dressing to retain it.

A mild caustic, in some cases, has the disadvantage of acting as a stimulant once the initial caustic action has ceased. It may be possible to accomplish destruction of the wart without producing any pronounced reactions in the underlying tissues, however, it is generally considered advisable to induce a mild degree of inflammation in order to make certain that nature's reaction against the abnormal growth has taken place and the area rejected. This ordinarily involves the formation of a small quantity of serum, and occasionally pus, beneath the growth. When this occurs the operator can reasonably assume that a cauterising action has taken place completely through the body of the growth. A wart cannot suppurate of itself, and consequently it must be an inflammatory reaction of the underlying tissue.

The following materials are of use when an energetic action is desired: monochloracetic acid, nitric acid, pyrogallic acid, the caustic alkalis potassium hydroxide, and sodium hydroxide. Less energetic materials are silver nitrate, trichloracetic acid, and salicylic acid.

Monochloracetic acid: This acid is favoured because of its powerful and reliable action, however, its use is rarely without some degree of pain but it is probably the most speedy agent available. Apply as much acid as the growth will absorb, continually applying it until the area is fully saturated and will not absorb any more. The area is then left for one week when, without removing any of the growth, a further dose is given. The conclusion will be indicated by a pronounced dark ring round the wart, indicating the reaction of the part and the formation of pus. An incision at this ring releases the blood-stained pus and allows for total removal of the growth. As the part is not denuded when the drug is applied for the second time the effect is not so painful, except at the termination, as one might imagine. In the majority of cases two applications will suffice.

Trichloracetic acid: This acid is used in much the same manner as monochloracetic acid. It is more superficial and much slower in action but it has the advantage of inducing very little pain and may be used with safety where a wart is situated in a difficult area such as around a nail or where the tissues are shallow.

The caustic alkalis: These are unpopular because they are sometimes difficult to control in their depth of action. They have a high capacity for diffusion and, if unwisely applied, will destroy more tissues than is intended as they not only penetrate downwards but also laterally. Following application, the continuity of their action must be terminated by neutralising the alkali with dilute acetic acid.

Silver nitrate stick: This may be used diagnostically when it assists in revealing the nature and limitation in area of growth or to touch up any suspicious spots which may remain following the application of a more vigorous substance.

Salicylic acid: This acid is of value in the treatment of multiple warts, as it may be conveniently applied in plaster form of high concentration with safety. It may need to be applied at frequent intervals. Salicylic acid is a keratinous exfoliating agent and is often useful in removing the calloused tissue covering the growth. Because it causes the cells to swell it relieves pressure on the nerve endings and is therefore useful to dispel the immediate discomfort of a wart. It also aids in stopping the throbbing sensation because it lessens vascularity without inducing pain. The devitalised tissue is easily removed after one week, when a further dose is applied if necessary. Salicylic acid alone may clear up warts in many instances but sometimes another drug may be indicated to complete the cauterisation. Salicylic acid has a tendency to whiten the tissues and consequently obscure the process of cauterisation, often making it difficult for one to be satisfied that the removal is complete. The acid often completely removes the growth without inducing an inflammatory reaction and is consequently a relatively painless method of eradication. Salicylic acid ointment is usually sixty per cent strength in a base of lead oleate or resin ointment.

2. *Fulguration*
The destruction of a wart by fulguration using monopolar, high frequency spark is extremely successful. The overlying callus is removed and anaesthetic is then injected into the base of the growth, injecting the growth from each side and allowing sufficient time for the area to become anaesthetised. The high frequency cautery electrode is then directed on to the growth; care must be used to confine the spark to the affected area. The area first turns white and then darkens, the length of application being approximately half to one minute. The wart will then be desiccated and can be removed with a scalpel and a gauze dressing, with a suitable healing agent, applied.

3. *Cryotherapy (dry ice therapy)*
This form of treatment is also very successful and is useful where there is limited time available in which to eradicate the wart. In America, Dr William Ignatoff did much to popularise this technique, the Ignatoff cryokit being named after him. If it is conservatively and skilfully used, carbon dioxide snow is both a safe and simple technique and produces a thorough, penetrating freezing. The preparation of the tissues consists of cleaning the area and removing the superficial callus. The prepared carbon dioxide snow has a temperature of $-70°C$. A pencil of carbon dioxide snow is made in a special apparatus in which the gas is released to form snow. The snow is formed in a chamber to which a pencil-shaped mould is attached into which the snow is packed to form a solid pencil. It is then removed from the mould and is ready for application. It should not be held with the bare fingers. The pointed end of the pencil should be trimmed to the exact size of the wart to which it is directly applied with reasonable pressure for about 60 seconds. However, the length of application is dependent on the individual lesion. The usual practice is to hold it against the lesion until a surrounding whitened ring appears. Experience enables the veterinarian to determine the degree of pressure and length of application. The freezing itself is painless, but the pressure on the growth causes discomfort. Removal of the affected tissues will reveal any remaining wart tissue and, if there is, further treatment is indicated. In the majority of cases a single application will suffice. The area should be protected

with a suitable dressing following treatment. Two weeks between visits appears to be a suitable interval.

Normally, a blister-like formation appears which separates the wart from the underlying tissue and which may be readily removed with a scalpel. The dog should be rested while under treatment, especially on the second day when the pain is at its acute stage. A severe reaction may take place and the wart may be contained within a painful bulla and in such cases the area is drained and a dressing applied. This eradicates the symptoms and effects a cure.

Cryotherapy is contra-indicated when a wart lies immediately over a joint or where there is a paucity of subcutaneous tissue. Cryotherapy is applicable to the well-defined, isolated wart.

With the use of fulguration or cryotherapy, recurrence of the lesion is far less likely than with milder, prolonged forms of treatment. The virtue lies in the speed of these two methods.

4. *Surgical treatment*

Surgical treatment consists of curetting the wart from its fibrous capsule, accompanied by the use of anaesthetic. Another method is excision by cutting around and below the wart, the edges then being sutured. A slight scarring is inevitable with this technique, and should the wart reform together with the scar tissue, the condition is much worse than before.

INFLAMMATION, INFECTION, AND REPAIR

Inflammation is the condition into which tissues enter as a reaction to injury. Inflammation is marked by hyperaemia (an excess of blood in a part), stasis (stoppage of the flow of blood or other body fluid in a part), changes in the blood and walls of the small vessels, and by various exudations. Inflammation may be the result of an infection of the tissues with pathogenic bacteria which may gain entry into the tissues by way of an abraded surface, a wound, or mucous membrane. Tissues may also become inflamed as a result of infection with viruses and fungi and as a consequence of irritation of the tissues by physical and chemical poisons. Trauma or injury, such as a blow, sprain, fracture, or burn, may result in inflammation.

Inflammation is characterised by:
1. Redness—due to extra blood flow in the area.
2. Swelling—due to the formation of the exudate.
3. Heat—due to extra blood flow in the area.
4. Pain—due to the pressure of the congested tissues on the nerve endings.
5. Impairment or loss of function.

In certain stages of inflammation some of these signs may be absent.

The distinction between acute and chronic inflammation is worthy of discussion. First the meaning of the words should be discussed. Acute (L. acutus. sharp) in the relevant sense, means 'having a short and relatively severe course' and chronic (L. chronicus, from Gr. chronos. time) means 'persisting over a long period of time'.

Cells may become damaged as a result of:
1. A single event, e.g., a sprain, a clean cut, a burn.

   The entire damage is done at the outset and the sequence of events which follow cell destruction will be uninterrupted provided that the general condition of the dog is satisfactory. This may be termed acute inflammation.
2. Repeated irritation, e.g., repeated trauma to the tissues as occurs in 'track leg'.

   All of the damage does not occur at once. Following the initial injury, the inflammatory and repair processes are set in motion, but while they are taking place fresh damage is inflicted on the tissues. If the net rate of cell damage in tissues which are being repeatedly injured is greater than the rate at which the damaged cells are replaced, the total number of damaged, unreplaced cells will increase and necrosis, or death of the tissue, may occur. If the defence and repair mechanisms are more effective than the irritant, the number of damaged cells which have not been replaced will remain reasonably constant but some unreplaced damaged cells will always be present for as long as the irritation continues. The inflammation will persist over a long period of time, i.e., the inflammation will be chronic. All stages of the inflammatory and repair processes may be going on at the same time in chronic inflammation.

Chronic inflammation and acute inflammation differ in the length of time during which the inflammation lasts, but they cannot be defined in terms of time alone. In summary, chronic inflammation differs from acute inflammation mainly in that:
1. In acute inflammation there is a fairly

straightforward series of events as a consequence of a single injury.

2. In chronic inflammation all stages of inflammation and repair processes are found synchronously because the irritation persists over a long period. Where the normal tissue response to injury is impaired in any way, chronic inflammation may occur.

The outcome of inflammation may be:

1. Resolution, when the irritated tissues are restored to normal without permanent changes being produced, the products of the inflammatory reaction being absorbed by the lymphatic system.
2. Organisation, when the involved tissues are replaced, to varying degrees, by connective tissue produced as a consequence of the organisation of the products of inflammation.
3. Tissue destruction (necrosis), which is generally followed by repair through granulation, as in healing by second intention.

Reparative processes

Reparative processes differ vastly according to the nature of the tissues involved. Reparative processes commence almost immediately an injury is incurred; they do not wait for the defensive processes to subside. It is obvious that it is necessary for defensive processes to continue while repair is being carried out. The two repair processes are known as 'union by first intention' and 'union by second intention'.

Union by first intention

This repair process takes place when there is no infection and when the wound edges are in close apposition and become stuck together by a thin layer of clotted blood released from the cut blood vessels. The acute inflammatory reaction is slight because tissue damage is minimal. After approximately 24 hours a section will generally show a mild inflammatory reaction on both sides of the wound. Phagocytes, both neutrophil granulocytes and macrophages, migrate into the fibrin meshwork of the clotted blood where the neutrophils ingest any foreign matter and the macrophages ingest extravasated red blood cells. About the second or third day fibroblasts in the tissues at the periphery of the lesion enlarge and a few may mitose and then migrate into the wound coagulum. Small buds of endothelial cells grow from the capillaries surrounding the wound edges at about the same time. New vessels are formed both by multiplication of the

endothelial cells of the blood vessels and by rearrangement of existing endothelium. Lymphatic capillaries grow into the blood clot at the same time as the blood capillaries. During the course of the next few weeks the new vessels develop muscular walls and so become arterioles or venules.

In time, the wound coagulum becomes completely colonised with cells and this process is known as organisation and the final condition of granulation tissue. Two things happen to the intercellular material and debris, namely, dead cells liberate an enzyme which digests the dead cells and exudate into soluble peptides and amino acids which are utilised by the fibroblasts and endothelial cells for their nutrition and growth. Secondly, intercellular collagenous fibres are laid down and it is thought that the fibroblasts play an important role in their formation. The collagenous fibres do not develop properly if there is an ascorbic acid (vitamin C) deficiency.

The complete repair processes may occupy several months, although temporary repair is much more rapid. Collagenous fibres become tougher and arrange along the lines of tension in the scar. A few of the capillaries remain in the scar but usually, when the need for the existence of a certain capillary ceases, the vessel is gradually absorbed into the parent vessel exactly reversing the process by which it was formed. This affords an excellent example of how a vascular arrangement adapts itself to the metabolic requirements of the tissues it serves.

Union by second intention

This repair process takes place when the edges of the wound are not in close apposition and some bacteria accompany the wound, causing the inflammatory reaction to be more pronounced than in a wound which heals by first intention.

A histological section through a wound which is healing by second intention will exhibit, from the wound surface:

1. A layer of pus.

   Because the wound is infected, exudate is abundant and leucocytes migrate towards the bacteria on the wound surface. Many leucocytes die and in doing so liberate an enzyme, called trypsin, which digests dead bacteria and also leucocytes and tissue cells which have been killed by bacteria. The fluid known as pus is formed by the mass of leucocytes contained in the fluid resulting from the digestive action of trypsin.

2. A layer composed largely of fibrin, leucocytes, and a few capillaries.
3. An extremely vascular layer with fibroblasts and capillaries.
4. A layer in which the capillaries are narrower and fewer in number and where fibroblasts are plentiful.
5. The deepest layer consists of relatively avascular fibrous tissue.

Granulation tissue slowly grows from the base and sides of the wound and each part will undergo the series of changes outlined above until the entire cavity is filled with fibrous tissue. The epidermis grows over from the margins of the wound when the granulation tissue has reached the former skin level. Occasionally, the granulation tissue forms at a faster rate than the epithelium can cover the wound and when the granulation tissue protrudes beyond the former skin level it is referred to as 'proud flesh'.

Increased permeability of the vessel walls accounts for the exudate which functions to:

1. Dilute bacterial toxins and so render them less likely to damage the tissues.
2. Form a barrier around the focus of infection. Increased capillary permeability allows fibrinogen to pass into the tissue spaces and, after being converted into fibrin, to form a meshwork which permits the filtering of tissue fluid but which retains the bacteria and so localises the infection.
3. Carry natural antibacterial antibodies to the area of bacterial infection, the production of which is initiated by bacterial presence.

These three functions refer to bacteria but it should be noted that exudation occurs whether bacteria are present or absent.

Regeneration of specialised tissues

The liver is a good example of stable tissue with considerable power of regeneration. In certain circumstances, e.g., severe virus infection, much tissue may die but when the infection is brought under control, the surviving cells may regenerate so effectively that the liver may become larger than it was prior to the infection, a number of new nodules of liver tissue being formed.

The outcome of the repair of an uncomplicated fracture is bone which is indistinguishable from normal. There is no scar formation and consequently bone repair is the most efficient possible. If the two broken bone ends are in alignment, the intervening space is initially filled with blood clot which is rapidly invaded by fibroblasts extending from the periosteum of the broken bone ends, followed by osteoblasts. The broken ends will consequently become embedded in a strong mass of specialised 'osteoid' tissue which is frequently more bulky than the adjacent bone and referred to as 'callus'. Osteoclasts aid bone absorption and help mould the bone as the bone-forming tissues become calcified. Calcification is also aided by the continuing activity of the osteoblasts which lay down bone.

If a nerve cell dies, the neighbouring cells are incapable of proliferating to replace the loss. Limited regeneration, however, occurs on occasion when the nucleus of the nerve cell is unaffected and, with the guidance of the fibrous sheath, the axon re-establishes the continuity of the nerve.

To reduce inflammation one endeavours to relieve the congestion and this may be achieved in a number of ways. Cold compresses afford relief by causing contraction of the vessel walls. Heat in the form of hot fomentations, radiant heat, or infra-red radiations, may be applied to stimulate the local circulation and reduce the congestion by carrying off the products of inflammation. Massage in the form of light effleurage (stroking in the direction of the lymphatic flow) may be implemented, except in cases of acute inflammation, as a means of assisting the lymphatic circulation to dispose of excess lymph in the affected tissues. When pus is present the tissue should be lanced to provide an outlet for it, care being exercised to prevent spread of infection by using a suitable antispetic.

6

NUTRITION

Metabolism is the sum of all the physical and chemical processes by which a living organism is produced and maintained and also the transformation by which energy is made available for the uses of the organism. In other words, life processes may be grouped under the heading of metabolism.

Broadly speaking, any constructive processes by which simple substances are converted by living cells into more complex compounds resulting in utilisation of food and promotion of growth are considered to be building-up processes and are often referred to as anabolism, or constructive metabolism. Catabolism, on the other hand, refers to any destructive process by which complex substances are converted by living cells into more simple compounds; destructive metabolism.

Energy in the body may be used in various ways, e.g., to synthesise chemical compounds; some of these compounds, such as glycogen and fat, represent a stored energy source. Let us take the work performed by the contraction of muscles. In this case only a small amount of energy is used in work and a far greater amount is given off as heat. Other body cells utilise energy and perform work in various ways, e.g., the production of a secretion by secretory cells represents work and requires an energy outlay. A convenient way to demonstrate and measure the energy derived from foods is to measure it in the form of heat. A joule is an energy unit defined in terms of heat. The basal metabolic rate is usually calculated in terms of joules per square metre of body surface per hour.

The energy derived from the breakdown of foodstuffs is not directly applied to metabolic functions, but is stored. Such chemical energy can be released, with the aid of certain enzymes, to catalyse various chemical reactions that come under the heading of metabolism.

The dog that consumes the greater volume of oxygen should have the greater rate of metabolism, but a large dog should be expected to utilise more oxygen than a small dog. A large dog, having a greater body surface, should give off more heat than a small dog, in the same way that a large radiator gives off more heat than a small one. Obviously, body size must be taken into consideration in the determination of the basal metabolism.

Mental work requires only a very small energy outlay. Muscular work has a pronounced effect in raising the metabolism and hence the need for more food energy. The production of heat is a result of muscular activity. Some of this heat may be implemented to keep the body warm and some is lost from the body. Muscular exercise on a hot day produces more heat than necessary and the heat-regulating mechanism of the body adjusts to provide more heat loss, e.g., through sweat. In very cold weather, it is often necessary to keep the dog moving just to keep him warm. Muscular activity is the most important single factor affecting energy expenditure and therefore in determining the amount of food required to maintain balanced metabolism. Consumption of more food calories than are expended in energy should result in an increase in weight, and conversely, a dog that is working harder and eating less should lose weight. Even though this is basically correct, losing weight by working the fat off a dog is usually a difficult way to reduce weight. The best method to reduce weight is to limit the intake of food calories to a level somewhat below the energy requirement. This will enable the dog to lose weight slowly, at a rate of about half a kilogram per week. Severe dieting can be harmful to the animal's health. The dog cannot simply stop eating; although the body can supply some reserve fats for fuel, it cannot supply sufficient protein, vitamins, and minerals essential to health. A reducing diet should contain the dietary essentials, but with the amount of carbohydrate and fat reduced.

A proper balance between the kinds of food is desirable. Carbohydrates represent a readily available energy source and should constitute approximately twenty per cent of the dog's diet. Fats are the best food for conversion to heat and they also supply certain essential acids. Various sources recommend that fats compose up to ten per cent of the daily diet. Protein is used for growth and tissue repair, and the diet should provide protein foods containing all the essential amino acids.

METABOLIC ACIDOSIS

Metabolic acidosis is a buildup of lactic acid and carbon dioxide in the muscles and associated tissues of the body as a result of the breakdown of proteins and sugars such as muscle glycogen. If an imbalance in body salts is present, these breakdown products cannot be removed from the muscular tissues as quickly as they should and consequently they hamper the nerve impulses to either small or large muscle groups. The nerve impulses can continue while muscle fibres are still contracted, causing the muscle to further contract and resulting in cramp. The cramp is extremely painful and may last for several minutes before the nerve impulses are blocked and the muscle is permitted to relax. As a consequence of the damage afforded the individual cells of the muscle, soreness generally develops about 24 hours after the cramp. The cramp may involve either small or large muscle groups. 'This condition is thought to be directly related to metabolic acidosis and can vary in degree from a mild cramp to extensive "tying up" in the muscles to a condition which can be fatal known as the "Grueller Dog" syndrome.' The dog may collapse or be quite unable to walk, the most dramatic sign of this condition being when the dog either cannot pass urine or the urine passed is pink to dark-reddish brown. Within 24 hours the back and flank muscles become so tender that the slightest pressure causes severe pain to the dog.

Some of the contributing factors of metabolic acidosis are:

Dehydration

This is most frequent in the hot weather and generally there is a balanced loss of water and concentration of the blood. The condition may be confirmed by a packed cell volume test. If a dehydrated animal is given an unbalanced electrolyte, it may disrupt the normal balance of body salts. In addition, if a dehydrated animal is given diuretics, this can lead to excessive loss of sodium which then increases the concentration of chloride which in turn will tie up bicarbonate and result in metabolic acidosis. If the dog's skin is dry and lacks elasticity and does not quickly return to normal when the skin is pinched up, then this is an indication of dehydration.

The degree of fitness of the dog

As the dog becomes progressively fitter the size of the muscle fibres and blood vessels increases and this makes the pathways of the body fluids easier as well as assisting the removal of breakdown products. Frequently trainers will run their dogs before they are sufficiently fit and often muscle fibres are torn or damaged by over-exertion which causes a build-up in unwanted chemicals.

Heat stress and hyperventilation

The respiratory rate increases markedly on hot, humid days. As a consequence of the rapid expulsion of carbon dioxide via the lungs a series of events take place in the body, and the kidneys excrete bicarbonate which leads to a buildup in body fluid acids and a lowered reserve of bicarbonate. When this occurs the animal cannot excrete the waste products of exercise sufficiently quickly. It is of paramount importance not to transport dogs in hot cars or trailer, particularly excitable dogs.

Diet

As a consequence of the high protein diets fed to greyhounds they have more acid breakdown products in their system and it is therefore necessary to keep a check on the balance of body salts. If the pH of the urine rises above 7, this implies that more sodium or bicarbonate than normal is being excreted via the kidneys, and in hot weather the presence of increased acid body fluids (which tie up bicarbonate) could give rise to metabolic acidosis following exercise. This condition can occur in fit dogs in good racing condition but, generally speaking, it is usually related to humid conditions and the excitability of the dog prior to the race.

It is interesting to note that greyhounds with ability are generally good performers if their blood bicarbonate levels are high, while dogs with lowered bicarbonate levels are usually poor performers. Therefore, a blood test which includes tests for bicarbonate levels will afford an indication of the dog's potential to cope with a given race. This should be evaluated in the light of the dog's fitness, the atmospheric conditions, and the dog's temperament. There are balanced electrolyte powders available with high bicarbonate levels which may be administered to the dog during the summer months in accordance with directions. Metabolic acidosis may also be present during the colder months as a consequence of over-excitement, over-exertion, or over-heating of kennels. Treatment is concomitant with the degree of acidosis. In severe cases intravenous fluids are administered and in less severe cases the imbalance must be located and the diet adjusted accordingly.

It may take up to six or eight weeks to bring a dog back into full work following metabolic acidosis. Massage is of value in relieving soreness from the muscles. The blood bicarbonate level is an important indication of the acid base balance of body fluids. High bicarbonate levels may be present if the dog has been panting excessively and is hot and this can lead to metabolic acidosis. Because there is too much bicarbonate present in the blood, it is excreted via the kidneys in order to rectify the imbalance. If the blood bicarbonate level is lowered naturally by the kidneys and the dog is suddenly subjected to a race, metabolic acidosis may result as a consequence of the lowered blood bicarbonate level and the inability of the body to remove the acid waste products from exercise. It is possible to give rise to this chain of events by exercising a dog too soon following biling, when the vomiting causes excess loss of chloride both from the stomach and the general system, which leads to metabolic alkalosis, which in turn leads to excess excretion of bicarbonate. If the dog is raced before the bicarbonate level has built up again, differing degrees of metabolic acidosis can occur.

The importance of maintaining a high blood bicarbonate level in the racing greyhound should now be apparent. Even mild degrees of cramping should be viewed as an indication that the acid base balance of the dog's body fluids is unbalanced and the possible causes must be sought.

In the wild state nature ensured that dogs obtained a balanced diet. The whole of any animal caught is usually consumed. Calcium and minerals are obtained from the bones, lecithin and amino acids from the brain and unlaid eggs, vitamins from the liver, proteins from the muscles, and carbohydrates from grass and seeds in the stomach. The greyhound, however, is dependent on man for his food and frequently the diet is limited. A dog has a comparatively short digestive system and any shortage of vital nutrients in his food will become apparent more quickly than in man and will be more harmful. It is well known that storage and processing of foods can destroy essential vitamins and even though vitamins may be added to the processed food at the time of manufacture, there is no guarantee that these vitamins retain their potency at the time that the food is fed to the dog. Nevertheless, many thousands of household pets are apparently thriving on what could be labelled a deficient diet. It might be argued therefore that the addition of vitamins and minerals to a greyhound's normal diet is unnecessary, but one must remember that the greyhound is not a household pet. The greyhound is a scientifically bred, efficient racing machine and as such must be afforded proper attention. His fuel, which is of course his food, is of paramount importance if he is to be expected to race at his maximum capability and enjoy good health. It is these increased requirements due to strenuous racing that are of interest to the trainer.

Dogs of the same size and breed frequently require different amounts of food, even when maintained under apparently identical conditions. Feeding thus becomes an individual matter and this is also the case with supplements. Multi-vitamin supplements are available for greyhounds requiring a daily minimum maintenance dose. Frequently raced dogs require all the principal vitamins but in larger daily doses than a minimum maintenance dose. Tables of minimum vitamin requirements should not be interpreted as final and absolute. There is no basis for the assumption that vitamin requirements in racing greyhounds are uniform, even in good health. In disease there is even greater likelihood that the need will vary.

It is inadvisable to feed large quantities of vitamins to greyhounds as an excess will achieve no purpose and may cause complications as well as proving very costly. By means of blood tests a veterinarian will give advice on the dosage to be administered in order to correct deficiencies and/or improve performance. The effects of all of the vitamins overlap and interlace to a large extent. The action of the B complex vitamins is

Trainer, Neil Freeman, with his 26·6-kg champion stayer, Palmerston Lass (Venetian Court—Cappy's Girl), who registered best time of the night on twenty-two occasions and broke the 762 metres, Strathalbyn (South Australia) track record on four occasions *(Courtesy of South Australian Greyhound Trainer)*

synergistic, i.e., they cooperate with each other, and better results are obtained by administering them together than by giving large doses of a single B complex vitamin. It is reasonable to expect that an overdose of any single B complex vitamin would throw the other B complex vitamins out of balance, and probably nullify their activity.

Vitamins are either fat soluble or water soluble and this action is important within the body. Generally speaking, excess water-soluble vitamins are disposed of in urination, while excess feeding of fat-soluble vitamins may result in problems of usage and disposal, and a nutritional imbalance or increased weight may be the consequence.

Excess feeding of a particular vitamin may cause severe complications, side effects, imbalances, and deficiencies of other vitamins, and consequently one should not attempt to deviate from the recommended dosage schedule without

the supervision of a veterinarian. Deficiency of any one vitamin can upset the balance of the dog's metabolism and so disturb bodily functions, resulting in complications. Excess feeding of vitamins appears to be brought about by a lack of understanding or by the naive concept that if a little is good, more is better and in addition, by the desire of manufacturers to impress the public with high-potency labels in order to compete with other products. Products which are non-vitamin in nature may be added to a supplement, e.g., calcium to growing puppies or bitches in whelp or lactation. High on the list of over-fed vitamins is the oil-soluble vitamin D. The body's natural mechanism takes care of slight excesses, but when these excesses are too great, storage occurs. The B vitamins are water soluble and not so detrimental when fed in excess because they are not so difficult to eliminate from the body via the urine—the main channel of waste disposal. Even with minerals problems may arise. Calcium must be fed with phosphorus in the ratio of $1 \cdot 2$ of calcium to $1 \cdot 0$ parts of phosphorus. Excessive calcium without phosphorus increases the need for vitamin D and so throws things out of balance and starts a chain reaction. Leave the use of high potencies to the veterinarian for clinical reasons. Read the label carefully and do not mix supplements.

Feramo D for greyhounds is an excellent, correctly balanced, totally safe vitamin-mineral conditioning formula containing prescribed amounts of the following ingredients:

Iron aminoates 70 mg

Lysine $99 \cdot 6$ mg

Vitamin B_1 $0 \cdot 9$ mg

Vitamin B_2 $0 \cdot 9$ mg

Nicotinamide 4 mg

Vitamin B_6 $0 \cdot 6$ mg

Calcium pantothenate 3 mg

Vitamin B_{12} 1 µg

Vitamin A 2500 i.u.

Vitamin D 240 i.u.

Vitamin E 3 i.u.

Choline $3 \cdot 7$ mg

Yeast 600 mg

Calcium and phosphorus 100 mg

Trace elements, including cobalt, copper, manganese, magnesium, zinc.

Plus protein to make 30 per cent, and poly-unsaturated fatty acids.

Despite constant research, there has been little alteration to the Feramo formula over the years. The formula is comprised of tested ingredients such as those supplied to medical practitioners and hospitals. Iron pills suited to human requirements have a serious toxic effect on the digestive system of the dog. The iron in Feramo D is chelate iron aminoates, an exclusive formula developed by Medical Research Pty Ltd. Theoretically, it has the advantage over all other iron preparations in that it is completely non-toxic. Its utilisation is extremely high, vying more than favourably with expensive iron injections. It is very potent and fast-working. The formula is patented and manufactured solely by Medical Research Pty Ltd in Australia. Large overseas concerns also produce this form of iron under licence to Medical Research Pty Ltd.

Feramo D is best sprinkled or mixed with the evening meal (if cooked, wait until cool). As humans respond to food in various ways, so some dogs on Feramo D respond with increased condition sooner than others. If after a few months the dog begins to put on too much condition, as occasionally happens, the dosage should be adjusted at the discretion of the trainer.

Daily dose: Pups — ½ teaspoon daily.

Bitches in whelp and nursing bitches — 2 teaspoons daily.

Greyhounds in training and racing grayhounds — 1–2 teaspoons daily depending on weight and general condition.

Large quantities of vitamin E are not included in the Feramo formula for a number of reasons, the two main ones being:

1. Iron, which inhibits the effect of vitamin E, is a most important integral part of Feramo. When giving Feramo simultaneously with White-E, to ensure maximum activity, it is advisable to give the White-E in the morning feed and the Feramo in the evening feed (by which time the White-E will be absorbed into the system). Each product should be mixed into the feed just prior to feeding time.

2. The dosage of White-E varies with the individual dog, depending on the response and the condition of the animal. Thus it is impossible to dose effectively with vitamin E in a multi-vitamin prescription, such as Feramo. Only the minimum daily requirement of vitamin E is included.

Lysine has been incorporated in the formula because investigation has revealed that high-potency lysine (one of the amino acids) in conjunction with vitamin B complex improves the blood picture.

Feramo D is a powder; this ensures maximum stability of the vitamins in the presence of minerals. Liquid vitamin-mineral tonics are, in the opinion of many authorities, useless, as the minerals cause the vitamins to deteriorate very rapidly. Authorities are also of the opinion that pelleting, unless used quickly, causes a breakdown of vitamins by minerals, even considering that the vitamins may have a special protective coating. The pelleting process tends to break this coating and force the vitamins into contact with the minerals.

VITAMINS

At the beginning of the twentieth century it was generally assumed that the correct proportion of carbohydrates, proteins, fats, and minerals should provide the essentials of a good diet. Around 1911 it became evident that something more was needed to provide for normal growth and nutrition. There were contributions toward a knowledge of food chemistry before 1911, but the period since that date has been particularly noteworthy for the discovery of many essential chemical substances known as vitamins.

Vitamins are a class of dietary essentials and are necessary for the proper maintenance of health. There are many different vitamins, all of which tend to have a specific action on some part of the body's metabolism. Lack of a vitamin usually leads to certain well-recognised changes in the body.

Deficiency of a vitamin may arise in several different ways:

1. Inadequate diet is a frequent cause of vitamin deficiency.
2. Deficient absorption from the gastro-intestinal tract, because of some disease in the tract, may lead to vitamin deficiency, even if the diet is entirely adequate.
3. Increased demand for vitamins may arise at certain times, which if not met may give rise to vitamin deficiency. It is for this reason that vitamin deficiencies are most frequent during periods of active growth, during pregnancy, in the course of severe, prolonged illness, and after major operations.

Vitamins are not necessarily closely related chemically, nor are their physiological effects necessarily closely related. Before the chemical nature of vitamins was determined they were designated by the letters of the alphabet as A, B, C, etc. This practice is still followed, but now that the chemical structure of vitamins is better understood, it is considered good usage to refer to them by their descriptive names, such as thiamine, ascorbic acid, or niacin. We are not able to break away completely from alphabetical classification, and it is often convenient to use it. Vitamin A affords a good example. Although the chemistry and the structural formula of vitamin A is known and has been extensively studied, no chemical name for this vitamin has been generally accepted.

Vitamins should not be confused with drugs. Vitamins are readily assimilated and belong to the field of nutrition. Drugs, on the other hand, are foreign to the body and may have trouble-some side effects, as well as destroying vitamins in the system. According to Dr E. S. Bayrd of the Mayo Clinic, U.S.A.: 'Every drug is poten-tially harmful.'

Vitamin A

Vitamin A is formed from precursors, or provitamins, of which carotene is perhaps the best known. These substances are hydrolysed by the animal organism to produce vitamin A. Any excess of vitamin A is excreted in the urine. Strictly speaking, plants do not contain vitamin A, but only the substances from which an animal organism can manufacture the vitamin. In general, the carotenes are found in yellow vege-tables and fruits and in the green leaves of vegetables in which the yellow colour is covered over by the green of chlorophyll. Vegetable sources of vitamin A are parsley, carrots, broccoli, celery, lettuce, turnip greens, spinach and tomatoes. Apricots are richer in vitamin A than any other fruit; bananas, oranges, and yellow peaches also contain vitamin A.

It is not advisable to rely entirely upon fruit or vegetables as sources of vitamin A because carotene is by no means as effective nutritionally as vitamin A obtained from animal sources or dairy products. Egg yolk, cream, butter, and fish-liver oils are particularly good sources of this vitamin.

Vitamin A is destroyed by exposure to oxygen, slow cooking, and by some preservatives.

Vitamin A and the carotenes are fat soluble and their absorption and metabolism within the body is similar to that of fats. Since animals have the ability to store vitamin A in the liver, this organ may contain relatively large amounts. Cod-liver oil has become an important commer-cial product containing the two fat-soluble vitamins A and D.

Research has revealed that vitamin A has special functions relating both to the skin and the epithelium. The latter lines the inside of the mouth, nose, sinuses, throat, bronchial tubes, lungs, stomach, intestines, gall-bladder, urinary bladder, kidney tubules, mastoids, and inner ear, and also the inner surface of the eye lids and conjunctiva.

Laboratory tests with animals have shown that when their diets are adequate in all respects except for vitamin A, they develop infections in one or other of those parts of the body already mentioned. Other test animals fed adequate vitamin A, remained free from these infections.

Investigations have shown that, when there is a vitamin A deficiency, the cells forming the epithelium multiply at a faster than normal rate. When these cells die, they become hard and dry. Other cells growing beneath them, push them upwards and they also die, so that layers of dry, dead cells present, as occurs with dandruff. Healthy epithelial cells secrete a moisture that ensures normal growth, but dead cells do not. The surface of the dry cells is thus not washed with mucus, but is roughened and tends to retain bacteria. These bacteria exude enzymes which are toxic and which break down the cellular structure of the body. Healthy cells produce anti-enzymes which destroy the enzymes released by bacteria. One of these anti-enzymes, lysozyme, is contained in the mucous secretion found in the nose, and also in tears, and has a strong antiseptic action. After vitamin A had been added to the diet of laboratory animals previously deprived of this vitamin, healthy changes in the epithelium were observed within seven days.

Deficiency conditions express themselves in several different ways. Night blindness is a recognised symptom of vitamin A deficiency. There is a substance in the retina of the eye called rhodopsin (visual purple) upon which normal night vision depends. When light enters the eye some visual purple is used up and the products of such destruction bring about nerve impulses which inform the brain what the eye sees. Replacements of visual purple, which is composed of vitamin A and protein, are normally conveyed by the bloodstream to the eye to make good the losses mentioned, but if the intake of vitamin A is deficient, there is a diminished supply of visual purple and this gives rise to dim vision in a poor light, or night blindness. However, all cases of night blindness cannot be traced to vitamin A deficiency.

Adequate vitamin A is necessary for normal growth, for formation and preservation of healthy bone structure, for the integrity of the enamel of the teeth, for good appetite, and for the normal production of red and white blood cells. It is also needed for healthy skin and mucous membrane and for good eyesight. A dry mouth may indicate lack of vitamin A.

Vitamin A is essential for greyhounds of all ages. The minimum daily requirement of vitamin A for the average racing greyhound is approximately 100 international units per kilogram of body weight.

It has been discovered that stored vitamin A becomes more effective when vitamin E is taken daily.

Too much vitamin A is very dangerous as it can cause malformations of unborn pups. Pups may be stillborn. In growing pups excessive vitamin A may cause bone deformities and increased risk of fractures. These problems have arisen when excessive amounts of cod liver oil and kidney have been fed to pups.

Vitamin D

Some vitamin D is contained in dairy produce, but fish-liver oil is the most reliable source. Another form of vitamin D is produced by the action of the sun's ultra-violet rays on the hair of the dog. When dogs lick their coat, it is considered that they thereby absorb vitamin D, as do birds when they preen their feathers.

Surveys reveal that dogs kept in areas where bad weather conditions prevail (with accompanying cloud, fog, haze, and smog, which prevent the sun's ultra-violet rays from reaching the earth) are more liable to rickets than dogs kept where the skies are clearer and there are more hours of sunlight.

Extensive research has been carried out to establish the relationship between vitamin D and the teeth. It has been found that even mild forms of rickets interfere with normal development of the teeth of puppies and also with the shape and structure of the jawbone, causing crooked, overlapping, and protruding teeth, defective bite, and faulty teeth alignment. Vitamin D helps to prevent tooth decay and plays an important role in preventing pyorrhea.

Vitamin D is considered to control the enzyme phosphatase, which appears essential to bone formation. This enzyme acts upon fats and sugars that are combined with phosphorus and releases the phosphorus for the purpose of bone-building. This detached phosphorus then unites with calcium, brought along by the bloodstream, and both substances share in building and hardening the bone structure. These complicated processes fail to occur when vitamin D is lacking in the diet. Instead, phosphatase leaves the bone formation and enters the bloodstream. Phosphorus is then not released from fats and sugars and is not available to combine with calcium, hence these minerals are not deposited in the young bones and growth may cease. Half of the phosphorus in the body is normally found in bones. If inadequate vitamin D is supplied, some phosphatase is present, but bone growth is slowed down and teeth formation is disorganised and delayed.

Vitamin D is perhaps the most important of all vitamins, for deformity of the bony framework in puppies due to a shortage of this vitamin can cause irreparable damage. Puppies deprived of calcium and phosphorus in their diet become stunted and develop bony malformations.

One of the functions of vitamin D is to release energy within the body. Phosphorus carries blood sugar through the intestinal wall, as well as to the liver, which stores it as glycogen. Blood sugar is 'burned' to supply energy and when there is a lack of vitamin D, sugar cannot combine with phosphorus, hence energy diminishes. Research has shown that puppies lacking vitamin D burn less blood sugar and display less energy than normal puppies. The combination of sugar and phosphorus in the muscles is reduced and the pups with this condition lose blood sugar in the urine, and their blood contains more than normal amounts of sugar. There is consequently an incomplete storage of blood sugar as glycogen, and an incomplete absorption of it in providing energy.

Vitamin D is important to the maintenance of healthy eyes. Experiments with puppies show that when they are fed on a diet deficient in vitamin D, changes occur in their eyes, comparable with changes observed in the eyes of humans. These alterations give rise to short-sightedness and myopia.

The use of paraffin oil as a laxative prevents the absorption of vitamin D as it does with other fat-soluble vitamins. Moreover, it damages the liver, according to authorities, who also state that fluoride (used in some water supplies) retards the action of vitamin D in preventing rickets.

The best source of vitamin D is fish-liver oil. Like other fat-soluble vitamins, vitamins D and A are best assimilated after a meal containing some fatty food, such as butter, cheese, milk.

There are several forms of vitamin D, of which vitamin D_3 (calciferol) is the most active in the dog. The daily requirement of vitamin D for the average racing greyhound is approximately 6·6 international units per kilogram of body weight. Massive doses of vitamin D or prolonged administration at high levels may lead to calcification of the soft tissues, excessive mineralisation of the bones, and deformation of the teeth.

Vitamin B_1 (thiamine) has a protective action against a possible overdose of vitamin D.

Vitamin B_1 (Thiamine)

Thiamine is essential for growth, nutrition, and energy. It plays an important part in the proper utilisation of carbohydrates. The function of thiamine appears to be that of a co-enzyme, i.e., it promotes the conversion of blood sugar into energy. When blood sugar is utilised to produce energy, pyruvic and lactic acids are formed. Thiamine is associated with enzymes which oxidise pyruvic acid and turn lactic acid into glycogen for subsequent conversion to blood sugar.

When thiamine is deficient in the diet, these changes are incomplete. The two acids mentioned accumulate in and irritate the tissues and retard the production of energy within the body. Wide repercussions follow. In more serious thiamine shortages the nerves may be damaged. Other nerve troubles are experienced, e.g., headaches, nervousness, neuritis, and irritability. Digestive processes are slowed down because contractions of the stomach become less vigorous, hence food is not so effectively mixed with digestive juices. In addition, the flow of hydrochloric acid, needed to digest proteins, slackens off or may cease altogether. There are diminished secretions of bile, pancreatic, and intestinal juices, all virtually necessary for healthy digestion. Digestive enzymes, which act as ferments, are also released in smaller quantities. The net result is experienced in gas pains, flatulence, stomach trouble, and poor appetite, frequently resulting in loss of weight.

Thiamine deficiency also slows down the wave-like motion of the large intestine and this delays food wastes in their journey to the rectum. As a result, the faeces become dry and hard, giving rise to constipation, which may lead to a haemorrhoid condition.

Overweight may be due to thiamine shortage because starchy foods are only partially converted into energy owing to a paucity of enzymes, and tend to be stored as fat. As less blood sugar is available for conversion into energy, the overweight dog tires easily, soon becomes breathless, and suffers from palpitation.

Thiamine deficiency may result in loss of appetite which, in turn, reduces the intake of food. This sequence complicates studies of vitamin deficiency, since some of the observed effects may be due to malnutrition rather than to the deficiency of any particular vitamin.

When thiamine is inadequate, it has been shown by experiments with laboratory animals that the heart is the first organ to be affected. A

Trainer, Des Delaine, with Just Biddy, a brindle bitch by Venetian Court out of Darra Linen, after her South Australian Champion of Champions win *(Courtesy of South Australian Greyhound Trainer)*

thiamine deficiency initially slows down the heart beat and, as this vitamin lack becomes more serious, the heart muscle, hampered by an accumulation of pyruvic and lactic acids, becomes irritated. This causes the heart to race and may result in heart failure.

Authorities state that thiamine deficiency impairs the function of the heart and increases its tendency to collect fluid and also causes a degeneration of the heart muscle.

Dogs whose intake of thiamine is inadequate suffer from poor memory, lack of initiative, confused thinking, and (frequently) from depression and fear. The reason is that the brain cells depend upon blood sugar for their energy and blood sugar cannot be transformed into energy without thiamine. The accumulation of pyruvic and lactic acids which follows a poor supply of thiamine, has a toxic effect upon brain cells. Tests carried out by American medical scientists put this matter beyond doubt.

The value of thiamine is reduced or destroyed by cooking, food processing, and by alcohol. It is also vulnerable to heat and air.

Sources of thiamine include liver, whole grains, wheatgerm, rice, bran, soya beans, brewer's yeast, nuts, potatoes.

The daily requirement of thiamine for the average racing greyhound is approximately 90 micrograms per kilogram of body weight. Some success has been achieved with vitamin B_1 in the treatment of nervous disorders of dogs.

Vitamin B_2 (Riboflavin)

Like other B complex vitamins, riboflavin is soluble in water. It is lost by sweating, panting, and in urination. Although unharmed by oxygen and the heat of cooking, it is leached away in the water used for cooking. Exposure to light destroys riboflavin, thus a bottle of milk left standing in bright daylight loses most of its riboflavin content within a few hours.

Good food sources of this vitamin include leafy vegetables, fruits, yeast, milk, and liver. It is also supplied in heart, beef muscle, veal, chicken, apricots, and tomatoes. Beer contains significant amounts of riboflavin.

Riboflavin is essential for growth and maintenance of a healthy nervous system. Riboflavin aids carbohydrate utilisation, i.e., in turning the sugar and starches eaten, into energy. Riboflavin combined with protein and phosphoric acid, forms enzymes needed for the breaking down of blood sugar and its conversion into energy. Riboflavin is concerned with several different enzymes and is essential to life. Relatively large amounts of this vitamin are stored in the liver and kidneys and a certain level is maintained in the tissues.

The following deficiency ailments can result from a shortage of riboflavin: inflamed, fissured tongue with possible difficulty in swallowing; cracking, scaliness, and softening at the corners of the mouth. Nervous symptoms include numbness, muscular weakness, dizziness, rolling of the eyeballs, difficulty in walking, tremor or shaking, and mental apathy. Eye ailments include roughness of the eyelids, watering, sensitivity to light, blurred vision, disorders of the cornea, inflammation of the iris, and dilation of the pupil. Tests have disclosed that adult laboratory animals will die on a riboflavin-deficient diet and growth can be slowed or stopped in young animals. Female animals deprived of riboflavin may produce deformed offspring.

The daily requirement for the average racing greyhound is approximately 0·044 micrograms of riboflavin per kilogram of body weight.

Niacin

Niacin is known variously as nicotinic acid, niacinamide and nicotinamide. Niacin is water soluble, resistant to oxygen in the air, and relatively heat stable. Alcohol and the water used for cooking reduce or destroy the value of niacin. Among the best sources of niacin are liver, kidneys, salmon, brewer's yeast, wheatgerm, soya beans, and peanuts. Other foods containing niacin include eggs, milk, whole wheat and lean meat.

Niacin occurs in all living cells and forms part of the enzyme system of the body. It promotes oxidative processes. Niacin is present in almost all tissues, chiefly as a co-enzyme, and more is contained in liver than in any other organ.

Tryptophane is an essential amino acid which is a precursor of niacin. The conversion of tryptophane to niacin is considered to occur in the tissues, not as a result of the action of intestinal micro-organisms.

After years of study concerning the curative effects of liver extracts on dogs with an experimentally induced condition called 'blacktongue', Elvehjem and his colleagues, in 1937, discovered that niacin would cure canine blacktongue. Blacktongue in dogs, or canine pellagra, closely resembles pellagra in humans and several investigators then discovered that pellagra could be cured, or its symptoms relieved, by the administration of niacin.

Pellagra denotes a condition characterised by red lesions of the skin especially on the backs of the hands and on the forearms, legs, and feet. The tongue assumes a bright-red colour and eventually there are symptoms of depression and derangement of the nervous system.

In greyhounds on diets lacking in niacin there is redness and ulceration of the mouth with a copious flow of saliva. Gastro-enteritis is also a common deficiency ailment. Niacin deficiency is generally concomitant with a deficiency of B complex vitamins such as riboflavin and thiamine.

The daily requirement for the average racing greyhound is approximately 240 micrograms per kilogram of body weight. Nicotinic acid (niacin) should not be confused with nicotine.

Vitamin B_6 (Pyridoxine)

Pyridoxine is a water-soluble vitamin and is not stable in heat and light. It is widely distributed in foodstuffs such as yeast, liver, rice, peas, beans, and lentils. Wheatgerm and peanuts are rich sources. Fish is a moderately good source, but milk and vegetables contain little.

Experiments with laboratory animals have revealed that skin lesions, anaemia, cardiovascular ailments, fatty degeneration of the liver, kidney trouble, and nerve lesions have resulted when animals were kept on diets deficient in vitamin B_6. It was noted, in some instances, that antibody formation was defective and that there was increased susceptibility to infection, e.g., pneumonia. Deficiency of this vitamin in greyhounds may cause itching of the skin and licking of the feet. Pyridoxine is needed to prevent a particular form of anaemia. Deficiency will cause erratic heart function, nerve degeneration, and appearance of convulsions. There is loss of appetite, poor growth, and diarrhoea. Pyridoxine is required for blood regeneration and normal growth in young puppies.

Pyridoxine appears to be essential in the formation and breakdown of certain amino acids. It may play an essential part also in the conversion of proteins to fats and in the metabolism of some of the fatty acids. No doubt further study will afford a much better understanding of the part it plays in animal nutrition. Pyridoxine seems to play an important role in the health of muscle tissue and nerves.

The daily requirement for the average racing greyhound is approximately 165 micrograms per kilogram of body weight.

Pantothenic acid

Reports on the significance of this substance in nutrition began to appear about 1940. It is apparently necessary for proper growth in all animals.

While this vitamin plays some part in nutrition, clear cut cases of deficiency have not been demonstrated. This may be largely because this vitamin is well distributed in foodstuffs, the best sources being yeast, liver, kidneys, wheatgerm, peas, soya beans, and peanuts. There is a need for further research to establish clearly the function of pantothenic acid in greyhound nutrition.

The work performed in the body by pantothenic acid is that of a co-enzyme concerned with the synthesis of fats from starches or proteins. It also stimulates the oxidation of amino acids that are converted to pyruvic acid. Pantothenic acid plays an important role in the prevention of chronic loss of body weight, anaemia, and nervous disturbances since any or all of these symptoms may occur when there is a deficiency of this vitamin in greyhounds. The vitamin is lost in sweating, panting and in urination. Dogs deficient in pantothenic acid exhibit erratic appetites, intestinal disorders and poor growth. Severe cases result in convulsions, collapse, coma, and liver damage.

The daily requirement for the average racing greyhound is approximately 550 micrograms per kilogram of body weight.

Inositol

Inositol appears to be associated with choline and biotin. This vitamin is supplied in heart muscle, liver, yeast, wheatgerm, oatmeal, molasses, beans, grapefruit, oranges, peaches, potatoes, peanuts, strawbrries, spinach, tomatoes, and turnips. Like choline, inositol is richly supplied in lecithin. Inositol is present in all animal and plant tissues. The highest concentration in animal tissues occurs in skeletal muscle, brain, red blood cells, heart, kidneys, and the lens of the eye.

Inositol aids in preventing the accumulation of fat in the liver and may also have some function in preventing hardening of the arteries. Inositol has been used with benefit on dogs whose hair was falling out.

Authorities state that caffeine and lindane create an inositol shortage in the body.

Biotin (vitamin H)

Biotin is found in small amounts in many foods. It is present in fairly large quantities in yeast, milk, liver, kidneys, and raw potatoes. Other sources include egg yolk, carrots, tomatoes, molasses, spinach, cauliflower, salmon, turnips, and mushrooms.

The discovery of biotin was due to a casual observation made in 1916, by Bateman, that a high concentration of egg white in experimental diets is toxic. The relationship between biotin and a protein in raw and dried egg white was investigated. The protein in egg white is called avidin and it apparently enters into a chemical combination with biotin in the intestine and prevents the vitamin from being absorbed and utilised. If the egg white is cooked there is no interference with the action of the vitamin.

While biotin appears to be essential in nutrition, deficiency conditions are produced only when a considerable part of the diet (nearly one-third of the total caloric intake) is raw or dried egg white. The intestinal flora are capable of producing biotin synthetically, but apparently not in sufficient quantity.

There is evidence that biotin takes part in several specific reactions, but there is need for further investigation. It is considered probable that biotin assists in the metabolism of fatty compounds and that it also plays a part in the growth process. Biotin, even in large amounts, is non toxic.

Deficiency can be produced in experimental animals, not only by feeding them a diet containing a great deal of raw egg white, but also by administering sulphanilamides. Biotin deficiency may cause muscular pain, poor appetite, dry skin, a disturbed nervous system, lack of energy, and sleeplessness. Laboratory animals deprived of biotin lost their fur, especially around the eyes, and suffered from an itchy dermatitis and retarded growth. Puppies fed on a diet deficient in biotin suffered from a progressive paralysis. Biotin is considered by some research scientists to activate lysozyme, the bacteria-digesting anti-enzyme found in tears, mucus, and body fluids.

Folic acid (pteroyl glutamic acid)

This vitamin was originally isolated from the green leaves of plants such as spinach, peas, and clover. Since its source was the foliage of plants, it was first called folic acid. Various investigators working on different aspects of the problem have called it the liver lactobacillus casei factor, vitamin M, and factor U. It is found in liver and yeast concentrates and was shown to be essential for the growth of certain bacteria and protozoa. Since its chemical structure is known, it is more correct to refer to it as as pteroyl glutamic acid.

A good deal of folic acid in foodstuffs is lost during storage by exposure to light, and almost all of it by the heat of cooking.

Folic acid produces a feeling of well-being and increased appetite.

Folic acid is not effective in certain kinds of pernicious anaemia which are accompanied by nerve degeneration, particularly of the spinal cord. In such anaemias, vitamin B_{12} is generally used. Conversely, there are other forms of anaemia which remain unaffected by B_{12}, but respond to folic acid. Various studies indicate that there is a physiological relationship between folic acid and the long-sought erythrocyte maturation factor, vitamin B_{12}.

A deficiency of folic acid can give rise to any of the following ailments: anaemia, diarrhoea, glossitis (inflammation of the tongue), gastro-intestinal disorders, lack of hydrochloric acid in the stomach, and a decrease in the normal number of white blood corpuscles.

Folic acid has been used with success in the treatment of anaemia associated with rheumatoid arthritis, celiaca (a disease of the abdominal organs, which is probably identical with sprue), and in disorders arising from the use of sulpha drugs.

A lack of folic acid in the diet results in a fall in blood count accompanied with rapid fatigue after the initial 200 metres of a gallop.

The daily requirement for the average racing greyhound is approximately $4 \cdot 4$ micrograms per kilogram of body weight.

Vitamin B_{12}

Why this vitamin enjoys such popularity with trainers is a mystery to authorities. Perhaps because in the early days of its availability the raw material cost more than $200 a gram (today it is as low as $5 per gram). Perhaps its dark-red colour gives it the appearance of a strong tonic.

Vitamin B_{12} is a red, crystalline substance isolated as a liver fraction, and it exerts a powerful effect in promoting the maturation of red cells and also is capable of relieving nervous and digestive disturbances associated with pernicious anaemia. Vitamin B_{12} is apparently the erythrocyte maturation factor (extrinsic food factor) that has been long sought. It is a cobalt compound. Cobalt has been shown to increase the number of red blood cells and the amount of haemoglobin, but cobalt alone has not proved of value in treating pernicious anaemia. Vitamin B_{12} is effective in minute amounts and is many times more effective than folic acid in promoting the production of red blood cells.

Chronic intestinal disorders may result from an impaired absorption of vitamin B_{12} and consequently lead to anaemia. In 1951 it was shown that the stomachs of animals with this form of anaemia do not produce a certain substance called the intrinsic factor, essential to the assimilation of vitamin B_{12}. Other factors which tend to nullify vitamin B_{12} are lack of hydrocloric acid in the stomach, and the use of laxatives (which hurry half-digested food through the intestines before the process of assimilation has been completed). A shortage of dietary calcium will also retard absorption of vitamin B_{12}.

Vitamin B_{12} is well supplied in liver and kidneys. Fair sources of supply include milk, eggs, cheese, fish, and meat.

Vitamin B_{12} may be deficient during heavy worm infestation in dogs and also following frequent, hard racing. The gums will be pale, the dog will lose stamina and become lethargic, and there may be a weight loss after a hard gallop.

The daily requirement for an average racing greyhound is $0 \cdot 55$ micrograms per kilogram of body weight.

Vitamin B_{12} is virtually non-toxic and large doses have been administered to laboratory animals without ill effect. Owing to the fact that this vitamin was discovered comparatively late (1948) it is still subject to scientific research. What is known, however, indicates that it has a variety of uses. It is not found, even in minute quantities, in plants.

Injectable B_{12} is widely used in racing greyhounds and is available in two forms. Cyanocobalamin is rapidly absorbed yet it is excreted within a few hours. Hydroxycobalamin is absorbed more slowly and has a long acting affect. Both types are usually injected under the skin.

Vitamin B_{15}

Vitamin B_{15} is a controversial 'vitamin' known also as pangamic acid, B_{15} calcium pangamate, and DADA. However, most authorities consider it a mixture of various substances. Many claims have been made for vitamin B_{15}. It is said to increase the oxygen supply to the blood and consequently improve stamina, finishing ability, and racing performance. Other claims include hastened recovery from fatigue and protection of the liver. However, many of these claims have not been substantiated and, in fact, the Health Commission has recently banned the import of B_{15} in its various forms and it is not registered for use in many states of Australia. It appears that the B_{15} fad is almost over.

Para-amino-benzoic acid (PABA)

PABA was only admitted to the B complex group in 1940 after research work by Ansbacher.

According to authorities, PABA is unique in that it is a vitamin within a vitamin in as much as it forms an integral part of the B complex vitamin, folic acid. It has some antibacterial activity. However, it reduces the action of sulphonamide antibiotics.

The richest sources of PABA are liver, brewer's yeast, and wheatgerm. Its occurrence in foodstuffs is concomitant with that of folic acid. PABA is found in meat, nuts, fresh fruits, and vegetables. PABA appears to play an important role in normal growth, skin health, hair pigmentation, and the health of the intestines.

The exact daily requirement for the average racing greyhound is not yet known.

Choline

Choline has been known for many years and was first isolated from bile in 1894. Only recently has investigation revealed that it plays an important role in nutrition.

Choline is present in many animal and plant tissues; good sources include wheatgerm, brains, liver, kidneys, and eggs. The richest source of choline is lecithin. Soya beans, asparagus, brussels sprouts, cabbage, carrots, peas, spinach, turnips, and potatoes also contain choline. The normal diet contains adequate quantities of choline.

Choline prevents excessive accumulation of fat in the liver of experimental animals when they are fed on diets containing a high fat content. Choline also plays a part in the various phases of metabolism. Acetylcholine, a derivative, is the chemical substance that provides for the transmission of a nerve impulse across a synapse.

The prevention of choline deficiency appears to be linked with an adequate intake of thiamine (vitamin B_1). A lack of choline may cause dyspepsia. If of long duration, this deficiency will cause permanent liver injury. A deficiency of choline can also result when too little protein is given.

The amino acid, methionine, can be converted to choline in the liver, thus allowing the liver to synthesise choline and reduce the build up of fats. Frequent racing and hard work increase the stress on the liver and liver function may be depressed, resulting in a build up of fats in the liver.

Vitamin C (ascorbic acid)

The discovery of vitamin C was the result of scientific investigations made to find the cause and cure of scurvy. In 1912 Funk postulated a scurvy-preventing vitamin, vitamin C, and efforts were made to isolate it from orange and lemon juice, which have proved most effective against scurvy.

Scurvy is characterised by weakness and lassitude. There is a marked tenderness and swelling of the joints. The gums are red and swollen, and the teeth become infected around their bases, causing them to loosen. There is a change in the capillaries, permitting haemorrhagic conditions beneath the skin, in mucous membranes, and under the periosteum.

The structural formula of vitamin C was established in 1933 by Haworth and Hirst and it was given the name of ascorbic acid. Vitamin C is very vulnerable to the presence of air or oxygen, but if kept dry and away from light it remains stable for a considerable time. Vitamin C is lost to the body by inhaling D.D.T. as contained in insecticides and pest sprays, also by inhaling cigarette smoke, and by inhaling the fumes of petrol, molten lead, cleansing solvents, and smog. It is interesting to note that 'Smoke from an idling cigarette contains almost twice the tar and nicotine of an inhaled cigarette and thus may be twice as toxic as the smoke inhaled by the smoker' — *N.H.F. Bulletin*, February 1974.

Vitamin C is synthesised in the gut. It is a water-soluble vitamin, the role of which is poorly understood. Vitamin C is stored in the liver and adrenal glands. The vitamin is important for the metabolism of carbohydrates and amino acids and appears to be involved in the absorption of iron from the gut. Extra vitamin C has been shown to enhance the uptake of iron in dogs and aid in the conversion of folic acid to folinic acid, which is important for haemoglobin production. Vitamin C also appears to be required for synthesis of haemoglobin and is necessary for the development of teeth, bone, skin, and cartilage. Wound healing can be delayed if vitamin C is deficient. Vitamin C also seems to reduce the requirement for vitamin E.

The adrenal glands produce hormones (e.g., corticosteroids) that counteract stress. Animals under stress have reduced adrenal levels of vitamin C, which authorities believe may be involved in the production of corticosteroids. Vitamin C may assist a racing dog to cope with stress, but there is no experimental evidence to indicate this action. Prolonged training increases the stress on racing dogs, and so extra vitamin C may assist a dog to perform more consistently over a long period.

Various claims have been made for the human use of vitamin C; these include the prevention of colds and increased resistance to infection. Research in dogs indicates that extra vitamin C has little benefit in preventing or aiding recovery from illness.

Current research evidence suggests that dogs synthesise sufficient vitamin C in their bowels. Pups, even during the first few weeks of life, can synthesise their own vitamin C and consequently the majority of vitamin mineral supplements for dogs do not contain vitamin C. Vitamin C is rapidly destroyed by copper salts. Some vitamin mineral supplements contain copper and vitamin C, and consequently the vitamin C would be destroyed during storage and would not be available to the dog. Therefore, it is of paramount importance to read the formula on the can before purchasing a supplement. As most trainers routinely use vitamin and mineral supplements and iron tonics which contain copper, it is best to add the vitamin C to a separate feed (e.g., morning feed). Vitamin E (e.g., 'White E') does not destroy vitamin C.

Vitamin C is also destroyed by cooking. Air and light accelerate the destruction of vitamin C. The salts of vitamin C (e.g., sodium ascorbate) are less affected. Nevertheless, it is best to store vitamin C powder or tablets in a refrigerator in a dark container.

Injectable vitamin C is popular and many trainers claim that it improves performance. However, there is no evidence to substantiate this. Oral vitamin C is well absorbed.

Several drugs cause vitamin C to be lost rapidly by excretion, namely, aspirin, the barbiturates, salicylates, sulphanilamide, insulin, thyroid extract, atrophin, anti-histamine drugs, adrenaline, etc. Animals who lack hydrochloric acid in the stomach cannot properly absorb vitamin C. Vitamin C is lost by perspiration and urination and excessive water drinking.

Vitamin C is well supplied in fresh fruit and vegetables, the richest sources being rose hips, black and red currants, strawberries, and citrus fruits. Cooking destroys this vitamin, both by heat and by leaching away the vitamin in the water used for cooking. Baking soda is detrimental to vitamin C.

Research indicates that vitamin C is essential to form and maintain healthy connective tissue. The cells that make up an animal's body are held together by this tissue, called collagen, and when it breaks down, not only the supporting connective tissue, but the cartilage, ligaments, and walls of blood vessels, weaken. This facilitates the admission of bacteria and viruses that cause infections. Vitamin C assists the animal to deal effectively with these foreign attackers, because strong connective tissue offers a powerful barrier. Vitamin C also strengthens the phagocytes and antibodies.

Vitamin C promotes healthy bone growth, and the knitting of bone fractures. When the vitamin is lacking, bones become soft, porous, or brittle, and break readily after a minor fall or injury. Bone fractures heal badly when vitamin C is deficient.

The rate of efficiency of wound healing depends upon the quantity of vitamin C and protein that is concentrated in the tissues.

Vitamin C is needed to maintain the thyroid gland in good health and helps the animal's body to assimilate iron, needed to ward off anaemia.

According to Professor E. V. McCollum: 'There is evidence that iron utilisation is defective when the body's reserves of ascorbic acid are depleted.'

Research workers have shown that vitamin C is particularly abundant in the adrenal glands, the pituitary, and other glandular tissue, and it seems to be essential for the efficient working of the endocrine system of glands and the production of hormones.

There is a high concentration of vitamin C in the fluid within the eyeball, and also in the lens of the eye, the iris, the retina, and the cornea. Treatment of corneal ulcers with vitamin C is reported to have resulted in dramatic improvement. Experimental cataracts have been produced in aged animals by restricting their intake of this vitamin. Administration of vitamin C daily to animals with cataracts caused marked improvement.

The daily requirement of vitamin C for an average racing greyhound is 2·2 micrograms per kilogram of body weight. Under normal conditions a dog can manufacture his own requirements of this vitamin.

Vitamin P (bioflavonoids)

There are several substances in addition to vitamin C that affect the integrity of the capillaries, and these substances are grouped under the name bioflavonoids, or vitamin P. The term, bioflavonoids, refers to flavonoids possessing biological activity.

The bioflavonoids are a group of carbon-hydrogen-oxygen compounds which have the property of correcting fragile capillaries and protecting their integrity. The capillaries form an important part of the transport system of the animal's body and they convey food, oxygen, and hormones to every cell in the body, as well as removing the waste products of metabolism and disease. When the capillaries are strong and healthy, infections are quickly thrown off.

The history of vitamin P began in 1926 when Gyorgyi and his associates found that a substance extracted from paprika (red pepper), and also from lemon juice, was superior to vitamin C in preventing capillary permeability and fragility. Gyorgyi named this active substance 'citrin' and research revealed that it contained the bioflavonoid hesperidin, and the glycoside of eriodictyol. Later the bioflavonoids were found, namely, quercitrin, quercetin, naringin, esculin, and hesperidin methyl chalcone. In 1944 another bioflavonoid, called rutin, was discovered by Griffith. Of those mentioned, hesperidin and rutin appear to possess the greatest biological activity. Rutin is obtained from a herb called buckwheat and also from eucalyptus. Vitamin P may therefore be regarded as a complex, similar to vitamin B complex.

The value of vitamin P is reduced by storage and destroyed by boiling.

Capillary fragility appears to be an accurate term to describe the condition of capillaries as a result of bioflavonoid deficiency. Vitamin P reduces the tendency to bruising and haemorrhaging.

It is accepted by science that vitamin P is an essential nutritional factor and that it produces a rise in capillary resistance which cannot be obtained from vitamin C alone. Vitamin P has been used with some degree of success in diseases marked by decreased capillary resistance, namely, hypertension, rheumatic fever, diabetes, allergies, bacterial infections, and toxicity arising from the use of drugs. Bioflavonoids and vitamin C have been used successfully to help prevent the common cold. Tests have shown that vitamin P enhances the biological effect of vitamin C by stabilising the latter and protecting it against the destructive action of oxygen. Vitamin P has a detoxicating action upon benzene and phenol and when used with vitamin C protects against the toxic effects of arsenical poisons. Unlike vitamin C, vitamin P appears to play no part in the healing of wounds.

The richest source of vitamin P is fruits, particularly lemons and oranges. It is in the pulp and peel of these fruits, rather than in the edible fruit, that vitamin P is contained. Vitamin P is also found in rose hips, black currants, grapes, buckwheat, prunes, apricots, and cabbage.

Vitamin K

In 1934 Dr Henrick Dam, of the University of Copenhagen, suggested that haemorrhagic disease resulted from lack of a fat-soluble vitamin which he named 'Koagulations vitamin', and it has become known as vitamin K.

There are two natural compounds of vitamin K. The first was isolated from alfalfa and is known as vitamin K_1. Vitamin K_2 was isolated from fishmeal which had been subjected to bacterial putrefaction. Bacteria are able to synthesise this vitamin, not only in bacterial preparations but also in the living intestine. As with other fat-soluble vitamins, bile promotes absorption from the intestine.

Vitamin K is richly supplied in green plants, such as lucerne and spinach, in which there may be some relationship between the vitamin and the chlorophyll. Vitamin K is also supplied in cauliflower, carrot tops, cabbage, soya beans, seaweed, and pine needles. Most animal sources of vitamin K are only comparable with the poorest vegetable sources.

Without vitamin K blood will not coagulate—but the vitamin will not arrest haemorrhage, either in normal dogs or those suffering from haemophilia. Vitamin K is necessary for the formation of prothrombin, which is one of the substances involved in a series of complicated reactions concerning the clotting mechanism of the blood. Prothrombin is formed in the liver. Any condition that prevents the normal flow of bile into the intestine results in inadequate absorption of vitamin K into the bloodstream. Pancreatic insufficiency, severe diarrhoea, ulcerative colitis, and intestinal obstruction can also result in inadequate absorption of vitamin K.

Some vitamin K is produced in the large intestine by bacterial action, but the amount is inadequate and must be supplemented by a dietary source. The administration of unsaturated fatty acids enables intestinal bacteria to synthesise vitamin K.

The new-born pup, during the first few days of life, requires a supply of vitamin K from external sources because the prothrombin level falls after birth and only returns to normal at the beginning of the second week, due to bacterial action. New-born pups are therefore subject to haemorrhage, which may result from accidental minor injury to blood vessels, while there is a lack of vitamin K. For this reason, vitamin K should be given to the mother shortly before whelping so that the vitamin passes from the mother's bloodstream to that of the pups. Experiments have shown that a rise in temperature increases vitamin K requirement.

A deficiency of vitamin K can be produced by the use of sulpha drugs, salicylates, aspirin, and arsenical preparations.

Vitamin K is unaffected by air and/or heat. The average minimum daily requirement of vitamin K for a racing greyhound is 0·11 micrograms per kilogram of body weight.

Vitamin E (the tocopherols)

Vitamin E was isolated from wheatgerm oil in 1936 by Evans and his associates. Vitamin E occurs as alpha, beta, gamma, delta, and three other tocopherols, but only alpha tocopherol exhibits marked biological activity, the other tocopherols being virtually inert. The following remarks concerning vitamin E refer to alpha tocopherol specifically.

Vitamin E is quickly and completely destroyed by rancid fats and inorganic iron preparations. Liquid tonics with vitamins and minerals mixed together should be suspected as it is a fact that iron will destroy vitamin E. Vitamin E is also destroyed by liquid paraffin.

Wheatgerm is the richest natural source of vitamin E. It is also found in lettuce, tomatoes, carrots, egg yolk, nuts, turnip greens, cereal, and vegetable oils.

Vitamin E appears to be essential for muscular health. It also helps to utilise fat and prevents vitamin A, linoleic acid, and perhaps other nutrients, from destruction by oxygen within the body. Vitamin E also performs several other important functions within the body.

Vitamin E exhibits the following properties:
1. It is a vasodilator, i.e., it permits the diameter of blood vessels to increase, thereby improving the blood flow to the tissues. It improves the blood supply in injured areas and stimulates wound healing.
2. It decreases the oxygen requirement of muscular tissues by approximately fifty per cent, which is equivalent to an enhanced blood flow. It therefore diminishes breathlessness and cramp and increases stamina. Vitamin E also has a direct effect on heart muscle. The heart has a stronger, more forceful beat.
3. It is an antithrombin, i.e., it dissolves blood clots and prevents the formation of blood clots but does not interfere with the normal blood-clotting mechanism.
4. It prevents excessive scar tissue formation.
5. It promotes urine excretion.
7. It improves the collateral circulation and capillary permeability.
8. It increases the power and efficiency of muscle tissue and has a very beneficial effect on tired heart muscle.
9. It increases the fertility of dogs and bitches. It is often recommended for fertility problems in bitches showing no signs of, or irregular, oestrus.

Veterinary authorities have proved by experimentation that high doses of vitamin E definitely increase speed and stamina in the greyhound.

'White-E' was developed and formulated under special conditions by Medical Research Pty Ltd and is stable to air, light, and moisture. This is a pure, natural form of vitamin E, its chemical name being d'alpha tocopheryl acid succinate. Most vitamin E on the market is synthetic, and as such is not as high in biological activity as natural vitamin E succinate on a weight basis. (Tests in Canada have proved conclusively that the degree of success of vitamin E therapy depends upon the use of medically stabilised products. Also vitally important are high consistent dosage levels and an absence of antagonists in the dog's feed.) Many vitamin E formulas on the market are not medically stabilised and deteriorate rapidly as soon as the container is opened.

White-E is considered, in this country, to be the leading vitamin E, which is consistent with opinions in Canada and the U.S.A. It is interesting to note what the eminent veterinarian, N. H. Lambert, M.R.V.Sc., of Dublin, stated at a

British Veterinary Congress: 'My early work was carried out using the synthetic vitamin E, but later I found the natural more effective and generally better tolerated.'

For trainers trying to win races, it is a false economy to save money by purchasing synthetic vitamin E. It is easy to differentiate the natural from the synthetic by the chemical formula. The natural is written with the letter 'd', e.g., d'alpha tocopheryl acid succinate; the synthetic is written with the letters 'dl', e.g., dl'alpha tocopheryl acetate.

White-E may be used right up to and including race day, and will not show in a swab. Some trainers give a double dose of White-E the day before the race and also on race day. It is generally fed in the morning feed and kept well away from iron and mineral tonics, which will cause vitamin E to deteriorate.

It is important to note that animals should not be raced for 4–6 weeks once started on vitamin E because of the tremendous beneficial change in metabolism caused by the high dose of White-E. In the early weeks of this change, the animal will become lethargic and disinterested in racing. During the following 2–3 weeks the lethargy gives way to a new-found energy and vitality. If the trainer wishes to give White-E while he is still racing the animal, he should follow the Immediate Dosage Schedule in the pamphlet, which reads as follows:

'Immediate dosage schedule:
(To be used only for dogs in training who have not previously received vitamin E therapy) 25 i.u. (⅛ teaspoon) every alternate day for 10 days; then 50 i.u. (¼ teaspoon) every alternate day for 10 days, increasing to 50 i.u. daily for 7 days, then to 100 i.u. daily during racing period. Then 200 i.u. (1 teaspoon) for two days prior to race.'

'The dog will reach its maximum performance in approximately six weeks of White-E therapy. Best results are achieved if 50 i.u. of White-E (¼ teaspoon) are administered daily three or four months before racing. The dosage for racing dogs is:
Training: 50 i.u. daily (¼ teaspoon)
Racing period: 100 i.u. daily (½ teaspoon)
Two days prior to race: 200 i.u. daily (1 teaspoon)
Dosage may be adjusted individually, depending on the condition of the dog. Older animals usually require more White-E than young dogs. There is no sudden "let down" after discontinuing the treatment, in fact, improvement is maintained for some considerable time after cessation of White-E.'

In large-scale experiments extending over several years, Canadian veterinarians showed conclusively that the breeding performance of both dogs and bitches improved remarkably under continuous vitamin E therapy. The effects may be summarised as follows:

1. White-E increases the whelping percentage, if given to dogs or bitches only. However, the response is much greater if both dogs and bitches are given White-E therapy for four months prior to mating.
2. Thoroughbred dogs on White-E can cover more frequently.
3. When White-E is given to old dogs and bitches their fertility is often restored to normal and even increased over earlier performance.

The recommended daily dosage for animals in the breeding season is 50 to 100 i.u. of White-E, depending on the size of the dog. Higher levels may be given if necessary.

Sterility in the male animal (based on a 14-kilogram dog)
50 i.u. daily for fourteen days increasing to 100 i.u. daily. In severe cases it may be necessary to administer an androgen in conjunction with White-E.

Sterility followed acute infections resulting in a chronic semino-vesiculitis should be treated with a course of broad spectrum antibiotics (Tetracycline, etc.) before commencing treatment with White-E. Consult your veterinarian.

Sterility in female animals (based on a 14-kilogram dog)
50 i.u. of White-E daily until oestrus occurs. In obstinate cases, a luteal hormone should be given 24 hours before mating.

Excessive exposure to sunlight has a direct bearing upon the vitamin E requirement of animals. Recent experiments in Italy were reported in the *Journal of the American Medical Association*. When animals are exposed to sunlight the body immediately produces ergosterols (vitamin D_1 and D_2). An excess of these D vitamins can be detrimental as they cause a destruction of vitamin E in the muscles and a shortening of the muscle fibres.

The Italian research revealed that if animals were over-exposed to ultra-violet rays of sunlight for long periods, the result was complete destruction of muscle fibre, terminating in the death of the animal. This would indicate that Australian dogs require a greater daily intake of vitamin E than English, Canadian, and American dogs, where the summers are shorter and the winter months mostly overcast.

Unsaturated fatty acids (vitamin F)

In 1929 Burr and Burr described the essential unsaturated fatty acids which are sometimes referred to as vitamin F. These three unsaturated fatty acids, linoleic acid, linolenic acid and arachidonic acid, quickly become rancid when exposed to air. Chief sources of supply include wheatgerm oil, safflower seed oil, cotton seed oil, maize germ oil, sunflower seed oil, soya bean oil, peanut oil, linseed oil, palm oil, and olive oil. Poor sources of supply are represented in butter, margarine, lard, fish oil, milk, beef fat, and mutton fat.

The unsaturated fatty acids play an important role in the maintenance of health and appear to be involved in the normal functioning of the adrenal glands, the thyroid gland, and the reproductive processes. They aid in phosphorus assimilation, cooperate with vitamin D in making calcium available to the tissues, and nourish the skin. Another function of the unsaturated fatty acids is to lower the blood cholesterol level. Excessive cholesterol may restrict the passage of blood through the blood vessels by forming deposits on the inner walls of the vessels. In time, the blood vessels harden and lose resilience and this gives rise to hardening of the arteries and high blood pressure. A coronary occlusion or thrombosis may result if a hardened cholesterol particle should break away and block an important artery.

The unsaturated fatty acids contain lecithin, which is also found in liver, brains, and egg yolk. Lecithin is able to emulsify cholesterol, thus preventing it from silting up blood vessels or forming a thrombus. Lecithin helps keep the skin and nails in healthy condition and is also a rich source of two B complex vitamins, namely, inositol and choline. It also contains vitamins K and E and zinc. Lecithin helps keep the body free from diarrhoea and other bowel ailments and is important to the health of the intestinal flora. Lecithin forms part of the fatty myelin sheath around nerves which insulates and nourishes them. Lecithin prevents rancidity, thus preserving the fat-soluble vitamins from destruction.

Lack of unsaturated fatty acids produces a dryness and scurfiness which spreads over the body; cold weather accentuates the condition. It has been discovered that there is a relationship between lack of unsaturated fatty acids and two B complex vitamins, namely, pyridoxine and pantothenic acid. There may be a failure to put on weight, the coat may be brittle, and there may be excess falling out of hair.

PROTEINS

The main sources of protein in the normal diet of the greyhound include meat, fish, fowl, eggs, and milk. All protein foods do not exhibit the same nutritional value. Protein foods are of value primarily for replacement of the normal wear and tear of tissues and for new tissue growth. Like carbohydrates and fats, they can also be utilised as a source of energy. Some protein should be included in every meal if the animal's health is valued. The word protein comes from the Greek, 'I stand first', an appropriate word for this important group of foods.

Amino acids may be regarded as the building blocks of proteins. Food proteins are considered to be derived from twenty-three amino acids in various combinations. Essential amino acids are those which the animal is unable to synthesise in the body and which must therefore be available in the diet. If adequate amounts of the ten essential amino acids are provided in the diet, then the animal is able to synthesise the others. Experimental evidence verifies this. Essential amino acids are arginine, histidine, isoleucine, lysine, leucine, methionine, phenylalinine, tryptophane, threonine, valine.

Egg protein (ovalbumin), milk, cheese (lactalbumin and casein), meat, and glutenin of wheat contain all the essential amino acids and are thus designated as complete proteins. The proteins of gelatin and corn and various others are called incomplete proteins because they do not contain all of the essential amino acids.

Amino acids are absorbed from the intestine and carried via the blood to the various tissues and organs and they may combine with other substances within the cells. Those amino acids which are not utilised directly may undergo a process called deamination, in which the NH_2 groups are removed. The nitrogen is combined with carbon dioxide to form urea, which is excreted in the urine. Deamination can take place in the kidneys and in other tissues, but the liver is the main organ concerned with this process. The molecule after deamination can be oxidised to carbon dioxide and water with a resultant release of energy, or the chain of carbon, hydrogen, and oxygen atoms can form the framework for conversion to fat or carbohydrate. Conversion of protein to fat enables the animal to store the energy from excess amino acids not utilised directly by the tissues. Not all amino acids form glucose or glycogen after deamination.

CARBOHYDRATES

Carbohydrates are compounds of carbon, hydrogen, and oxygen. They form an extensive group, comprising starch and its derivatives, various forms of sugar, and cellulose. A large amount of carbohydrate consumed by the dog is turned into fat, or is oxidised into carbon dioxide and water during the time it is supplying heat and energy to the body.

Generally speaking, carbohydrate is supplied in the diet by feeding a fabricated product known as 'kibble', the ingredients of which may include wheat meal, bone meal, meat meal from mutton and/or beef and/or lamb, milk powder, wheat germ, liver meal, salt, molasses, and vitamins. In addition to being one of the main sources of energy, carbohydrates provide most of the bulk, or roughage, of the diet, being derived from cereal grains and many vegetable materials. As in the human subject, this roughage ensures healthy activity of the digestive system.

The dog has little or no digestive enzyme (ptyalin or amylase) in its saliva, as do humans, and the carbohydrates it consumes do not undergo any degree of digestion in the mouth. This is one reason why dogs do not chew their food but swallow lumps of meat and biscuit almost whole, giving merely one or two bites to reduce the food to a size that enables it to pass down the oesophagus. Food digestion is left to the activity of juices derived from the stomach, the pancreas, and the glands present in the lining of the small intestine. The dog is capable of digesting and utilising large quantities of starchy foods, hydrolising the carbohydrate primarily by means of amylase derived from the pancreas.

Cellulose is partly broken down in the dog's intestine, but is finally rendered almost completely digestible by fermentation. This fermentation does not occur so much in the intestine of the dog as in the stomach of the animals the dog would normally devour in the wild. In the first stomach of a deer, for example, the cellulose is broken down by fermentation into glucose and fatty acids. This liberates carbohydrates and proteins in a condition in which the digestive apparatus of the dog is readily able to deal. This is one of the reasons why dogs derive enormous benefit from eating the stomach contents of a ruminant or smaller herbivorous animal (such as a rabbit) whenever the opportunity arises. This is why the larger carnivora such as lions, kept in captivity, do not retain their condition or thrive as they would in the wild, unless they are supplied not only with meat, but also with uncleaned tripe and paunches of the animals upon which they would normally feed.

Whether the dog thrives and maintains good health and condition depends on its ability to secrete sufficient digestive juices of good quality from the pancreas and intestinal glands into the small intestine. Any defect or abnormality of the pancreas, hereditary or acquired, may result in lack of insulin and sometimes, also, in a deficiency of pancreatic digestive juices, resulting in the dogs being unable to make full use of starchy foods. This is a frequent cause of loss of condition in dogs and their inability to put on weight in spite of heavy feeding.

Regulation of carbohydrate metabolism is dependent on several factors.

1. Insulin

Insulin, a hormone secreted by the islets of Langerhans of the pancreas, plays an important role in ensuring the proper use of glucose in the body. Insulin enables the glucose to be stored in the liver and muscles in the form of glycogen and also to be utilised as necessary.

When the pancreas fails to produce sufficient insulin, a serious derangement of carbohydrate metabolism occurs — the condition known as diabetes mellitus in which glucose is neither utilised nor stored so that it accumulates in the blood. High blood sugar is called hyperglycemia. As the sugar level of the blood rises above normal, the kidneys begin to excrete this substance. Since the kidneys do not ordinarily excrete sugar, a chemical test for sugar in the urine is routine procedure in the diagnosis of diabetes. The kidneys do excrete sugar after a high carbohydrate intake, but this is a temporary glycosuria.

The sugar reserves of the body are rapidly

depleted in diabetes. Proteins are then utilised and there is also a disturbance of fat metabolism. The oxidation of fats is increased, resulting in the accumulation of certain organic acids (ketone substances) in the blood and urine. One of the breakdown products of fatty acids is acetoacetic acid, a toxic substance which may be responsible for the development of diabetic coma in extreme untreated cases.

Early investigators removed the pancreas from dogs and discovered that there was then a large increase in urine production, that the urine contained sugar, and that these animals were unable to live more than a month without the pancreas. These workers also determined that it is not the digestive portion of the pancreas that is essential to life. Investigators tied off the pancreatic ducts, causing the glandular cells producing digestive enzymes to degenerate, leaving only the islets of Langerhans still active. The dogs lived and were not diabetics. Many attempts were made to extract a hormone from the pancreas but these attempts were unsuccessful until 1922, when Banting and Best prepared an extract of pancreatic tissue from islet cells that was free from digestive enzymes; when injected into depancreatised dogs it reduced their diabetic symptoms. This outstanding work was executed at Toronto, Canada.

Insulin does not cure diabetes, but it does regulate carbohydrate metabolism to such an extent that diabetics can live essentially normal lives. Diabetics usually exhibit increased thirst, a large amount of water being necessary to provide for the filtration of the quantity of glucose and salts excreted.

Too much insulin causes a fall in blood sugar which, if severe, produces coma (insulin coma).

2. Liver function

Normal liver function is essential for the proper storage of glucose (as glycogen). Absorbed glucose is carried by the portal system to the liver, where it is stored as glycogen (animal starch). The process of converting glucose to glycogen is called glycogenesis. As the tissues utilise glucose in their metabolism, the liver converts some of its stored glycogen back to glucose, thus helping to maintain a constant blood sugar level. The process of breaking down glycogen to glucose is called glycogenolysis. The blood carries a small amount of glucose and the liver contains a little, but there is no storage of glucose in the body. Glucose is converted to glycogen not only by the liver but also by skeletal muscles. The majority of the glycogen, however, is stored in the liver.

The intermediate stages between glucose and glycogen, consisting of phosphorylated compounds, are largely reversible. The initial stages of breakdown of glycogen in the liver are similar to the process that occurs in muscle, but lactic acid or carbon dioxide and water are not ordinarily produced as end products. The liver contains phosphatase, a very active enzyme which splits a glucose–6 –phosphate compound into glucose and inorganic phosphate. The glucose is then absorbed by the blood and transported to the body tissues. The blood would be unable to absorb glucose unless its own sugar level were lower than the concentration within the liver. Phosphatase is not exclusive to the liver; it occurs in tissues throughout the body.

3. Endocrine glands

Certain of the endocrine glands, notably the thyroid and adrenals, play a role in glucose metabolism. Overactivity of the thyroid gland, e.g., in thyrotoxicosis, may give rise to an excess of glucose in the blood and excretion of it in the urine. The adrenals secrete cortisone, which can convert protein into carbohydrate. When excessive cortisone is produced, the blood sugar level may be permanently elevated and diabetes mellitus results.

Like other carnivorous animals, the dog may convert a portion of the carbohydrates consumed into fats so that the total body fat may be in excess of the amount of fat consumed, and more than can be accounted for by the transformation of some of the fat eaten by the dog, into body fat. This occurs through particular amino acids derived from proteins being converted into sugar within the body and the subsequent conversion of this sugar into fat. Generally, nearly all the protein consumed by a normal dog is burnt up to provide energy, and the main source of body fat is carbohydrate plus any excess fat fed. However, all dogs, like all men, are not normal, and it is possible for a dog to become too fat on an almost total protein diet, even when protein is employed for the purpose of reducing its weight. Healthy dogs with a normal supply of pancreatic juice are readily able to digest cooked starch, as present in biscuit, with the output of a useful number of calories.

It has been discovered that dogs fed primarily

on carbohydrates develop skin disorders, but this need not be the case provided they are not deprived of essential vitamins, notably vitamins of the B complex and vitamins A and D in the form of cod-liver oil or halibut-liver oil. This is probably the reason for the popularity of yeast products which are the most prolific source of vitamin B. One disadvantage of feeding carbohydrates is that, unless exercise can be unlimited, carbohydrates sufficient to provide energy may result in the laying down of surplus fat.

FATS

Fat is necessary to ensure efficient production of lipase (a fat-splitting enzyme) and bile. The fat-soluble vitamins A, D, E, F, and K cannot be assimilated in the absence of fat and bile.

Fat is essential to health and a small quantity of stored fat is needed for several purposes. Fat beneath the skin serves to protect nerves and muscles and acts as an insulator to maintain warmth in cold weather. The kidneys are supported and protected by a surrounding layer of fat. A fat reserve is also beneficial as a source of energy during illness. These uses should not encourage the heavy feeding of fats because if one feeds in excess of that which is required by the animal for warmth and energy, the fat will be stored and become over-abundant and will then be objectionable.

Fats are composed of similar basic elements as carbohydrates, but these elements differ in their proportions. There is less oxygen in the fat molecule. When totally oxidised, both carbohydrates and fats yield energy and break down to carbon dioxide and water. A greater amount of energy can be derived from the combustion of a specific quantity of fat than from the same amount of carbohydrate.

Fats are absorbed primarily by way of the lymphatic system. During digestion they are broken down into glycerol and fatty acids. Evidence reveals that some fatty acids are essential and others are not. Following digestion, fats are absorbed and deposited in the various body tissues and this fat constitutes a reserve energy source. The greatest quantity is stored in the subcutaneous connective tissue, although considerable amounts may be stored around the kidneys.

It is well known that carbohydrates can be converted to fat by means of the chemistry of the animal's body. Evidence is not equally clear for the conversion of protein to fat in the diet.

Some deaminated amino acids can be converted to fat, but the quantity of fat derived from protein would probably be small in normal metabolism.

The average dog requires not less than five per cent fat in its diet if it is to exhibit a good coat. A dog that has survived on a fat-deficient diet, or been half-starved, may temporarily be fed as much as ten per cent fat in the diet without causing digestive disturbances, except perhaps in a few cases in which there is a fat sensitivity. However, every dog appears to have its own specific fat requirement. In the absence of a fat ration, the dog utilises fat already stored in its body, until the fat content of the whole body falls to six per cent, after which emaciation becomes observable. The ability to maintain the balance between the laying down of fat and its regular rate of absorption often spells success and it is not a particularly easy thing to achieve.

Although both fat and carbohydrate foods provide energy, they play quite different roles in body metabolism, and one cannot be substituted for the other, both fat and carbohydrate being necessarily present in the same diet. The inclusion of sufficient fat in the diet has been shown to have definite value in maintaining bitch fertility, but the proportion of fat fed to brood bitches should never exceed five per cent of the total ration. This is applicable also to lactating bitches during the summer, but more may be fed to them when the weather and the accommodation are cold.

Fat is essential in connection with the nourishment and general health of the skin, including the ears, which are lined with skin even in the ear canal. Experimentation has proved that a number of skin diseases, notably cases of chronic ear canker, respond to treatment consisting of feeding fat in the daily diet.

Excess fat fed to dogs lessens the appetite for other essential foods, may give rise to biliousness and vomiting, and may retard growth in young animals. Young dogs and recently weaned puppies are much less able to digest meat proteins or fats than older animals. Rancid fats are capable of destroying vitamins A and E in the body. A store of fat within the body may help to combat certain types of infection, particularly those attacking the skin.

MINERALS

Dogs require calcium, phosphorus, iron, copper, potassium, magnesium, sodium, chlorine, iodine, manganese, cobalt, and zinc. Most minerals and trace elements are obtained by the greyhound from an adequate diet, fresh water, and contact with the soil. Some minerals are more necessary than others, especially to the racing greyhound, and therefore should be given in the form of a supplement to ensure that the dog has sufficient to meet his needs. The more important ones are now discussed.

Sodium chloride has an important function in helping to maintain the osmotic pressure of the blood. Salt is lost by excretion in the urine and sweat.

Iodine is needed only in minute amounts, but is essential to the normal functioning of the thyroid gland. Thyroxine, the hormone of this gland, is an amino acid containing iodine. If an iodine deficiency arises, the thyroid gland may enlarge and result in simple goitre. This does not necessarily result in endocrine disturbance such as an alteration in the metabolic rate, although a low rate of hormone production is indicated. Pups and pregnant bitches should receive an adequate supply of iodine in the food and drinking water. The use of iodised table salt in the dog's food (sprinkled on the food in much the same manner as we use salt on our own food) should provide an adequate amount of iodine. Kelp tablets and seaweed meal are other products available which may be used.

Calcium is essential to the development of the bones and teeth. Calcium is a common element in food, but many foods contain only minute amounts and it is apparently not readily absorbed from some foods. Growing puppies require an abundant supply of calcium for the development of sound skeletal structures. Growing puppies from six weeks onwards should be given additional calcium and phosphorus until about six months old. The bones of the new-born pup are soft in order to prevent damage to the bitch during whelping. Hardening gradually takes place as the pup grows older and his body lays down calcium supplied to him in his diet. There will already be a certain amount of calcium in the bloodstream which will have been supplied by his mother before birth and this is why, in pregnancy, plenty of calcium is needed in the bitch's diet. Calcium is present in the body mainly as carbonate or phosphate salts. Calcium, potassium and sodium salts are maintained at a nearly constant level in the bloodstream and tissues. The diet is more apt to be deficient in calcium than the other elements. Vitamin D is essential to the proper absorption and utilisation of mineral salts deposited in bone. Too low an intake of calcium and phosphorus will lead to poor calcification of bones and other symptoms of rickets. Calcium is more effectively digested when administered with honey.

Phosphorus is a requirement of all living, growing tissue and is as important as protein for body building. For puppies, a diet low in phosphorus is detrimental because they have a considerable amount of growing to do. Phosphorus and sulphur are largely obtained from protein foods and if adequate amounts of protein food are included in the diet there should be sufficient phosphorus and sulphur for physiological requirements. Sulphur is a necessary element in the formation of the amino acids, methionine and cystine.

Iron, copper, and cobalt are needed to prevent iron deficiency anaemias. A normal haemoglobin level is necessary for all dogs, but is absolutely vital to the racing greyhound. The greyhound's diet is often deficient in iron because milk and grain products are extremely low in iron. Meat may also have a low content due to iron depletion of pastures and soils. These dietary facts combined with intensive artificial care and kennelling may lead to an anaemia in the dog. Schalm (1961) states that iron, copper, and cobalt are the principal minerals required for red blood cell production. Iron is an integral part of the haemoglobin molecule (i.e., it is responsible for the red colour) and therefore it is absolutely essential for haemoglobin synthesis.

To comprehend the importance of iron in the greyhound's diet, one must consider the following facts:
1. Haemoglobin consists basically of protein and iron, and in every gram of haemoglobin there is 3·36 mg of iron. Iron is essential to haemoglobin formation.
2. Red cells are responsible for fifty to seventy per cent of the total blood volume.
3. The amount of blood in a dog is approximately ten per cent of its body weight.
4. Blood cells are continually dying and being replaced. The red blood cells (erythrocytes) derive their red colour from haemoglobin which is composed of a pigment, heme, containing iron, and the protein, globin.
5. Haemoglobin is said to possess a chemical affinity for oxygen. As the blood passes through a capillary network in the thin air

sacs of the lungs, oxygen enters into loose chemical combination with haemoglobin, becoming oxy-haemoglobin, and is distributed to the tissues of the body. There, as blood passes through tissue capillaries, the haemoglobin loses oxygen to the tissues and is referred to as reduced haemoglobin. Haemoglobin not only functions to carry oxygen to the tissues, but also carries carbon dioxide and the waste products of muscular exertion away from the tissues. It is clear, therefore, that insufficient iron = less haemoglobin = less oxygen supply to muscle = build up of muscle toxins = consequent loss of speed and stamina.

Anaemia is a deficiency of red blood cells and/or haemoglobin due to an iron-deficient diet or poor absorption of iron and therefore the animal will suffer from a lack of oxygen. Lack of iron in the diet causes the dog to become lethargic, and so his tolerance to exercise decreases. He blows hard following a gallop. The mucous membranes of the eyes and lips are pale and the coat is poor. The dog often becomes distressed and is unable to attain his peak. This is a common condition in the racing dog and is most significant when maximum muscular activity is required. The anaemia may be present in varying degrees:

1. Severe or acute anaemia—the dog exhibits obvious clinical symptoms, i.e., the dog is obviously unhealthy, with poor coat, lethargic condition, pale mucous membranes.
2. Chronic anaemia—the dog may exhibit no obvious symptoms except that he is unwilling to work or race, which is shown by a decreased tolerance to exercise in that he pulls up blowing hard, is distressed, and cannot attain a peak condition.
3. Mild anaemia—this condition is difficult to detect as it may prevail in quite fit dogs. It can be shown only by several blood counts and expert determination. Correction of mild anaemia may be all that is required to turn a minor place-getter into a winner.

Anaemia is frequently the result of some other problem, such as the presence of blood-sucking parasites (hookworm), acute blood loss, and incorrect diet (i.e., lack of protein, iron, copper, and cobalt).

Treatment aims firstly at eradication of the cause of the anaemia and secondly at the effect, which is lack of haemoglobin and therefore iron. The majority of cases respond to administration

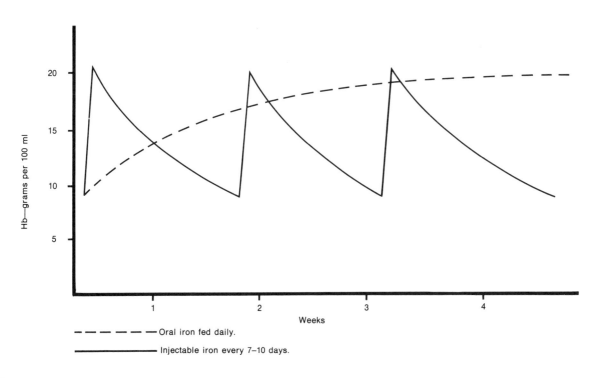

Hb—grams per 100 ml

Weeks

— — — — — Oral iron fed daily.

——————— Injectable iron every 7–10 days.

of oral iron aminoates. When fed as iron protein chelate it is extremely safe and effective. The dog regulates the intake of iron through the gut and any iron administered orally that is not needed can be excreted, except in the case of extremely large doses. One must exercise caution in regard to the use of oral inorganic iron salts which are toxic in large doses. By daily oral administration of iron the availability of iron to the bloodstream is constant, whereas with injections it is erratic, as indicated by the graph on page 83.

In deciding which oral iron tonic to use, three points should be afforded consideration:
1. Effectiveness in improving haemoglobin values.
2. Some forms of iron tonic can cause irritation of the stomach wall and, as the dog is unable to admit to stomach ache, it is an important selection point.
3. Traces of copper and cobalt should be present in the correct proportions. For maximum utilisation of iron to form haemoglobin, traces of copper and cobalt must be administered simultaneously.

Ironcyclen has been developed by Medical Research Pty Ltd specifically for the treatment of anaemia in greyhounds. Since haemoglobin is an iron chelate, scientists have developed an iron protein chelate as near to haemoglobin as possible. This is achieved by digesting protein in large vats until amino acids are produced (similar to normal digestion). This process takes approximately one week in the laboratory. The amino acids are then combined with a freshly prepared iron colloid to form iron aminoates. From this stage the final powder is produced following controlled and lengthy vacuum drying. The entire process takes more than two weeks and commences with an iron compound normally used in iron tonics. Traces of copper and cobalt are added during processing as it is well known that formation of haemoglobin from iron is retarded without their presence.

An alternative method to oral administration of iron is injection. Iron injections are used in critical cases of anaemia which have not responded to oral therapy due to metabolic disturbance. Iron injections should be administered in correct dosages and only by a qualified veterinarian, as serious side effects may arise. Iron administered incorrectly via intravenous route may kill a dog in seconds; overdose via intramuscular route will lead to serious liver necrosis (death of the liver) because the dog has no natural defence to this method of overdosage. The advantage of oral iron administration as compared with injection is that the dog's natural control mechanism, the liver, is still operative, whereas with injections this safety measure is bypassed. Iron injections can be extremely painful and can often cause muscle soreness and muscle abscess if administered unprofessionally using unsterile equipment.

There are also minute amounts of other minerals in cells; these have been called trace elements. Some of these are apparently essential for specific enzymatic reactions. Copper, manganese, and zinc are examples. Trace elements are not to be confused with radioactive substances referred to as tracers.

ROUGHAGE

Roughage is indigestible and usually adopts the form of fibrous plant matter, or cellulose. The value of roughage lies in the fact that it is indigestible. Cellulose adds bulk to the food and enables the muscles of the alimentary canal to grip the food and keep it moving, particularly in the large intestine. Rhythmic waves of muscular contraction and relaxation, called peristalsis, help to propel the food along the canal. Absence of roughage is likely to lead to constipation and its attendant disorders.

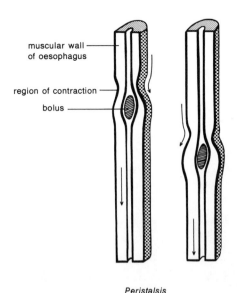

muscular wall of oesophagus

region of contraction

bolus

Peristalsis

WATER

Water plays an important role in the chemical reactions involved in metabolism and it must be considered in relation to the study of a proper diet. Water accounts for a large proportion of the body tissues and is an important participant in protein and carbohydrate digestion, disposal of waste matter via the urine and faeces, synthesising processes, physiological functions, and regulation of body temperature. Lack of water results in dehydration and may prove fatal. The proper functioning of the body tissues, notably the kidneys, enables the animal to maintain normal water balance. Water loss takes place primarily through the urine, as water vapour in expired air, as sweat, and in faecal matter. Generally speaking, greyhounds will only drink as much water as their system requires.

The aim of nutrition is to provide sufficient energy for maintenance and sufficient additional energy for work. Weight limits are imposed on racing greyhounds and there is an allowance of 1 kilogram variation in racing weight. If a greyhound has a declared racing weight of 30 kilograms, then its allowable racing weight is between 29 and 31 kilograms. To supply nutrition to this greyhound to meet its maintenance requirements along with its high energy requirements, and at the same time maintain a definite weight limit, is not an easy task.

The basic diet comprises a morning meal and an evening meal as greyhounds are almost invariably fed twice daily. To form a basis for discussion, I have chosen a greyhound weighing 30 kilograms and undertaking a walk of 8 to 10 kilometres per day and galloping twice a week, once in a race and once from a hand slip.

Morning meals for greyhounds are many and varied and generally contain no meat. They contain low-protein, low-fibre constituents that have reasonable energy levels. Fluid balance is of paramount importance in the racing greyhound. Racing dogs at peak fitness do not drink much water and consequently water, milk, soup, etc., is added to the diet. Greyhounds can dehydrate very rapidly during hot weather and extra fluid may need to be added to their diets, if they will not drink adequate water. Electrolytes, in particular, may need to be administered in milk. Each 100 grams of kibble or biscuits should be mixed with 200 to 300 millilitres of fluid. The 1:3 ratio, or higher, should be implemented in hot weather and the fluid mixed evenly throughout the meal just prior to feeding.

A suitable morning meal consists of:
- 200 millilitres of milk, 'Bonox', soup, or vegetable water.
- 120 to 150 grams of kibble, or two dog biscuits (e.g. Farrell's 10 × 5 centimetres), toasted wholemeal bread, or about three 'Weetbix'; 'Vitabrits' can also be fed. Milk should be fed with these products as their calcium content is low.
- 3 grams (1 teaspoon) of calcium carbonate, gluconate lactate, or 5 grams of D.C.P. If your dog is prone to cystitis or crystals, it is advisable not to use D.C.P.
- 3 grams of glucose, 'Glucodin', 'Sustagen' or 15 millilitres (1 dessertspoon) of honey.
- 2 grams (½ teaspoon) or 100 i.u. of 'White E' or one capsule of 'White E'.
- 3 grams of 'Betacel' electrolyte replacer or other good quality electrolyte mixture.
- 5 millilitres (1 teaspoon) of 'Fortex' for racing dogs twice weekly. However, remember that 'Fortex' and other tonics must be withdrawn at least 72 hours prior to the race.
- Some trainers like to feed a vitamin mineral supplement as well. However, if you are feeding vitamin E it is advised not to feed iron tonics or mineral mixtures containing iron in the same meal because vitamin E is made less available by iron.

Evening meals generally contain the protein, added minerals, and vitamins, and often the vegetable part of the daily ration. Traditional meat-based meals can have several variations. The amounts given depend on the weight of the dog and the amount of exercise undertaken. If the amount of work increases, or a cold change sets in, the ration amount may need to be increased.

A typical evening meal may contain the following ingredients:
- 750 grams of minced lean beef for bitches, 850 grams for dogs. The beef should not contain too much fat but at the same time should be minced without being excessively trimmed. Occasionally other meats may be substituted for variety.
- 350 grams of kibble for bitches, 450 grams for dogs. 'Farrell's Kibbled Dog Meal' is suitable. It may be necessary to increase the amount of kibble by up to 100 grams in cold weather to maintain body weight.
- Iron supplement. Racing dogs may require additional iron in their diets. Iron supplements and tonics are many and varied. 'Iron-

cyclen' tablets (two per day) or liquid (1 teaspoon per day) are widely used by trainers.

- Mineral and vitamin supplement. A combined vitamin and mineral supplement is perhaps the most economical. As previously mentioned, don't feed vitamin E with the iron or mineral supplement; feed vitamin E in the morning meal. A balanced supplement such as 'Feramo D' for greyhounds is suitable.
- Vitamin B—complex supplement. 'Amino-B Vet' tablets (six to eight per day) are a good source of vitamins although the choice is dependent upon availability and price. Some trainers prefer to feed only a vitamin mineral supplement.
- Vegetables. Add fibre, minerals, vitamins and variety to the diet. A mixture of vegetables, such as pumpkin, carrot, celery, parsnips, beans, peas cooked with a pinch of salt is commonly prepared. Approximately a cupful per dog is the usual amount, although a little more may be offered. Retain the cooking water. Vegetables may be fed raw if preferred.
- Fluid to moisten the meal. Approximately two cups of fluid for bitches, two and a half cups for dogs. The vegetable water is ideal as it contains more nutrients than water or milk. Mix the ingredients and fluid just prior to feeding to avoid sodden, mushy food. In hot weather more fluid can be added together with an electrolyte replacer such as 'Betacel'.

Selection of alternate meats and feeding programme is important. The most widely used meats are beef, horse, kangaroo, mutton, buffalo, and chicken. It is good practice to vary a dog's diet occasionally to freshen the dog between races. However, when changing over entirely to different meat types, it is a good idea to introduce it slowly over a week or so. Feed about half beef mince with the substitute meat for three to four days and slowly increase the amount of alternative meat until it is the sole meat source. This is especially important in the case of horse meat as it may cause diarrhoea in dogs when introduced quickly.

To prevent the dog putting on weight one should reduce the amount of mutton fed to about eighty per cent of the normal beef ration, that is, 800 grams instead of 1 kilogram. Mutton does not cause digestive upsets, but dogs used to beef may not accept it immediately.

Horse meat is lower in fat content than beef but has about the same protein content; generally speaking, the food value is about the same as lean beef.

Chicken mince has more protein and fat than beef; 1 kilogram of chicken is equal to about 1100 grams of beef. Chicken offal or pieces are not as good in value, about 1200 grams of chicken bits and pieces being equal to 1 kilogram of lean beef.

Fish may also be used but it varies considerably in protein content, depending on the type of fish. Fish is suitable as a change for racing dogs. Boil about 1 kilogram of mullet in water with a pinch of salt, remove the bones carefully, and feed to the dog as an evening meal with two cups of milk mixed into 200 grams of kibble. Rabbit stew is also suitable for variety.

Investigation reveals that many authorities advise against feeding of offal, sheep offal in particular, as it can transmit various diseases to dogs. All offal must be carefully inspected prior to feeding and examined for lumps, fluid-filled sacs, white threadlike lines, or fatty cysts, as these growths could be due to parasites. Fresh liver requires extra preparation prior to feeding in that it should be sliced into 1-centimetre thick slices before mincing to ensure that there are no internal cysts. The liver should then be lightly washed in warm water to remove bile, fluke, etc., and about 200 grams mixed with meat. Liver can contain high levels of copper, mercury, and vitamin A. Avoid feeding large amounts of liver for prolonged periods.

Special meals are often fed to racing dogs prior to a race. Sometimes these meals replace the normal breakfast. Remember to withdraw any tonics at least 72 hours before a race. Occasionally trainers give a tablespoon of 'Agarol' two nights before a race as this acts as a mild laxative. Special pre-race meals are designed to provide high energy levels with minimal bulk. They should also be attractive to the dog and should be well digested by the time of the race. A special meal instead of the normal breakfast may consist of 500 grams of lightly grilled steak and 30 to 40 grams (2 tablespoons) of glucose ('Glucodin') sprinkled over it. During hot weather additional fluids and electrolytes will be required. Two cups of water with one teaspoon of 'Betacel' may be offered two hours later. A non-meat diet may also be fed as it has a high carbohydrate content rich in energy and is easily digested prior to the race. It consists of forty grams of 'Sustagen' or 'Actavite' mixed as directed on the label. Do not use chocolate flavoured 'Sustagen' etc., because it shows on a swab—it contains theobromide from the chocolate.

- One cup (250 millilitres) of kibble.
- Half a cup (100 millilitres) of non-fat powdered milk e.g., 'Diploma', 'Dutch Jug'.
- 30 grams (2 tablespoons) of glucose, e.g., 'Glucodin'.

If a normal breakfast is given, then a special meal can be given either 8 or 4 hours before a race.

The eight-hour pre-race meal consists of:
- 200 grams of lightly grilled steak.
- 30 to 40 grams of 'Glucodin' sprinkled over it.
- Water and electrolytes if necessary.

The four-hour pre-race meal consists of:
- 20 grams (1 tablespoon) of 'Sustagen' or 'Aktavite; mixed as directed on the label. Milk can be used to mix it.
- 10 grams (2 teaspoons) of non-fat powdered milk.
- Electrolytes and fluids if necessary.

These diets vary considerably; if the dog is successful, then usually the particular pre-race meal is adopted.

Special meals after a race are often fed. It is of paramount importance that the dog be allowed to cool down before feeding. Fluid and electrolyte replacement is important, especially in hot weather. These meals are designed to provide moderate energy and protein levels, with particular attention to dehydration and fluid balance. Normally about 2 hours is required for the dog to cool down. If the dog is distressed as a consequence of racing under hot conditions, 2 cups of water or milk with a teaspoon of a suitable electrolyte replacer may be required. Severe dehydration should be treated by a vet.

Dogs exhibiting cramp or other muscular problems should also undergo veterinary examination and treatment. Some dogs pass a red-coloured urine after racing; this is due to muscle 'myoglobin' pigments and indicates that stress or slight cramping has occurred. If this does not clear up within 24 hours after a race, one should seek veterinary advice.

Frequently a kidney tonic such as 'Neutradex', given with the morning meal each morning for three days after a race will help to flush out the kidneys.

It is important to add electrolytes, in addition, to ensure adequate levels for maximum recovery after racing.

When the dog arrives home and has cooled down, the normal evening meal can be fed. This meal should be well moistened to ensure replacement of fluids and thus correct any dehydration.

Other alternatives include:
- A bread and milk meal; 500 millilitres of warm milk with half a loaf of wholemeal bread—break up the bread and mix in the milk; 10 millilitres (2 dessertspoons) of honey in warm water; 10 grams (2 teaspoons) of 'Glucodin'. A vitamin and mineral supplement is sprinkled over this.
- A stew. This is quite common and usually consists of chopped beef and vegetables, and sometimes cereal, added in the form of barley or rice. A vitamin mineral supplement is added.
- A white meat meal. This may consist of fish or boiled tripe, perhaps with some vegetable.
- The customary evening meal (which should be well moistened).

Dried dog foods are becoming more popular. The meat content may be reduced to a low level or cut out completely. Careful monitoring of the dog's body weight and performances will help you select the product you find most suitable. If the dog puts on weight, the amount of dried food should be reduced. If the dog loses weight, check for worms, and then increase the dried food.

A minimal meat evening meal could contain:
- 200 grams of lean beef.
- 350 grams for bitches, 400 grams for dogs, of dried prepared foods with twenty per cent protein or above.
- 200 millilitres of meaty gravy or 'Bonox'.
- 200 grams of cooked vegetables (optional).
- A vitamin and mineral supplement and extra electrolytes and water in hot weather.

A total dried food diet with no meat is usually best decided on how much the dog can eat, response to the ration and its acceptance.

A vegetarian racing dog could be fed:
- 500 to 600 grams of dried, expanded food with twenty per cent protein or above.
- 200 millilitres of meaty gravy or 'Bonox' or vegetable water.
- 200 grams of cooked vegetables (optional).
- A vitamin and mineral supplement and extra electrolytes and water in hot weather.

COMPLETE DRY FOODS by Stefan Brasch

In general terms complete dry dog foods are composed of one-third high-quality protein meal and two-thirds cereal or cereal by-products. This composition is coated with animal fat. Flavours may be added, either into the base composition or as a coating. Animal fat itself acts possibly as the flavouring most attractive to dogs.

The protein meals in the dry foods are either substantially of animal origin or from oil seed meal, most commonly soybean meal.

Animal protein meal

Meat meals: The most common ones are meat meals. These are the by-products of fat rendering after the tallow has been extracted by cooking processes. The tallow has a variety of industrial applications such as the manufacture of soaps, cooking margarines, fats, and cosmetics.

The meat meal residues which are left from these processes are dry, light-grey to dark-grey powders which can still contain up to twelve per cent fat. Basically meat meals have two main sources. There are those left after the fat-rendering of butchers' returns, that is, meat remains collected from butchers after the saleable meat has been removed. Essentially these remains are of muscle meat with, predictably, a good proportion of bone. The meat meal residues after fat-rendering therefore are rich in calcium and phosphorus, especially calcium. The other main source of meat meal is that directly from abattoirs, from the fat-rendering of animal organs removed during the dressing of the carcass and classified as unsuitable for human consumption. This meat meal is lower in calcium content than that from butchers' returns. By the same token, butchers' returns meat meals have a lower protein content than those from abattoirs, the analyses showing forty-two per cent and fifty per cent respectively. Manufacturers of the lower protein meals may choose to raise the protein content by adding blood meal (i.e., dried blood), or mixing in abattoir meat meal. Because the higher protein meat meals are made from organ meat, or the result of other meal supplementation, it is these which have the darker colour. The quality of the higher-protein meat meals is also higher than that of the lower-protein ones.

Fish meal: These are an even better protein source than meat meals and are produced by fundamentally the same process, with the same end in view. Fish oils have a large number of industrial applications. Important sources of fish meal throughout the world include South America, South Africa, and certain parts of Asia and the Pacific. The quality of fish meal protein is better than that of meat meals, and the calcium and phosphorus contents of the meals also occur in a suitable ratio.

Other animal meals: There are various other animal protein meals available, but of lesser importance mainly because of their relatively limited availability. Those made from the drying and powdering of poultry by-products, including feathers, are perhaps the best known of these, but are mostly converted back directly into poultry feed. Powdered milk or milk by-products are used to a limited extent.

Vegetable protein meals

Oilseed meals: Here again these are the residues from oil extraction processes. In these cases, however, the oil extraction method is basically one of pressing out the oil with as little heat as possible so as not to endanger the quality of the oil. The most common use of these oils is in the manufacture of table margarine. Soybean oil however has important industrial uses in paints and plastics.

Soybean meal: This is the most common and important of all the vegetable protein sources, its quality approaching that of meat meals. It is a pale-coloured, free-flowing, gritty powder and, depending on the extraction process, has a protein content between forty-five and fifty per cent. It is probably the only vegetable oil meal which is produced as much for its use as a protein feed as it is a by-product of vegetable oil production.

Sunflower and other oilseed meals: Depending on the amount of fibrous matter present, sunflower meal may have protein contents of thirty-three to thirty-eight per cent, and a quality close to that of soybean meal. Together with other oil seed meals like safflower meal, rapeseed meal, and peanut meal, its availability is not as plentiful as soybean meal because of the lesser acreage planted.

Other vegetable protein meals: These include dried lucerne meal, various dried beans, and certain residue products from brewing processes. In almost all cases vegetable proteins have an unsuitable calcium to phosphorus ratio for nutritional purposes and this may need to be compensated for in a dry food composition by calcium supplementation.

Cereals

These mainly provide carbohydrates in the form of starch as an important source of expendable energy. Wheat is naturally the most common of these, while others include oats, barley, and maize. Whereas wheat is a commodity available the year round because of relatively large harvests, other cereals are more limited in their availability.

Apart from being a valuable energy source, cereals also represent an important source of linoleic acid, especially through the medium of wheatgerm or bran and pollard, when these are used.

Other major ingredients

As one can imagine there are always a number of lesser materials available with quite useful nutritional qualities, be they primarily as contributors of proteins, minerals, or energy. These are often by-products from other food processes or lesser vegetable crops which may be available from time to time. Their usefulness at any one time is strongly dependent on the current price relative to that of the more commonly used materials.

A very important ingredient, of course, is fat, for reasons both of providing energy and flavour. Animal fat is used almost exclusively for this purpose. There appears to be no distinct preference shown by dogs between the different qualities of animal fats which are available from renderers.

Minor ingredients

From a nutritional standpoint the two important classes of additives are essential amino acids to enhance protein quality and vitamin–mineral mixtures. The specific roles of these has been discussed earlier, but in regard to amino acids, the two most important ones are lysine and methionine. Certain vitamins, particularly vitamin A, B_1, B_6, are somewhat sensitive to the heat used in processing of dry food. Thus they are added to the mixture of ingredients in sufficient quantity to ensure that the amount lost due to heat damage in processing still leaves the required amount in the final product.

FORMULATION OF DRY FOODS

The nutritional requirements of dogs have been gradually established on a scientific basis over a period of about the last fifty years. Some of the research contributing to this body of information has been carried out on other animals, but has been sufficiently relevant to be applicable to dogs. A vast amount has been carried out directly on dogs.

The international guidelines set for dog nutrition are published periodically by the National Academy of Sciences in the U.S.A., acting through one of the sub-committees of its Committee on Animal Nutrition. This publication is a compilation of the most relevant past and recent published results in these areas and on this basis gives recommendations on the values of the various nutritional parameters and quantities of the various nutrients required to fill these recommendations. To this information reputable manufacturers will add that derived from their own direct research as well as that gathered from other reliable sources. Thus a comprehensive framework is available around which to formulate sound diets.

It can be a fairly complex mathematical task to calculate the best combination of ingredients to achieve an optimum diet, since most of the major ingredients contain a number of the nutrients to some extent. There is much analytical data available about the nutrient contents of the ingredients available for feed formulation.

Another factor to be considered is that of achieving the best nutritional results in the most economical way. Ingredient prices can change quite significantly from one period to another and those ingredients which may provide an economic source of a particular nutrient on one occasion may not do so on another. In line with commonly accepted practice in a modern animal feed mill, the best formulae are obtained through computer calculations which provide the best combination of the nutrient standards set, ingredients currently available, together with the corresponding analytical data about their nutrient contents, and current costs of ingredients.

Such calculations can be done without the aid of a computer, but the time taken is very much longer and the accuracy somewhat less. The nutrient standards to which the computer is asked to work include principally: protein content, calcium and phosphorus content, amino acid content, and linoleic acid content.

MANUFACTURE OF THE DOG FOOD

Once a formula has been calculated, the following broad sequence of processing steps takes place: weighing of ingredients, mixing of ingredients, grinding, extrusion, drying, and coating.

1. Weighing

Materials may be stored either in bulk in large bins or silos which could hold anything between perhaps 20 tonnes and 100 tonnes, or in bags. They are fed either by direct tipping of bags or by a suitable conveyor system (most commonly screw conveyors) into large weighing units which are essentially suspended hoppers attached by a system of levers to counterweights and scale-reading units. Depending on the sophistication of the plant, addition of any one ingredient may be stopped when the correct weight is registered on the scale, or the cut-off can be operated manually. Again depending on the size of the plant, several major ingredients may be added to the hopper in succession and then dropped together into a mixing unit, or each ingredient may be dropped into the mixing unit separately.

2. Mixing

This may take no longer than several minutes. There are various types of mixing equipment, which may range from the principle of circulating the material through the apparatus or, more commonly, by rotating a blade of one design or another through the body of material. In either event, mixers can handle quantities of quite a few tonnes at a time.

Trace ingredients, already discussed earlier, and other small-quantity additives such as salt and possibly some flavouring are usually added into the mixer separately, having been weighed out on more-sensitive weighing equipment beforehand.

3. Grinding

In order to achieve the best texture in the final product, the mixture of ingredients needs to be reduced to a suitably small particle size in preparation for the cooking and forming process. This is achieved by a hammer mill. In this piece of equipment a large number of metal pieces, attached at one end to a fast-revolving cylinder flail against a perforated metal screen and the materials to be ground are fed into this in such a way as to pass between the flails and the screen, where they are crushed.

The particle size is determined by the size of the perforations in the screen. From the hammer mill, the ground material is passed continuously to the most important stage of the process, the extrusion and expansion.

4. Extrusion

There are various types of extrusion equipment by which the ground ingredient mix is converted into cellular pellets of various shapes and sizes, as desired. Although these different extruder types vary in a number of details, they work according to a common basic principle.

The 'business' portion of an extruder is a heavy metal barrel in which rotates a heavy screw, somewhat akin to a meat mincer. The ground dry mix is fed in at one end and is transferred through the barrel by means of the screw, exiting at the other. During this transfer stage considerable pressure is generated, and at the exit the material is forced through a plate with appropriately-sized holes. The difference in pressure between the inside of the barrel and the normal atmosphere as the material comes out of the holes causes the composition to 'pop' and develop a textured, easily-digestible consistency.

All extruders have means by which steam and water can be added to the ingredient mix, either inside the barrel or in a separate section of the whole equipment before the barrel. In addition it may be possible to heat or cook the barrel without directly injecting steam or water. The addition of water and/or steam is essential for the formation of a dough-like consistency inside the equipment and the mix then lends itself to shape formation as it comes out of the die holes. A further more important role which the water and steam play is that of cooking or gelatinising the starches in the cereal components of the mix. As is well known, uncooked starches are not as readily digested as cooked ones, and for this reason do not make available their full potential to supply energy. The cooking and extrusion process ensures that this is achieved to the greatest possible extent. In addition, the cooked starches form a continuous gel or 'glue' by which all the ingredients are able to be held together in one homogeneous form.

The temperature attained inside the extruder barrel will reach somewhere above the boiling point of water. The length of time any section of ingredient takes to pass through the barrel may not be more than about 30 seconds. The size of extruders will obviously vary depending on the model, but most usually produce at a rate of about 4 tonnes per hour or better.

On exiting from the holes in the die plate at the end of barrel, the extruded dough is cut to size by means of fast-rotating knives, and the pellet shape can also be determined as a result of this cutting process.

5. Drying

The pellets come from the barrel with about twenty-five to thirty per cent moisture which needs to be removed to ensure absence from bacterial and mould growth in the final product. This allows storage for virtually indefinite periods. Drying takes place immediately after extrusion in large ovens, some 12 metres long, either indirectly, by steam, or directly, fired by gas or oil.

6. Coating

The final stage, before packing is that of coating the pellets with animal fat and, in some cases also with flavouring. For this purpose the pellets are tumbled as they pass through a revolving drum while hot fat is sprayed on to them. An even coating is thus applied and flavouring may also be sprayed or sprinkled on at this stage.

TESTING OF DRY FOODS

There are three essential areas of testing.

1. Regular quality control by chemical analysis to ensure that any product fulfils the formulation criteria, principally with respect to fat and protein content. In Australia, some State Departments of Agriculture also require that dog foods be registered as Stockfeeds and under these regulations basic analytical data must be disclosed on the packs. Quality control by chemical analysis therefore also ensures that actual product analysis at any time conforms to these declarations. Essential amino acid analysis, because of its complexity, is not carried out on a regular basis, but rather from time to time. In any event, because the essential amino acid content of ingredients is well known and because the ingredients are mixed in known proportions, one can be confident that the essential amino acid content in the final product is as intended. Much the same can be said of calcium and phosphorus content although their chemical analysis is a relatively simple matter. Again, vitamin content determination represents a fairly complex process and because added vitamins and minerals are bought from specialist suppliers in a con-

sistent form and are accurately weighed in, their regular analysis is not warranted.

2. Testing for nutritional value is a very important feature of product control and new product development. Such testing is a fairly long-term exercise and, depending on the particular information needed, may be done on growing pups, adult dogs in work or at rest, pregnant bitches to see the effect on subsequent litters, or even through several generations.

   The most common measurement carried out in this connection on growing pups is that of measuring their weight increase over a period of time, while measuring accurately the amounts of a particular food consumed per day or per week or per some other convenient measuring period. No food can be considered in isolation, and a control diet, for comparison purposes, must always be used at the same time. In carrying out such comparisons it is always best to use several groups of litters and to split up each litter in such a way that some of the puppies are fed the control diet and some the diet under test. The arrangement of tests of this type in this way is for the purpose of ensuring that the resulting information is as far as possible due to the effect of feeding and not to genetic or environmental factors.

   From information obtained in such a way one can also calculate the amount of growth for every kilogram of food eaten (the so-called 'food conversion factor') and this serves as a very useful measure of the effectiveness of foods relative to each other.

   More detailed information can also be obtained by taking X-rays of bone development during such trials, as well as doing blood tests, as two further important indicators of the efficiency of the particular foods. Tests can be elaborated further through, for example, the omission or reduction of certain vitamins or minerals in diets and the observation or measurement of the consequence over a period of time. In this way minimum requirements of critical ingredients can be established.

   These types of tests carried out on adult dogs, either under prolonged stress conditions or at rest, will yield corresponding information through the measurement of weight losses or gains or even bone degeneration, for example. Thus the adequacy of exiting formulations or modifications can be assessed here also. In addition, if the stools of dogs are analysed, particularly for their content of nitrogen, one can learn to what extent a particular food is utilised by the body.

Tests of the above type can stretch from several weeks to many months, but generally any significant effect of dietary difference becomes noticeable within two to three weeks.

3. Testing for palatability of foods is the other important procedure in product development and evaluation. This can be done in several ways but the underlying technique is always to measure in a controlled way the amount of a particular food eaten by a dog compared with a control food fed under the same conditions. Naturally strong preferences between foods can be noted simply from observation of the dog's feeding pattern, but subtle differences require more extensive testing, using something like twenty dogs over a period of about one week or more.

—Stefan Brasch

7

THE DIGESTIVE SYSTEM

THE PROCESS OF DIGESTION

The digestive system, comprising the alimentary canal and its accessory organs, extends from the mouth to the anus. The more herbivorous an animal the greater the length of the digestive tract. Food is chewed in the mouth, then swallowed via the pharynx and oseophagus through the neck and thorax into the abdomen, where the stomach digests a whole meal to a certain stage before its transmission to the small intestine for further digestion and absorption. The residue passes to the last part of the intestine, the large intestine, for retention until excreted through the anus. The majority of the digestive tract is located in the abdominal cavity with the important organs, liver and pancreas, concerned with elaborating food into forms suitable for storage and assimilation by the tissues. Some regions of the canal have specific functions and accordingly different structures. Juices are secreted in the alimentary canal from glands in its lining or are secreted into it through ducts from glandular organs outside it. As food passes through the alimentary canal it is broken down in stages until the digestible material is dissolved and absorbed. The musculature of the digestive tract appears to be adapted to the specific functions that it performs. The muscles of the mouth provide the voluntary motive force for chewing and swallowing. Involuntary smooth muscles propel food along the tract and provide churning movements in the stomach and intestine.

The glands of the digestive system produce digestive enzymes which act as organic catalysts, i.e., substances which accelerate the rate of chemical changes in the body without altering the end products. The digestive enzymes accelerate the rate at which insoluble compounds are broken down into soluble compounds. Enzymes occur in great numbers and varieties in all protoplasm and without them the chemical reactions would be too slow to maintain life.

Each enzyme possesses the following characteristics:
1. Because it is protein in nature, it is destroyed by heat.
2. It acts most efficiently within a confined temperature range.
3. It acts most rapidly in a fixed degree of acidity or alkalinity.
4. It acts on only one kind of substance.
5. It always forms the same end product or end products, since an enzyme affects only the rate of reaction.

The different sections of the digestive tract are modified to alter the character of food material by the addition or removal of certain substances.

The mouth

The mouth extends from the lips to the pharynx, which is a membranous pouch extending from the articulation of the two jaw bones back to the opening into the oseophagus, or gullet. The mouth consists of the vestibule, the space between the inner sides of the lips, cheeks, and teeth, and the mouth cavity, contained within the dental arches and the gums. The mouth cavity is bounded above by the hard and soft palates and the floor of the mouth is formed by the tongue and its accompanying tissues, which bind the tongue to the lower jaw. Mucous membrane, continuous with that of the mouth, lines the inner surface of each lip. In the midline of the mouth the mucous membrane develops a small fold which attaches the lip to the gum and this is referred to as the fraenum of the lip. The skin meets the mucous membrane at the margins of the lip. The lips include muscular tissue and glands. At the level of the carnassial tooth, the inner surface of each cheek is pierced by the parotid duct which conveys saliva into the mouth. On either side of the fraenum of the tongue there is a small opening through which the submaxillary glands convey their saliva.

Food is chewed in the mouth to reduce its particle size and is mixed with saliva, a watery secretion serving to lubricate the food and hold particles together. Digestion of starch does not take place in the dog's mouth, although it does in man's, since the saliva of the dog lacks the starch-splitting enzyme. In man, the enzyme contained in saliva is known as salivary amylase and it acts on cooked starch and begins to break it down into maltose, a simple sugar. In the dog, water and mucus are added to the food while it is being chewed and swallowed. Food is delivered to the stomach by sequential muscle contractions.

Swallowing

Swallowing consists of the muscular propulsion of food from the mouth through the pharynx and into the oseophagus. The oseophagus is the tube leading to the stomach. During swallowing the following actions take place:

1. The tongue presses upwards and back against the roof of the mouth, forcing the mass of food, called a bolus, to the back of the mouth, or pharynx.
2. The soft palate, the movable partition between the mouth and the pharynx, closes the opening between the nasal cavity and the pharynx.
3. The laryngeal cartilage round the top of the trachea, or windpipe, is pulled upward by muscular action so that the opening of the larynx lies beneath the back of the tongue.
4. The epiglottis, a cartilaginous flap, closes over this opening during the passage of food materials and in this way food does not enter the trachea.

Liquids and solids are propelled through the oesophagus by wave-like contractions of its muscular wall, a process referred to as peristalsis. Liquids are moved very rapidly and since the dog drinks with his head down, peristalsis evidently overcomes the force of gravity. The dog has striated muscle throughout the length of the oesophagus and can swallow extremely quickly. However, in man, food passes through the upper striated portion of the oesophagus more rapidly than through the lower smooth-muscle portion. As the mass of food approaches the cardiac sphincter muscles, which guard the entrance to the stomach, these muscles relax, permitting the entry of food into the stomach.

Digestion in the stomach

The dog presents a true muscular stomach and one not unlike that of the human. The situation of the stomach of the dog differs from that of the human subject in lying much more longitudinally to accommodate itself more perfectly to the abdominal cavity. The digestive pouch is proportionately much larger in the dog than in man so that a large supply can be consumed when the opportunity offers. In the greyhound, the stomach holds from 2·5 to 3 litres, but when contracted and empty appears relatively small. Both man and the dog are able to draw nutriment from animal and vegetable matter, but probably best from a mixture of the two.

The stomach represents a dilatation of the alimentary canal and has flexible walls enabling it to be distended by the accumulation of a relatively large quantity of food, which is retained by the closure of the cardiac and pyloric sphincters at each end of the stomach. The pylorus is the terminal end of the stomach, acting like a valve, dilating sufficiently to permit partially digested food to enter the duodenum and closing tightly at other times. The stomach constitutes that section of the alimentary canal which lies between the oesophagus and the small intestine. The wide body of the stomach rests mainly in the concavity of the diaphragm, while the narrow pyloric portion extends into the duodenum on the right side of the body.

The food in the stomach is moved back and forth by muscular contractions and is mixed with gastric juice. By means of the action of digestive enzymes and hydrochloric acid, the food becomes partially liquified, or of a creamy consistency, and is called chyme. When it reaches the correct consistency, it is forced out through the pyloric sphincter and into the duodenum, a little at a time. The length of time that food remains in the stomach is dependent, to a certain degree, on its nature. Water may pass through in a few minutes, a carbohydrate meal may be retained less than an hour, and a meal of protein and fat may remain in the stomach from one to two hours.

Pepsin is the principal digestive enzyme in the stomach. It acts on proteins and breaks them down to more soluble compounds called peptides. The stomach wall also secretes hydrochloric acid, which provides the proper medium for the pepsin to work in, and also kills many bacteria taken in with the food. Hydrochloric acid is not an enzyme. Hydrochloric acid,

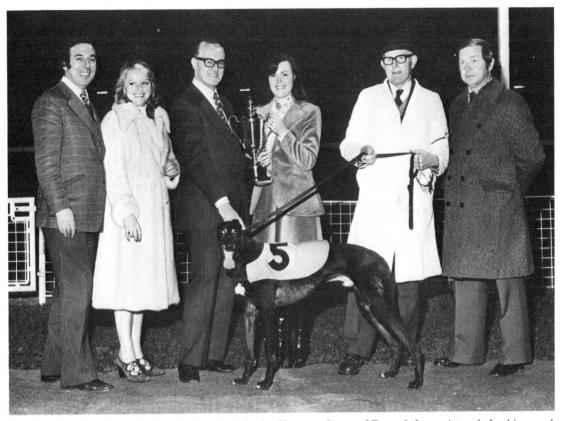

Wembley flyer, Knockrour Bank, a 33·4-kg black dog by Clomoney Jet out of Damsels Lass, pictured after his record-breaking win of 29·01 seconds in the 1976 Wembley Spring Cup *(Courtesy of Wembley Stadium Limited)*

secreted by parietal cells, is derived from sodium chloride of the blood, but the exact nature of its derivation lacks a complete explanation. The concentration of hydrochloric acid in gastric juice as it is secreted by the glands is approximately 0·5 per cent. However, the acidity of the contents of the stomach is seldom as great as this since the hydrochloric acid is diluted by saliva, food, and mucin. In addition, the secretion of glands in the pyloric portion of the stomach is slightly alkaline and so exerts some neutralising effect. Hydrochloric acid is capable of swelling and softening protein, such as meat fibres, and curdling milk.

The glandular lining of the alimentary canal is continually secreting mucus, which helps lubricate the passage of food materials between its walls but which also prevents digestive juices from contacting and digesting the alimentary canal itself. The cells which produce the protein-digesting enzymes would themselves be digested by these chemicals were it not for the fact that the enzymes are made in an inactive form, thus prohibiting them from working until they reach the cavity of the alimentary canal, where they become activated by the chemicals present. Pepsin, which is secreted as an inactive substance called pepsinogen, affords a good example. When pepsinogen is released in the stomach the hydrochloric acid present converts it into active pepsin which cannot then digest the walls of the stomach because of their protective coating of mucus. After death, however, digestive enzymes do attack the stomach.

The small intestine (duodenum, jejunum, and ileum)

Partially digested food leaving the stomach enters the duodenum or upper section of the small intestine. The duodenum, after leaving the pylorus, curves firstly upwards and to the right, making contact with the liver. It then descends and passes along the right side of the abdomen, bending again to the left and becoming continuous with the remainder of the

95

small intestine, which comprises the jejunum followed by the ileum. The coils of the small intestine are suspended from the dorsal wall of the abdomen by the mesentery, a fold of peritoneum which resembles a thin, transparent fan, carrying a large number of blood vessels. When uncoiled, the total length of the small intestine is approximately five times the length of the dog's body.

An alkaline juice from the pancreas, and bile from the liver, are secreted into the duodenum. The pancreas is an elongated, lobular gland with two limbs that diverge from the region of the pylorus, the right limb being contained within the mesentery of the duodenum. The pancreas may have two or three ducts which open into the duodenum, generally with the bile duct. The pancreas secretes three major enzymes:

1. *Trypsin*

Trypsin is a protein-digesting enzyme which is secreted by the glandular cells of the pancreas in an inactive form called trypsinogen. When permitted to combine with intestinal juice, trypsinogen becomes active trypsin. It is activated by the co-enzyme enterokinase, produced by the cells of the intestinal mucosa. Calcium also activates trypsinogen. Trypsin digests proteins in an alkaline medium and breaks them down to peptides or small amino acid groups. Trypsin does not normally complete the breakdown of proteins to amino acids; apparently this is accomplished by the peptidases of the intestinal juice.

2. *Amylase*

Amylase is a starch-digesting enzyme which is secreted by the glandular cells of the pancreas. In an alkaline-to-neutral medium it has the ability to hydrolyse starch to dextrins and to maltose. Recent investigation reveals that it is possible that glucose may also be formed.

3. *Lipase*

Lipase is the enzyme concerned with fat digestion. Lipase splits fat molecules into fatty acids and glycerol and is aided in its action by bile salts from the liver which appear to assist emulsification, thus presenting a greater surface area for the action of the digestive enzyme. The fatty acids concerned are organic acids and are highly insoluble in water, but are soluble in bile salt solutions. Glycerol is soluble in body fluids and therefore presents no problem.

Control of secretion of pancreatic fluid is nervous and hormonal. Hormonal control con-

cerns the hormone secretin, which was discovered in 1902. When the acid contents of the stomach enter the alkaline medium of the duodenum, a hormone is released from the duodenal mucous lining which is absorbed by the blood and carried to the pancreas, causing the pancreas to secrete. The hormonal mechanism stimulates the pancreas to secrete when there is food present. Investigations reveal that another hormone is involved, called pancreozymin, which stimulates the flow of digestive enzymes into pancreatic fluid. The pancreas also produces the hormone insulin, which is involved in carbohydrate metabolism. The hormone is produced by groups of small cells called the islets of Langerhans. Insulin is not dispersed via the pancreatic duct, but is absorbed and distributed by the bloodstream, as occurs with all hormones.

Bile is a green, watery, alkaline fluid made in the liver, stored in the gall bladder and conveyed to the duodenum by the bile duct. The colour is derived largely from the breakdown products of the red pigment in decomposing red blood cells. Bile contains organic bile salts and sodium bicarbonate, which partially neutralise the acid chyme from the stomach and create a suitable working environment for pancreatic and intestinal enzymes. In addition to diluting the contents of the intestine, bile affects the surface tension of fats and emulsifies them, resulting in the formation of a suspension of tiny droplets, the increased surface so presented allowing more rapid digestion. Many of the bile substances are reabsorbed in the ileum.

The glands in the lining of the small intestine secrete enzymes which complete digestion by reducing unchanged peptides to amino acids, maltose and other sugars to glucose, and unchanged fats to fatty acids and glycerol. All digestible material is now reduced to soluble compounds which are able to pass through the intestinal lining and into the bloodstream.

Nearly all absorption of digested food occurs in the ileum as the characteristics of this section of the small intestine are favourable to the process of absorption. The internal surface area of the ileum is greatly enhanced by thousands of minute, finger-like projections called villi, each containing a dense network of blood capillaries. The epithelial lining of the ileum is very thin, thus allowing fluids to pass through readily. The ileum also offers a large absorbing surface to the digested food by virtue of its length.

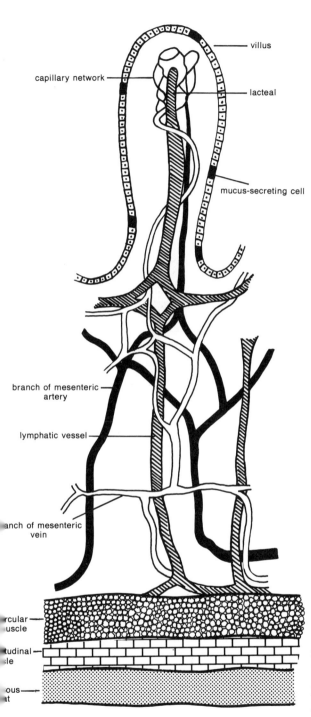

capillary network ———

——— villus

——— lacteal

——— mucus-secreting cell

branch of mesenteric artery

lymphatic vessel ———

anch of mesenteric vein

rcular uscle

udinal le

ous t

Longitudinal section through a villus
The internal surface of the ileum is greatly increased by thousands of tiny, finger-like projections, called villi, which are an important adaption to the absorbing properties of the ileum.

Small molecules of digested food, predominantly amino acids and glucose, diffuse through the epithelium and the capillary walls and enter the blood plasma. They are then carried away in the capillaries which unite to form veins and eventually join up to form one large vein, the hepatic portal vein, which carries all the blood from the intestine to the liver, which may retain or alter any of the digestive products. The digested food then reaches the general circulation.

Fatty acids and glycerol from the digestion of fats do not appear to enter the blood capillaries but pass into the lacteals, by which time they have recombined to form fat droplets. Some authorities believe that the fat droplets may pass through the intestinal wall without being digested. From the lacteals they enter the lymphatic system, which forms a network throughout the body and eventually empties its contents into the bloodstream. Food may spend from three to four hours in the small intestine before passing into the large intestine.

The large intestine (caecum, colon, rectum)

The large intestine is only a little greater in calibre in the dog than the small intestine and the length is only one-sixth of that of the small intestine. The large intestine follows the small intestine and commences at the ileocaecal valve, the point at which the terminal section of the small intestine enters the caecum approximately at a right angle. The caecum in the dog is small compared with that of herbivorous animals and it adopts the form of a blind bag, with its free end directed backwards, rather than being a true continuation of the digestive tract. In the dog, the large intestine assumes the shape of a large 'question mark' which occupies the length and width of the abdominal floor. It is divided into three sections, an ascending, a transverse, and a descending portion.

The material passing into the large intestine consists of water with undigested matter, predominantly cellulose and vegetable fibre (the roughage), bacteria, mucus, and dead cells from the lining of the alimentary canal. The large intestine secretes no enzymes and can absorb very little food, although it does absorb much of the water from undigested residues. The semi-solid waste, known as the faeces, is passed into the rectum by peristalsis and is then expelled at intervals through the anus. The residues may spend from 12 to 24 hours in the intestine.

97

Bacterial decomposition gives rise to a number of gases, acids and amines characteristic of the faecal matter. Carbon dioxide, ammonia, hydrogen sulphide, hydrogen, and methane are some of the gases. Lactic, acetic and butyric acids are commonly present. Amines are the breakdown products of amino acids, indole and skatole being two such products which contribute to the odour of the faeces. Some food materials, such as plant pigments derived from beets and spinach, affect the colour of the faecal matter.

The rectum is normally void until just prior to defaecation, when the faeces enter this region of the intestine. The anal canal is closed by an internal and an external sphincter muscle. When faeces enter the rectum, sensory nerve endings are stimulated and awareness of impending elimination becomes apparent. Muscular pressure exerted by the diaphragm, the abdominal muscles, and strong peristaltic movements of the colon accomplish the act of passing faeces.

It is generally considered that regular daily bowel movements are conducive to good health and that it is good hygenic practice to provide regular times for the animal to eliminate waste. An adequate amount of vegetables in the diet aids in avoiding constipation and there is no reason to believe that it is good practice to administer laxative medicines regularly in order to avoid constipation. Consumption of a reasonable amount of water is beneficial to the animal. Every effort should be made to secure proper elimination habits by training, correct diet, and the maintenance of good health habits. Pleasant surroundings, good food, and peace of mind favour digestion in the animal body.

The digestive system is a complex system which may be subject to many physical and chemical abnormalities. It is imperative that expert advice be sought should an abnormal situation arise. Any alteration in the dog's normal eating habits should be treated with suspicion. It is important to observe the colour and consistency of the motions and note any abnormality as this may indicate a disturbance in digestion. Dogs normally pass the same kind of motion each day, depending on the diet.

Sufficient roughage, in the form of undigestible fibre, must be fed in the diet. Roughage adds bulk to the food and keeps it moving by peristalsis, particularly in the large intestine. Absence of roughage is likely to lead to constipation and its attendant disorders.

DISEASES OF THE DIGESTIVE SYSTEM

Vomiting, diarrhoea, abdominal pain, and diminished appetite may be indicative of digestive disease involving the stomach, small intestine, pancreas, and liver. Many other diseases are characterised by these signs and hence expert advice must be sought.

Growths, infections, particles causing blockages, and poisons may affect the functions of the stomach as well as influencing the length of time that food remains in the stomach and what portions of it are actually digested.

Simple gastric irritation is commonly caused by the diet. Perhaps the next most common cause would be foreign objects such as stones. Malfunction of the pyloric sphincter, where the stomach opens into the intestine, results in vomiting and frequently requires surgical correction. Although stomach cancer can occur in older dogs, it is not common. All of these abnormalities interfere with digestion because food is vomited. The majority of the diseases of the intestine are caused by parasites, bacterial and viral infections, scavenged food, and foreign objects. All intestinal diseases cause digestive disturbance because the intestinal lining becomes irritated, peristalsis becomes more active, and the rate of passage may become so rapid that nutrients and water are not properly absorbed. Loss of weight may be extremely rapid, most notably in puppies.

The digestive tract, particularly the lower portion, is a natural habitat for roundworms and tapeworms. It is, therefore, important to give the dogs under your care a thorough worming at regular intervals. A dog cannot thrive when he is infested with worms. Roundworms and tapeworms interfere with digestion by virtue of their actual mass. Roundworms mainly inhabit the intestines but occasionally invade the bile ducts, liver, and trachea. Migration of the young worms through the lungs of puppies produces fluid in the pulmonary (lung) cavity. The main symptoms are abdominal pain, diarrhoea or constipation, loss of appetite, and unthriftiness. With many dogs the first sign of the presence of worms is in the motions. Adult or immature worms may be vomited. Regular treatment with piperazine drugs and regular faecal examinations are necessary to prevent and control roundworms. Tapeworms grow to a length of many feet. The worm, which has a flat white appearance, consists of a head and individual small segments which usually drop off in turn and are passed in the faeces. Segments about 0·5 to 1 centimetre in length are seen in the dog's faeces. The symptoms of tapeworm infestation are unthriftiness, mild abdominal colic, excessive appetite, staring coat, and loss of weight. There are several effective anthelmintics available for the treatment of tapeworm.

Partial or complete blockage of the intestine by foreign objects results in the accumulation of gas and fluids in the stomach, in addition to that part of the intestine preceding the blockage, and the obstruction almost invariably demands surgical removal. Blockages of the digestive tract can cause severe pain, shock and rapid death.

If the dog consumes a poisonous substance or eats food which is either too hot or too cold, and it reaches the stomach, the animal will attempt to expel it by reverse muscle activity and consequent vomiting. Should it get past the stomach muscle, increased activity occurs in the small and large intestines to attempt to expel the irritant substance via the anus as rapidly as possible, resulting in diarrhoea. Consequently, vomiting and diarrhoea are signs of a disturbance in the digestive system which can lead to general body dehydration.

Stomatitis

Stomatitis, or inflammation of the mucous membrane of the mouth, may be caused by unclean feeding utensils, prolonged general illness, fungus infection, or prolonged use of antibiotics (these destroy the normal bacteria in the mouth and so allow the fungus to flourish in their absence). The mouth is red, swollen, and sore, rendering the dog reluctant to take in food. In severe forms there may be ulceration, excessive salivation and bleeding. Local treatment consists of gentle swabbing with a mild solution such as bicarbonate of soda, permanganate of potash, or hydrogen peroxide. Any specific cause must be dealt with. It must be stressed that in all cases of stomatitis prevention is better than cure.

Gingivitis

Inflammation of the gums is known as gingivitis and may arise under the same conditions as stomatitis. The presence of dental diseases in dogs predisposes them to the development of gingivitis and is precipitated by accumulation of tartar, or scale, on the teeth with consequent irritation and infection of the gums adjacent to the tartar. Gingivitis may also be precipitated by inadequate mineralisation of the bony tooth sockets.

Bleeding from the gums is present in certain blood diseases, notably leukaemia and purpura. Scurvy due to vitamin C deficiency is another cause of such bleeding.

Glossitis

In health the tongue is normally clean but in most general illnesses it is dry and coated with a thick fur. Inflammation of the tongue, or glossitis, may be the result of anaemia or vitamin B deficiency, particularly of the B complex. The tongue is red and sore and appears rather glazed. The treatment of glossitis is that for the underlying cause.

Diseases of the oesophagus

As a consequence of birth defects, infection, inadequate nerve-muscle action, and obstruction by solid materials such as wood or bone, the oesophagus may be unable to transport food efficiently. Rapid return of food or water into the mouth within a few seconds or minutes following eating may indicate disease of the oesophagus, particularly if the act is regurgitation, which is passive rather than active, and accompanied by vomiting. Oesophageal disease should be treated and corrected quickly as enlargement due to muscular weakness and distention by food generally occurs and the greater the distention, the less likely it is that the oesophagus will return to normal size and normal peristaltic action. Most diseases which affect the oesophagus give rise to difficulty in swallowing, or dysphagia.

Dysphagia

Dysphagia may be caused by a foreign body in the oesophagus, carcinoma of the oesophagus, pressure on the oesophagus from outside, stricture of the oesophagus (this usually follows the swallowing of corrosive poisons), or disturbance of the nervous control of the sphincter of the oesophageal opening into the stomach. A foreign body is removed by operation. In many cases of dysphagia only symptomatic treatment can be given. A suitable diet, consisting of food which can be easily swallowed, is important.

Oesophagitis

Oesophagitis may arise as a result of reflux of the contents into the oesophagus. It may occur without gross anatomical disorder, but is especially common when there is a hiatus hernia, i.e., partial herniation of the stomach through the diaphragmatic hiatus. The chronic inflammation may become complicated by ulceration of the mucous membrane, and eventually this may lead to fibrous stricture of the lower end of the oesophagus.

Oesophageal obstruction

Obstruction of the lumen may take place in the oesophagus as a consequence of a functional disorder (achalasia) or from a malignant epithelial tumour (carcinoma) either of the oesophagus itself or of the cardiac end of the stomach. The oesophagus above the obstruction will undergo hypertrophy and dilatation, dilatation being much the more conspicuous because the swallowed food becomes increasingly retained and occurs more strikingly in achalasia than in carcinoma.

Obstruction of the stomach

Obstruction of the stomach arises when the pylorus ceases to relax at the time the rest of the organ undergoes peristalsis. This may develop in a newborn pup as a congenital defect of uncertain origin (congenital pyloric stenosis). The initial effect of the obstruction is usually increased peristalsis, which can be detected clinically. Later the stomach becomes increasingly dilated. It is not difficult to appreciate that large vomits, often projectile in nature, result from this disorder.

Gastritis

Gastritis means an inflammation of the lining mucous membrane of the stomach. It occurs in two main forms, acute and chronic.

1. Acute gastritis is usually caused by some severe dietary indiscretion. Bacteria ingested in food or water, internal parasites, or poisons may cause an acute gastritis. In most cases there is also an accompanying inflammation of the intestines (enteritis) and gastroenteritis is the result.

   Acute gastritis is common in a mild self-limiting form. The mucous membrane exhibits increased shedding of epithelium and signs of regenerative activity.

2. Prolonged dietary indiscretions, such as maintaining constantly irregular feeding times or eating indigestible foods, and certain chronic infections are a common cause of chronic gastritis.

Under microscopic examination the mucous membrane appears more flattened than normal, and it is heavily infiltrated with chronic inflammatory cells. The glandular epithelium exhibits varying degrees of atrophy, the specialised secretory cells disappearing, the remainder secreting mucus and showing a tendency to metaplasia to glands of the intestinal type. Acid secretion decreases and eventually fails. In a minority of animals the chronic inflammation is accompanied by hypertrophy rather than atrophy of the mucous membrane.

Symptoms of gastritis include thirst, and any pressure on the stomach will cause pain. The tongue is frequently covered with a white, furry matter and in such cases the mouth often becomes dry. Loss of appetite and vomiting are features of most cases. Flatulence and heartburn may also occur. The treatment is, firstly, to clear up any infection or correct the dietary indiscretion. Mild gastritis may be treated by the owner. Kaomagna or a similar preparation may be obtained from the chemist. Should diarrhoea be an additional symptom, Kaomagna will be useful for this as well as for the vomiting. Chlorodyne is another substance which will halt diarrhoea, and there are several reputable commercial products which may be administered.

Gastroenteritis

Approximately 8 litres of fluid reach the lumen of the intestine each 24 hours, but only 100 millilitres of this remains to be excreted in the faeces, the remaining having been absorbed mostly in the small intestine. It is not surprising therefore that when diffuse lesions arise in the small bowel, there should be some imbalance between fluid accumulation and removal within the bowel lumen, resulting in diarrhoea. The most common cause of diffuse lesions in the small bowel is infection, producing gastroenteritis or enteritis, which lead to diarrhoea and vomiting or to diarrhoea alone. In the majority of cases of gastroenteritis the cause remains unknown, either because it has not been sought or because the agent remains bacteriologically unidentified. The most common causative agents are Salmonellae of which there are approximately 700 varieties. Food poisoning is a common way by which the organisms exert their effects; the other is by cross-infection.

Gastroenteritis may be discussed under two main headings:

1. *Gastroenteritis in the adult dog*
The predominant symptoms in all cases are acute vomiting and diarrhoea, often accompanied by abdominal colic. Unsuitable food, food infected with salmonella (food poisoning) organisms, and duck's eggs are common causes of gastroenteritis. Rarer causes of acute gastroenteritis are arsenical and mercurial poisoning. Severe enteritis may also occur during the administration of broad spectrum antibiotics, such as the tetracycline antibiotics.

The animal should be kept on a fluid diet until the vomiting and diarrhoea stop and then be fed a non-irritating diet for a few days. In any case which does not settle within a day or so or whenever several cases occur together, the stools must be sent to the laboratory to find out whether any organisms of salmonella food poisoning, dysentery, or enteric fever are present. In all such cases strict isolation is necessary, especially with regard to disposal of stools.

2. *Gastroenteritis in puppies*
Gastroenteritis presents a special problem when it arises in puppies because it may have a serious effect on the animal and also in many cases is extremely infectious. The digestive system of a puppy is very easily disturbed, not only by diseases of the gastrointestinal tract itself but also by disease of any other part of the body. Gastroenteritis of puppies may be divided into two sections:
a. Cases due to disease outside the gastrointestinal tract—parenteral gastroenteritis.
b. Cases due to diseases of the gastrointestinal tract itself—enternal gastroenteritis.

a. Parenternal gastroenteritis
Any general infection of a puppy may be accompanied by vomiting and diarrhoea. The gastroenteritis usually responds to treatment of the primary disease. Where vomiting and diarrhoea are severe it may be necessary to give weaker milk feeds. In less common cases, where the gastroenteritis is severe, with dehydration also present, treatment is the same as for acute infective gastroenteritis and it should be regarded as an emergency involving strict isolation, curative measures (warmth and initial starvation period during which time only boiled water or glucose water is given by mouth), treatment of dehydration using intravenous therapy, special feeding, and drug therapy.

b. Enternal gastroenteritis
In puppies, gastroenteritis which is due to disease in the gastrointestinal tract is often caused by improper feeding. Simple overfeeding may upset the digestive system and so give rise to colic, vomiting, and diarrhoea, while too strong a milk solution or excessive use of sugar in the feeds is also a common cause. These dietetic forms of gastroenteritis usually respond to correct feeding.

There are three main symptoms which usually arise when the intestines are the seat of disease:
1. *Abdominal colic*
Pain is a constant feature of most intestinal diseases and is usually 'colicky' in nature. By this is meant pain which gradually increases in intensity and then completely eases off. The pain comes and goes in frequent spasms, although pain in intestinal disease may be of a more persistent nature.

2. *Constipation*
Constipation refers to delay in evacuation of the bowels. One must remember, however, that the bowel habit varies considerably from dog to dog. When definite constipation is present the motions passed are not only infrequent but also generally hard and dry. Causes of constipation are extremely numerous, the most usual being:
a. Habit
  Normally the desire to empty the bowel is experienced following a meal owing to the reflex bowel action called the gastro-colic reflex. If the desire to defaecate is ignored, the reflex impulse loses its force and as a result the faeces are retained. The retained faeces become hard and dry from loss of water and hence more difficult to pass. Habit constipation is seen most often in cases where dogs are not let out of their kennels at regular intervals to eliminate waste. The dog will not empty out in his kennel and hence becomes constipated.
b. Inadequate diet
  If the diet contains too little of the foods which resist complete digestion, the faeces become too small to excite normal peristaltic action and constipation occurs. Foods which resist complete digestion and which form sufficient bulk to stimulate intestinal peristalsis are usually termed roughage, and include green vegetables, cereals, and fruits. In addition to deficient roughage, insufficient fluid intake, by rendering the stools hard and dry, will cause constipation.
c. Any acute general illness.
d. Local causes in the intestines.

Butcher's Trac, a 30·8-kg dog by Butcher's Tec out of Outcast Trac, established the 845-metre track record of 52·44 seconds at Wembley in April 1976 *(Courtesy of Wembley Stadium Limited)*

i. inflammation of the rectum, e.g., haemorrhoids or anal fissures may cause constipation owing to the pain of evacuation.

ii. tumours of the bowel may cause obstruction and lead to constipation.

iii. Adhesions may cause obstruction.

In the commonest types of constipation due to faulty habits and bad diet, correction of these usually leads to rapid improvement. Any organic cause, such as tumours or anal fissures, should be treated by appropriate surgical measures. In the initial stages drugs to aid bowel evacuation (purgatives) may be used but should be discontinued as soon as possible. In severe cases of constipation, particularly in puppies or older dogs, a suppository or an enema may be used to induce evacuation.

3. *Diarrhoea*

When unformed stools are passed, diarrhoea is said to be present. Diarrhoea is a common and important symptom of intestinal disease and its severity and nature vary with the disease.

Dietary diarrhoea is a non-infectious diarrhoea always associated with a change of diet. It is not accompanied by a rise in temperature, but dehydration is the common feature. Treatment is simple and the animal usually responds readily. Exercise is reduced for a period of 24 hours, after which the normal exercise programme may be resumed. An appropriate preparation is administered to control the looseness of the stools. The animal is returned to the customary diet. Hard, abrasive foods are avoided for two to three days so that the inflamed bowel wall is not damaged. An electrolyte supplement is administered to treat the dehydration.

Acute diarrhoea may be caused by food poisoning, chemical poisoning, infective gastroenteritis, acute gastroenteritis, or it may be precipitated by dietary indiscretions. Enteric fevers, dysenteries, or functional causes (simple nervous diarrhoea) are other causes.

Chronic diarrhoea may be caused by inflammatory diseases, carcinoma of the bowel, or vitamin B deficiency.

It is impossible to give all the causes of diarrhoea, but mention has been made of a few of the more common ones. For the purpose of diagnosing the cause of diarrhoea, and also of watching the effects of treatment the nature of the stools is of great importance and a summary of the main characteristics of the stools in different diseases is given.

a. Number

The number of stools passed daily varies from dog to dog. Constipation is not necessarily present if the bowels are not opened daily. Frequent, semi-formed, or watery motions are observed in diarrhoea.

b. Colour

Normal stools are dark-brown. Pale stools are often seen:

i. when no bile reaches the intestine, e.g., the clay-coloured stools of obstructive jaundice.

ii. if excessive fat is present.

iii. if the animal is on a purely milk diet.

Black stools are credited to:

i. administration of iron, bismuth, or charcoal.

ii. altered blood from bleeding in the upper intestinal tract.

Green stools may be observed when there is severe, acute inflammation of the small intestine. Green stools are particularly characteristic of acute infective gastroenteritis in puppies.

c. Consistency and formation

i. in constipation the stools are hard, dry, and often in the shape of round balls.

ii. in all types of diarrhoea the stools are unformed, while in severe cases the stools are watery and contain little faecal matter.

iii. stools containing a great deal of mucus are slimy in appearance.

iv. ribbon-shaped stools are observed in intestinal obstruction such as carcinoma of the bowel.

d. Abnormal substances in the stools.

i. in diarrhoea undigested particles of food may appear in the stools.

ii. blood may be observed in the stools and it varies in accordance with the site of the bleeding in the gastrointestinal tract and also in accordance with the amount of blood present.

A large haemorrhage from the upper part of the gastrointestinal tract produces black, tarry stools. A small haemorrhage from the upper part of the gastrointestinal tract causes little change visible to the naked eye and chemical tests are necessary.

Blood from the large intestine is usually of a bright-red colour. If the bleeding is in the upper section of the large intestine, the blood may be partially mixed with faecal matter. Bleeding from the rectum (due to haemorrhoids, carcinoma, or anal fissures) produces a streaking of the outside of the motion.

Blood accompanied by mucus or pus is seen in severe inflammation of the intestines. No faecal matter may be present, the stools consisting of blood and mucopus only.

iii. the presence of mucus in the faeces indicates disease, usually inflammation of the large bowel. The mucus may coat the outside of the motion or be mixed with it.

iv. pus, either as pus or mucopus, is present in the stools in severe inflammation and ulceration of the large bowel.

v. the most common parasites found in the faeces are intestinal worms, especially roundworms and tapeworms.

In gastroenteritis the dog loses body fluid and it is of paramount importance that this be replaced or conserved. It is for this reason that products such as Electrolyte C are very useful adjuncts to treatment. The dog suffering from gastroenteritis derives little value from food, as it is either vomited or alternatively liquified and scoured out.

A 24-hour period of fasting is generally useful in assisting treatment of gastroenteritis. In instances where worm infestation is the underlying cause, treatment of the stomach infection should be rapidly followed by worming with an effective anthelmintic. The dog should be presented to a veterinarian for treatment as, if left unchecked for several days, or unsuccessfully treated, the condition will produce severe dehydration and there will be lengthy disruption to the dog's working programme.

Malabsorption syndrome

This condition is due to failure of essential foodstuffs to be absorbed from the surface of the small intestine. Most are absorbed from the upper end, but some, such as vitamin B_{12}, are absorbed from the ileum. Deficiency states may arise as a consequence of certain lesions in the small intestine which interfere with proper absorption of these foodstuffs. The animal is undernourished, wasted, and easily fatigued. Loss of appetite is a marked feature. The characteristic feature is a chronic diarrhoea with very large, bulky, pale, offensive stools. The appearance of the stools is credited to the large

excess of fat that they contain. Well known aspects of this malabsorption syndrome are iron deficiency anaemia, vitamin B_{12} and folic acid deficiency (megaloblastic anaemia), calcium and phosphorus deficiency (osteomalacia and rickets), and intestinal failure of fat absorption (steatorrhea). The lesions in the bowel which are known to produce these deficiency syndromes are those of idiopathic steatorrhea, fistulae between the bowel loops, and blind loops of the bowel, of which the former is the most frequently encountered. Macroscopically, the mucous membrane in idiopathic steatorrhea appears more flattened than normal; microscopically, the villi are greatly shrunken and there is increased inflammatory cell accumulation in the connective tissue coat of the mucous membrane.

The diet is of the utmost importance in the treatment of this syndrome. Food is best afforded in small quantities at frequent intervals, the quantity gradually being increased as the condition improves. A reputable vitamin-mineral supplement must be added to the diet.

Pancreatitis

Failure to take in food, vomiting, or diarrhoea may be indicative of pancreatitis, a painful abdominal disease, the inflammation of which may cause destruction of cells that produce digestive enzymes. The pancreas may atrophy without previous outward signs of the disease. The end result, in either instance, is frequently intractable diarrhoea, rough coat, large pendulous abdomen, and a ravenous appetite.

In acute haemorrhagic pancreatitis the pancreas is swollen and blotchy red, and creamy yellow flecks of fat necrosis may be observed in the surrounding fat. Microscopically, the pancreas is largely autolysed and areas of recent haemorrhage are present with some exudation of polymorph leucocytes. High levels of serum amylase clinch the diagnosis.

Chronic pancreatitis is of obscure aetiology, though some cases follow obstruction of the main duct by carcinoma or a concretion formed in the pancreatic duct from calcium carbonate with other salts and organic materials. The pancreas feels diffusely firmer than normal on palpation. The histological picture is one of surviving islets of Langerhans and some ducts in fibrous tissue containing a few chronic inflammatory cells.

The faeces are more fluid in the caecum than

the rectum because water is absorbed to some extent in the large bowel. Secretion of mucus is more active in this part of the intestine than higher up and becomes excessive under conditions of diffuse stimulation such as infection with dysentery organisms, in ulcerative colitis, or in cases of nervous irritability (mucous colitis).

Colitis

Dogs can suffer from inflammation of the colon, or colitis. The disease will not necessarily cause the dog to become very ill, but it will definitely exert some effect on his performance, if it is permitted to continue unchecked. Generally, the symptoms are quite discernable in the considerable quantity of mucus passed. Diarrhoea may alternate with constipation. The animal usually continues to eat well and look bright, but the disease brings on an anaemia and general weakness. A diet which will be completely digested in the small intestine and leave no irritating residue in the colon is best. In severe cases a milk diet is desirable.

Chronic ulcerative colitis is a distressing disease of obscure cause which leads to the passage of a large number of stools in the day, usually containing blood and mucus. Spontaneous regression can take place, but the disease is prone to become chronic and to require extensive surgical excision to improve the symptoms. The disease may affect any part or all of the large bowel, with the proximal colon the most frequently affected. The affected bowel may be contracted, but the wall is not usually thickened. The macroscopical picture is similar to that of bacillary dysentery, the bowel being congested and covered by shallow ulcers. In severe cases the neighbouring ulcers may blend together, leaving tags of surviving mucous membrane to project from the ulcerated surface. Despite the extensive ulceration and inflammation, reactive fibrosis of the underlying wall is rare. Occasionally the ulcers may penetrate the wall into the peritoneal cavity. Carcinoma may develop in long-standing cases of ulcerative colitis.

Diverticulosis and diverticulitis

Diverticula, consisting of herniations of mucous membrane and submucosa through the muscularis, are common in the colon, where they are usually multiple and most frequently located at the distal end. Excessive bowel contraction is considered to be an important factor in causing them to become larger. Diverticulosis is the name given to the presence of multiple diverticula, when present in the symptomless state. The mucous membrane is, however, liable to ulcerate and the surrounding serous coat then becomes the seat of episodes of inflammation or diverticulitis which may lead to abdominal pain. On occasions, the ulceration is followed by stricture formation or by perforation into the peritoneal cavity.

Peritonitis

Inflammation of the peritoneum (peritonitis) is one of the more serious ailments in the abdominal area. The symptoms are sudden in onset and quite severe. The condition is marked by exudations in the peritoneum of serum, fibrin, cells, and pus. It is attended by abdominal pain and tenderness, constipation, vomiting, and rising temperature. Restlessness and a rapid pulse, which may be very light and almost imperceptable, are further signs of peritonitis.

Although diseases of the anus and rectum do not directly influence digestion, they may cause extreme distress and result in bleeding, constant irritation by the dog, and painful defecation which will affect the general attitude and performance of the dog.

Glandular occlusion

The anal glands are enclosed in two pear-shaped sacs, located under the skin on each side of the anus, in both dogs and bitches. These glands produce a foul-smelling secretion which is normally discharged through a tiny opening at each side of the rectum. They are of no use to the civilised dog and may be surgically removed if necessary. In the wild state it is thought that the glands probably emptied as a result of the pressure of hard, bulky material in the bowel, but with modern soft foods the glands may fail to empty, causing considerable irritation and discomfort. A dog with anal gland trouble will typically slide along the ground on its bottom and/or continually lick or bite under its tail. Glandular occlusion is frequently confused with worm infestation and it is important to be sure of the cause before carrying out treatment. In the greyhound, in contrast with many other breeds, there is little chance of the hair matting in such a manner as to cover the anus.

The anal gland can be expressed easily by a veterinary surgeon and the owner can learn to do this if shown the procedure. Treatment simply involves the removal of the cause of the obstruction by the application of pressure with the fingers on the sides of the anus. If the gland is not evacuated it will become inflamed and perhaps abscessed. Infected anal glands may produce a foul-smelling and sometimes blood-stained discharge. Antibiotic treatment is indicated.

In the case of anal gland abscesses the duct becomes blocked and the anal sac fills with septic matter. A red swelling is observed at the side of the tail and the dog is generally in considerable pain. A veterinary surgeon should be consulted as soon as possible.

Anal prolapse

Anal prolapse is most commonly seen in young pups and is a consequence of excessive straining, usually following an attack of diarrhoea. A portion of the bowel extrudes from the rectum and rapidly becomes swollen, red, and painful. In some cases the bowel may become telescoped upon itself and this is referred to as an intussuseption. Having first lubricated the prolapse with liquid paraffin, it may be possible to return the prolapse but in most instances the dog will immediately begin to strain. A veterinary surgeon should be consulted as soon as possible.

Haemorrhoids

These are dilated submucosal venous channels which lie immediately below the mucous membrane in the anal canal. They are extremely common in older animals and are liable to give rise to recurrent slight haemorrhage especially after defaecation. The cause in most cases is obscure, but straining at defaecation is an important factor.

Dysentery

Members of the genus Shigella are responsible for bacillary dysentery. Mild forms of dysentery usually produce only diarrhoea. The more severe cases result in the passage of increased amounts of blood and mucous also. Macroscopically the large bowel is congested and, in severe cases, is covered with many shallow ulcers containing purulent exudate. Microscopically, the mucous membrane is infiltrated with inflammatory cells.

Small intestine obstruction

Obstruction of the small intestine, because of its length, its mesenteric attachment, and free movement, most frequently results from a band of connective tissue lying across it, or because it becomes twisted. The initial effect of obstruction of the small intestine is increased peristaltic activity of the viable intestine proximal to the obstruction, often detected clinically because of the increased intensity of the intestinal sounds. Later the intestine will dilate and the sounds will become reduced. When peristalsis ceases in the dilated intestine, this segment now becomes a source of obstruction to the alimentary canal higher up, and this is what happens in paralytic ileus. Small intestine obstruction is an extremely dangerous state and will cause death within a few hours unless relieved because the obstructed intestine is very prone to infection from bacteria within the lumen and general peritonitis will ensue.

Large intestine obstruction

Obstruction of the large intestine tends to differ in cause and effects from that of the small intestine because it is more attached to its surroundings and because the faeces become more solid, especially at the distal end. Particles of faeces may become so large and hard as to impact the lumen. Otherwise the most common cause of obstruction is a malignant tumour (carcinoma) which has stimulated the production of fibrous tissue causing the lumen to constrict considerably. Hypertrophy of the muscle is a conspicuous feature of large intestine obstruction; dilatation also occurs but rarely reaches massive proportions. The frequent complication of infection which may spread to the peritoneum is brought about by ulceration of the mucous membrane.

8

RESPIRATION

THE RESPIRATORY SYSTEM

The nose is the common pathway for air entering or leaving the lungs, the air being filtered, moistened and warmed as it makes its way over the warm, moist membranes which line the nasal cavity. The epiglottis is a movable cartilaginous lid that opens during breathing and closes during swallowing. Below the epiglottis is the glottis, across which are the vocal folds. The sounds made by the dog are caused by air being forced over the vocal folds causing them to vibrate; their vibrations, in turn, affecting a column of air above.

The glottis leads into the trachea, a long tube supported by rings of cartilage (which are not quite complete and are often described as resembling the letter C), and fibrous connective tissue. The trachea thus exhibits great flexibility and yet is sufficiently strong to resist compression. The trachea is lined with numerous minute protoplasmic hairs, called cilia, that constantly flick to and fro. Mucus is secreted by glandular cells in the lining of the tracheal tube. Dust particles, bacteria, etc., that are carried in with the air during inspiration become trapped in the film of mucus. By the movement of the cilia they are swept away in it upward toward the larynx. Choking and coughing are reflex actions which tend to remove any foreign particles which accidentally enter the trachea or bronchi.

The trachea divides into two bronchi which enter the lungs and divide into smaller branches called bronchial tubes and eventually into bronchioles. These terminate in a thin-walled sac with numerous pouches known as alveoli and they resemble a bunch of grapes clustered around a stem. The alveolar walls are very thin and highly vascular and it is through the capillary walls in the alveolus that the exchange of gases between the blood and the air takes place. The pulmonary artery divides into smaller branches and eventually dissipates in capillary networks around bronchioles and alveoli. Pulmonary capillaries anastomose to form venules as the blood leaves the alveoli and gives rise to pulmonary veins which transport freshly oxygenated blood back to the left atrium of the heart. The lung tissue is supplied by bronchial arteries directly from the aorta. The lungs are two thin-walled, elastic sacs occupying the thoracic cavity. A thin serous membrane, called the pleura, covers each lung and continues over the thoracic wall and the diaphragm.

The pleura consists of two layers. The pulmonary pleura covers the lung; the parietal pleura lines the wall of the chest and covers the diaphragm. These two layers are in contact and the pleural cavity between them is normally only a potential one since the lungs fill the thoracic cavity. The serous membrane secretes sufficient serum to moisten the surfaces that move upon each other during respiratory movement.

Respiratory movements occur rhythmically and breathing constitutes two respiratory movements:

1. **Inspiration** is accomplished by drawing air into the lungs and is said to be active because it requires that the ribs and diaphragm move from their normal position. The muscles of the diaphragm contract, causing it to lose some of its convexity. The ribs are moved outward by the contraction of the intercostal muscles which run obliquely from one rib to the next. Both these movements increase the volume of the chest cavity and also the volume of the lungs which follow the movements. The increase in volume raises the lung capacity so that atmospheric pressure forces air into them by way of the nose and trachea.

2. **Expiration** forces air out of the lungs and results mainly from the relaxation of the muscles of the ribs and diaphragm and is consequently said to be passive. Forced expiration, such as coughing or sneezing, is active. A deep inspiration must precede a forced expiration. Muscles

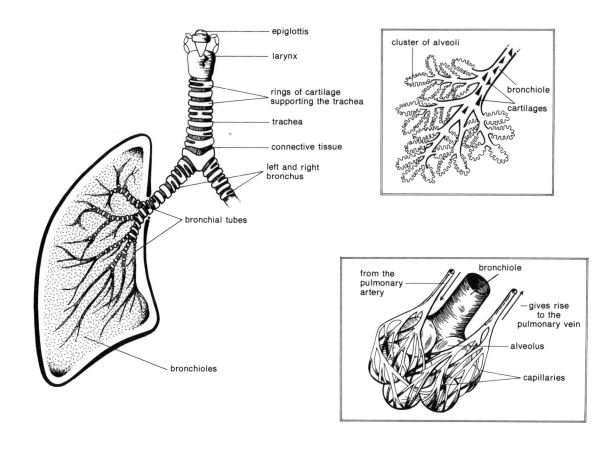

epiglottis

larynx

rings of cartilage
supporting the trachea

trachea

connective tissue

left and right
bronchus

bronchial tubes

bronchioles

cluster of alveoli

bronchiole

cartilages

from the
pulmonary
artery

bronchiole

gives rise
to the
pulmonary vein

alveolus

capillaries

Structure of the lungs

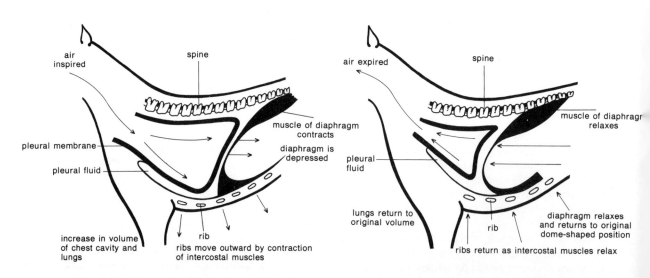

air
inspired

spine

muscle of diaphragm
contracts

pleural membrane

diaphragm is
depressed

pleural fluid

increase in volume
of chest cavity and
lungs

rib

ribs move outward by contraction
of intercostal muscles

a. Inspiration (drawing air into the lungs)

air expired

spine

muscle of diaphragm
relaxes

pleural
fluid

lungs return to
original volume

rib

diaphragm relaxes
and returns to original
dome-shaped position

ribs return as intercostal muscles relax

b. Expiration (expelling air from the lungs)

that depress the ribs and others that act to compress the abdomen then support a forcible expulsion. The diaphragm also assists in such acts as vomiting, defecating, passing urine, and in whelping. As a result of the relaxation of the muscles of the ribs and diaphragm and by virtue of their elasticity, the lungs return to their original volume. The intercostal muscles relax and the organs posterior to the diaphragm, under pressure from the muscular walls of the abdomen, push the relaxed diaphragm back into its domed position.

Certain factors influence the respiratory rate and the depth of breathing. There are two nerve control centres in the medulla, an inspiratory and an expiratory centre, which lie beneath the posterior part of the floor of the fourth ventricle. These respiratory centres have been determined as a result of work on experimental animals and are believed to exhibit reciprocal inhibition of each other. Motor tracts from the inspiratory centre descend through the cord to the level of the third, fourth, and fifth cervical vertebrae, where they synapse with motor neurons to form the phrenic nerves which innervate the diaphragm. Stimulation of the phrenic nerves results in contraction of the muscles of the diaphragm and an increase in the volume of the thoracic cavity during inspiration. Another set of neurons descending from the medulla, synapse with thoracic motor neurons supplying the external intercostal muscles which move the ribs outward and in so doing enlarge the thoracic cavity during inspiration. A similar set of neurons innervates the internal intercostal muscles, but their function is expiratory. The vagus nerves afford a pathway by which afferent impulses arising from sensory receptors within the lungs can provide rhythmical expiration. Elastic lung tissues become stretched during inspiration and the sensory receptors in these tissues are stimulated, producing afferent impulses and an ever-increasing flow of impulses passes over the vagus nerves to the expiratory control centre. Because the expiratory centre has a high threshold and is less readily stimulated, the lungs continue to inflate until the control centre is eventually stimulated. The inspiratory centre is then alternatively inhibited and expiration follows. This is an important mechanism by which the lungs are protected from over-inflation. When both vagus nerves are severed, breathing becomes deeper and slow but still retains its rhythm, thus indicating that

some other centre must be influencing respiration. A third control centre situated in the upper part of the pons is capable of substituting as an inspiratory inhibitory mechanism when the vagal reflexes have been eliminated. The existence of this third centre has been proved experimentally. In normal breathing, the afferent impulses from the lungs maintain rhythmic breathing but when there is increased respiratory activity (stimulated by a rise in body temperature) this third centre becomes more dominant.

Apart from nerve control over breathing, there are chemical mechanisms that enable the animal to adapt respiration to metabolic changes. A rise in carbon dioxide concentration, increased acidity of arterial blood, or a decrease in oxygen content stimulates chemoreceptors (a receptor adapted for excitation by chemical substances) and increases respiration reflexly. Generally speaking, all chemical and neural mechanisms are coordinated in the control of respiration, but if any factors are to be singled out for special note, alterations in carbon dioxide concentration and alterations in blood acidity (carbonic acid) are perhaps the most important in considering control of breathing. Reduction in the carbon dioxide concentration of arterial blood can be effected by deep, rapid breathing lasting a couple of minutes. It is thought that during normal breathing the chemoreceptors afford only a slight regulatory effect, but when the oxygen content of the arterial blood is lowered they afford a more important source of stimulation of respiration. Furthermore, they control the deep, powerful respiratory movements that one may observe when a dog is under the influence of ether anaesthesia.

A pressoreceptor is a receptor nerve ending which is stimulated by any element or agent which affects the calibre of a blood vessel. Pressoreceptors located in the walls of the aortic arch and the carotid sinus exert an influence on respiration, but do not appear to be as essential as chemoreceptors. The carotid sinus is the dilated portion of the internal carotid artery.

As with the heart rate, the respiratory rate varies in accordance with the age and the physical fitness of the dog as well as many other factors. During vigorous exercise respiration increases notably and all the factors which stimulate respiration are brought into play. These factors include a rise in the body temperature, increased blood acidity, and

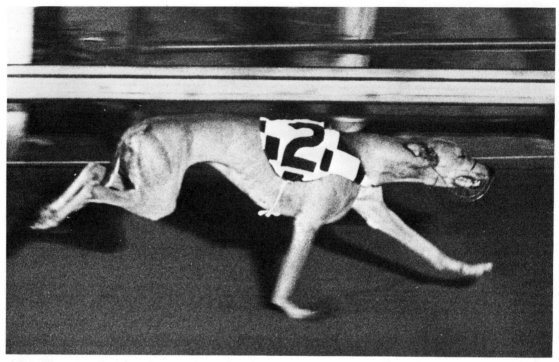

Bolta's Gift, a 28-kg fawn bitch by Second Stage out of Bolta, winner of 1976 National Distance Championship over 731 metres in 44·66 seconds conducted at Angle Park, South Australia *(Courtesy of Melbourne Greyhound Racing Association)*

increased secretion of epinephrine into the blood. Epinephrine is a hormone secreted by the adrenal glands. It is also produced synthetically and is the most powerful vasopressor substance known, increasing blood pressure, stimulating the heart muscle, accelerating the heart rate and increasing cardiac output. Nerve impulses from the cerebral motor area, the heart, the lungs, muscles, and joints, affect the respiratory centre.

The air breathed contains oxygen, nitrogen, water, and carbon dioxide as well as rare gases which may be considered as inert gases along with nitrogen. Inspired air loses oxygen to the blood and takes up carbon dioxide, this interchange being effected through the thin capillary walls in the alveoli of the lungs. Oxygen is absorbed by the tissues from tissue fluid. The tissue fluid is supplied by richly oxygenated capillary blood. Oxygen passes through the walls of the capillaries and the tissues take up only sufficient oxygen to meet their metabolic requirements. One should realise that the oxygen content of the blood is not increased as the oxygen demand increases during muscular activity; a greater amount of blood flows through the tissues because of the dilation of the capillaries. Carbon dioxide, continuously produced by the tissue cells, diffuses through the cell membrane into the fluid of the lymph spaces, through the walls of the capillaries, into the blood plasma, and into the red cells, to be transported to the heart and lungs in the venous blood. When oxyhaemoglobin (oxygen in loose chemical combination with haemoglobin) reaches the tissues, the oxygen is readily given up and diffuses into the tissues, aided by the lower oxygen pressure in the tissues. Carbon dioxide enters into loose chemical combination with haemoglobin by combining with an NH_2 group in the haemoglobin molecule and is then called carbaminohaemoglobin. A small quantity of carbon dioxide (about five per cent) is carried by the plasma in the dissolved state or in combination with the water of the plasma as carbonic acid. The carbonic acid dissociates into bicarbonate ions and H^+ ions. Only a small quantity of bicarbonate is formed in the plasma because the reaction of carbon dioxide with water is relatively slow. This same reaction within the red cell is catalysed by an enzyme called carbonic anhydrase and takes place in a fraction of a second. Approximately seventy-five per cent of the carbon dioxide in the blood is transported as bicarbonate ions. The reaction of carbon dioxide and water is a very important one within the red cell in contrast to the reaction in the blood plasma. The bicarbonate concentration within the red cell soon becomes higher than the concentration outside in the plasma and excess bicarbonate ions therefore diffuse outward through the membrane of the red cell. When the blood reaches the lungs, the carbon dioxide pressure is greater in the venous blood than in the alveolar air and this results in the diffusion of carbon dioxide from the blood into the alveoli. The chemical reactions in the capillaries of the lungs are the reverse of those taking place in the tissue capillaries.

Internal respiration (cellular respiration) is a process which involves the oxidation of nutrient materials with a consequent release of energy and with carbon dioxide being given off as a by-product. The energy derived from the breakdown of nutrient materials is not directly available but is transferred to the ADP–ATP system in the form of high energy phosphate bonds.

PNEUMONIA

In this very common condition there is an inflammation of the alveoli of the lungs caused by various micro-organisms. These include the different types of pneumococci and also streptococci, staphylococci, the influenzal bacilli, and certain viruses. In addition, the tubercle bacillus causes a specific type of pneumonia. Long periods of exposure to cold, wet conditions is perhaps the worst environmental factor to which a dog may be subjected. Physical and chemical agents may give rise to inhalation pneumonia. Foreign bodies such as vomit or water can irritate lung tissues, resulting in inflammation. Incorrectly administered chemicals, medicines, and anthelmintics may find their way into the lungs and irritate the tissues. Migrating parasite larvae, such as hookworm and particularly roundworm larvae, may end up in the lungs, causing physical damage to the lung tissues. Hypostatic pneumonia is a consequence of the failure of the blood to pass readily through the blood vessels which pass through the lung tissues. This condition is most commonly observed in old debilitated dogs and in dogs which become paralysed, dogs under anaesthetic, and dogs which are unable to move voluntarily for a lengthy period. Hypostatic

pneumonia is secondary to other conditions. The respirations are rapid and the nostrils may be observed to move with them.

Coughing is an important sign, as the type of cough may indicate the type of pneumonia. The cough may vary from a dry, hacking cough to a deep, fluid cough. This is dependent on the amount of exudate present in the lungs. If there is tissue damage, the dog will have a foul-smelling breath as a consequence of the decayed tissue. Severe lung damage may render breathing very painful and the dog may try to breathe using the abdominal muscles rather than those of the chest; consequently there will be little movement of the chest and increased movement of the abdomen. If the pain in the chest is sufficiently severe, the dog will remain standing with its front legs positioned wide apart. A discharge from the nose, and sometimes from the eyes, may be observed, but this is dependent on the cause and the degree of the pneumonia. If the pneumonia spreads from the lung tissue to the pleura, the thin layer of tissue enclosing the lungs, the consequence will then be pleurisy. Ultimately toxaemia and death may result if the cause of the pneumonia is not accurately diagnosed and correctly treated.

Inhalation pneumonias are difficult to treat as there is often no means of removing the foreign matter from the lungs. When washing a dog's mouth out at the track with a hose, care must be exercised not to allow water to get into the lungs. Special care should be taken following hydrobaths to ensure that the dog is properly dried and adequately rugged. The trainer should exercise care to see that his dogs are kept in a reasonably constant temperature environment, particularly during transit to and from the track. Young pups and elderly dogs have somewhat less resistance than middle aged dogs. Particular care should be taken with pups under three months of age as their immune responses are not fully developed until they have attained three months of age.

Only after the pneumonia has been correctly classified can the proper antibiotics, anti-inflammatory preparations and decongestants be administered. The great danger with pneumonia is that where lung tissue has been damaged some of the tissue will be replaced by scar tissue which, if extensive, results in inefficiency in the transfer of oxygen from the air to the body and removal of carbon dioxide from the body.

9

THE LIVER

The liver is a large, solid, reddish-brown organ, fitting precisely into the concave abdominal face of the diaphragm. Although a considerable quantity of its bulk projects into the abdomen behind the last ribs, it lies largely under cover of the ribs. The liver is supplied with blood from the portal vein and the hepatic artery, and within the liver these vessels give off numerous branches. The blood filters through the liver sinusoids, a more or less open capillary network, and eventually flows into the hepatic veins which empty into the inferior vena cava.

FUNCTIONS OF THE LIVER

The liver has many important and complex functions. The following listing makes no pretence of affording a complete summary of its functions.

1. Protective function (detoxication)

The protective function of the liver is associated with its ability to detoxify products of catabolism which may accumulate in dangerous quantities. These substances undergo chemical changes which enable them to be excreted by the kidneys or through the intestinal tract. Located in the liver sinusoids are large, stellate Kupffer cells which are phagocytic macrophages capable of ingesting bacteria or other foreign material from the blood.

2. Formation of bile

The liver continually forms a yellowish fluid called bile, which is alkaline and which contains bile pigments, bile salts, cholesterol, mucin, and other organic and inorganic constituents. The alkalinity and salt content of bile help to provide favourable conditions for digestion in the duodenum and small intestine. Bile is stored in the gallbladder and discharged down the bile duct into the duodenum when food passes from the stomach.

Bile is not as concentrated when it leaves the liver as it is after being held in the gallbladder, this fact indicating that the gallbladder is capable of absorbing a considerable quantity of water and some salts while the bile is stored there. The inner lining also possesses the ability to secrete mucous into the bile. Bile contains a green pigment which is derived from decomposition of the haemoglobin in old red blood cells. The disintegration of red blood cells, which is a continuous process in the bloodstream, releases the haemoglobin. It is broken down in various tissues, such as the liver, spleen, and connective tissues, where it is converted into bilirubin–biliverdin being formed as an oxidation product of bilirubin. These pigments are then transported by the bloodstream to the liver where they become bile pigments. The majority of the bile pigment is excreted with the faeces but a small quantity is absorbed through the capillary network in the intestinal lining, this pigment being returned to the liver by way of the portal system to be used again.

Bile salts, sodium glycocholate and sodium taurocholate, play an important role in fat digestion. These salts are formed in the liver by the chemical combination of cholic acid with the amino acid glycerine in one case and with the amino acid taurine in the other case. Fat digestion by pancreatic lipase is increased in the presence of bile but bile contains no enzymes. Apparently bile aids in the emulsification of fats. Bile salts play an important role in the absorption of insoluble fatty acids and glycerol. Bile salts are also absorbed and re-used by the liver.

Cholesterol, present in tissues and body fluids, is related chemically to vitamin D, sex hormones, and hormones of the adrenal cortex. It is highly insoluble in water but reasonably soluble in bile and is usually considered as an excretory product in the bile. Concentrations may form in the gallbladder, referred to as gallstones, and are largely composed of cholesterol.

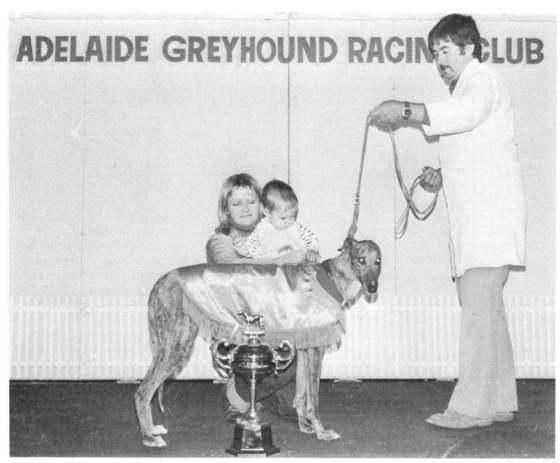

1978 Adelaide Cup winner, Riviera Moss (Clay Moss—Cursorial) *(Courtesy of South Australian Greyhound Trainer)*

3. Blood sugar regulation

The portal system carries absorbed glucose to the liver where it is stored in the form of glycogen. The liver helps to maintain a constant blood sugar level by converting some of its stored glycogen back to glucose as the tissues utilise glucose in their metabolism. This process is not simple and each step is catalysed by enzyme action. The blood carries a small quantity of glucose and the liver contains a little, but there is no storage of glucose in the body. Not only the liver, but also skeletal muscles, convert glucose to glycogen. However, the majority of glycogen is stored in the liver. The active enzyme contained in the liver, phosphatase, is responsible for splitting certain compounds into glucose and inorganic phosphate. The glucose then becomes absorbed by the bloodstream and transported to the body tissues. Phosphatase is present in other body tissues and is not exclusive to the liver.

The liver also has the ability to form glucose from specific amino acids. During starvation, glucose may be derived from the protein in the tissues themselves. Glycerol, which has been split from the fat molecule during digestion, presents another source of glucose. The liver thus has the ability to form glucose from noncarbohydrate sources.

Any marked fall in the blood sugar level gives rise to serious disturbances leading to convulsions and coma, but a rise in the blood sugar level, as in diabetes mellitus, affords no discomfort. When the blood sugar rises above a certain level the kidneys excrete the excess sugar. Since the kidneys do not ordinarily excrete sugar, a chemical test for sugar in the urine is routine procedure in the diagnosis of diabetes.

4. Deamination of protein

Excess protein is not stored in the body. Amino acids which are not built up into protein and utilised for tissue growth and replacement are converted to carbohydrates by a process referred to as deamination in which the nitrogen ($-NH_2$) group is split off the molecule. The enzyme deaminase catalyses the reaction. Some of the amino acids that have undergone deamination are converted to glucose, stored in the liver as glycogen, or utilised to release energy. The nitrogen is converted in the liver to urea and is excreted by the kidneys.

5. Utilisation of fats in the body

The liver plays an important role in fat metabolism. In the liver, fats brought in the bloodstream may undergo chemical changes which enable them to be more readily oxidised in the tissues when they are utilised for energy production.

6. Storage of blood

The numerous capillaries and blood spaces in the liver enable it to hold a large volume of blood, this being of value in instances when the circulatory system is overloaded.

7. Maintenance of body temperature

Many chemical changes take place in the liver, many of which release energy in the form of heat. This heat is distributed, by way of the circulatory system, throughout the body and thus aids in the maintenance of body temperature.

8. Storage of iron

The decomposition of red blood cells is completed in the liver and the iron from the haemoglobin is stored. This anti-anaemia factor gave rise to the practice of feeding liver and liver extracts in the treatment of anaemia.

9. Formation of blood proteins, serum albumin, and serum globulin.

10. Formation of fibrinogen and heparin

These are some of the substances concerned with the clotting mechanism of the blood.

DISEASES OF THE LIVER AND BILIARY TRACT

The liver receives by way of the portal vein the blood which has drained the gastro-intestinal tract, pancreas, and spleen, and following admixture with that in the hepatic artery, the blood passes via the hepatic vein almost immed-

iately into the right atrium of the heart. It is not surprising, therefore, that the liver should frequently exhibit degenerative changes arising as a consequence of disturbances of circulation and nutrition. Cloudy swelling, fatty degeneration, atrophy, necrosis, fibrosis, and chronic venous congestion are all reactions which take place in the liver. This organ is capable of considerable regeneration following necrosis of the component cells by various agents.

Hepatitis

The most frequent specific infections of the liver are the viral diseases, acute infective hepatitis, and homologous serum jaundice. Acute infective hepatitis, the most common form of hepatitis, usually occurs sporadically but at times takes epidemic forms. It has an incubation period of approximately 30 days and the virus usually spreads via the intestinal route, as it is excreted in the faeces. Homologous serum jaundice is a very similar type of viral hepatitis, clinically and pathologically indistinguishable from acute hepatitis, transmitted by transfusions of serum or by the use of inadequately sterilised syringes. The incubation period is about 100 days.

The onset of symptoms and signs is usually gradual over a matter of days, with marked loss of appetite and nausea as the predominating symptoms—the sight of food, particularly fats, being sufficient to cause nausea or vomiting. The dog is generally off colour, with headache and slight fever. Following a few days of these symptoms the urine becomes dark as a result of the presence of bile, and the faeces clay coloured. The conjunctiva and skin become yellow. The severity of the attack varies. In severe and fatal cases, necrosis may involve almost all of the liver cells and the liver seen at post mortem will then be yellow, flabby, with a wrinkled capsule, and the cut surface will exhibit blurring of the normal pattern. In those cases which do recover, there will be total restoration to the pre-existing normal architecture, provided that the reticulin framework of the liver cells has remained intact. If collapse of this framework has occurred, the acute disease is likely to develop into a more chronic stage.

Diagnosis is usually simple. The absence of any severe pain or history of previous attack of pain usually distinguishes it from the common type of jaundice caused by gallstones. Various liver function tests are available which show whether the jaundice is the consequence of damage and obstruction in the liver, as in cases of hepatitis, or by obstruction outside the liver such as gallstones or carcinoma of the head of the pancreas, in which case there is no actual damage to the liver itself. The liver has to be fairly severely damaged before these tests are positive and this is consequently the drawback with these tests. Sometimes a liver biopsy is necessary to determine diagnosis. A needle is inserted into the liver and a fragment withdrawn and examined under the microscope. The specimen will show whether the liver cells are inflamed or whether the damage is a result of obstruction. Differentiation is of paramount importance for an operation may be indicated if obstruction is the cause.

Complete recovery may occur or damage to the liver may be so severe that complete recovery is impossible and death takes place. Young pups between the ages of 6 weeks and 6 months are the most frequent victims of the disease. Older dogs may also become infected if they have not previously been protected from the disease. Pups should be vaccinated against hepatitis at 8 weeks, 16 weeks, 18 months, 3 years, and 5 years. Following vaccination it takes up to 14 days for the pup to be protected. Until full protection is achieved, the pup should be kept away from other dogs.

Treatment involves complete rest as this lessens the damage to the liver and hastens convalescence. The diet must be very light. Since fats are not tolerated they should be omitted. Glucose provides adequate calories and places no strain on the liver and so is particularly useful when nausea and vomiting are present. The glucose can be administered in non-fat milk. The diet is gradually increased as the jaundice subsides and the appetite improves.

Weil's disease (*Leptospirosis*)

Weil's disease, or leptospirochaetal jaundice, results from a spirochaetal infection originating from rats. The spirochaete is excreted in the urine of infected rats. Infection may occur by contamination of food or through abrasions in the skin. The disease varies in severity from moderate attacks to acute fulminating cases which gravely damage the liver. Signs of severe fever with extreme exhaustion are present. Severe conjunctivitis is a frequent feature. An obstructive form of jaundice, with pale stools and dark urine, develops after about 4 days. Albuminuria is often present in addition to the

bile in the urine. Haemorrhages from the nose, bowel, kidneys, or into the skin develop in severe cases, these being so predominant that Weil's disease is also called infective haemorrhagic jaundice.

Treatment is concommitant with that for acute infective hepatitis, with abundant glucose and copious fluids. Additionally, penicillin and the tetracycline antibiotics have proved effective in some cases.

Acute yellow atrophy (*acute hepatic necrosis*)

With the exception of tropical countries, this condition is relatively rare but mention is made of it because it is sometimes caused by severe forms of acute infective hepatitis or by severe attacks of Weil's disease. There is severe liver damage with cell necrosis, the liver becoming shrunken and atrophied. The liver adopts a yellow colour, hence the name. Acute yellow atrophy may be caused by a severe infection such as infective hepatitis, Weil's disease, toxaemia of pregnancy, or by severe arsenical or benzene poisoning.

The animal is usually very ill with a high temperature, sweating, and rigors. Jaundice and sometimes haemorrhages, are present. The animal may lapse into unconsciousness, and death is common. Unfortunately, there is no specific treatment. A very light diet with an abundance of glucose is indicated. Intravenous glucose saline infusions are frequently given. In all cases of severe acute liver failure protein must be excluded from the diet until the animal exhibits signs of recovery. Many animals are never fully restored to health owing to permanent liver damage.

Jaundice

Jaundice is a condition which can occur in dogs as readily as in humans. Jaundice is a common and frequently predominant sign in most diseases of the liver and biliary tract. Jaundice is the term given to the yellow discoloration of the skin and conjunctiva as a consequence of excess bile pigment in the blood stream. Jaundice can be divided into two main groups, according to the manner in which the excess bile pigment develops in the blood.

1. *Obstructive jaundice*

Excess of bilirubin occurs in the blood stream as a result of a blockage or disease in the liver or biliary passages. Since the bile cannot pass down its normal channel it is reabsorbed into the bloodstream, thus giving rise to jaundice. Gallstones or stricture may obstruct the ducts or there may be obstruction and pressure on the ducts from outside as in carcinoma of the head of the pancreas or secondary carcinoma of the lymph glands. Obstruction or disease in the liver caused by inflammatory diseases such as hepatitis, by certain drugs (notably chlorpromazine), by cirrhosis, or carcinoma of the liver may give rise to obstructive jaundice.

The jaundice is easily recognisable and generally first observed in the conjunctiva. The faeces are pale because the bilirubin is not reaching the intestine as a consequence of the obstruction. The normal dark-brown colour of the faeces, which is due to the bile pigment, is replaced by clay-coloured stools. The urine is dark-brown because of the presence of bilirubin. There is pruritis or itching of the skin caused by the accumulation of bile salts in the blood. In chronic obstructive jaundice the absence of bile salts, which prevents absorption of vitamin K from the bowel, gives rise to prothrombin deficiency. This deficiency results in a prolonged blood clotting time and is the cause of the excessive bleeding sometimes seen in operations on animals with obstructive jaundice.

2. *Haemolytic jaundice*

Excess of bile pigments in the blood, due to excessive destruction (haemolysis) of the red blood cells, gives rise to haemolytic jaundice. The liver can cope with a certain excess of bile pigments and hence jaundice does not necessarily develop with haemolysis of the red cells. When the haemolysis goes beyond a certain level, however, the liver cannot deal with the consequent large excess of bile pigment and therefore the bile accumulates in the blood and jaundice is the result. Haemolytic anaemia is usually associated with haemolytic jaundice.

The presence of excess bile pigment in the blood giving rise to staining of the skin and conjunctiva is common to both obstructive and haemolytic jaundice. As there is no obstruction in the liver or biliary tracts in haemolytic jaundice the bile pigment is present in the faeces which are not therefore clay coloured as in obstructive jaundice. The stools are frequently darker than normal because there is an excess of bile formed. Since bile salts do not accumulate in the blood, as in obstructive jaundice, there is no itching of the skin. Because there is an excess of bile pigment in the intestine there is also a marked increase in the amount of bile pigment absorbed from the intestine and excreted in the urine.

Gallstones

The mechanisms leading to the development of gallstones are still largely obscure. They arise through the precipitation of some of the three main ingredients of bile, bile pigment, cholesterol, and calcium salts, either because one or more of these components is in excess, or because there is altered absorption by the gall-bladder of water and some of the other constituents of bile.

In all cases in which gallstones are causing symptoms an operation to remove the stones is necessary. If obstructive jaundice is present, vitamin K is administered prior to the operation to prevent haemorrhage.

10

THE
CIRCULATORY SYSTEM

THE HEART

The vascular system, a continuous series of tubes ramifying throughout the body, circulates a constant flow of blood conveying nutrition in food and oxygen to the tissues and carrying away their waste products. Interposed in this tubular circuit is the hollow, muscular pump of that vital organ, the heart, which beats for a lifetime.

The heart is shaped like a flattened cone and is enclosed in a fibro-serous sack, the pericardium. The heart is placed obliquely in the chest, the base looking toward the thoracic inlet and the apex being in close contact with the diaphragm. The heart of a medium-sized dog weighs about 180 grams. Generally speaking, a large dog can be expected to have a proportionately large heart. The heart is divided by partitions into four chambers, the right and left atria and the right and left ventricles. The atria receive blood from veins. The muscular wall of the atria is very thin. The ventricles have thick muscular walls which enable them to force the blood out into the arteries.

The path of blood through the heart

Large caval veins (venae cavae) bring deoxygenated blood from the body and empty into the right atrium. The blood flows on down into the right ventricle, even prior to the contraction of the atrial walls. Between the right atrium and the right ventricle is a cylindrical valve composed of three cusps, the tricuspid valve, which permits the blood to flow from atrium to ventricle but which closes as the ventricle commences contraction. Valves increase the efficiency of the heart action by preventing the blood from moving backward into the space it previously occupied. Tendinous strands attached to small mounds of muscle projecting from the ventricular wall support the atrioventricular valves. The strands, chordae tendineae, attach to papillary muscles. These chordae tendineae prevent

the valve from being forced back into the atrium by the pressure of the blood as the ventricular wall contracts. Because the tricuspid valve prevents the blood from being forced back into the atrium, the only exit for the blood is through the pulmonary artery to the lungs.

One might imagine that a column of blood would flow back into the ventricle as it relaxes, but valves at the base of the pulmonary artery prevent this. These valves are called the pulmonary semilunar valves. Their concave surfaces are directed upward like cups to hold the column of blood in the pulmonary artery. When contraction of the muscular ventricular wall forces the blood upward, the valves collapse and thus offer little resistance to the passage of the blood into the pulmonary artery. Immediately this forward flow has ceased, the valves close and prevent the blood from flowing backward.

The pulmonary artery leads to the lungs where it divides into numerous small branches. Arterioles eventually subdivide into a capillary network traversing the walls of air sacs in the lungs. It is in this heart-lung cycle that carbon dioxide is given off by the blood to be exhaled and oxygen is taken up.

The capillaries of the lungs give rise to small veins, or venules, which, in turn, give rise to larger veins. The blood passes through the left atrium down into the left ventricle. The thin atrial walls contract and this action is followed by a strong contraction of the ventricles. The mitral, or bicuspid, valve lies between the left atrium and left ventricle and closes as the left ventricle begins to contract. The blood is forced up through the only exit available, the large aortic artery, branches of which distribute blood all over the body. At the base of the aorta are three aortic semilunar valves which prevent backflow of a column of blood in the aorta into the left ventricle as it relaxes.

The heart and bases of the great blood vessels

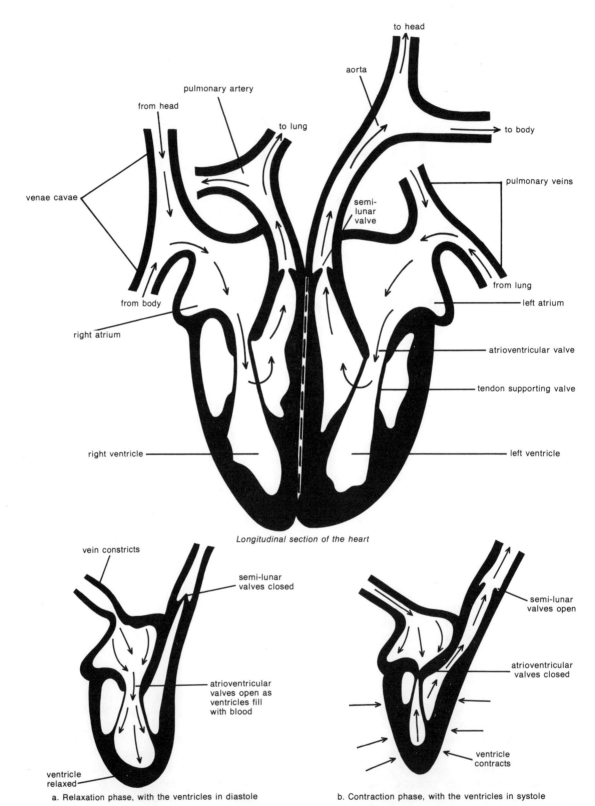

to head

aorta

pulmonary artery

from head

to lung

to body

semi-lunar valve

pulmonary veins

venae cavae

from lung

left atrium

from body

atrioventricular valve

right atrium

tendon supporting valve

right ventricle

left ventricle

Longitudinal section of the heart

vein constricts

semi-lunar valves closed

semi-lunar valves open

atrioventricular valves open as ventricles fill with blood

atrioventricular valves closed

ventricle relaxed

ventricle contracts

a. Relaxation phase, with the ventricles in diastole

b. Contraction phase, with the ventricles in systole

Diagram illustrating the heart cycle

118

are enclosed in a two-layered membrane called the pericardium, the outer layer being composed of fibrous tissue and the more delicate inner layer being a serous membrane. The serous membrane is closely applied to the heart, but it also lines the fibrous pericardium. The serous section forms a closed sac — the pericardial cavity. The heart is not in a cavity, it is merely covered by two layers of membrane. A very small quantity of pericardial fluid prevents friction as the heart beats.

The cavities of the heart are lined by a serous membrane called the endocardium, which is continuous over the valves and chordae tendineae and fuses with the membrane lining the large blood vessels of the heart. Since the endocardium covers the valves of the heart, in addition to lining the openings guarded by the valves, inflammation can alter the shape of either so that they no longer close tightly. In this case a small quantity of blood may get back past the valves, causing a low sound in a stethoscope referred to as a murmur. The valvular opening may become restricted as a result of inflammation, the condition being referred to as stenosis. Ordinarily, the heart will compensate for considerable loss of efficiency from valves that do not close tightly. The heart with valvular deficiency will often perform sufficiently well to permit normal activity, but it will attain its peak load earlier than the normal heart. It is inadvisable to subject dogs with well-defined heart murmurs to strenuous activities that may overtax their heart. Such dogs should either be put to sleep or kept as household pets.

The musculature of the heart is referred to as the myocardium and is composed of involuntary cardiac muscle tissue and has branching fibres. The muscles of the heart are arranged in complex patterns of irregular whorls, the heart contracting with a wringing motion. The atrial walls are relatively thin. The ventricular walls are thick and strong, this being especially pronounced in the left ventricle which forces the blood out to be distributed through the body. Its walls are much thicker than those of the right ventricle, which only moves the blood through the lungs.

The nerve supply to the heart is considered to be largely regulatory. The heart receives motor impulses through branches of the right and left vagus nerves. There is a very high degree of automatism about the beating of the heart. The distention of the muscular wall as the chambers of the heart fill with blood provides one type of stimulus, while certain salts in the blood provide a chemical stimulus. There is also an inherent rhythmic contraction characteristic of cardiac tissue.

The wave of contraction that spreads over the atria originates in an area of specialised tissue called the sinoatrial node (S A node). This area is considered to be the pacemaker and the heart beat originates here. The wave of contraction passes through the musculature of the right and left atria. The musculature of the atria is separate and distinct from that of the ventricles; a band of connective tissue separates the two sets of muscles. A strand of differentiated muscular tissue in the wall, or septum, which separates the right and left sides of the heart, affords a pathway by which excitation can reach the ventricles. The atrioventricular node (A V node) is another area of specialised tissue located in the septum between the atria. The bundle of His, a neuromuscular bundle, extends downward from the A V node and divides into right and left branches, conducting impulses to the right and left ventricles. The atria are first to contract since their muscles are the first to be stimulated. The muscular wall of the ventricles then contracts immediately subsequent to contraction of the atria.

Heart movement exhibits a regularity of rhythm. The contraction phase, during which blood is forced out of the chambers of the heart, is called systole (this word refers to contraction of the ventricles unless specifically designated as atrial systole). Diastole refers to the dilating (relaxing) of the chambers of the heart so that they fill with blood. (Unless atrial diastole is indicated, this term refers to relaxation of the ventricles.) The pressure within the ventricles is high during systole and since it becomes higher than the pressure in the arteries leaving the heart, blood rushes out into these arteries as the semilunar valves are forced open. The atria are then in their diastolic phase, the pressure within low, and blood flows into them from the large veins.

Heart sounds

If one listens to the heart by means of a stethoscope or by placing ones ear against the chest over the heart, two distinct sounds may be heard, the first being of lower and longer duration than the second. The sound is primarily associated with the closure of the atrioven-

Above: Which Chariot (Cheerful Chariot–Which Side), imported from England to Australia in 1960 by F. J. Schock, winning his first race at Harold Park, New South Wales, by ten lengths *(Courtesy of F. Schock). Below:* Clifden Times (The Grand Prince–Pink View), aged eleven years. England's leading authority on breeding, Alan Ross, reported that 'Clifden Times must, by breeding and performance, be the best yet to be sent to Australia'. The owner claims that he was at least twenty-five lengths faster than Which Chariot *(Courtesy of F. Schock)*

tricular valves but it may be caused by vibrations arising from various sources. The second sound is associated with the closure of the semilunar valves as the ventricles enter their diastolic phase. This sound is louder, sharper, and of higher pitch than the first sound. The sounds are altered if the valves of the heart are defective.

Heart rate

A great many factors influence the heart rate and thus statements concerning rate are only relative to various conditions. The digestion of a meal increases the strength and rate partly because of the muscular activity of the stomach and intestine. Muscular exercise increases the heart rate. Excitement affects the heart. One may have felt the pounding of a dog's heart as a result of fear or have felt the depressing effect from overwhelming fear. Age and size influence the heart rate since as the dog grows older and larger the heart rate becomes slower. The secretions of the endocrine glands also affect the heart rate.

An electrocardiograph is an instrument which amplifies and records the small voltages produced by the beating heart and provides an accurate record of heart action which may be implemented in the diagnosis of various heart conditions.

Blood supply to cardiac tissue

The right and left coronary arteries supply the cardiac tissue. The heart does not receive its oxygen and nutrition from the blood that passes through its chambers. Blocking of the coronary arteries is therefore extremely dangerous because of the inability of the heart muscle to continue its work without proper nourishment. No other tissue in the body is nourished by such a complete distribution of blood vessels as is cardiac tissue. The blood, after passing through a dense capillary network, passes into a venous system that finally empties into the coronary sinus and into the right atrium.

Arteries, veins and capillaries

The heart is the motive force and the arteries, veins, and capillaries are the tubes through which the blood is pumped to all parts of the body. The arteries are responsible for carrying blood from the heart to the tissues via small branches. We may refer to an artery as a trunk with its branches becoming successively smaller in diameter, like those of a tree. The total diameter of all the branches is much greater than the diameter of the trunk artery and hence the blood flows with decreasing pressure and velocity through the smaller arteries and arterioles to the capillaries.

The arterial wall consists of three layers:
1. the endothelial lining which contains some elastic tissue,
2. an intermediate layer of smooth muscle and elastic tissue,
3. an outer layer of loose connective tissue composed of collagenous and elastic fibres.

The walls of the large arteries, such as the aorta, are composed largely of elastic tissue and contain little muscular tissue. This elastic tissue presents a tough, resilient wall exhibiting extensibility and elasticity.

Gathering of blood from the tissues and its return to the heart is the concern of the venous system. From the smallest venules the branches become increasingly larger as one vein unites with another. The veins bringing blood into the heart are large trunk blood vessels and frequently lie alongside arteries of similar size.

Veins exhibit the same three layers in their walls as the arteries but because the intermediate layer is poorly developed the walls of the veins are thinner and contain little muscular or elastic tissue. Following death the walls of the veins tend to collapse while the thicker walled arteries retain their shape. Some veins, particularly those of the extremities, exhibit flaplike valves which prevent the backflow of blood.

The capillaries are minute tubes lying between the smallest arteries (arterioles) and the smallest veins (venules). The diameter of a capillary is smaller than that of a hair and many capillaries are so minute that even the red blood cells must pass through in single file.

Flat endothelial cells only one layer thick comprise the capillary wall through which oxygen and food materials pass to the tissues, while carbon dioxide and other breakdown products of metabolism enter the bloodstream and are transported away.

The vascular system may be divided into two main systems:
1. The systemic circulatory system is composed of the aorta and its branches, which supply blood to the tissues of the body, and the capillaries and veins which return blood to the heart.
2. The pulmonary circulatory system consists of the pulmonary artery and its branches,

the capillary network in the lungs, and the pulmonary veins. Unlike other arteries, the pulmonary artery carries venous blood from the right ventricle to the lungs. It divides into right and left pulmonary arteries which supply the right and left lungs respectively. After passing through the capillary network in the lungs the blood flows into venules and small veins, eventually giving rise to the pulmonary veins. These are short veins containing no valves and returning oxygenated blood from the lungs to the left atrium of the heart.

THE CIRCULATION

It is important to differentiate between the functions of the blood as an internal fluid, and the circulation which distributes it. The following account is concerned principally with the circulation as a transport system, rather than with the properties of blood fluid as an internal environment.

1. *Transport of oxygen from the lungs to the tissues*

As the blood passes through the capillary network in the thin air sacs of the lungs oxygen enters into loose chemical combination with the haemoglobin of the red blood cells, forming oxyhaemoglobin, and is carried to the tissues. There, as the blood passes through the tissue capillaries, the haemoglobin loses oxygen to the tissues and is then referred to as reduced haemoglobin. Arterial blood, after passing through the lungs, is somewhat brighter red than that found in the veins.

2. *Transport of carbon dioxide from the tissues to the lungs*

Carbon dioxide, a product of cell metabolism, diffuses through the capillary walls and dissolves in the blood plasma. Some of it enters the red blood cells and some of it forms sodium bicarbonate in the plasma. It is released in the lungs, diffuses into the air sacs, and is expelled.

3. *Transport of nutrient materials, absorbed from the intestine, to the tissues*

The soluble products of digestion diffuse into the capillaries of the villi lining the small intestine and are carried in solution by the plasma and, after passing through the liver, enter the general circulation. Glucose and amino acids diffuse through the capillary walls into the cells of the body. Glucose may be oxidised in a muscle, e.g., to play its role in muscle contraction; amino acids will be built up into proteins to fabricate new cells and fresh tissue.

4. *Transport of organic substances representing breakdown products of metabolism (urea, uric acid, creatinine, purine wastes) from the tissues to the kidneys for excretion*

Many of the chemical activities of the body form by-products or end-products of a poisonous nature. These substances diffuse into the capillary or lymphatic systems and are carried away in the plasma. Eventually, they reach the kidneys where a large proportion of them is removed and excreted.

5. *Distribution of hormones, the secretions of ductless or endocrine glands, throughout the body*

Hormones are chemicals which affect the rate of vital processes in the body. They are carried in the blood plasma from the glands which secrete them all around the body and when they reach specific organs, e.g., the heart, they affect the rate at which these organs operate.

6. *Distribution of heat and temperature control*

Muscular and chemical activity release heat and these processes are taking place far more rapidly in some parts of the body than in others, e.g., chemical activity in the liver and muscular action in the limbs. Locally produced heat is distributed more evenly to all parts of the body by the bloodstream.

Surface blood vessels in the skin can be dilated so that more blood can come to the surface, heat thus being lost more rapidly. Conversely, surface vessels can constrict to keep blood away from the cold exterior and so reduce heat loss. The blood, therefore, plays an important role in the regulation of body temperature.

7. *The ability of the blood to form a clot*

The ability of the blood to form a clot and thus reduce bleeding has been of survival value to animals and man. The mechanism of clot formation protects the animal from excessive bleeding from minor wounds and is essentially a chemical and physical process. The breakdown of blood platelets releases a lipoid substance called thromboplastin which initiates the clotting process. Subsequent to the release of thromboplastin; thromboplastin, calcium ions, and accelerator globulin interact with prothrombin causing the release of thrombin which, in turn, interacts with fibrinogen to fabricate threads of fibrin which form the framework of the clot. Blood cells and blood platelets are held in this framework as the clot develops.

122

8. Prevention of infection

The blood plays an important role in protecting the body from harmful bacteria and organisms that may cause disease or abnormal states. Certain of the white cells of the blood afford protection by ingesting bacteria or foreign matter appearing in the blood stream. If, however, the skin is broken and bacteria enter the cut, these white cells migrate through the capillaries in that region and engulf any invading bacteria and localise the infection, destroying most of the bacteria before it enters the general circulation. These bacteria which escape into the lymphatic system are trapped by white cells in the lymph nodes or in the spleen and liver. Certain virulent strains of bacteria cannot be ingested by the white cells until they have been acted upon by chemicals called antibodies.

9. Maintenance of correct fluid balance throughout the body tissues

The capillary wall acts as a semipermeable membrane, permitting constant filtration into the tissues of water molecules and other substances in solution. Small molecules, such as those of oxygen, glucose, and amino acids, pass readily through the capillary wall but the larger protein molecules pass through extremely slowly, if at all. Filtration, in this instance the movement of water and dissolved substances out of the bloodstream, is assisted by capillary blood pressure.

The blood contains a number of proteins in colloidal state that have a tendency to attract fluid from the tissues into the blood stream and retain it there. Food proteins undergoing digestion are broken down to amino acids, in which state they are absorbed. Investigation indicates that amino acids can enter into the formation of plasma protein, including albumin and globulin. Plasma protein plays a significant role in building up osmotic pressure if osmosis is taken to mean the movement of water through the capillary wall toward the protein. Abnormal conditions such as increased permeability, increased capillary pressure, or reduced plasma protein content of the blood, may allow excessive filtration of fluid into the tissues. The tissues literally become water-logged and swollen, the condition being referred to as oedema. Subsequent to severe blood loss, water moves from the tissues into the bloodstream and the volume of blood may be rapidly restored in this way. In this instance the blood is able to draw on a water reserve normally held in the tissues.

10. Maintenance of the acid base balance of the body tissues

The majority of the tissues, blood inclusive, are slightly alkaline in their reaction. The pH of arterial blood ranges between $7 \cdot 35$ and $7 \cdot 45$. Numerous acids and acid-like substances are constantly produced by body metabolism; the tissues themselves and the body fluids remain remarkably constant and at a slightly alkaline pH. The main reason for this chemical stability lies in the fact that the blood contains a number of alkaline substances, sodium bicarbonate being the principal one. Weak acids produced by metabolic processes are buffered by alkaline substances in the blood and tissues, while excess alkalinity is buffered by acids. A buffer solution is comprised of substances that afford a reserve of acidity and alkalinity. If a weak acid or base is added to the solution, either substance is buffered by the appropriate reserve and chemical equilibrium is maintained.

There is a tendency to emphasise the buffering action of alkaline substances against the acid products commonly formed by metabolic processes. The bicarbonate of the blood readily neutralises carbonic acid, a weak acid which breaks down into carbon dioxide and water.

Carbon dioxide constantly formed in metabolism is regularly eliminated via the lungs and thus its influence on blood acidity is markedly reduced. The pH of the blood alters very little as the result of acids taken into the bloodstream. Sodium bicarbonate acts as an alkaline reserve to protect the body from acids produced by metabolic processes. Acid substances buffered in the blood are constantly removed by the kidneys and this assists the maintenance of the chemical acid base balance of the blood.

THE COMPOSITION OF THE BLOOD

The liquid portion of the blood is known as plasma, a straw-coloured fluid of complex chemical nature, containing a variety of substances. The red cells, white cells, and platelets are contained in this liquid medium and thus the blood may be referred to as a liquid tissue.

The majority of the functions of the blood exert a direct influence on the plasma. The chemical content of the blood is reasonably constant despite the fact that the blood is continually engaged in the transportation of absorbed food products and the receipt of waste products from cell metabolism. Plasma is approximately ninety-two per cent water, the remaining eight per cent being materials in solution.

Red cells (Erythrocytes)

Carried along in the fluid portion of the blood are minute, biconcave red cells so numerous that the blood itself appears red. Erythrocytes are fabricated in the red marrow of the short bones such as the sternum, ribs, and vertebrae. A hormone called erythropoietin controls the production of erythrocytes. The source of the hormone is unknown, although evidence indicates that it is formed in the kidneys. Erythrocytes derive their colour from a complex protein called haemoglobin which is composed of a pigment, heme (containing iron) and the protein globin. Haemoglobin has an affinity for oxygen and readily combines with it in conditions of high-oxygen concentration to form an unstable compound called oxyhaemoglobin which, in conditions of low-oxygen concentration, readily breaks down and releases oxygen. This property renders it most efficient in transporting oxygen from the lungs to the tissues. Erythrocytes not only function to carry oxygen to the tissues, but indirectly carry carbon dioxide away from the tissues.

Approximately forty-five per cent of the blood volume of the dog is comprised of red cells which are thrity-three per cent haemoglobin. A red blood cell lasts for about 100 days, after which it breaks down and is disintegrated by specific cells present in the liver, spleen, and connective tissues, known as the reticule endothelial system of cells. The haemoglobin is broken down into the pigment bilirubin which is then excreted by the liver through the biliary passages into the intestine. Consequently, a 35-kg dog would need to produce 30 mL of blood daily.

White cells (Leukocytes)

White cells are nucleated and variable in shape and size. They are far less numerous than red blood cells, red cells outnumbering the white by about 700 to 1. Leukocytes exhibit amoebid movement.

There are two main groups of white cells:
1. Cells that have granules in the cytoplasm and possess a nucleus of two or three lobes. These cells are referred to as granular, or polymorphonuclear, leukocytes. According to some authorities, this is the only group correctly referred to as leukocytes.

2. Cells without granules in the cytoplasm and with a spherical nucleus. These are nongranular white cells. This group includes lymphocytes and monocytes.

Granular leukocytes (Neutrophils)

These are the most abundant type of white cell, constituting sixty-five to seventy per cent of the total number of white cells. They are larger than erythrocytes and the nucleus tends to vary with age. Neutrophils are active amoeboid cells and are phagocytic (i.e., they have the ability to ingest bacteria or foreign material). They contain protein digesting enzymes which enable them to digest most of the materials they engulf. This phagocytic activity is important in helping to eliminate injurious bacteria from the body. Much of the protective function of antibodies is in their ability to react with infectious material, slowing it down or immobilising it, rendering phagocytosis more effective.

Eosinophils

Eosinophils resemble neutrophils but are slightly larger and the nucleus is bilobed. The granules in the cytoplasm stain bright red with acid dyes such as eosin. Although these cells may congregate in considerable numbers in the tissues, they constitute only two to four per cent of the total number of white cells in the blood. According to some authorities, eosinophils are less active and not as highly phagocytic as neutrophils.

Basophils

Basophils exhibit a bilobed nucleus and the large cytoplasmic granules stain deep blue with basic stains such as methylene blue. Basophils constitute only one-half per cent of the total number of white cells in the blood. Little is known concerning the phagocytic ability of basophils, but they are considered less active than eosinophils.

Granular leukocytes, like erythrocytes, arise in the red marrow of bone. Although various estimates have been made, the length of their active life is unknown. (It is thought to be a period of only a few days.) It is supposed that older leukocytes are removed from circulation principally by the liver and spleen, as are erythrocytes.

Nongranular leukocytes (Lymphocytes)

Lymphocytes are either small or large. The small

lymphocytes constitute twenty to twenty-five per cent of the total number of all leukocytes and are the smallest of the white cells. The nucleus is large and spherical and the cytoplasm is nongranular and stains light blue, while the nucleus stains a much deeper blue with Wrights stain. Large lymphocytes constitute about three per cent of the total number of white cells. They contain more cytoplasm and they exhibit a large, oval, indented nucleus. Lymphocytes arise in the lymphoid tissue of organs such as the spleen or lymph nodes. The life span of a lymphocyte is perhaps a day or less and consequently it is estimated that 5 to 10 billion new lymphocytes must be fabricated each day.

The exact function of lymphocytes is obscure. They exhibit some degree of mobility and congregate in large numbers around the focus of an infection that is accompanied by inflammation. Active phagocytosis is not apparent. Investigation has revealed that they are concerned with the production of antibodies.

Monocytes

Monocytes are about 15 microns in diameter and have a large, deeply indented nucleus which stains deep blue with Wrights stain. Monocytes resemble large lymphocytes but contain relatively more cytoplasm. Monocytes account for about five per cent of the total white cell count in the blood. Monocytes are active phagocytes and it is supposed that they function in contributing to repair and reorganisation of tissues.

The function of leukocytes

Unlike red cells, which must remain within a confined circulatory system, the white cells are able to pass through the capillary wall and move about in the tissues. They are most significant in protecting the body from bacterial invasion, since by virtue of their phagocytic ability they are able to ingest bacteria or foreign matter. The white cell count may rise remarkably as the protective elements of the body attempt to control infection. In the case of an abscess around the root of a tooth or in tonsilitis, and in many infectious diseases, the white cell count may reach the condition known as leukocytosis. A rise in the white cell count affords excellent corroborative evidence to a veterinarian that there is an infection located somewhere in the body. It is often true that the severity of the infection is indicated by the number of leukocytes present in the blood.

A rise in the white cell count does not imply that the various types of white cells retain normal numerical relation to each other. Inflammation and certain infectious diseases, notably those involving the coccus form of bacterium, cause an elevated neutrophilic cell count. Some chronic infections cause an increase in the number of lymphocytes, while certain skin diseases and some cases of infection by parasitic worms cause an increase in the number of eosinophils.

Some diseases, especially pneumonia, cause a reduction in the white cell count. Certain drugs reduce the number of white cells. Destruction or degeneration of red bone marrow also causes a reduction in number of white blood cells. Leukopenia is the term used to indicate a reduction of white cells below normal which in turn indicates a lowered resistance to infection.

The normal rise in the white cell count as the consequence of infection is called leukocytosis. However, leukaemia is an abnormal condition in which white cells are produced in tremendous numbers, but not in response to any known infection. The red bone marrow produces white cells at an uncontrolled rate. In another type of leukaemia, lymphoid tissues are overactive in lymphocyte production. A deficiency in the number of red cells (erythropenia) is often associated with leukaemia.

Blood platelets

Minute, granular, disc-shaped platelets, or thrombocytes, are present in the blood and little is known about them. Investigation reveals that they arise from the red marrow of bone together with other formed elements of the blood. They are not nucleated and are much smaller than erythrocytes. It is difficult to obtain an accurate count of the blood platelets because as soon as a sample of blood is taken, the platelets clump together in groups of thirty or more, and then proceed to slowly break down. It has been suggested that thrombocytes are fragments of giant cells of the red bone marrow (megakarocytes). Platelets play an important role in the control of bleeding and help to form a firm clot. If they were not present even a small cut would bleed continuously, while haemorrhages could occur spontaneously into the skin and internally.

The clotting mechanism of the blood

The clotting mechanism of the blood is essentially a chemical and physical process which protects the animal from excessive bleeding from minor wounds. It is difficult to determine all the causal factors that initiate the chemical reaction resulting in clotting. It is thought that a tissue extract exudes from injured tissues and promotes clotting upon coming into contact with the blood. Thromboplastin, a lipoid substance released by the breakdown of blood platelets, initiates the clotting process. Thromboplastin is a group of substances capable of initiating the interaction that results in the release of thrombin from prothrombin. Thrombin is an enzyme present in the blood in an inactive form called prothrombin.

The clotting process is extremely complicated but, generally speaking, may be roughly outlined as follows:

1. Platelet breakdown (or injured tissue substance) releases thromboplastin.
2. Thromboplastin, in the presence of free calcium ions and accelerator globulin (factor V), interacts with prothrombin, resulting in the release of active thrombin.
3. Thrombin interacts with firbinogen which comes out of solution as threads of fibrin. Fibrin plus blood cells and blood platelets form a clot.

Accelerator globulin, or factor V, is fabricated in the liver and is essential in the clotting process as it activates the change of prothrombin to thrombin.

The quantity of thromboplastin released from the disintegration of blood platelets is surprisingly small in comparison with the volume of blood plasma. Investigation reveals, however, that a globulin in the blood called the anti-haemophilic factor (AHF) enhances the breakdown of blood platelets, causing them to rapidly and completely disintegrate once the clotting process has begun.

Fibrinogen is formed in the liver. Fibrinogen is a protein in solution in the blood plasma and as such can be coagulated by heat or precipitated by specific salts, but its normal coagulant is thrombin. Fibrinogen comes out of solution as strands of fibrin when thrombin is present in its active state. Fibrin forms the framework of a clot and the blood cells and platelets are retained in this framework as the clot develops.

Mechanical defibrination can be achieved by whipping blood which causes the threads of fibrin to collect on the object with which it is being whipped. If the fibrin is removed, the blood will lose its ability to clot.

Under normal circumstances the blood does not clot internally in the body. Unless there is access to injured surfaces, there are insufficient thromboplastic substances liberated to convert prothrombin into thrombin and so induce the series of chemical reactions that produce clotting. Additional safety measures are also present in antiprothrombic substances such as heparin which is thought to be produced by the large basophilic mast cells found in tissues of various organs. Heparin blocks the change of prothrombin to thrombin and thus reduces the clotting ability of the blood. Heparin may be employed to assist in reducing clots in instances where internal clotting has occurred. Internal clotting is called thrombosis. A thrombus, or clot, can form in a blood vessel in the leg and do comparatively little harm but if it blocks the blood supply to the heart or brain it can be extremely serious. A clot which has become dislodged from its place of origin is known as an embolus.

THE SPLEEN

The spleen is a highly vascular organ applied on one of its surfaces to the wall of the stomach to which it is bound by means of a ligament. This surface is concave. The opposite dorsal surface is convex and is applied to the lower surface of the spinal bones and the under surfaces of the ribs, extending a short way behind their borders. It is often the first organ to exhibit itself when the abdomen is opened surgically along the midline. In the dog the spleen is approximately 12 centimetres long according to the size of the dog, greyish-pink in colour and somewhat freely moveable in the abdomen.

The internal structure of the spleen is complex. Immediately beneath the serous coat is a connective tissue capsule, from which a fibrous framework projects into the interior. Both the capsule and the internal fibrous structure contain smooth muscle. Splenic pulp constitutes the areas between the fibrous framework and occurs as loose reticular tissue supporting small arteries and veins and containing red and white blood cells in vast number. The splenic sinuses are a complicated network of blood spaces found in the splenic pulp. Lymphatic nodules, concerned with the development of lymphocytes, are also found here. Large phagocytic white cells of the reticuloendothelial system are numerous in the splenic pulp and function

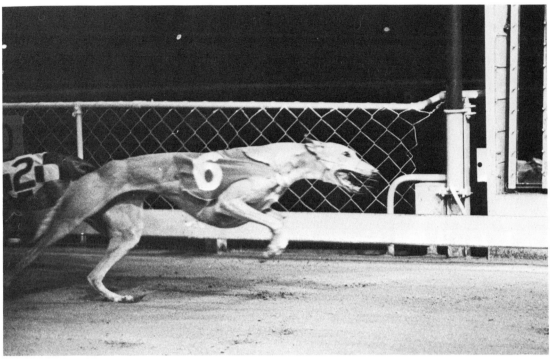

Young Moss, a 27·2-kg dog by Miller's Moss out of Rocket Site, winner of 1972 National Derby in 31 seconds contested at Wentworth Park, New South Wales, Australia over 530 metres *(Courtesy of Allan Quinn)*

in the removal from the blood of old or agglutinated red cells, fragments of red cells, and foreign material.

Three of the functions of the spleen are of primary importance:

1. The spleen acts as an accessory organ of the circulatory system. It is capable of directing a considerable quantity of reserve blood into the arteries in response to an emergency. This increases the oxygen carrying capacity of the blood. The spleen is strongly activated when the animal is under physical stress or emotional stress by impulses from the sympathetic nervous system and by epinephrine from the adrenal glands. The spleen assists in supplying additional red cells and in making up the volume of blood when there is a loss of blood.

   The spleen appears to be an organ one can live without, although it manufactures red cells. However, the spleen enables animals to meet emergencies more readily. Exercise and an increase in the external temperature cause the spleen to decrease its volume of blood. Investigations reveal that animals with their spleens removed are apparently less resistant to the toxic effects of disease.

2. The spleen has been referred to as the 'graveyard' for old blood platelets. The large phagocytic cells of the spleen are most useful in removing old red cells, fragments, and agglutinated masses of cells from the circulation.

3. The spleen is an important organ for the manufacture of lymphocytes and monocytes throughout life.

THE PHYSIOLOGY OF CIRCULATION

Blood flows rapidly from the deeper parts of the body to the extremities and returns to the heart in approximately 60 seconds. It may take various routes and some are longer than others, e.g., the heart lung cycle is a far shorter trip than that between the heart and the foot. The blood travels at various rates in accordance with the various sections of the circulation. The rate of flow is not uniform in all arteries, being somewhat faster in the larger ones. The flow is also faster at the crest of the systolic wave than it is during diastole.

The velocity of the blood reduces to approximately 0·5 millimetre per second as it travels through the capillaries. The diameter of a single capillary is extremely small but the total diameter of all the capillaries exceeds the total diameter of the arteries.

A proportion of the capillaries provide direct connection between the smallest arterioles and venules and are referred to as 'a v' capillaries for convenience. A small volume of blood always flows through these 'a v' capillaries even during vasoconstriction. These capillaries provide an important route for circulation between peripheral ends of arteries and veins.

Vasoconstriction in the smallest arterioles limits the flow through the capillaries. The blood flow into a typical capillary is controlled by a band of smooth muscle, at the point where it branches off the arteriole, called the precapillary sphincter.

The venous system collects blood from the great capillary bed. The velocity of the blood in the veins may increase to more than 250 times the velocity in the capillaries. One would not expect the velocity of the blood in the veins to be as great as in the arteries since the venous bed is greater than that of the arteries.

Many conditions influence the rate of flow:
1. Velocity will be greater in large vessels than in small ones.
2. Velocity will increase during exercise and will be directly proportional to the blood volume of a specific vein.
3. The beating of the heart assists the movement of blood in the veins, but other factors supplement the action of the heart.
4. The massaging action of the skeletal muscles is of value. The muscle action of exercise promotes return flow through the veins, but conversely, standing quietly for long periods exerts unusual pressure on the veins of the legs.
5. Inspiratory movements assist blood flow into the atria from the great veins. As the volume of the thorax is increased, air rushes into the lungs. The heart is situated in the thoracic cavity and the decrease in pressure within the cavity assists in filling the atria with blood.
6. Veins possess the ability to dilate or constrict. The veins of the skin, as other surface blood vessels, react to temperature by dilating when the skin surface is warm and contracting in response to cold. In excess of half the total volume of blood is contained within the veins alone.

The pulse

The pulse is a pressure wave which travels along the arteries at a much faster rate than the velocity of the blood itself. The pulse is lost as the blood filters through the capillaries. The pulse can be easily palpated where an artery lies near the surface, the most convenient place to feel this impulse being over the radial artery at the wrist. The pulse should not be confused with the movement of the blood itself.

The ventricles force blood out into the aorta as the heart beats. The force of contraction in the ventricles initiates a wave of increased pressure, which commences at the heart. If a large artery is severed, the blood escapes in spurts, but under normal circumstances, in the intact circulatory system, much of the force of ejection from the heart is absorbed by the arterial wall. If a circulatory system was fabricated from glass tubing, which is inelastic, the blood would move in spurts in the entire apparatus.

In taking the pulse three specific points are to be noted:

1. *Rate*

An increase in the heart rate above normal is known as tachycardia. There are numerous causes of tachycardia but generally speaking they may be divided into three groups.

a. Increased metabolism calling for increased oxygen requirements. Any increase in bodily function calls for an increase in oxygen, the essential fuel of the body, and to supply this the heart beats faster to increase its output. This explains the tachycardia of all physical and emotional effort. Severe pain also causes tachycardia.

b. Reduction in the oxygen carrying capacity of the blood. If the capacity of the blood to carry the necessary oxygen to the tissues is notably reduced, the heart beats faster. This increases the circulation rate and so makes the reduced number of red cells and haemoglobin present do more work. This accounts for the tachycardia in anaemias. In cases of shock and haemorrhage, where the blood volume is reduced and consequently the oxygen carrying capacity of the blood, a constant tachycardia is present. The increase in pulse rate is a valuable guide to the severity and progress of the shock or haemorrhage.

c. Heart disease.
   The third main cause of tachycardia is disease of the heart. In all instances of heart failure the heart is weakened and is unable

to pump out into the circulation the normal amount of blood at each beat. In order to compensate for this and supply sufficient oxygen to the tissues, the heart beats faster.

Overdosage of some drugs, certain diseases of the central nervous system associated with increased intracranial pressure such as cerebral tumour, meningitis and head injuries, cause a slowing of the pulse rate or bradycardia.

2. *Rhythm*

The pulse should exhibit a regular rhythm. When the pulse is irregular the term irregular heart action is used. There are many causes of this and it is sufficient to state here that when the heart's action is very irregular, the pulse rate may be a fallacious guide to the heart rate. In such instances, to obtain the true heart rate it is necessary to listen directly over the heart with a stethoscope.

3. *Force*

Much is frequently made of the degree of fullness or volume of the pulse and also of the compressibility or tension. If the pulse is very soft and thready it is a good indication that the blood pressure is low. A hard pulse indicates high arterial tension.

Blood pressure

The heart pumps blood against the frictional resistance of the blood vessels. Cardiac output is important in relation to blood pressure. If the heart rate is increased, the blood pressure is elevated, and vice versa. Pressure is highest in the large arteries near the heart and diminishes as the blood travels in the smaller vessels which are a greater distance from the source of pressure.

The viscosity of the blood is an important factor in resistance to flow since blood of high viscosity offers greater resistance to flow than blood of low viscosity.

The quantity of blood to be moved is a factor influencing the blood pressure. The animal can withstand relatively small losses of blood without an accompanying loss of pressure but the loss of a large quantity of blood causes the pressure to fall.

The elasticity of the arterial walls also affects the blood pressure. The elastic rebound of the arterial walls keeps the blood moving along and a steady flow is delivered to the capillaries.

Vasoconstriction and vasodilation

The smooth muscles in the walls of the arterioles are supplied with vasomotor nerves. If the muscle fibres are stimulated to contract, the diameter of the blood vessel becomes smaller and this process is referred to as vasoconstriction. If the muscle fibres relax, permitting the diameter to increase, the process is known as vasodilation.

The vasoconstrictor centre is situated in the medulla and, by means of vasoconstrictor nerves, maintains a constant flow of impulses to muscles of the arterioles maintaining them in a state of tonic contraction.

The vasodilator centre is situated in the medulla posterior to the vasoconstrictor centre. It is supposed that there is reciprocal inhibition between the two centres, i.e., when the vasodilator centre is stimulated, the vasoconstrictor centre is reflexly inhibited.

The blood pressure rises considerably during physical exertion. There is some increase in diastolic pressure, but the greatest rise is in the systolic pressure. Generally speaking, a greater effort produces an increased heart rate and higher blood pressure. The blood pressure of a greyhound quickly returns to normal, and frequently drops below normal, after a race. Racing over long distances produces a more moderate rise in blood pressure, but the recovery phase requires a longer time. The reason for the fall below normal of the blood pressure following exercise is apparently due to the slowing of the heart and continued vascular dilation in the blood vessels supplying skeletal muscles recently active. In addition, a rise in body temperature would be accompanied by vasodilation of blood vessels located in the skin to provide for heat loss.

The lymphatic system

Lymph is the medium of exchange between the blood and the tissues. Lymph is virtually tissue fluid but when it is contained within the lymphatic vessels it is referred to as lymph. Lymph is a clear fluid containing a low granular leukocyte count and a varying number of lymphocytes. A few erythrocytes may be present. The protein content and the total calcium and phosphorus content is less than that of blood. Lymph exhibits some ability to clot but the clot is soft and the process is slow. Nutrient materials can pass through the capillary walls and be carried by the tissue fluid to the cells. Waste materials from cellular metabolism pass from the cell into the tissue fluid and are then absorbed into the bloodstream and carried away. Lymph flows very slowly.

The larger lymphatic vessels eventually drain into veins, the lymph becomes part of the blood and is distributed by the arterial system. Lymphatic capillaries are the smallest vessels of the lymphatic system and they drain tissue fluid from extracellular spaces. Lymphatic capillaries anastomose readily and form elaborate plexuses. Lymphatic capillaries are distributed to the majority of tissues and organs of the body but no lymphatic vessels have been demonstrated in cartilage, bone marrow, the central nervous system, or in peripheral nerves. However, the periosteum of bone is well served with lymphatic capillaries. Larger lymphatic vessels, the walls of which resemble those of veins, drain the capillary network and exhibit valves on their inner surface which prevent backflow. Unlike veins, they do not unite to form larger and larger vessels but tend to adopt individual courses. The larger lymphatics are collecting vessels and flow from the capillary network toward lymph nodes, these vessels thus being the afferent vessels of the lymph nodes.

Lymph nodes are small bodies of lymphoid tissue distributed along the route of lymphatic vessels. The lymph stream widens considerably as it passes through the node and consequently the rate of flow is accordingly reduced. The lymph filters through passageways lined with phagocytic cells which engulf bacteria and foreign matter from the lymph stream. During severe bacterial infections the lymph nodes frequently become swollen and inflamed. Experimentation indicates that the lymph nodes and the spleen are involved in the formation of antibodies. The lymph nodes also produce lymphocytes. In specific parts of the body there are great collections of lymph nodes, e.g., in the neck and groin. Lymphatics in the region of the small intestine possess a special function in the absorption of digested fat from the intestine.

The lymph flow takes place in only one direction, from the tissues to the heart, and there is no specialised pump. The flow is created partly by the pressure of the lymph that accumulates in the tissues and partly by muscular exercise.

Blood counts

Blood counts or haemotology reports are a physical and biochemical analysis of blood and are usually carried out by a pathologist. A blood count may be used as a diagnostic aid in the case of a dog with disease or it may be used to interpret how well or fit a dog is in relation to his blood. Since we are concerned with blood counts from a racing point of view, we are primarily concerned with the oxygen-carrying capacity of the blood which, if deficient, is likely to cause a marked reduction in speed towards the end of a run.

RBC (red blood cells — erythrocytes) — million/mm^3

Hb (haemoglobin) — g/100 mL

PCV (haematocrit packed cell volume) — per cent

WBC (white blood cells — leucocytes) — thousand/mm^3

MCV (mean corpuscular or average RBC volume) — cu (cubic microns)

MCH (mean corpuscular haemoglobin or average RBC Hb) — Micro micrograms (2)

MCHC (mean corpuscular haemoglobin concentration or average RBC Hb concentration) — per cent

With the exception of the WBC reading all of the other readings above are concerned with RBC. RBC is the number of red blood cells in a specified volume of blood.

Hb is the amount of haemoglobin in a given volume. This should be in the order of 19 to 20 grams per 100 millilitres of blood.

PCV is a function of the RBC and Hb. It is the percentage of blood that packs out to be cells. This is done in a centrifuge. The average greyhound needs to be between fifty-eight and sixty per cent, i.e., the cells should occupy 58 to 60 millilitres in 100 millilitres of blood.

WBC is the number of white cells.

MCV is the actual volume of one red blood cell (RBC).

MCH is a measurement of how full each RBC is with Hb.

MCHC is a measure of the haemoglobin expressed as a percentage of the total PCV or haematocrit.

Analysis of the plasma protein is important because increases above 7 grams per 100 millilitres of blood generally infer that the animal is dehydrated or has suffered from a chronic infection, usually viral.

With an understanding of the foregoing it is not difficult to interpret the trend that the blood count should take. It is important to remember that every dog has a different optimum or maximum but an average range can be established. Blood tests are best taken 8 or more hours following feeding and 4 to 5 days following a race.

The main interpretation made from a blood count of this nature is in regard to the PCV, RBC and Hb. These three results would be either above normal, normal or below normal.

1. Above normal range is what is known as relative polycythaemia, i.e., too many RBC associated with high PCV and high Hb levels. These conditions can be caused by excitement, forcing the spleen to evacuate its reserve of RBC, and by dehydration due to sweating or refusal to drink (remember blood is the water balance system).
2. The normal range is best determined by practical analysis with individual dogs. The average is 45. Range 38 to 53.
3. The below normal range is most common and indicates anaemia. Deficiencies in the blood picture will reduce performance.

ANAEMIA

Anaemia refers to a condition of the blood in which there is a reduction in the number of red cells or reduced haemoglobin. Frequently both the red cell count and the percentage of haemoglobin are reduced. The oxygen-carrying capacity of the blood is reduced by the loss of haemoglobin. Many conditions and circumstances may lead to anaemia in greyhounds and an accurate diagnosis by the veterinarian is necessary to determine the type of anaemia and then to correct it.

The typical animal with anaemia becomes weak and lethargic following exercise. The mucous membranes, particularly those of the eye and mouth, become pale. In severe cases the pulse may become rapid and the dog may faint. The depth of respiration is frequently increased following exercise and there may be an enlargement of the heart as a consequence of the strain placed on it in chronic cases. The dog may lose weight and have a poor appetite.

Anaemia may present very rapidly as in the case of severe haemorrhage or it may take considerable time to develop as in the case of chronic infestation with fleas. Remember that fleas are blood suckers and in sufficient numbers can cause anaemia.

Correction of mild anaemia may be all that is required to turn a minor-place-getter into a winner. The initial step in the eradication or correction of anaemia is to find the cause and then to treat the effect.

Pernicious anaemia

The failure of the red bone marrow in the production of erythrocytes results in a very low red cell count, but individual cells may be normal or large and contain normal or even above-normal amounts of haemoglobin. The discovery of an anti-anaemic factor in liver has proved of great benefit to victims of pernicious anaemia or similar types. An understanding of the relationship between the erythrocyte maturation factor and vitamin B_{12} has been of great help in interpreting the factors involved. The reader is referred to previous discussions on pteroylglutamic acid and vitamin B_{12} in the section dealing with vitamins. In pernicious anaemia the intrinsic factor normally secreted by the stomach is absent with the result that vitamin B_{12} is not absorbed from the gastrointestinal tract.

There are a number of things known to be causative factors of failure of the red bone marrow in erythrocyte production. These factors include DDT, Lindane, arsenical preparations, benzene compounds, canine distemper, and some infectious diseases. Frequently the cause is unknown but treatment can be effected if the cause can be traced. Extensive bone disease may interfere with the marrow and consequently depress blood formation. In leukaemia vast numbers of abnormal white cells crowd the marrow to such an extent that red cell formation is greatly reduced and for this reason leukaemia always leads to anaemia.

Pernicious anaemia affects both sexes equally. The onset is gradual and typical remissions occur when the anaemia improves of its own accord. General symptoms and signs of anaemia are present and their severity naturally varies with the degree of anaemia, but usually they are marked. Glossitis is common. Symptoms and signs of involvement of the nervous system may be present, including difficulty in walking (ataxia) and pins and needles in the feet. These are due to the characteristic neurological complication of subacute combined degeneration of the cord met with only in pernicious anaemia. Examination often reveals an enlarged spleen. There is a characteristic blood picture in pernicious anaemia which is always a hyperchromic macrocytic (large cell) anaemia. Immature cells frequently appear in the peripheral blood and the white cells are reduced in number (leucopenia). If the blood picture is not definitely typical, examination of the red marrow is carried out and this affords a characteristic picture in all cases. This examination is referred to as a marrow puncture. The diagnosis of pernicious anaemia is readily made on the typical signs of anaemia, the blood picture, the complete achlorhydria and, if necessary, by a sternal puncture. Carcinoma of the stomach or intestine often gives rise to effects similar to those of pernicious anaemia.

The essential aim of treatment is to supply the missing vitamin B_{12}. In the early stages of treatment when there is severe anaemia, vitamin B_{12} is injected intramuscularly once or twice a week until the number of red blood cells and the amount of haemoglobin return to normal. Thereafter maintenance doses are administered every 2 to 4 weeks as the animal will relapse if vitamin B_{12} is stopped. Vitamin B_{12} will be necessary for the remainder of the animal's life and at periodic intervals a blood count is taken to ensure that sufficient vitamin B_{12} therapy is being given. If subacute degeneration of the spinal cord is present, much larger doses of vitamin B_{12} are necessary for the initial six to twelve months of treatment and then followed by the usual maintenance dose.

Iron-deficiency anaemia

This is the most common type of anaemia and is due to a combination of causes. The diet is frequently deficient in iron-containing foods and absorption of iron is inadequate because of the lack of hydrochloric acid in the stomach. Significantly, many of the east coast areas of Australia have iron-deficient soil types and consequently meat derived from stock reared in these areas may be low in iron content. Loss of blood from bitches in season and the increased nutritional demands during pregnancy and hard training further exacerbate the anaemia. A constantly low iron level may be due to internal or external parasites, bladder infections, uterine infections, bleeding ulcers, and cancers.

In addition to the general symptoms and signs of anaemia already mentioned, these dogs exhibit a dry skin and coat, the toenails may be cracked, and the tongue may be sore. Examination of the blood reveals a severe reduction in Hb content and the red cells are small and hypochromic.

The diet should contain adequate quantities of meat and other iron-containing foods. Iron must be administered regularly until the anaemia is fully corrected. There are many satisfactory preparations of iron mixtures and tablets available. The motions are always stained black when iron is administered and this is a noteworthy point to avoid anxiety. In instances where iron cannot be tolerated by the dog when administered orally an iron sorbitol compound is available for intramuscular injection. An intramuscular injection of 2 millilitres should raise the Hb level about four per cent. Generally speaking, there appears to be a tendency for trainers to overdose their dogs with iron preparations. This may have harmful effects as too much iron can be toxic.

Haemolytic anaemia

This type of anaemia is due to increased destruction of the red cells. In some diseases an over-destruction of red cells takes place, resulting in anaemia which is referred to as haemolytic anaemia. Any process which reduces the life of the red cells can also be responsible for depressing the activity of the red bone marrow, vitamin B_{12}, and folic acid. One of the features of this type of anaemia, in contrast to other types, is that it is usually associated with a form of jaundice called haemolytic jaundice. Excess of bile pigment accumulating in the bloodstream causes jaundice. In mild haemolytic anaemias the jaundice may be slight or even absent as the body is able to deal with a small excess of bile pigment without jaundice developing.

The most common causes of haemolytic anaemia are severe liver disease, blood poisoning, leptospirosis, lead and warfarin poisoning, and enlargement of the spleen. The poisonous venom of some snakes also causes haemolysis of the red cells, as do sulphonamide drugs. Incompatible or mis-matched blood transfusions cause agglutination and destruction of the transfused red cells with jaundice. There may be a congenital defect in the red cells which renders them more fragile than normal and thus more easily destroyed. This disease is chronic and usually recognised in the pup, although mild cases may be missed for many years. Recurrent attacks of jaundice of the haemolytic type, with anaemia, are the predominant features and the spleen is usually enlarged. The diagnosis of this disease can be confirmed by performing a fragility test, when the abnormally increased fragility of the red cells will be evident. In severe cases the only effective remedy is to remove the spleen and so increase the life of the red cells and decrease the amount of red cell destruction.

(The function of the spleen as one of the main parts of the reticulo-endothelial system is normally to destroy worn out red cells.) An accurate diagnosis by the veterinarian is important and treatment is aimed at the underlying cause.

Haemorrhagic anaemia

As can be readily appreciated, any sudden acute loss of blood is likely to result in a reduction in the red cells and Hb. It may take several weeks or more before the body can replace this loss, depending on the size of the haemorrhage. Haemorrhagic anaemia may be a consequence of ruptured blood vessels, cancer growths, foreign bodies, abortions, and injuries which rupture the blood vessels and skin, permitting haemorrhage.

It is only when a sufficient quantity of blood has been lost that any appreciable anaemia occurs. In the majority of cases of acute blood loss there is also associated shock which calls for treatment. Generally speaking, the shock is caused primarily by actual loss of fluid from the circulation, which leads to failure of the peripheral circulation. When the blood volume is severely reduced the blood pressure falls, and if the fall is too great the vital centres are affected and shock results. Consequently, in severe acute haemorrhage, fluid is vitally needed to restore the blood volume and raise the blood pressure. It is also essential to replace the severe deficiency in red cells and Hb otherwise the tissues will lack oxygen. Ideally, transfusions of whole blood replace the fluid lost from the circulation, the red cells and the Hb. The pulse is very rapid and difficult to palpate owing to the low pressure and there is marked reduction in urine output in animals suffering from severe acute haemorrhage.

It is convenient to mention here that the condition of shock with low blood pressure may be the result of severe injuries without actual haemorrhage. In these cases transfusions with plasma instead of with whole blood may be adequate. In these cases, also, it is essential to correct the low blood pressure by transfusions, but plasma instead of whole blood may be adequate.

Chronic blood loss also gives rise to anaemia and in these cases the Hb is reduced more than the red cells because the red cells can be replaced more rapidly than the Hb. Carcinomas may give rise to chronic blood loss. The anaemia is treated by clearing up the cause of the chronic blood loss and by administration of iron to manufacture Hb. The red bone marrow usually replaces the red cells without special treatment.

Red bone marrow failure

Blood formation in the red bone marrow may be depressed by chemical poisons such as benzol or arsenic, or by drugs such as chloramphenicol, phenylbutazone, or gold salts. Chronic sepsis, rheumatoid arthritis, chronic nephritis, and uraemia are frequently accompanied by anaemia due to depression of blood formation. Overexposure to X-rays, radium, and some radioactive substances may give rise to very severe anaemia. Extensive bone disease may interfere with the marrow and so depress blood formation. In leukaemia great numbers of abnormal white cells crowd the marrow to such an extent that red cell fabrication is greatly reduced. Consequently, leukaemia always leads to anaemia.

In some instances the marrow may become atrophied, resulting in severe and often fatal anaemia, known as aplastic anaemia, which may be secondary to the drugs mentioned, infections, or X-rays. A primary type of unknown aetiology also occurs.

LEUKAEMIA

In leukaemia the white cells are vastly increased in number and appear in the blood in immature forms. Three types of leukaemia may occur, according to the type of white cell affected:
1. Myeloid leukaemia (polymorphonuclear cells).
2. Lymphatic leukaemia (lymphocytes).
3. Monocytic leukaemia (monocytes).

The symptoms of all three types are similar. It is important to understand that leukaemia is a disease of the cells, of unknown aetiology, which gives rise to a great increase in the number of the cells. Leucocytosis refers to an increase in the number of white cells, generally as a result of infection by bacteria, and is the natural response of the body to overcome the invading organisms.

The general symptoms and signs of leukaemia are:
1. Purpura (haemorrhages into the skin and mucous membranes) is common, especially in the acute forms of leukaemia. Purpura is due to a deficiency in the formation of platelets, normally formed in the marrow,

but which are crowded out in the same manner as the red cells.

2. Anaemia. Leukaemia causes anaemia because of interference with the formation of the red blood cells in the marrow, as the vast number of white cells in the marrow crowd out the red cells. The animal exhibits the general symptoms of anaemia such as fatigue and loss of energy.

3. The disease may be acute, particularly in pups when the entire course may last only a few weeks or months. In the adult dog it is generally more chronic.

4. Examination of the blood reveals a vast increase in the white cells. In some rare forms the white cells may not have increased in the peripheral blood, but examination of the marrow reveals that the whole increase has occurred in the marrow, causing it to be completely packed with white cells. This rare form is known as aleukaemic leukaemia.

Predominant features of the different types of leukaemia are as follows:

1. In monocytic leukaemia, the rarest of the three types, there is severe bleeding and swelling of the gums.

2. In myeloid leukaemia the spleen is enlarged and the lymph glands slightly so.

3. In lymphatic leukaemia the lymph glands are generally more enlarged than the spleen.

There is no complete cure for leukaemia. Some of the acute forms are rapidly fatal. In the more chronic types deep X-ray therapy to the lymph glands and spleen frequently affords relief and prolongs life. Many different drugs are available which exert a temporary effect on leukaemia, busulphan (Myleran) apparently being the best drug available for treatment of chronic myeloid leukaemia. Nitrogen mustards and mercapto-purine are also used. Chlorambucil reduces the size of the spleen and temporarily relieves symptoms of chronic lymphatic leukaemia.

Irradiation therapy is never implemented in acute leukaemia because it exacerbates the disease. Initially, blood transfusions are indicated. Remission may be induced with cortisone or prednisone but the remission is generally short lived. As yet, no animal or person with acute leukaemia has ever recovered.

AGRANULOCYTOSIS

Agranulocytosis refers to either the complete absence or a severe reduction in the number of granular cells. Leucopenia infers a reduction in the white cells which does not necessarily give rise to harmful results and it is stressed that it is not the same condition as agranulocytosis.

The usual cause of agranulocytosis is a toxic depression of the bone marrow which results in the polymorphonuclear, or granular, cells not being formed in sufficient numbers. The most common cause of this toxic depression is drugs, notably the sulphonamides, thyroid drugs, phenylbutazone, chloramphenicol, and gold salts. In view of the liability of these drugs to give rise to agranulocytosis, early symptoms and signs of the condition must be observed. A deficiency in the white cells means that there is a lowered resistance to bacterial invasion so that infection is liable to take place, especially of the throat.

The most common early symptom is a sore throat, which may be severe and accompanied by marked swelling and exudate. The temperature rises, the animal becomes lethargic and the pulse is rapid. Sore throat and fever in an animal on sulphonamides should immediately raise the suspicion of agranulocytosis. The drug must be ceased immediately until a white cell count is taken and the condition confirmed or vice versa.

Penicillin is usually administered by injection in order to combat infection that is present or likely to arise. Since penicillin is non-toxic to white cells it can be administered with safety.

11

THE ENDOCRINE SYSTEM

GLANDS

The salivary glands, digestive glands, sweat glands, and mammary glands are exocrine glands, or glands of external secretion, in the sense that their secretions are carried to definite areas by means of ducts.

The endocrine glands, or glands of internal secretion, have no ducts; their products are absorbed and carried all over the body by the bloodstream. Glands such as the thyroid, hypophysis, and adrenals are all ductless or endocrine glands. Some glands such as the pancreas, testes, and ovaries produce both exocrine and endocrine products.

There is a delicate balance between the endocrine glands and if one of the glands is thrown out of balance by disease, the other glands may become more or less affected. Some of the glands are directly inter-dependent while others seem to be only remotely so. For clarity the glands will be discussed one at a time.

The specific secretions of glands of the endocrine system are called hormones. Hormones act as chemical regulators for many important functions and even though produced in minute amounts, deficiency or over-production of a hormone can cause profound effects on the body. Hormones are organic substances produced as secretions of cells but they do not belong to any one class of chemicals; some are proteins, while others are steroids or amines. Many hormones have specific functions, for example, the role of insulin in carbohydrate metabolism. Generally speaking, hormones are the chemical regulators of enzyme systems and many of them play an important role in the regulation of growth and metabolism. The effects of some of the hormones are less obvious; they contribute to the personality, intellectuality, and physical ability of the animal. The part played by the sex hormones in the development and maintenance of the reproductive system is perhaps better acquainted with.

The thyroid gland

The thyroid gland is situated in the neck and comprises two lobes, one on each side of the trachea (windpipe) joined by a middle section called the isthmus. The cells of this gland produce the hormone called thyroxine, the main function of which is to control metabolism in the body. One of the main substances required for the manufacture of thyroid hormone is iodine. Excess of the hormone leads to a general over-activity of bodily function and produces the condition of hyperthyroidism. Simple (nontoxic) goitre or enlargement of the thyroid gland is endemic in some areas and it is believed that in these areas this type of goitre is due to lack of iodine in the water. This form of goitre is not associated with over-secretion of thyroid hormones and consequently no signs of toxic goitre (thyrotoxicosis) are present. Treatment consists of the addition of a small quantity of iodine to ordinary table salt or the use of iodised table salt such as that packed and prepared by Salpak Pty Ltd, the contents of which are:

Sea salt—98·98%
Sodium silico aluminate—1%
Iodine—30 P.P.M.

In some instances simple goitre may persist and eventually grow so large as to become unsightly, or it may cause pressure symptoms such as difficulty in breathing. It may become toxic in later life and there is also the possibility of long-standing simple goitre becoming malignant.

When swelling of the thyroid gland (goitre) appears in conjunction with over-secretion of thyroid hormone it is known as toxic goitre. Exopthalmos is the term used for the characteristic abnormal protrusion of the eyeballs which is often caused by thyrotoxicosis. In the presence of such typical symptoms as wasting, sweating, tremor, exopthalmos, and tachycardia (persistent excessive rapidity of the pulse rate) in conjunction with enlargement of the thyroid gland, the diagnosis is easy. A basal metabolism test is implemented in less obvious cases to confirm diagnosis. The amount of oxygen used by the body at rest is markedly increased in thyrotoxicosis. A small tracer dose of radioactive iodine may be used in diagnosis of the disease. The amount of iodine excreted in the urine is very low because the over-active gland takes up so much iodine. The converse is true in myxoedema, where the output of radioactive iodine in the urine is high.

Under-secretion of the thyroid hormone causes a lowering of bodily function. The juvenile or congenital form of this deficiency is a chronic condition due to congenital lack of thyroid secretion and there is arrested physical and mental development and lowered basal metabolism. Myxoedema is the adult or acquired form of this deficiency.

The anterior lobe of the hypophysis produces thyrotropin, which is the main regulator of thyroid function. The thyroid substance, in turn, appears to influence the hypophysis in addition to the adrenal glands and the gonads.

The parathyroid glands

The parathyroid glands are four in number and are situated behind the thyroid gland. The cells comprising these glands do not closely resemble thyroid tissue nor are they closely related from a functional aspect. The hormone produced by the parathyroid glands is called parathormone. The main function of the parathyroids is the regulation of the calcium and phosphorus content of the bones and blood. One of its functions appears to be the regulation of the excretion of phosphates by the kidneys. Calcium metabolism and the blood calcium level seem to be regulated indirectly.

To comprehend the changes that arise as a result of diseases of the parathyroids, it is essential to appreciate the part that calcium plays in the healthy animal. The main functions of calcium are:
1. Bone formation (a disturbance in the level of calcium can lead to improper development of bones and deformities in bones).
2. Control of irritability of nerves and muscles.
3. Involvement in the clotting mechanism of the blood.

The absorption and usage of calcium is regulated by parathormone, which regulates the flow of calcium between the bones and the blood. Withdrawal of calcium from the bones into the blood, resulting in soft, spongy, deformed bone

which is prone to fracture, is a consequence of excessive secretion of the hormone. Deficiency of parathormone leads to a low calcium level in the blood which causes a form of tetany. Vitamin D controls absorption of calcium from the bowel, the majority of the calcium absorbed going to the bones to aid in proper formation and calcification. Deficiency of vitamin D obviously leads to marked bone changes such as rickets and osteomalacia.

Phosphorus, largely in the form of phosphates, is widely distributed throughout the body, but approximately eighty per cent is found in the skeleton. Phosphates are obtained from foods and are eliminated largely by way of the kidneys.

Approximately ninety-nine per cent of the calcium stored in the body is in the skeleton, where it is found in the form of carbonates and phosphates. Calcium is absorbed from foods through the intestinal wall and eliminated mainly by way of the intestinal tract, though a small portion appears in the urine.

The adrenal glands

The adrenal glands are divided into two main parts, the medulla and the cortex. The two parts are distinct in origin and function. In man, the glands lie on top of the kidneys and may be termed suprarenal glands, but in the dog they are separate from the kidneys, and hence adrenal is the term preferred.

1. *The medulla*

The medulla secretes two hormones:

a. Epinephrine (adrenalin, adrenin)

The action of epinephrine is said to be sympathomimetic, i.e., it mimics the action of the sympathetic nervous system which, when stimulated, causes a rise in blood pressure, mainly because the muscles in the arterioles are stimulated to constrict; peristaltic movements of the intestine are inhibited; pupils dilate; bronchial muscle relaxes. The rate of breathing and rate of oxidation of carbohydrates is increased. These changes increase the animal's efficiency in a situation that may demand vigorous exertion in running or putting up a fight. In humans, they do the same but produce, in addition, the sensation of fear, thumping heart, hollow feeling in the stomach, etc. In humans, epinephrine may be secreted in situations which promote anxiety or excitement. 'The theory that epinephrine comes to the aid of an animal in an emergency was proposed by

Odious, the flying 24·4-kg bitch by Proper Prince out of Oddnik, hit the pinnacle of her career with a gutsy win in the 1976 Australian Cup—richest race in the southern hemisphere *(Courtesy of J. Coleman)*

Cannon and his associates. While the evidence is largely indirect, it does seem to indicate that many of the effects produced by an emergency situation are beneficial. Still, it is doubtful that the evidence indicates that epinephrine is essential for survival in an emergency. The theory, therefore, does not necessarily explain the function of the adrenal medulla. There is still some question that the adrenal glands play a primary role in enabling an animal to resist shock and stress, although this concept is seemingly well established.'

Epinephrine increases the blood supply to the lungs and skeletal muscles in the normal animal.

Epinephrine as a vasoconstrictor has numerous uses in surgery. The hormone reduces bleeding in surgery in which the larger vessels are tied off and the smaller ones swabbed with epinephrine to induce vasoconstriction. It may also be used as a heart stimulant and to cause a temporary elevation of blood pressure. Epinephrine also finds a use in the treatment of bronchial asthma because it dilates the bronchioles. Increased hormone secretion or an injection of epinephrine increases oxygen consumption and respiration rate because it increases the basal metabolic rate.

b. Norepinephrine (noradrenalin)

The chemical structure of norephinephrine is slightly different from that of epinephrine. It is primarily a vasoconstrictor and has little effect on heart rate but may cause a sharp rise in blood pressure. Epinephrine, as secreted by the medulla, contains minute amounts of norepinephrine. 'Cannon and his associates stated that, when sympathetic post ganglionic fibres are stimulated, a substance resembling epinephrine, but not identical with it, is liberated at the neuromuscular junction. They called the substance Sympathin.' (Norepinephrine.) Little is known of the function of this hormone.

2. *The cortex*

The functions of the adrenal cortex are difficult to define and it is not a simple matter to determine even a primary function since many organs and tissues are affected in various ways and there are numerous secondary effects. If the adrenal cortex fails to secrete its hormones, the functions of the muscles, liver, kidneys, and various endocrine glands are affected. Investigation reveals that animals with adrenocortical insufficiency are unable to withstand stress and that they are more prone to infections and to the onset of fatigue. The adrenal cortices are of vital importance.

Originally it was thought that there was only one hormone, cortin, of the adrenal cortex. Some twenty-eight compounds have been discovered, although many are not physiologically active, and

137

there is evidence of still more to be discovered. The various compounds derived from the adrenal cortex are steroids and therefore related to such compounds as cholesterol and the sex hormones. Two of the more important active corticosteroids are cortisone and hydrocortisone. These two corticosteroids are called glucocorticoids because they affect carbohydrate, protein, and fat metabolism.

Because these steroids control the processes of inflammation and allergy, cortisone is often prescribed to suppress excessive inflammatory or allergic reactions. Unfortunately, in most diseases in which cortisone is beneficial, relapse occurs when the drug is discontinued. If steroids are administered in large doses or for too long a period, serious side effects may occur, in particular, salt retention with subsequent oedema (swelling) and hypertension (high blood pressure). Cortisone-like substances have been synthesised which exhibit less tendency to lead to salt retention. Many such steroids are now available (e.g., prednisone, triamcinolone, dexamethasone) and their main use is to suppress excessive inflammatory or allergic reactions and though they do not remove the cause of these reactions, they relieve the effects, similarly as an umbrella keeps one dry but it does not stop rain.

Hydrocortisone, prednisolone, and other steroids are available for local treatment to relieve specific areas of inflammation:

1. Eye drops for acute, inflammatory conditions of the eye.
2. Sprays and ointments for skin conditions such as eczema.
3. Injections for rheumatoid or osteo-arthritis. The toxic effect of steroids include:
1. Salt retention, leading to swelling and high blood pressure.
2. Conversion of protein to carbohydrate, leading to an increase in blood sugar, which may precipitate diabetes.
3. Lowered resistance to infection, due to suppression of inflammatory reactions which normally afford protection.
4. Obesity, and thinning of the bones.
5. Adrenal collapse. The natural secretion of the gland is suppressed and the gland becomes inactive when cortisone is administered. Consequently, if cortisone treatment is suddenly ceased, collapse due to adrenal insufficiency is prone to occur. Steroid therapy must be discontinued gradually.

By far the most powerful of the mineralocorticoids is aldosterone, which regulates the sodium—potassium ion balance of the body. If present in excess, there is a retention of excessive sodium and excretion of too much potassium.

The adrenal cortex also produces the following sex hormones—androgens, estrogens, and progesterone.

Adrenocorticotrophic hormone (ACTH) is secreted by the hypophysis and it influences the development of the adrenal cortex and its ability to produce its hormones. When it was discovered that cortisone proved useful in the treatment of certain types of arthritis, the possibility of stimulating the adrenal cortex to produce its own hormones in larger amounts, by using ACTH to stimulate production of adrenocortical hormones, attained some importance.

The hypophysis (pituitary)

This gland is often called the master gland of all the endocrines because it exerts a regulatory effect over the activity of the other endocrine glands. The hypophysis is a small gland situated within the skull and is divided into two main divisions or lobes:

1. *The posterior lobe*

The crude extract of the posterior lobe yields pituitrin. Injection of this extract into animals causes:

a. a rise in blood pressure (a pressor effect).
b. contraction of uterine muscle (an oxytocic effect).
c. reduction of water loss through the kidneys (an anti-diuretic effect).

These major effects are generally conceded to be controlled by two hormones present in the posterior lobe. Fractions of the original extract have been prepared that accentuate the pressor or oxytocic effect under particular conditions. Vasopressin causes a rise in blood pressure of the anaesthetised dog but has very little effect on the blood pressure of the human. The word 'oxytocic' is derived from the Greek language and means 'rapid birth'. The oxytocic fraction induces marked contractions in the muscles of the uterus and particularly in the pregnant uterus.

Diabetes insipidus is believed to be a manifestation of posterior lobe deficiency which can be alleviated by continual administration of posterior pituitary extract (ADH, anti-diuretic hormone).

Investigation reveals that the secretion of the

posterior lobe arises in the hypothalamus and that there are two hormones—vasopressin or ADH, and oxytocin.

2. *The anterior lobe*

The anterior lobe produces the following six hormones which are well verified.

a. Growth hormone.

The growth factor in the anterior lobe secretion is not solely responsible for growth. Genetic and nutritional factors exert an important influence on growth, while hormonal factors largely regulate or modify. Basically, growth is indicated when there is protein accumulation in the body tissues. Increased nitrogen excretion is noted when there is a loss in body weight or when the body fails to grow. Injection of growth hormone in animals retards nitrogen excretion and is thus favourable to protein retention for growth. Daily injections of growth hormone stimulates skeletal growth in young animals, which have been made to attain unusual proportions by this means. The body proportions are different from that of normally tall animals. Growth in height occurs only as long as the growth zones in the long bones remain open. In humans, an excess of this hormone gives rise to gigantism in young people and acromegaly in older people. Lack of growth factor causes dwarfism.

b. Gonadotrophic hormones

Careful experimentation has enabled investigators to differntiate three gonadotrophic hormones of the anterior lobe of the hypophysis.

i. FSH (follicle stimulating hormone)

In the bitch, this stimulates the development of the follicle cells surrounding each maturing egg in the ovary. In the dog, it stimulates development of the seminiferous tubules of the testes, which produce the sperm.

ii. LH (luteinising hormone)

This hormone stimulates the development of the corpora luteum in the ovary. The combined action of FSH and LH is essential to the development of the ovum and to ovulation. After the ovum ruptures through the surface of the ovary (ovulation) the follicular cells, which previously surrounded and nourished the ovum, change in appearance and function and form a glandular body called the corpus luteum, which then commences to

function as an endocrine gland in its own right. LH is believed to stimulate development of the ovarian follicle prior to ovulation as well as to stimulate ovulation and to provide for development of the corpus luteum. In the dog, LH is more appropriately called the interstitial-cell-stimulating hormone (ICSH) because it stimulates development of the interstitial cells of the testes which secrete the male sex hormone. The inequality in the names LH and ICSH arose when it was believed that these were two separate hormones. It has since been discovered that these are identical hormones in either sex.

iii. Lactogenic hormone (luteotropic hormone)

The nature of the luteotropic factor in the dog is not known. In other animals the development of the mammary glands is stimulated by the female sex hormones, but, once they are developed, their secretion is controlled by an anterior pituitary hormone called prolactin, or the lactogenic hormone. Prolactin possesses a luteotropic action and, in addition to LH, it stimulates secretion of progesterone from the corpus luteum. Investigation reveals that removal of the anterior lobe of the hypophysis in young females results in failure of the gonads to develop; the animal remains sexually infantile. Estrus cycles fail to ensue, indicating that the ovaries secrete little or no estrogen or progesterone.

c. Thyrotropic hormone (TSH)

The principal function of thyrotrophic hormone is to regulate the secretion of the thyroid gland. Excessive amounts of TSH may affect other tissues, in particular the tissues surrounding the eyeball. It is supposed that this hormone is responsible for the exopthalmos associated with thyrotoxicosis.

The gonads

The gonads are the reproductive organs that give rise to the sex cells. The ovaries of the bitch produce eggs (ova); the testes of the dog produce sperm (spermatozoa). The gonads function as endocrine glands producing the sex hormones which exercise control over development and function of the reproductive organs.

Female sex hormones

Hormones are secreted by various parts of the reproductive system of the female and may be listed as follows:

1. *The estrogens or female sex hormones*

The estrogens are secreted by the ovary and of them estradiol is the most potent. The estrogenic hormones are so named because they possess the ability to produce the estrus (or mating state) in female animals. Estrogenic substances are not produced exclusively by the ovary; they may be obtained from the urine of both male and female. The urine of the pregnant bitch contains more estrogen than the urine of non-pregnant bitches.

The female sex hormones are responsible for the development of the internal and external genitalia, development of the mammary glands, cyclic changes in the reproductive tract and the female body contour.

2. *Progesterone*

The corpus luteum of the ovary produces a pro-gestational hormone, the active principle being progesterone. Gestation (L. Gestatio, from gestare: to bear) means pregnancy, and the progestational hormone is concerned with changes in the lining of the uterus that are favourable to the implantation of the developing embryo (the developing product of fertilisation of an egg) and thus to pregnancy.

Progesterone is apparently dependent on estrogen for building up the lining of the uterus after metestrus but then is able to stimulate the maintenance of the lining, once it is developed.

Placental hormones

In addition to the production of a gonadotropic hormone called chorionic gonadotropin, the placenta secretes estrogens and progesterone. The foetal membrane that forms the embryonic portion of the placenta is called the chorion. The placenta is the nourishing organ that provides for the exchange of food and oxygen between the blood of the mother and the blood of the embryo. It also provides for the elimination of carbon dioxide and waste products from the embryo.

Chorionic gonadotropin prevents the decline of the corpus luteum during the early stages of pregnancy. It is obtained from the urine of the pregnant bitch and forms the basis for various pregnancy tests.

Male sex hormones

Testosterone is the male sex hormone and it is produced by the interstitial cells of the testes. This hormone possesses great androgenic activity (masculinising effects). Androgens (steroids) are breakdown products of the hormone that retain some androgenic activity and they can be obtained from the urine.

Much of the knowledge of the action of the male sex hormone has been derived from the castration of animals. Castration of meat animals renders them more docile and easier to fatten and the meat is of better quality. The male sex hormone influences the development of the sex organs and the internal genitalia such as the prostate gland and the seminal vesicles. It is also responsible for the development of the male body contour and the deep bark of the male.

Androgens and estrogens can be obtained from the urine of either sex, but the estrogens predominate in the female and the androgens predominate in the male. The adrenal cortex is capable of producing both androgens and estrogens. The ovaries also produce androgens.

Thymus

The thymus gland plays an important role in young animals and then gradually undergoes regression, the lymphoid tissue being largely replaced by adipose tissue. It seems to play no part in adult life. The thymus secretes a hormone which prepares the lymphocytes for the produc-tion of the various antibodies necessary to combat infections later in life. Like other lymphoid tissue, such as the tonsils, it produces lymphocytes.

Summary

Generally speaking, it may be said that the activity of the endocrine glands plays a major role in determining the temperament of the animal. Energetic dogs with plenty of initiative may have slightly over-active thyroid glands. A courageous dog may owe his intensive living to his pituitary glands. Timidity and tiredness may result from insufficient pituitrin. Energetic, muscular, virile dogs often have over-active adrenals. The administration of cortisone has produced remarkable cures for arthritis and fibrositis but has sometimes caused marked changes in the character of the animal as well.

12

THE
REPRODUCTIVE SYSTEM

THE MECHANICS OF REPRODUCTION by Noel Banks

The canine species of which our greyhound is a part, is a placental mammal — divided into two sexes, male and female. Both male and female are equipped with glands of reproduction called gonads. The two gonads of the female are located in the ovaries and contain her eggs. The gonads of the male are located in his testicles and contain spermatozoa.

When the female puppy is born her ovaries provide the potential for the development of all the egg cells (oocyte) that she will ever possess. When these eggs become fully ripe, they are flushed into the fallopian tubes which extend from the ovaries, and into the two horns (cornu = horn) of her uterus.

Copulation occurs with a 'tie', necessary because the male dog has no seminal vesicles to store sperm. Prolonged copulation is needed for semen to be pumped from the testicles of the male into the vagina of the female. About 600 million spermatozoa are released during one copulation.

The number of eggs expelled from the female ovaries at one heat period usually is the number of puppies that result. These eggs remain in the fallopian tubes, and spermatozoa from the male, with little propelling tails, have to make their way from the vagina through the cervix, the horns of the uterus, and up into the fallopian tubes where the eggs are waiting to be fertilised. The first sperm to touch one of the eggs buries itself and a zygote is formed. When the eggs all have been fertilised, the remaining spermatozoa die and are expelled or absorbed by the female. The zygotes, these little one-cell puppies, then descend from the fallopian tubes down into the uterus. There, they attach themselves to the uterine walls where heat, food, and protection is provided for their development.

The embryos are not attached to the mother's nervous system and her blood does not flow through them. Every inherited characteristic they ever will have is sealed when the sperm first touches the egg. The only part of the mother plays from here on is to serve as an incubator for the growth of this separate organism.

THE MECHANICS OF HEREDITY

Many people think the study of genetics is so technical that it is beyond the comprehension of anyone except a scientist. This is far from the truth. The basic principles are quite simple and straightforward.

Chromosomes and genes

Let it be emphasised that characteristics of any breed are not transmitted through the blood. There is no such thing as 'blood kin'.

The reproductive germ cell of each dog is the building material for future generations. If we combine this building material, which has a built-in blueprint, and give it a proper environment, it will develop into the exact building which its blueprint and specifications call for.

We know what bricks, cement blocks, and so forth, are. They are the materials with which architects and builders construct buildings.

We now look at the building material our dogs possess. Each male and each female has thirty-nine pairs of chromosomes, a total of seventy-eight in each of their reproductive germ cells. Chromosomes might be called the crates or boxes in which the genes are located; the genes are the building blocks and material. Within these chromosomes are the genetic factors — and it is estimated that each chromosome has 150 000 genes — that determine characteristics of the organism's progeny. To be a successful breeder, we must know in what manner these factors are transmitted from parent to offspring.

Genes are contained within the chromosomes like peas in a pod. And, the chromosomes of the parents split apart like hulls of a pea. One-half of one chromosome from the male united with one-half of one chromosome from the female. Thus, half the genes from the male have been combined with half the genes from the female and that seals the new individual.

This does not mean the sire has emptied half of himself to be mixed with half of the female, but they each have given one half of their genes to produce the puppies. It could mean the male gave his bad one half and the female her good one half, or vice versa. It also could mean both gave their good halves or both gave their bad halves.

We already have noted the male has about 600 million spermatozoa at one service. Only one spermatozoa is needed for a puppy. Therefore, one batch of genes a dog might have received from his sire could be passed on to reproduce the puppy. In that case, the particular puppy could be more related to his grandsire than to the immediate sire.

Dominant and recessive genes

The nerve centre of scientific breeding is right here. We must know what is meant by 'dominant' and 'recessive' genes, how they manifest themselves, and how to sort them out.

A dominant gene is one of a pair of genes whose effects are expressed to the exclusion of the effects of the other.

A recessive gene is one whose effects are undeveloped, or buried, when associated with a dominant gene.

Fortunately, most of the qualities we want to perpetuate in our dogs are produced by dominant genes.

We referred to genes as building material. Now suppose we call dominant genes the bricks; recessive genes, the timber walls. Driving

Influential sire, Newmore King (Newdown Heather–Wondermore), one of the best imports to Australia *(Courtesy of South Australian Greyhound Trainer)*

142

through a city we see a home that appears to be solid brick but actually is timber walls covered with brick. Next door is a house of solid brick all the way. We would call this house 'dominant' and the other, the house of timber walls and brick, a 'hybrid'.

The scientific breeder knows how to select this foundation stock, how to cross and re-cross, and sort out the genes, eliminating recessives and building dominants.

Finally, he comes up with a puppy that is solid brick through and through. The timber wall 'recessives' have been cast aside. When he has a sire and a dam, both with solid brick 'dominants', and mates them, every puppy will be solid brick. This principle holds true in every trait of the dog.

The mechanics controlling heredity

Selection is the keystone of animal breeding. Our ultimate success or failure depends upon our selection. Don't forget what we have already learned. We are not selecting individuals. We are not selecting bloodlines. We are not selecting pedigrees. All these are indispensable in our process of selection, but we actually are choosing a deposit of genes. The one purpose in selecting brood stock is to increase the bank, or backup, deposit of desirable genes.

The quickest, most economical and potentially successful way for beginners to start is to find a person who has spent years building up the breed in which the beginner is interested.

The experienced breeder will advise starting out by carefully selecting a brood bitch. There are good reasons for this:

1. The bitch contributes one-half of the chromosomes which determine every puppy. Here influence on the puppies is exactly one-half. But more care must be exercised in selecting her than the male, because she produces such a limited number of offspring as compared to the male.
2. It is simpler to find a match for the bitch than vice versa, since males produce a comparatively larger number of offspring and it is, therefore, easier to judge the quality of their progeny.
3. The cost is considerably less. Inexperienced breeders sometimes pay a large price for a stud dog, then assemble around him a kennel of mediocre bitches. They usually stay in mediocre business. The wise breeder carefully and scientifically selects a brood bitch

(often for much less than the cost of a top stud dog) with a breeding deposit of genes he wishes, and then chooses a stud to match her. From there, he ruthlessly culls the offspring and judiciously selects each generation of breeding stock.

We have three courses of investigation to determine quality in the prospective brood bitch; the individual herself, her pedigree, and her progeny, if any.

Having selected a brood bitch and stud dog following the above-mentioned procedure, we probably have come up with a sire and dam that are closely related to each other.

Inbreeding in humans or animals merely doubles up what we start with. Let me make it clear that we do not breed related animals just for the sake of inbreeding, but to combine a sire and dam whose banks of genes match each other.

When the stud dog and brood bitch have a good reserve of the same genes, the chances are these genes come from the same individual or individuals listed a few generations back in the pedigrees. This simply emphasises the fact that producing puppies with characteristics decided by certain genes means those genes must be selected from ancestors with the desired qualities.

This further means we are defeating our purpose in breeding the brood bitch to a grandsire, first cousin, half brother, or uncle with few or none of the exact kinds of genes we desire. But it also means that if such an individual is heavily endowed with the genes we want, breeding back to him goes to the source of genetic supply.

You must isolate the genes put into breeding stock, with more and more 'good' genes and fewer and fewer 'bad' ones. Most of the qualities that dogs have on the outside are inside, too, in their genetic makeup. There are exceptions, of course, so take an individual who appears to have what you want and test breed.

You cannot breed too closely if ruthless and sufficient culling is practised. But without culling, inbreeding or linebreeding will have a disastrous effect. It is a two-edged sword.

If you mean business and stick with it, every time breeding results in unwanted characteristics it simply means these traits have been boiled up to the surface where they can be skimmed off and thrown away. And then you can go on with your breeding programme. With

Best Sun's pedigree is an example of line breeding, the double cross of Chief Havoc denoting that Best Sun is line bred to Chief Havoc. Best Sun came from last to win the 1965 National Sprint Championship at Harold Park, New South Wales, Australia. Derived from a prominent male line, Best Sun produced outstanding progeny *(By permission of W. Bracht)*

outbreeding, problems would have been swept under the rug, but they'll still be there.

Remember, if you cannot cull, you cannot succeed. 'Selection' means selecting the lesser desirables for culling as well as the most desirable for propagating. We use the following schedule as a formula for culling: at birth, six weeks, six months, twelve months, and finally at two years with test breeding.

—Noel Banks

THE FEMALE REPRODUCTIVE SYSTEM

The vagina, the uterus, the Fallopian tubes (oviducts) and the ovaries constitute the internal reproductive organs of the female. The female reproductive cells or ova (eggs) arise and develop in the ovaries; when they are mature they rupture from the surface of the ovary and pass down the Fallopian tubes to the uterus. If the ovum is fertilised during its passage down the Fallopian tube, the developing ovum becomes implanted in the lining of the uterus; if it remains unfertilised it breaks down and becomes lost in mucous secretions. The uterus leads into the vagina, the canal which receives the penis in copulation.

The paired ovaries lie on either side of the uterus and below the Fallopian tubes and are attached to the uterus by ovarian ligaments. The internal structure of the ovary is composed of a supportive connective tissue framework, muscle cells, blood vessels, and nerves. A delicate membrane envelopes the ovary. The ova develop within the ovarian follicle, the follicles developing under the influence of FSH (follicle-stimulating hormone) and LH (luteinising hormone) originating in the hypophysis. Mature follicles approach the surface of the ovary and rupture mature ova through the surface in the process known as ovulation.

The corpus luteum replaces the old follicle. In the period between ovulation and proestrus the corpus luteum secretes the hormones progesterone and estrogen, which apparently sustain the lining of the uterus. If the ovum is not fertilised, the corpus luteum begins to degenerate during metestrus. If the ovum is fertilised, it is probable that the production of gonadotrophic hormones, following implantation of the developing ovum, is responsible for maintenance of the corpus luteum. After the placenta is formed, it is capable of producing progesterone and estrogens and this is thought to relieve the corpus luteum of its function. The corpus luteum slowly degenerates and is still present in the ovary at the time of whelping.

The oviducts conduct the ova from the ovaries to the uterus. The distal ends of the oviducts, near the ovaries, flare out in a funnel-like manner. These funnels exhibit fringed processes called fimbriae which aid in guiding the ovum into the tube. The fimbriae are erectile and at ovulation they and the funnel move closer to the ovary to receive the ovum. The movement of the ciliated epithelium (lining exhibiting hair-like processes) which lines the tube and the smooth muscle in the wall of the tube, move the ovum along toward the uterus.

The thick-walled uterus is located in the upper pelvic region, its function being to receive the developing ovum and to provide protection and nourishment to the developing embryo after implantation. The uterus is capable of considerable enlargement during pregnancy, extending high into the abdominal cavity. The uterus is supported by the broad ligament and the round ligament. The lower section of the uterus is more cylindrical in shape and is called the cervix, this then opening into the vagina.

The vagina is a muscular canal lined with mucous membrane and capable of considerable distention. During intercourse the vagina receives the penis of the dog; a seminal emission releases sperm near the opening of the uterus. At whelping the vagina becomes greatly distended to form the birth canal leading from the cervix to the exterior.

A fold of membrane known as the hymen partially occludes the opening of the vagina of the maiden bitch. It may be torn at the first mating, but it is not regarded as a reliable sign of a maiden bitch.

The mammary glands are modified skin glands present in both sexes but which develop under the influence of female sex hormones. The glandular portion matures and becomes secretory upon termination of pregnancy. Prolactin, the hormone of the anterior hypophysis, stimulates and maintains lactation. The initial secretion of the mammary glands is a substance called colostrum, which contains nutrient materials. The composition of colostrum differs from that of milk. Following the initial secretion of colostrum, milk is secreted which is best adapted for feeding the pups. Cow's milk is sometimes substituted but it should be realised that its composition differs from the milk of the bitch.

The female reproductive functions are greatly influenced by hormones, this having been discussed in the chapter dealing with The Endocrine System.

The cycle of the bitch is generally considered to consist of four phases:

1. Proestrus

Vulvular swelling (swelling of the external genital organs of the female) and haemorrhagic discharge characterise proestrus. This period usually lasts from seven to ten days but may vary considerably. Microscopic examination of a vaginal smear will reveal the presence of certain cells which verify this stage of the cycle. The ovarian follicles exhibit swelling prior to ovulation. Secretion of estrogen rises and is responsible for the characteristic changes in the vagina and external genitals.

2. Estrus

The discharge is now straw-coloured and the external genitals, although swollen, are less rigid. During this phase the bitch will accept the male. The majority of bitches exhibit an estrus period of four to twelve days duration, but this may vary considerably and has been reported to have ranged from three to thirty-one days in some cases. Once again, microscopic examination of a vaginal smear will exhibit changes which verify this stage of the cycle. Estrogen secretion increases and the ovarian follicles, under the influence of FSH, grow rapidly. When the ovarian follicles mature, the correct blood estrogen level is attained and FSH secretion is suppressed and LH is released, resulting in ovulation. The uterus becomes more vascular and its muscle tone is considerably increased.

3. Metestrus

Generally speaking, this phase of the cycle is from sixty to sixty-three days duration. Changes in the uterus take place, with uterine glandular development being at its peak during the second to fourth week of metestrus. The corpus luteum regresses during metestrus if conception does not occur and the mucous membrane of the uterus begins to regress from about the fourth to the twelfth week and glandular secretion ceases. The external genitalia return to their normal size and the bitch ceases to attract the dog. Pregnancy follows fertile matings while non-fertile matings are frequently followed by phantom or false pregnancy (pseudocyesis) during which the mammary glands and reproductive tract develop as in normal pregnancy. There is a short term of lactation.

4. Anestrus

This phase constitutes the period of sexual quiescence and ovarian inactivity which may extend from two to eight months. The proestrus phase interrupts anestrus and initiates a new cycle.

Microscopic examination of vaginal smears reveals the presence or absence of certain cells which exhibit particular characteristics during each phase of the cycle and hence the veterinary surgeon is able to define each stage. The use of these smears to determine the most favourable time for mating has greatly reduced infertility. The study of microscopic examination of vaginal smears has revealed marked variations in the estrus cycle of bitches and may help to explain difficulties in breeding with seemingly normal dogs and bitches.

Bitches vary tremendously in the frequency with which they come into season. Generally speaking, greyhound bitches commence to come into season from the age of sixteen months onward. Sometimes the bitch comes into season as early as eight months old and in other cases the season does not commence until the bitch is two years old. Many factors determine the period when the bitch commences to cycle, namely, environmental influences, hereditary factors, drugs and/or chemicals which have been administered to the bitch. A six-monthly estrus cycle is most usual but the interval is longer in many bitches. With a few bitches it is slightly shorter, and it is inferred that there may be some hormone imbalance which requires veterinary attention. No bitch should be mated before she has properly matured and this usually means not before her second or perhaps third season. It is inhumane to breed from a bitch at

every season, one litter a year being best for the general health of the bitch, except perhaps in instances where only a small litter has been reared with little strain on the bitch.

The coming into season of a bitch does not infer that she has to be treated as an invalid. As in all animals these periods affect each individual in a different manner. Some bitches exhibit no distress at their condition, but rather seem to be improved by it. Highly strung, temperamental bitches may decline both physically and mentally while in season and so require careful attention. Preliminary signs that a bitch is coming into season are a liveliness in her behaviour and her willingness to attract male dogs by wagging her tail and teasing them by backing up her hind quarters to them. When the dog sniffs at her in the usual manner of investigation she will generally not disapprove. A few days prior to the bitch coming on season and her first gallop following her seasonal rest are usually the times that she runs her best race. The knowledge of the date of the previous seasonal period is valuable to the gambler. After five weeks the milk begins to secrete and all violent exercise such as galloping is prohibited. A moderate amount of walking is sufficient to maintain health. One may find it necessary to increase the amount of protein and decrease the amount of carbohydrate in the diet so that the bitch does not gain too much weight during this period. The bitch may be galloped twelve weeks from the first date of coming into season.

Bitches on season should be removed from the close proximity of male dogs, especially in racing kennels, as she may upset them considerably. Bitches will generally urinate more frequently during a season and this enables suitors to track her down easily. Male dogs exhibit often unexpected resourcefulness in reaching a bitch in season and consequently complete confinement is the most certain method of preventing accidental matings. Rules for greyhound racing provide that a bitch in season cannot be presented to race.

A bitch requires supervision, even following mating, until the cessation of her season as she may still be willing to accept males. Should a mis-alliance take place, the unwanted pregnancy may be terminated within 48 hours of the mating by a veterinary surgeon. If dangerous side effects are indicated, then the bitch should be permitted to have the litter. It is a false assumption that a mongrel litter will ruin a greyhound bitch's breeding career, as subsequent litters with registered stud dogs are in no way affected.

The owner of the chosen stud dog should be contacted the moment the bitch comes into season so that he may make the necessary arrangements for the service. Many stud masters prefer to board bitches for a few days to ensure that the service takes place at the correct time. The most favourable period for mating is usually in the vicinity of the eleventh to thirteenth day but successful matings have been recorded from the third to the twenty-fifth day. Observation is of the utmost importance as signs of the bitch's readiness to mate must be noted.

The usual gestation period is fifty-nine to sixty-four days. X-ray examination at approximately fifty days will reveal a positive diagnosis of pregnancy. An expert may be able to feel the pups in the uterus between the twenty-fourth and thirtieth day of pregnancy.

The general health of the pregnant bitch is of paramount importance. The bitch should be maintained on a correctly balanced diet with the addition of a reputable vitamin-mineral supplement. The bitch should not be over-fed and permitted to become obese. Exercise should be adequate but very light in the last three weeks of pregnancy. The bitch's teeth require checking and it is imperative that she be free from all internal and external parasites. Failure to rid the bitch of worms will result in infested pups. A vaginal douch with a mild antibiotic is desirable several days prior to whelping: this is carried out by the veterinary surgeon. The bitch should be transferred to her whelping quarters several weeks prior to whelping so that she may become acquainted with her surroundings. Newspaper serves as a cheap, suitable bedding which may be easily replaced. An infra-red lamp suspended over the whelping box, out of reach of the bitch, provides warmth during the first few weeks.

The actual whelping generally commences on the fifty-ninth to sixty-fourth day and occurs in three recognised stages:

1. A reliable sign that whelping is imminent is a drop in rectal temperature from the normal 38·6 to about 36·7°C. The bitch may pant, become restless, and make a bed by tearing up her bedding. This stage may vary from a few hours to 24 hours and it is desirable that the bitch be accompanied by a familiar person throughout the whelping as she generally will become more contented.

2. The second stage is true labour commencing with rhythmic straining. Usually a pup is produced within several minutes.

3. There follows a period of rest which may last up to 60 minutes. Pups are frequently whelped in pairs and there is usually a longer rest period between the delivery of each pair.

Veterinary advice should be sought if the first pup is not delivered within 5 to 6 hours of commencing to strain. No longer than 2 hours should elapse between delivery of subsequent pups. Advice should be obtained if the pups are more than three days overdue. The pups are normally born head first, encased in a membrane and with the umbilical cord still attached. The bitch will instinctively break the membrane and vigorously lick the pup in order to stimulate it; she will nip the umbilical cord. If the bitch fails to do this the membrane should be removed from the pup's nostrils and the cord parted, care being taken not to cause a rupture by placing strain on the stomach wall of the pup. The afterbirth is expelled following each birth and it is normal procedure for the bitch to eat the afterbirth, which she will probably vomit after the birth of all of the pups.

Sometimes the bitch may have difficulty in expelling breech births (the pup is positioned tail first) or very large pups and, if this occurs, veterinary attention is required or, alternatively, the pup should be gripped with a piece of towelling and gently pulled outward and downward in rhythm with the contractions of the bitch. A normal litter may take from 2 to 24 hours to be whelped and, if the bitch is resting quietly between contractions, no anxiety is warranted. At the conclusion of whelping the bitch should be offered a drink of milk and glucodin and permitted to lie quietly, allowing her pups to suckle. The pups should be checked for abnormalities and, if present, the pup should be destroyed. Following whelping the bitch should be checked by a veterinary surgeon and administered antibiotics to prevent uterine infection. Close attention must be afforded to ensure that she does not develop mastitis or milk fever (eclampsia), the two most common ailments following whelping. The bitch's temperature requires checking over the next few days to ensure that it returns to normal. A warm, well-fed litter of pups generally makes little noise; constant crying from the pups may indicate that all is not well. The number of whelps in a litter varies tremendously and most authorities agree that eight is the maximum a bitch should be expected to rear unaided.

Cleanliness, patience, and correct feeding are of the utmost importance, particularly for the pregnant bitch and during whelping. Often normally quiet bitches will become savage when someone attempts to handle the pups and consequently care should be exercised when handling pups. If necessary, the dew claws should be removed with sterile scissors when the pups are three days old. The pups are best confined to dimly lit quarters for several days after their eyes open. If the pups eyes are gummed up with a mucus discharge, they may be gently bathed with a saline solution.

The majority of pups are infested with roundworms, the eggs of which pass via the bloodstream of the mother through the placenta into the foetus. Badly infested pups will appear pot bellied, lean, and exhibit insatiable appetites.

A false pregnancy may occur, the bitch producing milk and undergoing all the apparent stages of pregnancy, even to going through the motions of having pups at the end of the sixty to sixty-three day period.

Some trainers have the heat period suppressed in the racing bitch, but the decision is often governed by the situation at a given time, e.g., the bitch may be in the middle of a series of heats, semi-finals, or final of a feature event. It must be borne in mind that chemical interference with the natural function of the ovaries may have consequences at a later date in regard to breeding prospects. Suppression of one season may prevent the bitch from coming into season for several months or years. Injection of male hormone derivative drugs, or drugs of a similar nature, are administered to suppress the development of the mammary glands and prevent the bitch from coming into milk. It is imperative that any such treatment be supervised by a veterinary surgeon. One must be thoroughly aware of the intimate relationship of the various endocrine glands and realise the dangers of indiscriminate use of hormonal preparations.

Varying degrees of anaemia may be the consequence of heavy blood loss during the heat period and hence the bitch should be permitted to recover fully. Trainers often spell their bitches for a short time. The mammary glands develop in the few weeks following the heat period and a watery fluid may develop, the bitch being said to 'come into milk'.

The breeder is often confronted with the problem of hand-rearing and feeding orphan pups, which may arise from the death of the mother or as a consequence of ailments such as mastitis or metritis or some factor which renders the bitch incapable of feeding her pups. Anyone with orphan puppies should make every effort to find and introduce them to a foster mother rather than undertake hand-rearing. It is essential that the pups receive colostrum, or mother's first milk, in the initial two days of their life, as the antibodies in colostrum enable the pups to withstand bacterial invasion. If colostrum has not been received, it is imperative that an antibiotic preparation be added to the formula to prevent ailments such as diarrhoea and intestinal disturbances. Pups that have not received colostrum must be protected from distemper as they will have no maternal antibodies to protect them. Vaccination at four weeks is indicated. Pups that have received colostrum should be vaccinated at four to six weeks.

The veterinary surgeon will advise the breeder as to the correct formula for orphan pups. The pups may be fed with an eye dropper, a doll's bottle, or a feeding bottle for premature babies, but as one may imagine this can be very time consuming. A special kit and instructions are available from veterinarians, which enables a litter to be fed a measured feed within a few minutes. This method is called gavage and consists of feeding by means of a tube passed into the stomach. A flexible plastic tube of suitable size is passed down the pup's throat to the stomach. The tube is attached to a syringe, the required food is drawn up and the end of the tube is passed over the back of the pup's tongue and down the gullet into the stomach. Gavage has the advantage, once mastered, of quickness and there is no possibility of the pup inhaling food. Irrespective of the feeding method, all utensils must be thoroughly cleansed and stored in appropriate solutions following each feed. After each feed the pup's abdomen must be gently massaged with cotton wool dipped in olive oil in order to stimulate urination and defaecation. Normally the bitch licks her puppies to encourage elimination.

The amount of protein in the milk of the bitch is $11 \cdot 2$ per cent of the total weight of milk and this accounts for the rapid growth of the pups during the suckling period. The total amount of protein in cow's milk is $3 \cdot 5$ per cent and consequently a pup fed on cow's milk would need to consume large quantities of cow's milk for rapid growth and this would result in distention of the stomach and pot belly. Food closely approaching the quality of the bitch's milk is required and there are products available for hand-rearing pups which are quite adequate. The temperature of the formula administered to the pups should be approximately 37°C. Some breeders supplement the mother's milk supply so that a large litter does not drain her milk supply and also in order that the pups do not pull her down unnecessarily. If the pup's nose is dipped in the milk it will lick it off and without much trouble will lap from a shallow saucer. During the initial three weeks of weaning, the pups require feeding four to five times daily and at this stage one cannot adhere to any definite amount of food. Some require more than others and the individual response of the pups is the best measure as to their needs. One must be on the watch for gluttons which prevent the smaller and/or weaker pups from gaining their share of food. Gluttons should be fed alone from a separate bowl.

The environment of the orphans is quite important and the temperature for the first week should be maintained at 29·5°, dropping to 27° in the second week and being progressively lowered to 21° by the end of the fourth week. The bitch is not there to clean the pups and consequently they and their bedding must be cleaned several times daily.

It is important that the pups be weighed at the outset so that progress can be checked in regard to growth and the amount of formula to be administered to each pup calculated accurately. Calculation of the daily intake may be made on the following basis:
First week — 20–25 per cent of body weight
Second week — 25–30 per cent of body weight
Third week — 30–40 per cent of body weight

The calculated daily intake is then divided by the number of feeds administered daily which, generally speaking, consists of four to five times daily for the first week, four times daily until three weeks of age, three feeds daily until approximately half grown. An alternative method of calculation of food intake is 3 millilitres of formula for every 15 grams of body weight per day, e.g., if the pup is fed three times a day it receives 1 millilitre of formula per 15 grams of body weight at each feed. Under no circumstances should one attempt to feed puppies without prior instruction in the correct technique. Obviously hand-rearing is a real burden and very time consuming, but the effort can be most rewarding when the pups are finally sold.

When the pup is about 5 weeks of age, milk should form the bulk of its meals, but some attempt should be made to introduce more solid food — Farex mixed with milk and Glucodin with a little powdered brewer's yeast added. Lean, finely minced beef may be given as a solid supplement to the diet. It is absolutely essential that the pups receive an adequate intake of vitamin D, calcium, and phosphorus. From three to four months of age the pup should be fed four times daily with an increase in the amount of protein, milk, and the addition of a reputable vitamin-mineral supplement. From four to six months is a rapid period of growth and the pup must receive a balanced diet of carbohydrate, protein, vitamins, and minerals. The amount of carbohydrate fed is dependent on the amount of exercise enjoyed by the pup. The more strenuous the exercise, the greater the fuel requirements of the pup in the form of fats and carbohydrates to burn in order to produce energy. Always feed as the growth rate and exercise demand. A dog pup at ten months usually weighs within a couple of pounds of what he will weigh at eighteen months, although his tissue, by conditioning and balanced meals, includes more muscle tissue.

Diseases of the female reproductive system
Vaginitis
Inflammation of the vagina is marked by pain and by a purulent discharge. Veterinary examination reveals an irritated hyperaemic (excessive blood in a part) mucous membrane. If a bitch exhibits vaginitis at the time of breeding, then the mating should be avoided. Potassium permanganate douches (1:5000) followed by infusion of antibiotic ointments generally proves successful.
Metritis
Acute or chronic inflammation of the uterus may result in infertility. Because of the absence of symptoms and the imperceptible nature of low-grade uterine infections they are often overlooked and the stud dog is frequently blamed for failure to conceive. The discharge during proestrus may exhibit no indication of infection. The history of the bitch and physical examination constitute diagnosis. Some uterine infec-

tions subside with uterine infusion of antibiotics during the proestrus, but it is preferable to miss the mating and breed at the following cycle.

Endometriosis

Ovarian endometriosis is the occurrence in the ovary of tissue resembling the uterine mucous membrane, either in the form of small superficial islands or in the form of cysts of varying size. Endometriosis may also occur in the oviduct, on the outside of the uterus, the bowel, the bladder and the umbilicus, as well as in less usual sites. Multiple lesions are usual. Macroscopically, the main centres of endometriosis are usually small puckered scars containing tar-like, blood-stained fluid. The pathogenesis of the condition is obscure. It may be due to growth of particles of the mucous coat of the uterus (endometrium) transported from the uterus through the oviduct or by metaplastic transformation, i.e., changes in the type of adult cells in a tissue to a form which is not normal for that tissue. Neither explanation can account for all cases and it is probable that more than one factor is involved in the formation of these lesions.

Habitual abortion

The expulsion of a dead or non-viable foetus at about the same period of development in at least three successive pregnancies may be due to improper development of the corpus luteum occurring during the fourth to fifth week of gestation. Habitual abortion due to premature regression of the corpus luteum occurs during the sixth to seventh week. Malnutrition, infection, and other debilitating conditions should be eliminated before establishing faulty development or premature regression of the corpus luteum as the cause. Replacement therapy with progesterone is indicated and administration should commence two weeks prior to the anticipated abortion and ceased one week prior to expected whelping.

Nymphomania

Exaggerated sexual desire in the female appears to be associated with multiple follicular cysts resulting in excessive build up of estrogen. LH (luteinising hormone) deficiency is the cause of nymphomania. LH may be administered and given a trial if the brood bitch is valuable, but removal or destruction of an ovary or ovaries is the treatment of choice.

Silent heat (absence of gross proestrual bleeding)

This condition is due to low estrogen levels at the beginning of proestrus and frequently delays mating past the most favourable fertile period. These bitches are fertile when mated at the proper time and the cycle is apparently normal. Proestral bleeding may be initiated with diethylstilbestrol. Examination of vaginal smears is preferable to determine the correct bleeding time and is preferable to hormone therapy.

Prolonged proestrual bleeding

LH may prove successful in alleviating this condition. Many of the bitches so affected exhibit marked variation in their cycles and are sterile, while others ovulate regularly and are fertile. The bleeding continues into metestrus.

Prolonged anestrus

This condition may arise in old or young bitches and has two possible causes:
1. Primary diminished function of the ovary.
2. Diminished hypophysis gonadotrophic function, mainly FSH.

Estrogenic or FSH hormones are administered to produce visible bleeding and swelling of the external genitalia. Alternatively, proestrus may be confirmed by microscopic examination of vaginal smears. LH's are employed following the beginning of proestrus to assure ovarian follicle rupture and release of the ovum or egg.

Mastitis

Mastitis is the inflammation of the mammary glands or breasts, usually seen when the bitch is in milk following the birth of the pups. It is commonly due to infection. The characteristic signs of inflammation are present, i.e., redness, swelling, heat, pain and impaired function. The mastitis may be accompanied by a blood-stained pus fluid. The bitch's temperature rises and she usually becomes lethargic, loathe to eat and loses interest in her pups. The effect of mastitis on the pups is of paramount importance and it may be the initial indication of the presence of mastitis. The pups weaken and become restless and agitated. They cry frequently and may die. At the very first indication of mastitis the pups should be removed from the bitch and hand fed. Veterinary attention is essential since the longer the condition is left unattended the greater is the likelihood of abscess formation in the breast.

Preventative treatment is most important in later pregnancies. The bitch may undergo antibiotic therapy prior to whelping and perhaps for a week after whelping.

Galactostasis

Mastitis should not be confused with galactostasis (Gr. galacto = milk, stasis = halt) in which the breasts become congested, hard, and painful as a consequence of engorgement with milk and not because of inflammation due to infection as present in mastitis. Because galactostasis is due to cessation of milk secretion and consequent abnormal collection of milk, treatment is directed at removal of same. Handstripping of the breasts or restraint of the bitch, while ensuring that the pups suckle each breast respectively, may be implemented. If the condition is left unattended, the nipples are prone to crack and matters will be further complicated by suckling. If galactostasis occurs following weaning of the pups or after a still-born litter, the condition may be relieved by regular massage with camphorated oil. If pain and congestion do not subside, veterinary advice should be sought.

Infertility

The low fertility rate achieved by many stud dogs is probably the fault of the brood bitch in many cases. Investigation by authorities reveals that the incidence of infection in bitches from which vaginal swabs had been taken over a given period was approximately fifty per cent positive. A proven brood bitch is an extremely valuable asset and it will never cease to amaze that many breeders consider mating their bitch without first having a vaginal swab taken. Many stud masters insist on the swabbing of bitches prior to mating with their stud dog because the sire's reputation and fertility rating is very much at stake.

Infected bitches may frequently be held responsible for infection of the stud dog. It should be noted that maiden bitches can be infected. The swabbing of a bitch to establish whether or not infection or pathogenic bacteria are present is most important. Infected bitches require treatment. In the latter stages of treatment the bitch is re-swabbed and if the sample is clear then she may be mated. Many stud masters are aware of the frequent incidence of infection in brood bitches, with the result that we may now observe such insertions as 'swab test necessary' and 'it is necessary to have your bitch given an interuterus antibiotic douche by a vet, before service date' and '$10 reduction on vet's certificate' at the foot of stud dog advertisements.

Neoplasms (new growths), physical deformities and inbreeding may also be responsible for infertility in the greyhound.

A PEARL OF GREAT PRICE by Noel Banks

In the commercial world of greyhound breeding, the following statement has often been made by an enthusiast becoming attracted to the sport of the greyhound: 'I decided to get a bitch pup rather than a dog pup as if it is no good for racing at least I can breed a litter and get my money back.'

What a fallacy! No doubt in a majority of these cases, a later mating would be effected with a currently popular sire, with thoughts of ready sale of the progeny uppermost in the breeder's mind, without due regard to the needs of compatibility of bloodlines, temperament, conformation, and, of course, a continuation of inherited inability in relation to speed or pace.

Perhaps the following article, although it was originally written in relation to another species of canine, is equally applicable to the practical and proper approach to those deeply interested in the reproduction of the greyhound.

A horse breeder once told me, 'A good mare gives more than half to her foal.' This was a knowledgeable man, a long-time successful breeder. I started to object — genetically the inheritance gift must be half. 'No,' he went on to say. 'At the instant that the egg is fertilised, they have each given one half, stud and mare, but from that point on it is the mare's own healthy body that nourishes that newly created life. At the instant of fertilisation that organism acquired its total potential. From then on realisation of that potential will be up to the dam.'

This is as true for the brood bitch as it is for the mare. Man, the breeder of record, will assume the responsibility only at some time after the actual birth, and if that responsibility must be taken very early in the young life, it is very possible that no matter how diligent the care, it will never provide what could have been derived from a healthy, temperamentally sound dam providing from her own body the perfect diet, warmth, and security.

The creation of a fine brood bitch must begin generations before the day she first whelps. Not only must she come from stock notable for beauty of form and movement, and stability of temperament ideal for her breed, but there should be also behind her generations of dams granddams who whelped easily, normally, and who nourished their litters without assistance, and who never slackened their attention to the cleanliness and safety of their broods.

151

Laziness and weakness in the whelping box, enough to make the surgical birth, caesarean section, necessary, and irresponsible maternal attitudes seem to be inherited. A bitch puppy whelped naturally in peaceful, comfortable surroundings, and given the proper care by her dam from the first anxious lick, seems also to be 'programmed' for performance of the same duties when her turn comes.

Modern veterinary medicine coupled with the know-how of the experienced breeder have today made it possible to save many a pup, even many a litter that would a few decades past never have lived to maturity. This becomes a mixed blessing for it enables us to preserve the constitutionally inferior animal and from it propagate a weakened strain. The medical skills that can save the strong pup from epidemic viral disease and accidental post-natal injury are far too often employed to preserve a life that nature has marked as inadequate for continuance of the race. That body beautiful brought precariously into this world and maintained here solely through human effort and against nature's will to eliminate the weak may well survive to pass many essential weaknesses throughout subsequent generations.

Trust a good bitch. If she has six strong, wriggling, greedy puppies filled with the unlimited urge to survive, fighting for their nourishment, thriving, don't be upset about that seventh one that she has shoved off into a cool corner to expire. If she has been handling her personal affairs up to this point suitably, assume she knows something you don't know. Let that one go! And that littlest one who can't seem to hang on to a tit—let it go! Many a tiny one is unbudgeable as is the biggest in the litter. Vigour and ability to survive is unallied with size, large or small.

Long ago in the eager altruistic early days of my dog-breeding experience it was a matter of pride to 'save them all'. And many a time I was successful. One little female that I remember especially had to be fed minute quantities of food every two hours. Because she had thus become very dear to my heart as a result of our great battle together, I gave her to a very good home. Within four months she had succumbed to the worst all-over case of red mange I have ever seen; she grew bald and scarred. I recommended euthanasia but her owners persisted with the most time-consuming care. At the age of two-and-a-half years, after finally achieving an orderly estral cycle, she kicked the mite and haired out almost completely, except for a few areas permanently scarred as a result of secondary bacterial infections. Very much against my advice they bred her. Slow, difficult labour produced two pups and a caesarean section the remained four, of which one was dead and another dying. Massive infections followed and ultimately one pup survived. A few months later the bitch did finally have to be euthanised because of almost complete paralysis from back trouble. Full and half sisters of this same bitch, out of the same dam, bitches vigorous and strong from birth on are the best whelpers, the strongest, fiercest, most infection-resistant members of my kennel gang.

Without details, I will say that something like this did have to happen more than once before I became a believer.

Now, when someone mentions a lot of trouble with a litter, I ask questions about a bitch's family and make a mental note to follow the reproductive career of the survivors. Far too often the sad story is repeated in varying forms.

The inherent weaknesses having to do with reproductive capacity express themselves differently in the male. The undescended testicle is one thing, the low or non-existent sperm count another. The breed as a whole is luckier than the individual proud owner when a terrific performer fails to reproduce himself. It suffers sorely when the constitutionally inadequate male that has been kept alive at all cost and raised to maturity because of his famous parentage and sheer external beauty does succeed in reproducing himself prodigiously. 'We didn't want to lose the bloodline,' may be the excuse. If that bloodline is essentially sturdy, this weakling will not honour it, and if not, chances are that this line is one that nature, if left to her own devices, would have cancelled some generations earlier.

There is a bonus benefit. Inherent constitutional vigour carries with it in both the male and the female the ability to resist infection, disease, and even severe parasitical infestation. The animal will flesh out and grow glossy coated with only a good maintenance diet, not requiring a superfluity of dietary supplements as it is able to extract the maximum available in the food ingested. It will adjust readily to extremes of heat and cold, thus it will require less artificial heating and cooling in the kennel. This in turn reduces chances of illness from changes of weather and temperature in the course of shipping and travelling. This healthy animal will cost you a lot less in time and money to keep in top condition and may even spare you the heartache of an early demise, with possible disruption of carefully formulated breeding plans.

So, if your bitch is beautiful *and* healthy, strong and natural in her breeding behaviour, talented in the performance of her maternal duties—trust her. Pick your winners from the healthiest of her offspring. Honour her—she will honour you—this pearl of great price.

—Noel Banks

THE MALE REPRODUCTIVE SYSTEM

Generally speaking, canine reproductive problems have been largely neglected and most knowledge of infertility in dogs has been gained by way of clinical observation and response to treatment in contrast to preplanned experimental design, utilising adequate controls.

Spermatogenesis takes place in the testes and is the process of formation of spermatozoa or mature male germ cells. A spermatozoon (pl. spermatozoa) is the generative element of the semen which serves to impregnate the ovum. It consists of a head, or nucleus, a neck, a middle piece, and a tail with an end piece.

The testicles are slightly flattened, oval bodies, each contained in its own half of the hammock of the scrotum, suspended by the spermatic cord, a collective term for the vas deferens and accompanying vessels, nerves, and coverings. When the testes migrate through the inguinal canal into the scrotum they carry with them the vas deferens, blood vessels, lymph vessels and nerves. From the abdominal inguinal ring to the testis these structures comprise the spermatic cord. The enclosing fasciae contain muscle fibres of the cremaster muscle. Occasionally the testicles fail to descend into the scrotum. Undescended testicles are almost invariably sterile, although they produce the male sex hormone. The development of fertile spermatozoa appears to be contingent upon the normal migration of the testicles, ascribed to the need for lower scrotal temperature (an average of 2°C lower than the abdominal temperature) required for maturation. When the dog is subjected to a cold environment, the testicles are drawn up close to the body by the action of the cremaster muscle; in a warm environment muscular relaxation permits them to lie deep in the scrotum away from the body.

The roundabout position of the vas deferens, which extends upward from the testes through the spermatic cord, through the inguinal canal, over the pubic arch and posteriorly over the urinary bladder to terminate in the ejaculatory duct, can be explained when we recall that the testes have altered their location.

The testes consist of a radiating mass of sperm-producing tubules, lined with germinal epithelium, which meet and join to form sperm ducts leading to the epididymis, a long, closely wound, coiled tube on the outside of each testicle. On their way from the testicle through this tube the spermatozoa undergo many changes necessary for fertility. The duct of the epididymis is continuous with the larger duct of the vas deferens which conducts the sperm away from the testicles.

The inguinal canal is a short, oblique passage approximately 30 millimetres in length which has an internal opening amid the muscles of the belly wall and an external opening which also issues amid muscles. The canal contains no cord in the bitch, but the round ligament of the uterus passes from the tip of the uterine horn down the canal and is directly attached at its lower end within the skin of the vulva (the region of the external genital organs of the bitch).

The seminal vesicles are lobulated sacs located at the posterior surface of the bladder and they secrete a fluid that forms part of the semen and which is thought to contribute to the viability of the spermatozoa. This fluid passes down a small duct into the ejaculatory duct.

The prostrate gland consists partly of glandular matter, the ducts from which empty into the prostatic portion of the urethra, and partly of muscular fibres which encircle the urethra. The gland is located below the bladder and anterior to the rectum and the base of the urethra passes through it. The lobules of the gland discharge their alkaline, somewhat milky secretion via small ducts which open by minute pores into the urethra. The secretion of the prostate gland contributes to the odour of the semen.

Two small glands about the size of peas are located in the bulb region at the base of the penis and empty into the urethra. These glands are known as the bulbourethral or Cowper's glands and they secrete a clear, mucoid fluid which is discharged when the dog becomes sexually stimulated. The majority of this secretion precedes seminal emission and it has been suggested that it functions to lubricate the urethra and glans penis as well as to neutralise the uric acid in the urethra before the spermatozoa pass through. A small amount of the secretion contributes to the seminal fluid.

The prepuce (foreskin) is a tubular sheath, lined with modified skin, which communicates with the exterior by means of a slit-like orifice. Within lies the anterior glans of the penis which is composed of erectile tissue and is completely covered by the prepuce when quiescent. The skin which lines the prepuce continues backwards to behind the posterior glans of the penis and is then reflected forwards and covers the penis like a cap, joining up at the orifice at the tip of the penis with the mucous membrane of the urethra (the passage for urine).

The penis is the copulatory organ of the male. It is attached to the ischial bones of the pelvis and is covered with skin that is continuous with the integument covering the scrotum. The body of the penis is composed of longitudinal columns of erectile tissue called the corpus cavernosa. Erectile tissue is composed of blood spaces, which ordinarily are not distended with blood, the penis then being soft and flaccid. Sexual excitement causes the blood to pour into these spaces faster than it can be drained away by the veins. As a consequence, the tissue becomes distended with blood, and the penis becomes hard. It is in this state that it is inserted into the vagina in the act of coitus (sexual union between individuals of the opposite sex). When sexual excitement has subsided, blood is drained from the erectile tissue and the penis becomes soft again.

The penis consists of an anterior and a posterior erectile glans. The posterior glans is termed the 'bulb' of the penis. The anterior glans is not as large as the posterior glans which enlarges markedly during coitus and causes 'locking', the greatly swollen posterior glans becoming trapped within the vulva by the contractile circular muscle which surrounds the terminal portion of the vagina. The penis of the dog contains a small bone called the os penis which consists of two narrow plates several centimetres long which unite dorsally to form a gutter in which the urethra lies, surrounded by the corpus cavernosum. That section of the urethra within the os penis surrounded by the corpus cavernosum is smaller in diameter than the portion behind the os penis and this is where bladder stones (calculi) generally become arrested and render the dog unable to pass urine.

Semen varies in colour from grey to milky white in accordance with spermatozoa concentration, the more highly concentrated semen being of whiter colour. The average pH (the measure of alkalinity and acidity) of freshly ejaculated semen is 6·75. The neutral point is pH7; above 7 alkalinity increases; below 7 acidity increases. Under clinical conditions the volume of semen ejaculated at one time by a greyhound is approximately 10 to 25 millilitres.

The dog ejaculates in three well-defined phases:

1. The first fraction has a water-like consistency, contains no spermatozoa, and comes from the bulbourethral (Cowper's) glands. The required time for this ejaculation is approximately 30 to 50 seconds and the volume varies from 9·25 to 5 millilitres.
2. The second fraction is white and viscous and contains the spermatozoa. The time required for this ejaculation is approximately 50 to 90 seconds and the volume varies from 0·5 to 3·5 millilitres.
3. The third fraction has a water-like consistency, contains no spermatozoa, and comes from the prostate gland. The time required for this ejaculation is approximately 3 to 35 minutes and the volume varies from 3 to 20 millilitres.

Approximately 10 to 20 seconds elapses between the voiding of each phase of ejaculation. Ejaculation generally ceases a few minutes prior to the dog being released from the bitch.

The concentration of spermatozoa may vary within the one dog on different days and among different greyhounds. The number of spermatozoa varies from 4 million to 540 million per millilitre, but the average spermatozoa concentration is suggested to be 125 million per millilitre. Following ejaculation there is a relaxation of the reproductive organs and general lassitude. Coitus is not necessary to maintain the reproductive organs in a state of good health. Healthy young dogs may have occasional nocturnal emissions which serve to eliminate excess accumulations of semen.

Infertility

A number of conditions frequently cause infertility in the greyhound.

Cryptorchidism

Cryptorchidism is a developmental defect characterised by failure of the testes to descend into the scrotum. The condition is readily palpable and is usually unilateral (monorchidism) and is perhaps a consequence of inbreeding. The condition may be inherited and the retention of a dog for stud work does not appear to be warranted if he exhibits monorchidism. Retained testicles often descend between three and six months of age and hence dogs should not be declared unfit for stud duties until eight months of age. Although affected dogs frequently exhibit reduced fertility they are not necessarily sterile. However, bilateral cryptorchids are sterile because high abdominal temperatures are not favourable to spermatogenesis. Owing to the likelihood of neoplastic growths (e.g., a tumour), the surgical removal of retained testicles is advisable. There is an increased risk of malignant change developing if the testicle remains undescended.

Orchitis

Orchitis, or inflammation of the testis, occurs more frequently than is diagnosed and may also involve the epididymis. Careful palpation will reveal any involvement of the epididymis and differentiate it from testicular neoplasms. Involvement often results in strictures. Orchitis may be responsible for lowered spermatogenesis. The disease is marked by heat, pain, swelling, and a feeling of weight. It may be the consequence of a systemic infection such as canine hepatitis or secondary infection of the urogenital tract, notably prostatitis, or it may occur idiopathically (unknown causation). Orchitis may be associated with trauma to the testicles and scrotum.

Treatment involves the use of systemic antibiotics and proteolytic enzymes. Rest and hot applications prove beneficial. Treatment should be continued for about seven days in order to eliminate the possibility of relapse and subsequent fibrosis. If the condition is not correctly treated at the onset, abscesses or fibrosis may occur, resulting in reduced fertility or sterility.

Testicular neoplasms

A neoplasm is an abnormal or new growth such as a tumour. Testicular tumours generally occur in dogs over five years of age and there are three main types of tumour. The transfer of cells of testicular tumours to other parts of the body not directly connected with the reproductive organs (metastases) is of low incidence.

1. Seminomas
   A seminoma is a solid testicular tumour derived from germinal epithelium which has not been differentiated to cells of either male or female type. The seminoma causes swelling of the testis and on section is pearly grey.
2. Sertoli cell tumours
   Sertoli's cells are elongated cells in the tubules of the testes to the ends of which the spermatids become attached, apparently for the purpose of nutrition, until they become transformed into mature spermatozoa. Sertoli cell tumours produce a feminisation syndrome and are associated with marked bodily changes. Because of the absence of the inflammatory reaction, differentiation from orchitis is not difficult. Careful palpation of the testicles reveals the neoplastic organs which should be removed as soon as possible.
3. Leydig cell tumours
   Leydig's cells are the interstitial cells of the seminiferous tubules (L. semen = seed + ferre = to bear: producing or conveying semen) and of the connective tissue partition of the testes, believed to furnish the internal secretion of the testicle. Interstitial cell tumours are relatively rare and are benign.

Prostate gland involvements

Involvements of the prostate gland may be categorised under three main headings.

1. Benign hyperplasia (common in heavily booked stud-dogs)

Benign hyperplasia is the abnormal multiplication or increase in the number of normal cells in normal arrangement in a tissue and is not malignant. The major complications of this disease are acute or chronic retention of urine with or without superimposed infection. Obstruction to urinary outflow comes about most commonly as a result of the benign enlargement of the prostate which leads to stretching and narrowing of the prostatic urethra so that it becomes increasingly difficult for the bladder to empty. The bladder is capable of enormous dilatation to accommodate accumulating urine but, being a muscular organ, its wall will also undergo considerable hypertrophy so that when it is empty, after the urine has passed, the wall will be seen to be very thick and the inner muscular trabeculae will be prominent. If the bladder is unable to effectively compensate for the obstruction, the urine accumulates in the ureters and the pelves of the kidneys. Since these parts have relatively little smooth muscle they will dilate early, leading to the states of hydroureter (abnormal distention of the ureter with urine) and hydronephrosis (distention of the pelvis and calyces of the kidneys with urine as a result of obstruction of the ureter). With increasing degrees of hydronephrosis, the functional elements of the kidney become increasingly stretched, and its blood supply increasingly obstructed, so that fibrous tissue develops to replace the damaged nephrons (replacement fibrosis). The kidney thus becomes progressively less able to excrete urine and ultimately renal failure follows. This result of urinary obstruction is complicated in many instances by infection which is very liable to occur whenever urine becomes stagnant in the urinary tract.

Various degrees of hyperplasia may be observed and treatment as indicated for orchitis is implemented, in addition to massage of the gland, and the administration of small dosages of estrogenic hormones. Investigation reveals that the condition appears to be associated with excessive quantities of male hormone because of the fact that the administration of estrogens (the treatment of choice if the affected male is a stud dog) or the excision of one or both testes (orchiectomy) reduces the size of the gland. The pain associated with the enlargement of the prostate gland may cause the dog to be very reluctant to copulate.

Excessive quantities of estrogens reduce fertility and may actually cause enlargement of the prostate gland; consequently correct dosage is of vital importance. Diethylstilbestrol is the drug usually administered. It is an estrogenic compound which exhibits estrogenic activity similar to, but greater than, that of estrone (an estrogenic steroid). It may be necessary to maintain affected animals on a low maintenance dose of approximately 1 to 2 milligrams weekly following the initial dosage, which is aimed at regression in size of the gland.

2. Prostatitis (inflammation of the prostrate gland)

All of the characteristics of inflammation are present and the prevention of the spread of infection to adjacent structures is of the utmost importance. Pain diminishes the sexual drive of the affected dog and the quality of the semen is reduced. Various degrees of hyperplasia may be observed. Treatment is as indicated for orchitis. Massage of the gland and administration of

small doses of estrogenic hormones are warranted.

2. Neoplasms (new growths)

A neoplasm consists of a mass of cells which have undergone some fundamental and irreversible physiological modification which leads to continual, apparently unrestrained, proliferation. The rate of growth of neoplasms varies considerably. The expansible growth leads to compression of nearby structures and may seriously interfere, in one way or another, with normal bodily functions and should consequently be removed as early as possible. The tumour may be benign or malignant, the distinguishing features being as follows:

Benign

Remain localised.
Grow slowly.
Frequently has a capsule.
Closely resemble the cells of origin.
Cells are uniform in size and appearance.
Degenerative changes are relatively uncommon.
Mitotic figures are rare.

Malignant

May metastasise.
Grow more rapidly.
Capsules are rare and incomplete.
Less similar to the cells of origin and, in some instances, totally differentiated.
Cells vary in size and appearance.
Degenerative changes are relatively common.
Mitotic figures are frequent.

The distinction between neoplasms and other conditions which give rise to tissue hyperplasia is not easy. Neoplastic growth involves a fundamental cellular change and is an automatic process which, once started, is independent of the continued presence of the initially provocative agent in contrast to other hyperplastic masses which will cease to grow and may regress on removal of the stimulus responsible for the hyperplasia.

Balanitis (inflammation of the glans penis)

Balanitis is the inflammation of the glans penis and is usually associated with phimosis, or tightness of the foreskin, so that it cannot be drawn back from over the glans. Posthitis, or inflammation of the prepuce, may also be present. Balanoposthitis may be indirectly blamed for infertility because of the pain associated with copulation. The condition is characterised by a greenish-yellow discharge from the prepuce. Specific gangrenous and ulcerative balanoposthitis is marked by ulcerations and some times by gangrene and is caused by a spirochete (a spiral-shaped bacterium).

Because the affected dog will almost always endeavour to lick and clean himself, a close watch must be kept on the genital organs. The condition may become chronic and pass undetected until such time as it affects the general health of the dog. It is well to remember that the dog cleans himself by licking his genitals and that it is a natural habit. Unfortunately, the causative micro-organisms are consequently conveyed to the stomach. The discharge may appear on the inside of the thighs during the time that the dog is lying asleep.

Effective treatment usually involves irrigation of the prepuce with potassium permanganate (1:5000) followed by local instillation of antibiotics such as neomycin, polymyxin, or streptomycin. Increase in the severity of the symptoms of this condition is quite common and elimination is prevented because the dog continues to exercise the natural habit of licking himself.

Impotence

Impotence is the lack of virility or copulative power. This problem may be the consequence of an increase in the body weight of the dog, which is beyond the limitation of his skeletal and physical requirement, as the result of an excessive accumulation of fat in the body. Other factors which may result in impotence include lack of sufficient exercise, malnutrition, and poor general health. Strange surroundings may render the dog shy and authorities have discovered that, if animals must be transported to a strange environment, then bitches will generally adjust better than dogs. Some dogs become quite shy at the time of mating and manual assistance may be necessary or it may be found that the dog does better if left alone in a familiar environment with the bitch.

Although production of semen may be essentially normal, the reproductive activity is limited to such an extent as to render the affected males infertile in actual practice. Older stud dogs may be unable to copulate as a consequence of feebleness due to age. In such cases artificial insemination has proven extremely valuable but this method is not advised with males unable to mate because of inherited abnormalities. Small doses of testosterone (1 to 5 milligrams) afford results in 12 to 36 hours with stud dogs incapable of exhibiting erection. This, however, is prohibited in Australia.

Cysts

Cystic swellings may present in association with the testis and epididymis. A hydrocele is a circumscribed collection of fluid within the tunica vaginalis of the testis, the wall of which is thickened by fibrous tissue and may contain a few inflammatory cells. Some hydroceles may be a consequence of inflammation but the cause of most hydroceles remains obscure.

Cysts lined with flattened epithelium and containing clear fluid, in which spermatozoa may be identified, may also present in association with the epididymis. These cysts are frequently called spermatoceles because of the presence of spermatozoa.

The spermatic cord may undergo voluntary torsion (twisting) which occurs without external influence and which results in venous infarction. Venous infarction is an area of death in a tissue produced by sudden arrest of circulation in a vein.

Wasting of the testes, whether due to primary testicular failure or as a result of pituitary failure, frequently results in sterility.

CARE OF THE STUD DOG

The care and attention afforded the stud dog is of utmost importance and is equally as essential as that given to a top-grade racing greyhound. A good stud dog is a particularly valuable possession and should be maintained in the best possible condition whether or not in present demand. Patience and understanding, particularly with a young stud dog, are important. Feeding, exercising, grooming, medication, and punctuality all follow the same lines as training a racing greyhound. However, care must be taken not to overwork the dog. If the dog is not in demand as often as might be expected, he may tend to gain weight. This should be avoided as obesity will only serve to make the dog lazy and reduce his stud value. A stud dog which is confined to cramped quarters and which receives irregular exercise cannot be expected to possess the vitality which a well-cared-for stud dog will display. Regularity in all aspects of his maintenance is essential.

Time being a valuable commodity to the stud master, sound planning of the various routines involved in owning a stud dog is essential. There is no doubt that the intelligent application of management of stud duties enhances the value and work of the studmaster in the greyhound industry and to his stud dog almost immeasurably. As skill is acquired in various techniques of handling a stud dog, so the amount of time spent begins to assume manageable proportions, but the mating of the stud dog and the brood bitch should not be approached as a haphazard affair. A well-run stud is a smoothly busy, well-organised concern. To rely on cancellations or failure to keep an appointment to provide requisite opportunity to perform duties will usually result in failure in any business.

In order to 'sell', the stud dog must not only be functional but must also exhibit an attractive appearance. The dog must not only be able to 'do the job' for which he has been selected, but must also appeal to owners and handlers of prospective bitches to be mated. People gain satisfaction from using a dog which has an attractive appearance. In addition to the inherent utility of the dog himself, and the appeal made in the form of advertising and direct effort the dog must be attractively packaged. Poor general appearance of the stud dog and his quarters will soon deter prospective customers. The kennelling for the stud dog is the same as that described for the racing greyhound. As with racing greyhounds, adequate security must be provided to ensure that the dog is unable to escape from his quarters or injure himself, and that he is not interfered with. The kennel should be padlocked.

Generally speaking, greyhounds are not retired to stud until they are three years of age or more unless the dog has met with an accident which terminated his racing career. Regulations limit the services of the stud dog to fourteen matings per month. If the dog has had to serve a difficult bitch, it is advisable to allow him about two days rest before serving another bitch. Some bitches are extremely difficult to mate and the dog may become exhausted before he is able to serve her. Most authorities agree that it is preferable to have the dog serve the bitch in the morning, or, in hot weather, in the evening when it is cooler. Following completion of the service the dog should be returned to his quarters to rest. He should be exercised that evening and then be bedded down.

It is advisable to turn down a service, if need be, in both the interests of the studmaster and the stud dog. The dog then has time to recover his vitality and the owner of the bitch has sufficient time to book his bitch in to another stud dog as well as preventing the risk of a poor mating.

It is advisable to contact the stud master as soon as the bitch comes on season so that arrangements may be made. Most stud masters prefer bitches to be brought or sent to their kennels a few days prior to the actual date of service so that she may settle down. The stud dog is generally the best judge of time of service. No one except the studmaster and, if necessary, the owner or handler of the bitch, should be present at the mating. The number of services performed each week depends on the bitches to be served and to a large degree on the condition of the stud dog. It is advisable for stud dogs to be rested from all stud duties for six weeks per year.

The actual racing performance of a particular dog is not the essential factor in breeding; the importance lies in the ability of certain lines of dogs to consistently breed winners. It is of vital significance to realise that the mating of two champion greyhounds does not necessarily produce champion offspring. It is of value not only to study the brood bitch herself but also preceding generations. A bitch should be chosen which exhibits lines that have consistently thrown above-average offspring or offspring which are equivalent to or better than herself. The same applies to the stud dog.

Authorities have discovered that the mating of an unraced or lightly raced litter sister of a successful racing bitch frequently proves advantageous. Available evidence points to the theory that although a champion bitch may produce a few litters while still continuing to race, those offspring are seldom as successful as their mother. In most cases it has been wiser to choose a bitch which has won half-a-dozen good class races and has then been retired to stud.

Every stud master's intention is to achieve 100 per cent conception rate and to do this it is necessary to refuse bitches with a history of difficulty in breeding and to consider the medical and mechanical factors involved. Factors involving the bitch to be served which are due careful consideration are as follows:
1. Blood lines.
2. Breeding record of the bitch — non-conception, average number of pups per litter, number of litters, mortality rate of the pups, difficult whelpings.
3. Seasonal information — period between seasons, duration of season, induced season,

abnormal discharges, difficulty with seasons.
4. General health of pups produced — size and number.
5. General health of the bitch.
6. Proven breeding record of stock.
7. Conformation.
8. Temperament.

Experimentation by authorities has revealed that the volume, density, and mobility of the semen of the dog deteriorate following eight consecutive days of ejaculation. Semen maintains a good quality if the dog ejaculates only two to three times per week. More frequent usage of the stud dog over prolonged periods results in the production of semen which is of inferior quality.

The number of bitches served by a registered sire must not exceed fourteen in any one calendar month. If a registered sire fails to produce more than ten reported litters from each twenty bitches served the studmaster must, at his own expense, upon being notified by the N.C.A., present the sire to a professional person so that a veterinary test may be carried out. The N.C.A., may suspend the registration of services from the date of notification to the studmaster until a satisfactory test has been reported to the N.C.A. If the N.C.A. is not satisfied with the results of the test, it may, following a further test at the end of a specified period, suspend the stud registration of the greyhound for such period as it thinks fit, or indefinitely. The N.C.A. has the unrestricted right to publish the number of services by any registered sire and the number of litters produced from such services.

On the production of a bitch for mating with a registered sire, it is the duty of the studmaster to demand the registration certificate of the bitch and compare the identification particulars thereon with the bitch produced for service. Where the person producing a bitch for service is not the person shown on the registration certificate of the bitch as the registered owner, such person is required by the stud master to supply an authority signed by the registered owner, giving permission for the bitch to be mated.

All services by registered sires must be by natural methods and the impregnation of bitches by means of artificial insemination is prohibited.

The distinguishing characteristic of a stud business is that it is motivated primarily for the desire of profit, and accompanied by the risk of loss. If the goal is not profit, the activity is not a business one. Satisfaction of service, achievement of personal independence and of commanding the respect of colleagues and clients in the greyhound industry are of paramount importance.

ARTIFICIAL INSEMINATION

Barry Ward became involved with stud dogs six years ago when he imported Cheers For Akii and Agry from Ireland. Both stud dogs sired classic winners in their first crop and this initial success must have increased Barry Ward's credibility as far as Australian breeders were concerned as most of his later imports were well received and well patronised on their arrival in Australia, the one exception being Weston Pete, who was virtually ignored by breeders.

Over the past six years he has established one of the leading greyhound studs in Victoria and he credits his success to an unshakeable belief in Irish bloodlines. At his Cranbourne kennels Barry Ward offers breeders the largest selection of imported Irish sires at any stud in Australia. He stands seven Irish imports at stud and five of these have won classic track events in England or Ireland; they are Ballybeg Prim, Shamrock Point, Ashleigh Honour, Leaders Champion, and Weston Pete. This is the largest number of greyhounds that have won track classics in the British Isles standing at the same stud anywhere in the world.

After becoming involved with stud dogs Barry Ward became interested in artificial insemination which had been outlawed in Australia as far as greyhound breeding was concerned in the mid-fifties. After consulting several of Victoria's leading vets and reading everything he could get on the subject, the studkeeper was convinced that artificial insemination offered many advantages over natural servicing.

About three years ago Barry Ward set out to gain approval to use his stud dogs for AI — a venture that seemed to have no chance of success from the outset. There was considerable opposition to AI from most areas of the sport but Barry Ward was of the opinion that this was because breeders were misinformed. They were generally not aware of the advantages and he felt the objections put up by opposing factions were completely illogical.

He commenced his lone campaign to have AI legalised by writing to greyhound publications

Ballybeg Prim (Rockfield Era–Ballybeg Pride) 1975 Irish Greyhound of the Year *(Courtesy of Barry Ward)*

throughout Australia, listing the advantages of the artificial method and pointing out that the major objection of malpractice also applied to natural servicing. Gradually many breeders started to change their opinion concerning AI, but Ward's campaign never gathered momentum until the G.O.T.B.A. of Victoria got behind AI and finally applied to the National Coursing Association of Victoria to have artificial insemination legalised.

Following the annual conference of the Australian and New Zealand Greyhound Association in Auckland, New Zealand, in October 1980, Barry Ward applied to the National Coursing Association of Victoria to have three of his sires approved for servicing by artificial insemination. In February 1981 permission was granted and Ward became the first studmaster to gain approval for AI, enabling this valuable breeding aid to be used legally for the first time in Australia for nearly thirty years. Today Barry Ward restricts the services of his four oldest stud dogs, Ballybeg Prim, Cheers For Akii,

Leaders Champion, and Shamrock Point, entirely to the artificial insemination technique.

PROBLEMS CONFRONTING THE INTRODUCTION OF AI INTO AUSTRALIA
by Barry Ward

Within the past twelve months the progressive Australian Trotting Council has approved the use of AI for the trotting industry, and the Irish Coursing Club is currently investigating the advantages offered by the introduction of artificial insemination, but still Australian greyhound breeders are deprived of the legal use of this valuable mating and breeding technique.

AI has been used successfully with humans where conception has not been possible by natural methods, and AI has been used to overcome breeding problems in practically every breed of domestic animal on earth. I have spoken to veterinarians, breeders, and studmasters and I have yet to find one person that is able to give one logical reason why AI should not be legalised; in fact, logic overwhelmingly supports the usage of artificial insemination.

Breeders who do not support AI tend to reject its acceptance on one or more of three 'imagined disadvantages which can basically be described as split servicing, malpractice, and loss of nervous energy; however, each objection is illogical.

1. Split servicing has been condemned in greyhound breeding on the false premise that it would enable a popular sire to be used excessively and dominate breeding to the extent that future generations would be saturated with his bloodlines. However, the rule restricting a stud dog to fourteen bitches per month renders this situation impossible. Split servicing is, in fact, probably the most important (and misunderstood) advantage of AI.

2. Malpractice. It has been expressed that AI lends itself to 'cheating'. This claim is quite ludicrous. The integrity of studmaster and breeder is the ingredient that determines malpractice and, should the situation exist where skullduggery is likely, this would occur with either natural servicing or AI.

3. Nervous energy. Some breeders claim that AI removes the transfer of nervous energy from sire to progeny. They claim that nervous energy is the element that passes on the desire to chase and the natural mating instinct. Modern research in the equine field has proven that this is complete nonsense. The elements that determine nervous energy are still transmitted through AI. No matter how the sperm reaches the ovum, nervous energy is transmitted at the time of conception.

It is completely unnatural for a greyhound to have to perform fourteen services consistently every month. The demands placed on our leading studs are enormous; no other member of the canine species (show-ring, working, or gun dogs) ever has to cope with such a gigantic workload, apart from the greyhound. The stud dog that is able to adequately cope consistently with fourteen natural services every month is indeed a rare animal. His sperm count cannot be maintained at optimum level when performing matings at least every alternate day. Continual use at this rate must result in reduced sperm motility.

Some sires have been criticised for not possessing the natural instinct to mate. I have yet to see one. Admittedly the sexual drive in greyhounds varies, as it does in humans. Greyhounds that are recognised as poor servers generally have a low sexual drive and in many cases are grossly overworked. Others recognised as non-servers or completely lacking the mating instinct generally have suffered a mishap or injury at one of the mating attempts early in their stud career and generally at the hands of an inexperienced person. (How would you front up the second time if at the first attempt your partner dragged you around the paddock by your appendage or, alternatively, if it was almost removed by gnashing teeth?) Other non-servers are generally suffering from a hormone imbalance.

For this reason the benefits of artificial insemination to the practical breeder are immeasurable and include the following:

1. With AI, bitches can be mated at the correct time. With a stud dog that is heavily booked there are numerous occasions when bitches booked two days apart ovulate simultaneously. In these instances split-servicing enables both bitches to be served at the right time, greatly increasing the chance of both bitches conceiving and having reasonable-sized litters.

2. With split-servicing, a stud dog can perform his fourteen matings per month and greatly reduce his workload. The benefit to the breeder is that the bitch can be mated at the right time and the dog's sperm count is not depleted, thus providing a far greater conception rate than is possible to attain under present regulations. The average conception rate in greyhound breeding throughout the world is about sixty-five per cent; this would increase dramatically if AI was legalised.

3. With AI, the conception rate is further increased because all of the semen is distributed directly into the uterus. With natural matings the majority of semen never reaches the uterus and is wasted.

4. AI eliminates the risk of transferring infection from the dog to the bitch or vice versa.

5. Some maiden bitches have abnormally small vaginal passages and even with repeated dilation it is a physical impossibility to effect a proper mating. If a 'tie' could be effected in these circumstances, it would be a most traumatic experience for the bitch, with the risk of severe injury to both bitch and stud dog. This type of mating is a simple matter with AI.

6. With AI, matings can be easily effected between timid and shy partners. (With AI, the Taylors would not have lost their brood bitch, Renoka.)

7. It is possible with AI in many cases to inseminate a bitch with a stricture, adhesion, or growth in the vaginal passage. This should only be done on veterinary advice and the breeder should be prepared for a caesarean birth.

8. Stud dogs that are fully booked understandably become selective and at times refuse certain bitches. This problem is eliminated with AI.

9. There have been cases where heavily booked stud dogs have been treated with sex hormones to give them sufficient desire to continue serving naturally. This treatment invariably sends the dog infertile and the breeder is prematurely deprived of what is normally a very popular sire. This situation would not occur if AI was legalised.

10. The introduction of AI could mean that it was possible to obtain semen from Ireland's greatest sires directly, rather than via their unproven offspring. Imagine the benefit of obtaining semen directly from Monalee Champion or Newdown Heather. Semen could be taken under supervision in Ireland and administered under supervision in Australia, although the cost would be considerable.

11. AI would mean substantial savings for breeders in remote areas such as New Zealand, Western Australia, and the Northern Territory.

These are just a few of the many advantages of AI, without even considering the possibility of freezing semen from outstanding sires for future generations, which would necessitate strict control procedures by the N.C.A.

I do not advocate AI for all matings, but its introduction would provide a valuable tool to overcome practical breeding problems, it would mean better conception rates, save breeders money, and protect the fertility and longevity of leading stud dogs.

I am a keen supporter of AI and will continue to be so until someone can come up with a logical reason based on *fact* and not *supposition* as to why it should not be introduced.

The use of artificial insemination is widespread throughout the industry but has never been discussed openly because it is prohibited.

In fact, I have been approached by two of Victoria's most prominent breeders who have requested that their bitches be artificially inseminated because they have experienced far better conception rates in the past by this method.

One of our failings as humans is that we abhor change, because we feel comfortable with things the way they are. But if it was not for change the wheel would still not be invented. All progress in human endeavour comes about by change and *now* is the time for change to come to greyhound breeding. Supporters of AI should *stand and be counted*, and if the number is sufficient the N.C.A. will have to act to bring about this much-needed change.

—Barry Ward

IRISH BLOODLINES

Over the past eight years imported Irish-bred sires have been responsible for a dramatic change in greyhound breeding trends in Australia. In 1973 only three of the twenty leading sires in Victoria carried imported blood close up in their pedigree, and in each case the outcross had been provided by Which Chariot (Imp.).

The influence of Irish bloodlines has been so great that this pattern has changed completely over the past eight years. Today only two of the twenty leading sires in Victoria, Benjamin John and Busy's Chief, have pedigrees comprised entirely of Australian bloodlines.

The remaining eighteen leading sires are either greyhounds imported from Eire, or male-line descendants of Irish imports. In fact, fifty per cent of Victoria's twenty leading sires are Irish imports, while an additional forty per cent are direct descendants of imported greyhounds, predominantly Tivoli Dreamer (Imp.). The Australian contingent represents a mere ten per cent of the current twenty leading Victorian sires.

This phenomenon started initially with a handful of imports from the Emerald Isle, many of which had poor racing records in their homeland. After the initial success of the early import, studkeepers endeavoured to obtain better-performed greyhounds and today Australia has the largest number of Irish and English classic winners at stud, outside of the British Isles.

Barry Ward's kennels at Cranboune, in Victoria, stands a total of five greyhounds that have won Irish or English track classics, namely Ashleigh Honour, Ballybeg Prim, Leaders Champion, Shamrock Point, and Weston Pete. This is the largest number of Irish and English classic winners standing stud at the same kennels anywhere in the world.

13

THE
SKELETAL SYSTEM

BONES

Bone, or osseous tissue, is the hardest of the connective tissues, its hardness being primarily due to the deposition of inorganic salts in an organic matrix. Calcium phosphate and calcium carbonate are the two most abundant salts. The organic matter includes fibres embedded in a matrix that contains protein, bone cells, blood vessels, and cartilaginous substances. Bone may be decalcified by placing it in a weak acid solution to dissolve the inorganic salts. The bone retains its shape and is still strong, but flexible. It may be cut with a knife or tied in knots. This experiment may be reversed by exposing the bone to intense heat in order to drive off the organic matter. The bone retains its shape but is more brittle than porcelain and extremely liable to crumble and fracture.

Bone is not to be regarded as the solid homogeneous material that it may appear upon superficial examination. Longitudinal section of an adult long bone reveals that only the walls of the shaft are composed of hard compact bone; the ends are filled with a porous, spongy network called cancellous bone. A long medullary canal within the shaft contains bone marrow. There are two kinds of bone marrow. Yellow marrow is found in the medullary canal and contains connective tissue, blood vessels, immature blood cells, and a vast amount of fat cells, from which the yellow colour is derived. Red marrow is found in the ends of long bones in the cancellous tissue and is more abundant in the larger bones and in the ribs. Fat cells are present in the red marrow, but they are limited to individual cells distributed among a vast number of developing blood cells. Investigation has revealed that in the adult the red cells and the granular white cells of the blood originate in the red marrow.

Study of a thin transverse section taken from the shaft of a bone reveals that the osseous tissue is composed of concentric rings, the centres of the rings being canals—Haversion canals—that contain blood vessels and a small quantity of connective tissue. Cavities called lacunae contain the bone cells and are located between the concentric layers of bone. Tiny canals, referred to as canaliculi, radiate out in all directions from the lacunae and branch and anastomose, forming a network throughout the bone. Minute protoplasmic filaments grow outward from osteocytes into the canaliculi. Thus bone is living tissue, containing cells and connecting strands of cytoplasm even in the most compact portions of its structure. Haversion canals are not isolated but are joined by communicating canals. The concentric arrangement of layers of bone and cells around a canal is referred to as a Haversian system. Areas between Haversian systems are occupied with lamellae that do not exhibit a concentric arrangement.

The periosteum is a tough, fibrous membrane that envelops bone except at the articulating surfaces. There are two layers within the periosteum, although not clearly defined. The outer layer is composed of connective tissue filled with blood vessels, lymph vessels, and nerves. The inner layer is composed of elastic fibres, cells, and blood vessels, but is not as vascular as the outer layer. The majority of investigators consider that the cells of the inner layer are capable of becoming bone cells. In young greyhounds there are many osteoblasts in the inner layer of the periosteum next to the surface of growing bone, but in the adult the cells remain inactive unless an injury is sustained. If a bone is fractured, this osteogenic layer supplies new bone to replace the old and assists in repair of the break. Blood vessels and nerves from the periosteum pass through Volkmann's canals into the hard substance of bone. These minute passageways pass through the lamellae as secondary vascular canals. Some of them unite with blood vessels in Haversian

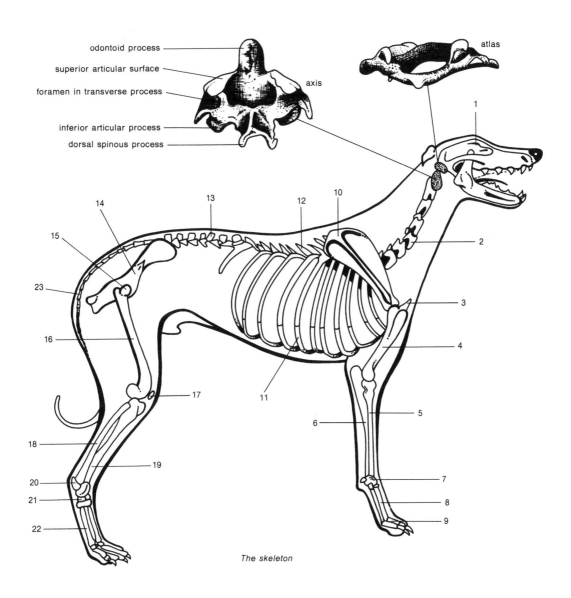

odontoid process

superior articular surface

foramen in transverse process

inferior articular process

dorsal spinous process

axis

atlas

The skeleton

1 skull
2 cervical vertebrae (7)
3 sternum
4 humerus
5 radius
6 ulna
7 carpus
8 metacarpus
9 phalanges
10 scapula
11 thorax
12 thoracic vertebrae (13)

13 lumbar vertebrae (7)
14 pelvis
15 acetabulum (cup shaped cavity in
    which head of femur articulates)
16 femur
17 patella
18 fibula
19 tibia
20 hock
21 tarsus
22 metatarsus
23 tail

canals, and others follow an irregular pathway through solid bone.

Most of the bones of the head develop embryologically between membranes and are called membrane bones. These bones do not preform in cartilage. The bones of the cranium develop from centres of ossification in connective tissue. Fibroblasts, located in fibrous connective tissue, change to osteoblasts (bone-forming cells). The intercellular matter adopts a gelatinous consistency. Spicules of bone appear and calcium salts are deposited in the matrix. Eventually, long, thin plates surrounded by osteoblasts appear in the connective tissue. Some of the osteoblasts become individually located in lacunae and are then referred to as osteocytes or bone cells. They maintain connections with each other and with the nourishing membrane by means of the canaliculi.

The connective tissue surrounding the developing bone also forms the periosteum, a nourishing membrane capable of producing bone. The inner layer of this fibrous covering is lined with osteoblasts and is called the osteogenic layer. More compact bone is deposited directly under the periosteum, whereas the intermediate portion is composed of spicules of bone in a spongy arrangement. The skull bones have not completed their ossification at birth and there are membranous areas called fontanels between them. The thickest portion of the bone is at the centre of ossification.

The skeleton of the developing embryo, with the exception of most of the skull bones, is formed of cartilage that is later replaced by bone. Bones formed in this manner are called cartilage bones. Cartilage is gradually replaced by bone. The perichondrium becomes the periosteum and forms a cylinder of bone at the middle of the shaft in the long bones. The cartilage within this ring of bone undergoes degeneration, the cartilage cells appear swollen and calcification takes place in this area. The cartilage cells die as they are released by the degeneration of cartilage. Endochondral bone then commences to replace the degenerating cartilage at the centre of ossification and the shaft is gradually converted into bone as ossification proceeds from the centre toward the bone ends. The cartilage ends continue to grow and the bone becomes longer while ossification progresses from the centre of the shaft. Understandably, there is necessarily considerable reorganisation inside the bone. The inward growth of perichondral

tissue into the degenerating cartilage brings about the formation of primary marrow cavities. Blood vessels accompany the periosteal buds. Eventually, the primary marrow spaces unite to form the single medullary cavity of long bones. The marrow cavity in the bone of the adult greyhound is considerably larger than its original cartilage antecedent in the embryo. Bones increase in diameter by successive layers of bone laid down by the periosteum.

The shaft of a long bone is called the diaphysis and the ends are called the epiphyses. There may be several centres of ossification which progress from the shaft to the epiphyses. The epiphyses are primarily cartilaginous at birth and commence ossification at various times after birth. Ossification can proceed from more than one centre in the epiphyses of the larger bones. Bone-forming tissue invades the cartilage and spicules of bone present, forming a network of spongy bone. The diaphysis and epiphysis convert to bone prior to completion of growth, but a cartilage plate—the epiphyseal plate— separates them during the entire growth period. Proliferation of cartilage cells and the formation of new matrix proceeds on the side of the plate toward the epiphysis and the cartilage toward the diaphysis is slowly replaced by bone. These growth zones are maintained in the long bones of the bitch for a shorter period than the dog. They are entirely replaced by bone and no further growth in the length of bones or in the height of the animal occurs.

Cartilage

Cartilage is a dense, white, connective tissue consisting of modified connective tissue cells surrounded by massive amounts of intercellular material which is composed of white fibres, yellow fibres, and a ground substance, or matrix. The ground substance is found in a limited area around the cells. The majority of the intercellular substance is composed of a dense mass of white fibres, the individual fibres not being visible under normal light. Cartilage is usually found in thin sheets covered by a connective tissue called the perichondrium which, being well-supplied with blood vessels, acts as a nourishing membrane. Nutrient fluids slowly diffuse through the intercellular substance to nourish the cells. Nerves and lymphatics are also confined to the perichondrium.

There are three types of cartilage which are differentiated primarily on the basis of variations in the structure of their intercellular substances into hyaline, yellow elastic, and white fibro-cartilage.

Hyaline cartilage structurally corresponds to the description of cartilage afforded previously. There are relatively few cells located in cavities called lacunae. The intercellular substance consists of white collagenous fibres which exhibit a pearl-like appearance, but in thin sections a slight bluish tinge presents. Hyaline cartilage is the most abundant and most widely distributed type of cartilage. It is the type of cartilage that, in the embryo, is the forerunner of bone. Hyaline cartilage is found in the nose, the larynx, and in the rings of the trachea and bronchial tubes. It covers the ends of bones at joints and promotes the smooth action of joints and assists in absorption of some of the shock of walking, galloping, and hurdling.

Yellow elastic cartilage develops from hyaline cartilage and is somewhat similar in appearance. Yellow elastic fibres are present in vast numbers within a network of white collagenous fibres. The cells are located in lacunae and a peri-chondrium is present. The elastic fibres impart a degree of elasticity to this tissue. Elastic cartilage is found in the external ear, the epiglottis, the Eustachian tube, and in some of the small laryngeal cartilages.

White fibrocartilage resembles fibrous con-nective tissue and is composed of bundles of wavy, white, collagenous fibres, the bundles being essentially parallel to each other. Cartilage cells are located in lacunae in the ground substance, surrounded by bundles of fibres. Fibrocartilage is found between the vertebrae in the inter-vertebral discs and in the cartilage between the two pubic bones. It is located around the outer borders of movable joints, where it tends to deepen the joint cavities. The tissue is frequently ill-defined, grading off into areolar or fibrous connective tissue. When associated with hyaline cartilage in a joint or in the inter-vertebral discs, the hyaline cartilage always makes contact with the bone and gradu-ally grades into fibrocartilage. The plates of fibrocartilage between the vertebrae act as padding that absorbs a great deal of the shock transmitted through the vertebral column as the result of walking or hurdling.

The skeleton

The skeleton forms the bony framework of the body and is the principal support for the various parts. In addition, it affords protection for vital organs. The skeletal muscles are attached to bones by tendons. Muscular contraction affords power of movement to the skeleton.

The bones in the skeleton are classified according to shape as long, short, flat, and irregular bones. The larger bones of the legs are examples of long bones. The bones of the carpus, or knee (corresponds with the human wrist) and hock, or tarsus, are short bones. The skull bones and shoulder blades are good examples of flat bones. Irregular bones include that not readily classified, such as the vertebrae. There are a few small round bones that develop in a joint or in tendons that are called sesamoid bones. The patella (kneecap) is the largest of these bones, which are usually found embedded in tendons of the feet. Projections from the surface of bones are referred to as processes. There are various types of projections, such as the condyle, which is defined as a rounded arti-culating surface forming a joint at the end of a bone. A tubercle is a nodule, or small eminence, on the surface of a bone that affords attachment to a muscle or ligament. Several other types of projections are afforded specific names. Cavities may also be of varying types. A foramen is a natural opening, or passage, into or through a bone through which blood vessels and nerves pass. A sinus is a cavity, or hollow space, such as the dilated channels for venous blood, found chiefly in the cranium, or the air cavities in the cranial bones. A fossa is a hollow or depressed area in the surface of a bone.

The skull

The greyhound possesses a dolichocephalic or long head. The main difference between the long-faced and short-faced skulls lies in the relative lengths of the superior maxilla, the nasal bones, and the premaxilla. The cranial division of all three types of head shapes—dolicho-cephalic (long head), mesocephalic (intermediate type), brachycephalic (short head)—is some-what similar apart from the fact that in the majority of brachycephalic skulls the cranial capacity is relatively slightly greater than in the long-headed skulls in comparison with the body weight of the dog. The orbit exhibits little difference in the various skull types, with the exception that in the brachycephalic heads the orbit is wider and the section which contains the eyeball is located closer to the midline of the skull, since the nasal bones occupy less space as

South Australian staying sensation Bayroad Queen (Tegimi–Village Swallow), 1982 Arnott–Spillers National Distance Champion and 731-metre track record holder (43·88 seconds) at Angle Park *(Courtesy of South Australian Greyhound Trainer)*

regards their width and length. This permits the dog to enjoy better frontal vision than is possible in the long-headed types. In the greyhound the eyes are set obliquely, and a little to the side of the head, usually at an angle of thirty degrees with a line drawn longitudinally through the midline of the head, i.e., midway between the eyes and the ears.

A ridge known as the sagittal crest which strengthens the cranium and affords attachment for the temporal muscles runs centrally and longitudinally down the cranium. It is prolonged at its upper end to join the occipital crest and at its lower end reaches the inferior limit of the parietal bones. In addition to playing a considerable role in shaping the head, the sagittal crest has a number of functions. It protects the roof of the cranium and minimises the effect of blows upon the upper surface of the head which might otherwise prove fatal. It affords attachment to some of the muscles which enable the dog to forcibly close its mouth and so increases

the power to bite and kill game. Generally speaking, a well-developed sagittal crest extending from occiput above to the frontal sinuses below, accompanies a long, narrow head, with a rather straight, slightly curved zygomatic arch, and long jaws well-equipped with teeth capable of killing and tearing prey to pieces.

The temporal fossa lies on either side of the sagittal crest. Although anatomically it is a cavity, the space in the living specimen is (with the exception of the coronoid process of the mandible or lower jaw bone) almost completely filled by the temporal muscle, the function of which is to close the lower jaw. The temporal fossa is continuous below in the dog, with the orbital fossa which contains and protects the eyeball. The dog, unlike the horse, is said to possess an open orbit. Whether the orbit be open or closed, it contains the eyeball, while the upper cavity, the temporal fossa, gives passage to the upper end of the lower jaw.

The outer boundary of these two fossae is a

continuous arch of bone formed primarily from the highly developed zygoma of the malar bone and is known as the zygomatic arch. The zygomatic arch, a lateral projection of bone which protects and encloses the eye, as well as providing increased surface area for the attachment of the muscles operating the jaws, is much less marked and the malar portion of the zygoma is much straighter in long-headed dogs than in the shorter-faced varieties. It is the variable degree of curvature of the zygoma which decides the width of the dog's forehead and it is false to assume, as so many people do, that a dog is likely to be more intelligent because it possesses a wide forehead and consequently has 'more room for brains'.

The frontal bone of the dog extends from the suture at the lower end of the parietal bone downwards to the upper ends of the nasal bones centrally and to the superior maxillae laterally. The frontal bone forms the inner casing of the orbit. A small projection from the centre of the inner edge of the frontal bone lies opposite a similar projection on the inner edge of the zygoma. Between these two projections stretches a thin, ligamentous band which separates the temporal fossa and the orbital fossa. The air chamber contained within the frontal bone is known as the frontal sinus. The two sinuses on either side of the head are separated by a bony partition in the majority of dogs. The frontal sinus is of considerable extent in hunting dogs which work by scent, but is rather less so in the greyhound, which hunts by sight.

Directly above eye level on either side of the lower end of the forehead is a raised prominence which contains an air chamber. Between the two prominences is a depression which extends downwards to the upper level of the nasal bones, referred to as the stop. The degree of development of the stop varies in different breeds. The stop acts as a separation between the forehead and the nasal passages.

The sinuses communicate with the nasal passages by means of the ethmoid meatus and also communicate with a second sinus located in the maxillary bone underlying the cheek. The maxillary sinuses lie within the bone just above the level of the cheek teeth and coincide in position with the last four of these. The roots of these teeth may lie within the sinuses or be separated from the chamber by a thin layer of bone. If an abscess develops as a consequence of infection of one of the tooth roots, the abscess

invariably breaks on to the surface of the face directly below the eye.

The function of the air chambers within the skull is mainly to add to the substance of the structure without resulting in too much additional weight. They afford sufficient width of face to permit the attachment of the upper jaw bones without interruption to the normal contour. The sinuses do not play an important part in respiration and they contain no nerve endings capable of conveying to the brain any impression of smell so, contrary to popular opinion, they do not influence the ability of an animal to recognise odours.

The upper ends of the basal bones are generally narrower than the lower. The nasal cavity is divided into two symmetrical halves in the longitudinal direction by a cartilaginous plate called the septum nasi. The nasal chambers contain three passageways through which air passes backwards to the larynx on its way to the lungs. The passages arise from the presence within the nasal chambers of the ethmoid bone and the upper and lower turbinated bones. These are thin plates of bone in scroll-like formation covered with a highly vascular mucous membrane containing nerve endings capable of analysing odours. The upper nasal passage lies between the upper turbinated bone and the lower surface of the nasal bones. The middle nasal passage lies between the two turbinated bones, and the third passage lies between the lower turbinated bone and the floor of the skull.

The mandible, or lower jaw bone, or inferior maxilla, is virtually straight from the incisor teeth back to its posterior angle, where it becomes erect, this upright section being termed the coronoid process. It articulates by means of the condyle with the glenoid cavity lodged in the temporal bone and underlying the upper end of the zygoma. The coronoid process enters the temporal fossa and moves freely within it. The two halves of the mandible, the rami, meet at their lower end half-way along the incisor teeth but the two halves do not fuse, except in very old dogs. The outer aspect of the mandible is smooth, with the exception of the coronoid process which is deeply recessed on the outer surface to give attachment to the masseter and temporal muscles.

The cranium, or braincase, is located between the upper level of the eyes and the occiput, or peak of the head. The bones which surround and support the cranial cavity comprise the cranium which contains the brain. Brain efficiency depends primarily upon the thickness and distribution of the 'thatch' of grey matter covering the underlying primitive brain and not upon the actual size of the entire brain. The grey matter carries the nerve structures and primary lines of communication between the brain and the various parts of the body and is spread out over and inserted into the substance of the brain in a continuous layer, giving rise to ridges and depressions, referred to as convolutions, on its surface.

The brain is comprised of a large anterior section, the cerebrum (the seat of knowledge), and a smaller posterior portion, the cerebellum (concerned with co-ordination of movement and balance). Beneath and posterior to this is the medulla, a continuation of the brain connecting it with the spinal cord, which travels down the body through each of the vertebrae giving off nerve branches at regular intervals. The interior of the cranial cavity is roughly divided to accommodate these three portions of the brain. A great many separate bones enter into the formation of the skull and are (with one or two exceptions) thin, flattened, or curved plates of bone of specific shape, united by closely applied edges, the lines of apposition being referred to as sutures. During the first year of life the majority of these sutures remain cartilaginous so that the separate bones are able to change their relative size and shape during the period in which the pup is growing into eventual adult form. Some of the cranial bones, such as the occipital bone, fuse prior to birth with the parietal bones lying directly below it, while the temporal bones also unite at an early age.

The cranium of the greyhound may be regarded as possessing a roof, lateral walls, and two extremities. The upper end is comprised of the occipital and interparietal bones, which are single bones. The upper end of the cranium is pierced by a large canal through which the brain and spinal cord communicate, known as the foramen magnum. The parietal and frontal bones form the roof of the cranium and are thin bones. The occipital, temporal, parietal, and frontal bones, which become integrated below with the floor of the cranium without visible sutures, form the lateral walls of the cranium. The floor of the cranium is formed by the basilar process of the occipital bone and the sphenoid bone. In some of the short-faced varieties of

dogs the front end of the sphenoid bone is poorly developed and the flattened plate of the palatine bone which supports the roof of the mouth (the hard palate) may be incomplete on the midline and consequently give rise to cleft palate. This is a genetical fault which may sometimes be associated with hare-lip and umbilical hernia, or it may be inherited. Only two or three pups in a litter may be affected, but the apparently normal pups may be carriers.

The vomer bone cuts off the nasal passages from the mouth and divides the right and left chamber of the nostrils.

The dentition of the dog

The importance of the teeth as organs of mastication and weapons of offence and defence renders some particular notice of them necessary. Hard, enamelled teeth located in the sockets of the jaw bones provide for cutting, tearing, and crushing of food. Three types of teeth are present in the dog—the incisive or cutting teeth, the canine or tearing teeth, and the molar or crushing teeth.

The newborn pup does not ordinarily possess any erupted teeth, but they are forming in the jaw bones. The dog later comes into possession of two sets of teeth—a deciduous or 'milk set' to accommodate the jaw of the pup and a permanent set for the adult jaw. The milk teeth are replaced, because they become inadequate in their function, as the length of the pup's jaw increases. The milk teeth correspond to their permanent namesakes except that they are whiter and smaller, their necks are more constricted, and the molar roots more divergent to bestride the crowns of the unerupted pre-molars. The milk teeth are shed as hollow crowns, breaking from their roots (now in the process of absorption), but loosely held for a time by the gum at the neck of the tooth.

The incisive teeth occupy the front of the mouth. The molar, or grinding teeth, are located at the back of the mouth and are advantageously placed as regards the action of the molar muscles, which are assisted by the tongue in placing the edible matter between the grinding surfaces. The temporary canines make their appearance at three to four weeks and all six should be present by the fifth week. The permanent central and lateral incisors appear at four months while the temporary corner teeth are replaced by permanent teeth at four to five months. The canine teeth should be changed at approximately this time but not infrequently the temporary canines remain long after the permanent teeth are present. The upper canines possess the longest roots of all the teeth. The adult dog should possess twelve incisors, four canines, sixteen premolars, and ten molars. The teeth of the upper and lower jaws are not numerically equal. Each tooth meets two in the opposite jaw as the opposing teeth are not directly opposite but at intervals between their opponents. The lower jaw carries three molars in comparison with the upper jaw which carries two. The fourth premolar of the upper jaw is matched with the first molar of the lower jaw, which it closely resembles. The first, second and third premolars appear at approximately three to four weeks and are changed between five and six months. Occasionally, the first premolar, a smaller tooth, does not appear until the second month. At about the same time the first molar appears in the upper jaw, while the second molar should appear in the lower jaw at six to eight months, but is often absent from the upper jaw. Absence of some of the premolars in the greyhound and other long-faced breeds, indicates a progressive hereditary weakness according to many, but perhaps it is more indicative of the tendency of breeders to direct more attention to outward appearance than to internal soundness.

A tooth may be divided into three regions—the visible section above the gums is the crown; the neck is a constricted portion between the crown and the root; the root is the part embedded in the socket in the jaw bone. The crown of the tooth is composed of enamel, the hardest substance in the body. The enamel is thickest on the wearing surface and becomes thinner as it terminates in the neck region of the tooth.

Teeth develop in sockets, or alveoli. The tooth socket is lined with a specialised connective tissue called periosteum, which assists in attaching the tooth to its socket, acts as a nourishing membrane, and is capable of forming the bone-like substance called cement over the root of the tooth. The cement is a thinner, softer layer than the enamel and covers the tooth from the termination of the enamel to the tip of the root. The greater bulk of the tooth is formed of a bone-like structure called dentine which is of a yellowish colour. Dentine forms slowly throughout the life of the tooth. Injury accelerates the formation of new, secondary dentine. Normally,

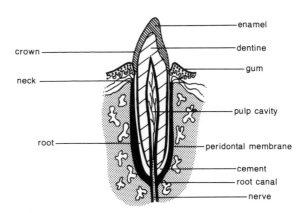

Longitudinal section of a tooth

in older dogs, the pulp cavity is reduced by the continued formation of dentine. The pulp cavity lies in the central portion of the tooth, extending down into the root. The pulp is composed of loose connective tissue and is highly vascular and contains a great many nerves. Blood vessels and sensory nerves enter through a minute opening at the tip of the root and pass through the root canal to the pulp cavity proper. The gums, attached to the necks of the teeth, consist of firm fibrous tissue fixed to the jaws and the overlying mucous membrane. Approximately a millimetre thick and richly vascular but sparsely innervated, the gum forms a free collar around each tooth just above the attachment to the neck. The collar, which recedes with age and in certain diseased conditions, exposing the neck, dips in a concave line on the labial (lip) and lingual (tongue) aspects of each tooth but rises between the teeth, where it is more readily damaged by trapped food particles.

Few abnormalities occur in the teeth of greyhounds as a consequence of the length of their jaws, although extra teeth, particularly in the upper jaw, may be observed. Sometimes the permanent teeth do not push out the milk teeth from behind, but erupt beside them, in which instance the milk teeth should be removed. Absence of some of the premolars is common. Gaps may appear in the cheek teeth and a congenital absence of tooth sockets may render it impossible for the dog to own a full set of teeth.

Proper occlusion of the teeth is important to their function. An undershot jaw or out-jutting lower jaw may be due to faulty occlusion of the teeth. Raising the upper and depressing the

171

lower lip will expose the incisor teeth and the canines. It will be observed that there is only a small interdental space, i.e., the space between the canine tooth and the first premolar. It can now be determined whether the mouth is level, possesses a scissors bite, or if it is undershot, overshot or normal. The number of each type of tooth may be checked to see if they are all present, if they are in correct alignment, or crowded or overlapping. By opening the mouth or drawing back the lips, the premolars and molars may be checked.

If a pup has contracted distemper and recovered from it, the permanent teeth are damaged prior to eruption. When the teeth do erupt, the enamel is generally pitted and exhibits brown marks which cannot be removed.

Since the greyhound's diet consists primarily of soft food, scale or tartar builds up on the enamel. Tartar from salivary salts may be deposited upon the teeth at the gum collar and may push up under the gums, lifting them away from the tooth surface, the end result being inflammation of the gums, tender mouth, and foul breath, which may render the dog unthrifty. If the condition is not checked, teeth may require extraction. If the dog is given a large shank bone once a week, the gnawing action on the bone will serve to cleanse the teeth and massage the gums and so prevent a build-up of scale. Bones should not be fed closer than four days prior to a race and a check should be made to ensure that the dog does not become constipated. If this occurs, a tablespoon of medicinal liquid paraffin will relieve the condition.

Generally speaking, broken teeth are painless to the dog, unless they become inflamed or infected. Split teeth should be extracted as food particles become trapped in the splits, causing irritation.

Probably the most important factor in producing good teeth is a proper diet in the early stages. A proper diet for the bitch during pregnancy will contribute to healthy teeth in the pups.

The vertebral column

The vertebral column is composed of individual bones called vertebrae and is divided into seven cervical, thirteen thoracic and seven lumbar vertebrae. Each vertebra has a spinous process projecting dorsad which affords attachment for the ligaments and muscles of the back. There are two transverse processes projecting laterad

and dorsad from a typical vertebra that also afford attachment for muscles. Articular processes unite the vertebrae into a column. Articular processes form joints, the articulating surfaces being covered with cartilage, which promotes smoothness in action. Each intervertebral disc consists of a cartilaginous fibrous section forming the peripheral portion of the disc, with a softer central part called the nucleus pulposus. This soft centre becomes squeezed out and may protrude at the upper part of the disc, causing pressure on the spinal cord as it passes between the two vertebrae which are normally united with its assistance. This is referred to as a 'slipped disc' and gives rise to pain and symptoms of paralysis. Intervertebral discs vary in thickness in different individuals of the same species and in accordance with the age of the animal. They are generally thicker in young dogs and become progressively thinner with age. In older dogs, they may become impregnated with calcium salts, producing fusion of adjacent vertebrae.

The length of the neck is largely dependent upon the degree of inclination of the scapula. An upright scapula shortens the neck and also influences the angle at which the neck is carried and, in addition, that of the head in relation to the neck. A long neck is seldom accompanied by an upright shoulder or a sloping shoulder accompanied by a short neck. The length of the neck is dependent upon the relative length of each of the seven vertebrae it contains, in addition to the thickness of the intervertebral discs.

There are typically seven cervical vertebrae in the neck region of mammals. The first cervical vertebra is the atlas, which is specialised, with large smooth surfaces that articulate with the occipital condyles for the support of the skull. The body of the atlas is not well-developed and occurs almost as a circular bone, with two transverse processes and a posterior tubercle in place of a dorsal spinous process. The articular surface of the atlas is convex in front where it meets the rear end of the skull and concave behind so that it can receive the odontoid process of the axis.

The axis is the second of the cervical vertebrae. A strong, bony process, the odontoid process, arises from its upper surface. The atlas pivots on this process when the head is turned and represents a striking specialisation to permit freedom of head movement. The dorsal spine of the axis is thick and strong in comparison with the spines of the other cervical vertebrae. A flattened elastic cord called the ligamentum nuchae is attached along the upper edge of the neural spine of the axis and extends down the entire length of the neck as far as the dog's withers, where it is attached to the tip of the spinous process of the first dorsal vertebra and becomes continuous with the supraspinal ligament, which extends down the spine as far as the sacram, being attached to each of the spinous processes. The ligamentum nuchae assists in support of the head and neck and effects a downward curvature of the cervical vertebrae.

The remaining five neck bones adhere to the general pattern of the other bones of the spine and carry spinous processes above and transverse and oblique processes laterally. The transverse processes afford attachment to the muscles of the neck and the oblique processes offer flat articular surfaces in front and behind each bone, which articulate with similar surfaces on adjoining vertebrae. The neural canal traverses each vertebra longitudinally and through this channel the spinal cord passes from the medulla of the brain to the last lumbar bone at its junction with the sacrum. The spinal cord sends off nerves to all parts of the body on its way down the neck and back, these branches leaving the spine by passing through a space between the bodies of adjacent vertebrae. Cartilaginous spinal discs, between the bodies of each pair of spinal bones, help to reduce concussion between the bones.

The neck is supported and moved by muscles passing between the transverse processes of the vertebrae and by muscles running the entire length of the neck and, in some instances, extending into the forelimb and helping to move and bring the limb forward, notably when the head and neck are extended at the same time, as in galloping. The brachiocephalic muscle originates at its attachment to the occipital bone of the skull and anterior aspect of the ligamentum nuchae and at its opposing end is inserted into the humerus. It is therefore apparent that a strong, lengthy, well-developed neck considerably assists forward movement of the forelimb. The cervical vertebrae do not run straight down the neck but curve downward in their lower third and then continue horizontally to unite with the first dorsal bone between the scapulae. When the scapulae are inclined from below upward toward the rear end of the body, a greater amount of the lower end of the neck presents. When the scapulae are set almost perpendicularly their front edges extend forward over the last cervical and occasionally over the sixth vertebra, and this makes the neck appear short. The point at which the neck joins the body will consequently appear abrupt rather than level and streamlined, and the neck will appear to be set almost perpendicularly instead of sloping gradually upward toward the head. In the cervical vertebrae the transverse processes on either side form a foramen which transmits the vertebral artery.

The thirteen thoracic vertebrae are larger and stronger than the cervical vertebrae. The transverse processes are large and assist in supporting the ribs while the dorsal spinous processes are long and extend downward.

The seven lumbar vertebrae are also large and their dorsal processes are similar in shape to an axe. The transverse processes are thin. The seventh lumbar vertebra is not typical, since it is modified for articulation with the sacram.

The vertebral column is not a rigid support and the column normally is not straight but exhibits natural curvatures which are present at birth. The vertebrae are bound together by ligaments. Muscles are attached to the dorsal spines and to transverse processes that act as levers and allow limited movement.

The thorax

The thorax is formed by the thoracic vertebrae, the ribs, the costal cartilages, and the sternum and affords protection for the heart, thoracic blood vessels, and lungs, as well as assisting in supporting the bones of the shoulder girdle. A dome-shaped, muscular, and tendinous partition, known as the diaphragm, forms the floor of the thoracic cavity. The chest walls are lined and the lungs covered by a membrane called the pleura. The thorax is divided longitudinally by a partition of pleura called the mediastinum. The thorax is suspended between the scapulae and ribs entirely by muscular attachment without any form of bony union.

There are thirteen pairs of ribs in both the male and female, nine pairs of which are united below to the sternum. The tenth, eleventh, and twelfth pairs are united below to each other by means of a cartilaginous prolongation of each rib, while the thirteenth pair, known as floating ribs, are free at their lower termination. A typical rib is a long, slender, curved bone, which articulates dorsally with two vertebrae, except in the case of the first rib, which articulates with the last cervical and first dorsal bones. There is a tubercle just beyond the neck region of the rib, where it articulates with the transverse process of the vertebra. The articular head and tubercle diminish in size from the first rib to the last. Generally speaking, the eighth pair of ribs are the longest and the ribs become progressively shorter as they run forward and backward from the eighth pair. The longer the ribs, the deeper the chest and the greater the degree of curvature the greater will be the cubic capacity. Long ribs provide a deep chest.

The sternum

The sternum is the breastbone and is located medially below the first nine pairs of ribs which unite with it on either side. Although described as a single bone, it is composed of a number of bony segments united by cartilages which become calcified into bone late in life. In the dog there are eight of these segments which, in greyhounds, as a consequence of selective breeding, are becoming deeper with a tendency toward the development of a cartilaginous keel, which affords the chest a fictitious appearance of greater depth without increasing the cubic capacity of the thorax. The terminal portion of the keel of the sternum is slightly flattened to form a xiphoid process and just above this, in the thorax, the apex of the heart is located. One may have heard about the need for 'heart room', but what is really needed is lung room and this is possible only when there is sufficient space between the ribs. Depth of chest is of far less consequence.

The forelimb

The majority of people concerned with greyhounds appear to pay great attention to the hind quarters, their grace of movement and their role in propulsion of the animal. Far less attention, however, is afforded the part which the forelimbs play in propulsion. There seems to be a fixed belief that the hind legs do the pushing and that the forelegs are concerned predominantly with support and play only a minor role in moving the body. If a greyhound sustains a serious injury to its hind leg it will soon learn to elevate the hind part of the body and walk about on its forelegs with ease. If an accident is incurred to the forelimb the hind limbs will be quite incapable of lifting the front end and moving the animal about in an erect or semi-erect attitude. It can be demonstrated, by means of an apparatus which measures the force of the impact conveyed to the ground by each foot in turn, that the forelimb supports not only more than the weight of the front half of the animal, but that it also possesses propulsive power frequently greater than that transmitted by the hind limb. It is worthy of note, however, that the force of impact of the forefoot upon the ground varies in accordance with the attitude of the dog's head during motion. The propulsive impact is greatest in dogs which move with the head elevated and firmly anchored in that position by the contraction of the neck muscles. This is necessary in order to permit the muscles occupying the length of the neck, from skull to humerus, to draw the foreleg forward to its fullest extent. This permits a considerably longer total stride with corresponding increase in speed, provided that the number of strides for a given time is not appreciably lessened. The degree of propulsion exerted by the forefoot thrusting upon the ground decreases when the head is lowered and dogs that gallop with the head lowered propel themselves largely by the efforts of their hind limbs. For perfect front-end action the pasterns must be strong and straight, with appropriate spring and give. The pads of the feet should be firm and thick and sufficiently spaced so that the weight falls correctly upon them and there is no loss of power transmitted through them during encounter with the ground.

The scapula

When one can place two or more fingers between the two scapulae, with the head in the normal position in the standing animal, then almost invariably the shoulders will be both upright and too widely spaced at the withers. This type of shoulder is desirable in a coursing greyhound to enable the lowering of the head sufficiently, at a fast pace, to pick up a hare. If the space between the summits of the scapulae is able to accommodate only one finger, although the dog may be very fast it may be totally incapable of picking up the hare. It may be observed that many speed-track greyhounds with beautifully inclined shoulders and long necks are unable to feed from a bowl put on the ground in front of them unless they bend one knee, or straddle their front legs, so that they may reach down to the bowl. A long neck usually accompanies a well-inclined shoulder because the cervical and dorsal bones are equally lengthy. The angle of inclination of the scapula is dependent not only upon the relative length of the cervical and dorsal vertebrae, particularly that of the first six dorsal vertebrae, but also upon the point of greatest curvature of the first four ribs.

The scapula or shoulder-blade, the flat triangular bone of the shoulder girdle, presents a large surface to provide anchorage for a number of muscles which serve to operate the forelimb and attach it to the body, spine, and ribs, as well as assisting in movements of the neck. The scapula is attached to the body by muscles without any form of bony union. On either side of the body the scapula is attached to the spine and behind it is fastened to the ribs by muscle. The outer, or dorsal, surface is divided unequally by a raised prominent ridge of bone called the spine, which terminates as the acromion process, with which the clavicle articulates. The spine is subcutaneous and easily felt along its entire length in the living subject. Another process, the coracoid process, projects upward and forward underneath the clavicle. The smooth, depressed, circular area below these two processes is the glenoid fossa, or cavity, in which the head of the humerus articulates, forming the shoulder joint. The capsular ligament is attached to the circumference of both articular surfaces and completely surrounds and holds the joint together. The upper ends of the scapula are tilted slightly inward as a consequence of the pull of the muscles which attach them to the dorsal vertebrae. It is of great importance that the scapula be properly inclined in order to enable the dog to move freely and well. The degree of inclination of the scapula is dependent upon the length of the cervical and dorsal bones because, whatever the length or degree of inclination of the scapula, it is always attached to the same dorsal vertebrae by the muscles which communicate from the one to the other; the rhomboideus muscle is attached at one end to the fourth to seventh dorsal bones and at the other to the scapula at its upper anterior angle. Also, the cervical portion of the trapezius muscle is attached to the ligamentum nuchae and to the second to fourth dorsal bones and at its other end is inserted into the spine of the scapula. The dorsal portion, also attached to the spine of the scapula, inserts into the tenth dorsal bone. Although this may be difficult to comprehend without being in a position to view an actual specimen, the point to grasp is that the scapula has a number of fixed attachments. To attain the desired degree of inclination, the upper end of the scapula must lie as far back along the body as possible and this is dependent upon the neck and dorsal bones being of sufficient length to extend back to the necessary position.

The humerus

The humerus is the long bone of the upper forelimb, the rounded head of which fits into the glenoid cavity of the scapula and forms a ball-and-socket joint at the shoulder, permitting rotating movements. Just beyond the constricted neck region there are two bony prominences known as the greater and lesser tuberosities, the lesser tuberosity projecting anteriorly when the animal is in the normal standing position, a bony mass which can be felt through the skin as it is the most prominent point of the shoulder. The tendon of the long head of the biceps muscle lies in the groove between the tubercles. Between the groove and the tendon is a synovial bursa and this is frequently injured and becomes a source of lameness in greyhounds. The shaft of the humerus is not straight, but exhibits slight torsion. On the outer aspect of the humerus is a shallow groove, the musculospiral groove, which extends the entire length of the shaft and affords lodgement to the brachialis muscle, which aids the biceps muscle in flexion of the shoulder joint. The deltoid tuberosity is located about midway along the lateral margin and the deltoid muscle is inserted there. At the lower extremity of the humerus are two smooth articular surfaces. The outer capitulum articulates with the radius and the inner trochlea articulates with the ulna, the radius and ulna being the bones of the forearm. At the back of the lower end of the humerus is a deep fossa, known as the olecranon fossa, which receives the olecranon process of the ulna when the elbow is extended (straightened) and as this is the position that the limb assumes in the standing position when weight is borne on the foot it follows that the elbow joint locks and will remain so until the foot is relieved of weight bearing.

When moving off from a stationary position with both elbows locked, the greyhound usually transfers some of its body weight from the front end to the hind quarters by slightly flexing a hock and dropping the corresponding quarter, or alternatively, the animal may advance the hind limb and then flex the hock. Either of these attitudes relieves weight from the diagonally opposite forelimb and makes it easier for the dog to advance it. The length of the humerus is an important factor in determining the position of the elbows, as when the humerus is short the elbows are necessarily positioned farther forward. If the elbows are farther back under the chest, the humerus would necessarily be longer to make this possible. The length of the scapula also has a determining role in deciding where the elbows will lie. The degree of inclination of the humerus varies in accordance with differences in its length.

The radius and the ulna

The radius and ulna are the bones of the forearm, the ulna being the longer and larger of the two, largely as a consequence of its olecranon process, which extends considerably above the upper end of the radius.

The ulna can be felt along the forearm from the elbow to the wrist. The proximal end of the ulna exhibits two processes, the olecranon and the coronoid; between them is the trochlear notch, which articulates against the trochlea of the humerus and forms a hinge joint which permits movement only in one plane. On the inner aspect of the coronoid process is a smooth, articular surface, the radial notch, that articulates with the head of the radius. The distal extremity consists of the head of the ulna and a small lateral process, referred to as the styloid process, which can be felt just above the wrist on the outer side. The distal end of the ulna articulates with the cuneiform and pisiform bones of the carpus, or knee. The radius articulates at this extremity with the remaining bones of the upper row.

The head of the radius exhibits a smooth, hollowed-out disc which articulates with the capitulum of the humerus. As the foot is rotated, the radius pivots on the capitulum. Below the neck of the radius, on the medial side, the radial tuberosity affords attachment for the tendon of the biceps brachii muscle.

The radius and ulna are articulated at the inner aspect of the head of the radius and at the lower extremity at the outer aspect of the radius and between these two points is a narrow space which separates the two bones, the degree of movement between the two bones being practically negligible. In young dogs there may be a little rotation of the radial head upon the ulna,

but in older dogs a certain degree of fusion generally takes place. The carpus or knee corresponds with the human wrist.

There are seven small bones in the wrist of the dog, three in the upper row and four in the lower. The bones of the carpus are firmly bound together by ligaments; yet their arrangement in two rows permits some movement. In the upper row the scapholunar bone, formed from the fusion of the scaphoid and semilunar bones, articulates with the radius. The cuneiform bone articulates with both radius and ulna, and the pisiform bone with the ulna. The outermost bone of the upper row, the cuneiform, inclines downward into the second row to articulate with the external metacarpal bone. The trapezium articulates with the first and second metacarpals, the small irregular trapezoid with the second metacarpal, the os magnum with the third metacarpal, and the cuneiform with the fourth and fifth metacarpals. The bones of the carpus include the pisiform, scapholunar, cuneiform, unciform, trapezoid, and os magnum.

The metacarpus

The five metacarpals below the knee are miniature long bones, the innermost being the shortest, and the third and fourth the longest. The fifth metacarpal is the thickest of the metacarpal bones. All five bones are articulated at their upper end to their neighbours and diverge a little as they pass downward. Each metacarpal bone carries two small sesamoids behind it, i.e., on the aspect which corresponds with the palmar surface of the human hand.

The phalanges

The innermost digit, or dewclaw, corresponds with the human thumb and has only two phalanges and does not make contact with the ground while the dog is in the normal standing position. The other four digits each possess three phalanges. The proximal and middle phalanges of the digits are small long bones, while the distal phalanx is small and roughly helmet-shaped.

The feet

The feet of the dog are levers of paramount importance whereby the animal enjoys movement. The feet are required to support the body at rest, to provide a lever at once adequate for a gentle walk or a high jump, and to form a resilient spring absorbing jarring shocks in concert with muscles. Variations in general foot shape may present in accordance with the condition of the muscular, tendinous, and ligamentous tissue. The nature of the surface on which the dog is exercised has a great bearing on the feet. If the ground is rough, it will necessitate a bunching up of the toes in order to negotiate it; if it be smooth and soft, the dog will travel flat-footed across it. It is important to realise that the dog's feet will bunch up nicely under some conditions and slacken and spread under others and this is usually not due to a fault in the conformation of the dog. Muscles become stronger and firmer if adequately exercised. Pasterns may become relaxed and yielding if the dog is confined to a small kennel for the majority of the day and receives little exercise. The feet may be well bunched, like those of a cat, or they may be flattened and more lengthy. In some instances the forefeet may be cat-like and the hind feet of the hare type.

There are five pads in all which present as modified areas of skin. The largest pad inhabits the hollow of the digits between the other four pads and is roughly heart-shaped, with its apex directed toward the centre of the under surface of the foot. This large pad receives a section of the deep flexor tendon of the foot. If the large central pad of the foot becomes worn and thin, or is poorly developed, the tips of the toes may be directed slightly upwards, and consequently nail growth is excessive because the nails do not wear down from friction with the ground. Conversely, when the central pad is thick and well developed the nails tend to be directed downward and so become worn down by their contact with the ground. At the back of the limb at the level of the lower row of carpal bones is a well-developed, pad-like formation which is loosely attached by skin and directed downward. This pad is known as the 'stopper' and it acts when the dog is pulling up and reducing speed. Consequently, it is often partially torn away from the leg when acting in this capacity. The pads of the feet are generally darkly pigmented but in some white dogs they may be devoid of pigment, often in company with unpigmented nails.

The pelvis

The pelvic girdle is rigidly joined to the base of the spine so that in walking or galloping the force of the leg thrust is transmitted to the spine. This fusion of the pelvic girdle to the spine is very effective in transmitting force from the hind limbs to the body; the muscular attachment of the scapulae to the spine is less effective in transmitting force from the forelimbs to the body.

The pelvis of the dog consists of three bones — the ilium, the ischium, and the pubis — fused together. The hip bones are two large, flat bones that form the pelvic girdle. These are the broadest bones in the skeleton. The ilium is the uppermost and the largest of the three parts. Prior to the fusion of the three sections of the hip bone, the ilium is separated from the ischium and pubis by a suture that passes through the cavity that receives the head of the femur — the acetabulum. The upper end of the ilium articulates with the sacrum, which forms the roof of the pelvic girdle. The ischium is the posterior portion of the hip one. The obturator foramen, through which passes the blood vessels and nerves to the hind limb, formed by the ischium and pubis on either side, is the largest foramen in the skeleton. The lower anterior portion of each hip bone is the pubis, the pubic bones meeting anteriorly along a median line and a disc of fibrocartilage presenting between the two bones. The female pelvis differs from that of the male, the differences being largely due to the adaption of the pelvis of the bitch to whelping. The female pelvis is wider and the cavity is larger and shorter, the sacrum is shorter and broader, and the ischial tuberosities, as well as the acetabula, are farther apart. The pubic arch is also much wider.

The sacro-iliac joint is a synovial joint between the thick cartilage covering the auricular surfaces of the sacrum and ilium, but since the closely applied surfaces are undulating or even tuberculated, no movement is possible except a little rotation around a transverse axis, the primary function of the articulation being the transference of weight from the hind limbs to the body. Movement at the joint is more free in bitches, especially during whelping, when the ligaments become more relaxed. The bones are connected by the anterior sacro-iliac ligament, composed of a number of thin fibrous bands, and the much stronger posterior sacro-iliac ligament.

The femur

The femur, or thigh bone, is a strong, heavy bone the globular head of which is cupped in the acetabulum of the hip bone, forming a ball-and-socket joint. Below the long, constricted neck region are two processes—the greater and lesser trochanters—that afford attachment for some of the muscles of the thigh and gluteal regions. A ridge, known as the linea aspera, presents along the posterior aspect of the shaft, muscles being attached to this ridge. The articular capsule extends almost to the base of the neck of the femur and it should be noted that fractures of the femoral neck may be wholly intracapsular or partially extracapsular. The intracapsular head of the femur is covered with articular cartilage except at the fovea, the pit for the attachment of the ligament of the head of the femur; this pit presents one or two foramina for vessels transversing the ligament to nourish the head, vessels probably playing a minor role in repair of fracture of the neck. The lower end of the femur widens and at the extremity are two bony prominences referred to as the medial and lateral condyles. The smooth articular surfaces form a hinge joint with the tibia. The patella also articulates with the lower extremity of the femur.

The femur possesses the longest, thickest, and strongest shaft of all the bones of the skeleton. The upper end comprises a globular articular head which is enclosed by the acetabulum in a deep articulation which is securely designed and in direct contrast with the design of the shoulder joint in providing stability at the cost of some limitation in the range of movement. Flexion and extension of the thigh, the most frequent movements, though angular movements of the shaft, are at the hip converted to a rotation of the head in the acetabulum. If the neck of the femur were in the same straight line as the shaft, flexion of the thigh would rapidly cease as the neck came into contact with the rim of the acetabulum, but because the angular movement of the shaft is converted to rotation of the head the range of flexion is increased without being checked, until the thigh meets the abdomen. The attitude of the neck and the shaft ensures sufficient space for the large mass of muscles.

The patella

The patella is a flat sesamoid bone, the largest in the body, and is contained largely within the tendon of the rectus femoris muscle. The patella and bursae serve to protect the knee joint. The ligamentum patellae is a strong ligament extending from the patella to the tibia. The knee cap articulates in all its movements only with the femur and functions as a mobile lever, a kind of roller bearing that glides upon the femoral condyles, enabling the rectus femoris muscle to pull at greater advantage. The patella projects forward in extension and sinks downward and backward in flexion, securely fixed between the condyles. A limb functions more efficiently with a patella, but removal of the knee cap presents no serious impairment and is preferable to one which, due to fracture, prevents smooth articulation.

The tibia

The tibia is the larger bone of the leg below the knee. The upper, larger, expanded end articulates with the femoral condyles and the head of the fibula; a long shaft and a smaller, expanded lower end articulates with the fibula and talus (astragalus). The upper end of the tibia is formed of medial and lateral condyles. The long process at the lower end of the medial aspect is termed the medial malleolus. The shaft is narrowest at a level below its mid-point, the most frequent site of fracture and the area where rickets manifests itself early by accentuating the natural curves of the bone. Little movement is possible between the tibia and fibula, but the ligaments afford a resilience to the tong-like action of the malleoli on the talus.

The fibula

The fibula is a long, slender bone which articulates above, by its head, with the lateral condyle of the tibia and below, as the lateral malleolus, with the tibia and talus. The fibula serves, together with the attached interosseous membrane, to extend the area for muscle attachment and to act as a brace to the tibia.

The hock, or tarsus

Seven bones form the tarsus of the dog. They are the calcaneus (heel bone; os calcis), talus (astragalus), navicular (schapoid), cuboid, and the first, second, and third cuneiform bones. The calcaneus is the largest of the tarsal bones and helps support the weight of the hind limb and affords attachment for the muscles of the calf. The talus lies above the calcaneus and articulates with the tibia and fibula. The navicular bone is immediately anterior to the talus on the inner aspect of the hock. The cuboid bone is anterior to the calcaneus on the lateral

Kate's A Scandal (Temlee–Grotto's Babe), 1981 South Australian and National Greyhound of the Year and Arnott–Spillers National Sprint Champion. Created a new Australian record of fifteen consecutive wins, breaking a thirty-year-old record held by Harryed *(Courtesy of the* News, *Adelaide)*

aspect. The three cuneiform bones form a row in front of the navicular, with the first cuneiform being on the inner aspect. The most important joints of the hock are those of the talus, which act as a form of universal joint between the hind leg and the remainder of the foot.

Synovial bursae

Bursae are sacs of fibrous connective tissue lined with synovial membrane which are frequently located at joints to prevent the friction of surfaces. They may be subcutaneous, like the bursa over the patella or the olcranal bursa. Bursae are located wherever friction is likely to occur between tendons or between muscles and bones. The synovial membrane secretes a viscid lubricating fluid, mechanical injuries to the bursae or infections giving rise to accumulation of fluid. Bursitis refers to inflammation of the bursa, common sites of bursitis being subdeltoid (above the shoulder joint), in the vicinity of the Achilles tendon, and around the knee.

Articulations

Various types of joints or articulations have been mentioned in the discussion of the skeleton. Joints are usually classified according to the amount or type of movement associated with the articulation as:

1. *Immovable*
   The sutures between cranial bones afford an excellent example of immovable articulations. These bones are fitted together by means of an interlocking arrangement and are held together by fibrous connective tissue. The sutures generally become more ossified with increase in age.

2. *Slightly movable*
   These articulations exhibit a pad of fibrocartilage between the two bones. The intervertebral discs permit some movement between the vertebrae. The symphysis between the pubic bones is also of this type, although there is almost no movement. The sacro-iliac articulation affords a similar example. At the termination of whelping there is a slight degree of flexibility in these pelvic articulations occasioned by structural alterations in the fibrocartilage.

3. *Freely movable*

Hinge joints permit free movement in one plane but articulations of the ball-and-socket type are the most freely movable. Pivot joints permit rotary movements, for example, the atlas moving on the axis.

THE GREYHOUND IN MOTION

The spine of the greyhound, in contrast to that of the horse, is very flexible. In the dog the hind feet actually glide past the elbows or shoulders and land marginally ahead of the position occupied by the forefeet when the dog is stationary. If one has had the opportunity to study moving pictures of the racing greyhound it might be argued that the hind limbs perform most of the propulsion and that the forelimbs merely act as a support to the body at the cessation of each bound. In actual fact that section of the forelimbs above the elbows still adds to the forward thrust of the body through space, but does not exert nearly as much force as the hind limbs in galloping at considerable speed. Both the forelimbs and the hind limbs are active at slower speeds, but the dominance of the one or the other depends to a large degree on the attitude of the dog's head which, by virtue of being raised and lowered, brings about a change in the centre of gravity. When the head is lowered considerable strain is directed upon the forelimbs and most of the propulsion is produced by the loins and hind limbs. When walking or trotting on a level surface propulsion is fairly evenly divided between the hind limbs and the forelimbs. Owing to the fact that the greyhound exhibits highly developed loins and quarters, more weight lies behind and the centre of gravity is consequently further back. There must be perfect co-operation or balance between the two main portions of the body as this will tend toward ease of movement. Actual propulsion through space depends upon the particular attitude or gait of the animal and the acquired momentum.

During galloping there may be instances when only one foot contacts the ground and occasionally none at all, the body being propelled through space by the acquired momentum. When a greyhound gallops on a circular track the foreleg nearest the centre of the track (i.e., nearest the running rail) takes the greater weight and consequently becomes the leading leg. If for any reason the dog is thrown off stride and changes legs, as occurs by dogs colliding with each other

in running, by hitting racetrack structures, or by faultering due to the track surface, there will be a loss of speed and the winner is frequently the dog that is able to retain its balance and maintain the same gait throughout the race. Generally speaking, when a greyhound gallops on a straight track the tendency is to turn all feet slightly toward the mid-line of the body. When the greyhound negotiates a bend the body will be seen to lean toward the running rail at an angle of about 35° with the feet of the inclined side directed inwards and those of the opposite side directed marginally outwards.

It is well to remember that 'perfection of form does not ensure perfection of movement, nor necessarily any great improvement in stamina'. A vast number of greyhounds fulfil all the requirements of the most exacting standard until such time as they are called upon to move.

The inclined shoulder which permits upright head carriage, without which the muscles advancing the forelimb cannot operate to full advantage, is of paramount importance when considering the desirable movement of the greyhound. It is essential, also, that the dog be properly balanced. There may be an imbalance between the natural length of the fore and hind stride—perhaps a side effect of selective breeding. Poor coordination in the hind quarters may be a consequence of difficulty in flexing the spine. A sacrum which is low and inclined downwards gives rise to weak, sloping quarters, a badly fastened tail, and a poorly developed thigh, which is often concomittant with cow hocks.

It is incorrect to imagine that by increasing the angulation of the hind limbs that one can increase the power of propulsion operating through the hind limbs, because in four-legged animals the force derived from the pressure of the hind foot against the ground is transmitted to the pelvis at the acetabulum and then via the sacrum to the spine. This direct route affords negligible wastage of power. The dog with an almost-straight hock and stifle and standing over less ground can generally draw away from the dog with the over-angulated hind limb, 'owing to the fact that it is less wasteful to employ a shorter, straight hind limb and a greater number of shorter strides than to employ fewer longer strides'. This angulation has been retained in the show ring as it renders a more pleasing appearance to the outline of the dog. The pasterns should retain their width from below the knee downward as well as being strong and capable of bearing weight without permitting the feet to sprawl in a forward direction.

Causes of pintoeing

1. Excessive curvature of the upper third of the first four ribs causes the upper end of the scapula to be pushed outward, with the shoulder joints necessarily following suit. This frequently results in a corresponding off-setting of the elbow joints, the toes then turning inward in an attempt to restore balance.

The elbows of young puppies may point out due to slackness or under-development of the pectoral muscles which anchor the inner aspect of the forelimbs to the sternum. Growth, time, and exercise usually correct this elbow position.

2. An exaggerated degree of rotation of the shaft of the humerus in the region of the musculo-spiral groove may result in the lower articular extremity of the humerus being a little out of place, the consequence of this being a corresponding alteration in the position of the elbow joint and, in an attempt to maintain balance, the dog turns its toes inward.

3. Slight deviation of the outer trochlea of the lower extremity of the humerus may affect the attitude of the limb from that point downward and induce the toes to turn inward.

4. Pintoeing may present when the fore-end of the dog is either at all times, or momentarily, heavier than the hind end.

5. Pintoeing is sometimes a form of protection against skidding on a slippery surface, for example, when a dog negotiates a highly polished floor.

6. When the chest is wide and heavily muscled the elbows tend to be wide apart and there may be a tendency for the dog to pintoe. The degree of curvature of the first four pairs of ribs also determines, to some extent, the amount of width between the forelimbs. Ideally, the first three pairs of ribs should be slightly curved and from then on the curvation should gradually increase up to the tenth pair of ribs and then slightly diminish.

As an authority on dogs once commented 'whether you be owner, or merely an inmate, hold your head high and stride firmly forward, happy in the knowledge that you have sound reserves behind you'.

FRACTURES

A fracture has been defined as the interruption of the continuity of a bone. This interruption may be complete or incomplete. Fractures may be classified as follows:

Incomplete

1. Greenstick: in which the bone is bent, and broken only part of the way through its shaft. This type is found only in puppies.
2. Fissured: consisting of a mere split of the bone without displacement of the fragments.
3. Perforating: in which there is a hole such as is made by a bullet.
4. Depressed: saucer or gutter-shaped depressions, generally observed in fractures of the skull.

Complete

1. Simple: in which the skin is intact. This is sometimes referred to as a 'closed' fracture.
2. Impacted: in which the broken bone ends are driven into each other.
3. Comminuted: in which the bone is splintered or broken into several pieces.
4. Compound: in which the broken bone has pierced the skin. This is sometimes referred to as an 'open' fracture. There is great danger of infection.
5. Complicated: in which there is injury to an important organ or structure in the vicinity of the fracture.

Traumatic fractures are those which are caused by direct violence. In these fractures the bone is normal and the causative force maximal. The force causing a fracture may consist of:

1. Direct violence, as when a leg is broken by a blow.
2. Indirect violence, in which case the force is transmitted to the bone via some other part of the body, as when the tibia and fibula are broken by a fall on the feet.
3. Muscular action, as in fracture of the patella due to a sudden contraction of the quadriceps extensors.

Spontaneous fractures are always of pathological origin. Local or general diseases render the bone unduly brittle and liable to fracture with minimal traumatic force.

Fractures may be transverse, oblique, or spiral in their form of displacement, the transverse fractures usually being the result of direct, the oblique and spiral fractures of indirect, violence. There is generally a great deal of soft tissue damage in transverse fractures, while in spiral and oblique fractures soft tissue damage is frequently slight. The fragments may be displaced as follows:

1. Lateral displacement.
2. Angulation, in which the fragments form an angle with each other instead of being in a line.
3. Overlapping, resulting in shortening of the bone.
4. Rotation, or twisting of the distal fragment.

The symptoms of a fracture at the moment of injury, or shortly after, are unnatural mobility, crepitus (grating between the broken bone ends), deformity, pain, and subsequent loss of function. The muscles go into spasm and the more mobile the fragments, the greater is the spasm. This is a protective reflex designed to maintain the fragments in position and it disappears when the limb is supported and immobilised. Swelling soon follows and may be intense and widespread. It persists for a time and then gradually subsides.

The veterinary surgeon makes a diagnosis partly by observation of the symptoms, but fractures are X-rayed as a matter of routine. The X-rays are also employed later to ascertain whether the fragments have remained in the correct position after reduction, whether union is taking place, whether the screws or nails are holding in a bone which has been plated or nailed, or whether the bone grafts are taking in instances where bone graft is necessary.

When the bone is broken, swelling occurs within 24 hours and is due partially to haemorrhage into the tissues and partially to slowing of the venous circulation, with increased exudation of lymph. A clot, or haematoma, forms between the broken bone ends and organises into a soft mass into which new blood vessels grow. The new tissue is fabricated not only between the bone ends, but outside these beneath the periosteum, and the space where the medullary cavity of the bone would be is also filled with granulation tissue, the entire section constituting a rubbery mass. The bone ends become rarified and calcium is laid down in the granulation tissue, the new substance being referred to as callus. The fracture is clinically united at this juncture and the two ends move as one, although they are not yet sufficiently strong to withstand stress. When union by callus has been completed, the osteoblasts form a deposit of bone salts in the soft tissue, progressively hardening it. Osteoclasts pass into the new bone, and hollow out the cavities, rendering its structure less dense. This process is similar to the process of ossification in normal bone. The medullary cavity is reformed and marrow cells reappear, the process being referred to as consolidation. Finally, remodelling of new bone occurs.

The time required to obtain union varies in different bones in accordance with the thickness of the bone, the richness of its blood supply, and the degree of separation between the fragments. Transverse fractures generally unite later than spiral or oblique fractures and the forelimb before the hind limb. The time needed to obtain union also varies in accordance with the section of the bone injured. The blood supply in the vicinity of the joints is good, so that fractures in these regions unite more rapidly than those of the bone shaft. The time for union also varies in different dogs. The age of the dog is a factor; fractures unite more rapidly in puppies than in adult dogs.

Delayed union and non-union are terms used to denote respectively that union is taking longer than usual, and that callus has not formed. Delayed union frequently results in non-union. Delayed union may be the consequence of general disease, such as severe anaemia, of local disease of the bone, or of sepsis in the bone or surrounding tissues. Union will also be delayed if the blood supply to one fragment is impaired, since the ability of the non-vascular fragment to lay down callus is limited. If the blood supply of both fragments is impaired, the time required for union will be much longer. If one fragment is totally deprived of its blood supply, it is able to take no part in repair of the fracture, and eventually dies; this is referred to as avascular bone necrosis. The living fragment lays down tissue which invades and eventually replaces the dead section but this process is extremely slow. Non-union may be due to the same causes as delayed union, to extensive loss of bone substance as in a gun shot wound, to the fact that muscular or ligamentous fibres have become interposed between the fragments, to lack of immobility at the site of the fractures, or to too great disparity between the bone ends.

Complications

Complications include:

1. *Injuries to the skin*

This occurs in compound fractures and in these cases bacteria may enter and infect the wound and because of this danger a skin wound takes precedence over the fracture. Sometimes only temporary treatment is afforded to the fracture until such time as the wound has healed.

2. *Injuries to blood vessels*

These may occur as:

a. Haemorrhage, due to the tearing of large vessels.

b. Blocking of a large artery which, if partially occluded, results in ischaemic contracture and, if completely blocked, in such an area as to cut off almost the entire blood supply of the limb, results in gangrene. These conditions may also be brought about by over-tight bandages, incorrectly applied splints or plaster, or may be due to compression of an artery by bone fragments.

c. Thrombosis of veins in the vicinity of the fracture manifested by the sudden onset of cramp-like pain in the part, by increased swelling, and by marked tenderness along the line of the affected vein. In cases of suspected thrombosis, all treatment must cease.

3. *Injuries to muscle*

Fibres may tear or rupture as a consequence of the injury or myositis ossificans, post traumatic ossification, may occur. Myositis ossificans consists of formation of bone in structures surrounding a fracture, if the periosteum is torn. This condition is always a possibility following injuries in the region of the elbow, although it may occur in other parts, e.g., round the hip, or involving the quadriceps in injuries to the knee joint. Bone cells escape into the muscles and eventually ossify.

4. *Injuries to nerves*

A nerve may have been injured at the time of occurrence of the fracture, in which case the symptoms appear immediately. A deep nerve may become involved in forming callus, or be compressed by displaced bone, and in this instance the symptoms are gradual in onset. If the nerve is severed, there is immediate paralysis and anaesthesia of the parts supplied by it.

5. *Injuries to joints*

The fracture may extend into the joint and seriously restrict movement by imperfect replacement of the fragments, by excessive formation of callus or by the formation of adhesions. Osteoarthritis may later develop in the joint following on from the traumatic arthritis caused by the injury. The veterinary surgeon aims at exact anatomical alignment, which is not always possible, particularly if the surface is disrupted. In such cases movement may assist in moulding the surfaces and regaining joint congruity.

6. *Persistent swelling: adhesions*

Swelling is the consequence of the liberation of histamine from the injured tissues which causes neighbouring capillaries to dilate, thus increasing the flow of blood to the affected part, and slowing the circulation in the area. The walls of the vessels become more permeable and fluid passes out into the tissue spaces; if this is excessive, it can prevent treatment of the fracture, temporary measures only being possible. This serofibrinous exudate lays down fibrin, forming dense bands which may impair joint mobility, producing stiffness and pain. In the early stages the swelling is soft but later, when some of the fluid part of the exudate has been absorbed, it becomes harder and pits deeply upon pressure. In severe cases, especially in the hind limbs, the whole limb may remain permanently enlarged and muscle tone is lowered. The limb feels weighty and the dog fatigued and so it is essential to disperse the swelling as quickly as possible. Persistent swelling may be the consequence of recurrent injury, e.g., too early or too forcible movement of the injured joint or of the joint nearest the fracture; of functional inactivity which produces circulatory stasis, e.g., if the knee is immobilised and no movements of the hip or foot are given to maintain the circulation of the leg; of infection in or in the vicinity of the joint; or of injury to the vessels of the limb. Recurrent swelling may be the consequence of the action of gravity, e.g., when the dog commences to walk following a fracture of the hock.

Treatment

The aim of treatment is, firstly, to obtain accurate anatomical alignment in order to promote sound repair and, secondly, to restore the function of the limb.

The fragments of bone are hyperaemic, as a result of the inflammatory reaction which occurs as the result of the injury, while the soft callus is developing. This leads to decalcification of the fragments because the calcium in the bone is carried away by the increased blood flow. During the consolidation period the bone ends become ischaemic, i.e., their blood supply is greatly reduced, the calcium accumulates and the bone recalcifies. A certain degree of inflammatory reaction and consequent hyperaemia is necessary for callus formation but, if it is extreme or persistent, too much calcium will be lost from the fragments. A small amount of movement at the fracture site in the recent stage promotes callus formation by increasing the inflammatory reaction, but if movement is over-done undesirable results follow. In certain regions, such as the elbow, a large amount of callus may form which later ossifies and blocks the joint and dense fibrous adhesions develop which further limit mobility. If the movement between the fragments is continuous or excessive, the bones may unite extremely slowly or fail to unite. An authority has stated that 'if the young repair material is stretched, it ends up as a pliable scar; if it is compressed, it ends up as a rigid bone. One should therefore, during the mending of a fracture, encourage everything that compresses the embryonic callus, and discourage anything that stretches it'. Factors which contribute to compression are muscle tone, voluntary muscle action, and weight bearing. Factors contributing to stretching are traction, hinging, and rotation. Consequently, there are three major principles of treatment.

1. *Reduction*

Reduction may be closed, i.e., by manipulation under anaesthetic, or open, i.e., performed by operation. Reduction is undertaken to regain perfect alignment of the fragments. If there is no displacement, or if the fragments are impacted, there is generally no need for reduction.

2. *Fixation*

Fixation is designed to maintain reduction and to prevent harmful stress until union has taken place. In the past, treatment of fractures following reduction consisted of splinting and fixation of the whole limb until union was solid. This ensured a good anatomical result, but since the joint in the meantime had become stiff, and the muscles wasted, the functional result left much to be desired. Nowadays, the veterinary surgeon does not engage more extensive fixation than is necessary to ensure immobilisation of the site of the fracture and no joints which can safely be left free are included in the plaster, and in these free joints movement is encouraged. Fixation may adopt the form of external splintage, internal splintage, and traction. External splintage includes plaster of Paris casts, apparatus, strapping, or bandages which secure the fracture site. Internal splintage is applied by open operation, the fragments being fixed together by steel or silver plates, screws, or nails. Sometimes the fragments are sutured with wire or catgut or pegged together with pegs of bone. Many veterinary surgeons engage some form of external splintage in addition until union

has taken place. Others are of the opinion that internal fixation affords sufficient support. Operative measures may be employed initially or follow delay or non-union.

3. *Protection*

Although union has occurred the fracture cannot withstand stress until consolidation is established and it is thus necessary to protect the fracture if it may be subjected to a rotation strain, a hinging strain, or to traction by muscle action, such as takes place at the elbow or knee.

The method of fixation selected by the veterinary surgeon and the amount of physical treatment permitted is entirely dependent on his views. The importance of preventing joint stiffness and muscular atrophy is widely recognised. Most authorities agree that certain fractures do not require any fixation and that such fractures are treated as soft-tissue injuries, the stress being made on prevention of adhesions. These include fractures without displacement, some fractures in non-weight-bearing bones, some impacted fractures, and some minor fractures in weight-bearing bones. Some veterinary surgeons engage excessive splintage, others employ it sparingly, but whatever the views of the veterinary surgeon the principles of treatment are the same.

To assist repair and help restore function two points are of major importance:

1. *Adequate circulation*

This is of paramount importance if a haematoma is to form, if the uninjured tissues are to remain healthy, if trophic changes are to be avoided, and if adhesions are to be prevented. The circulation must be adequate for the formation of callus. In the early stages of fractures, factors such as swelling, the protective spasm of the muscles, and pain, which gives rise to a protective spasm, lead to a reduction in the circulation. It is therefore essential to relieve pain, spasm, and swelling as quickly as possible, in the interest of the comfort of the dog and to facilitate the repair processes. The fact that part of the limb is immobilised tends to exert an adverse effect on circulation because it reduces the activity of joints and muscles.

2. *Joint mobility and muscle power*

Joint mobility and muscle power must be maintained in all free joints and, as far as possible, in immobilised joints if the dog is to be restored to full functional activity as soon as possible. Care must be taken to ensure that nothing delays repair or leads to non-union. The soft tissues must be cared for in order to assist the process of union. Any softening of plaster or similar damage which may permit unwanted movement must be repaired. It is of paramount importance to maintain joint mobility and prevent adhesions and to maintain muscle power and prevent disuse atrophy. One must watch for complications such as ischaemic conditions, thrombosis, and skin infections.

Following removal of the plaster, massage may be employed to loosen or stretch adhesions or adherent scars, or to improve the condition of the skin. Olive oil or other lubricants are often used for the last purpose mentioned. Any joints which do not need to be fixed should be assiduously exercised in order to prevent stiffness in these joints and atrophy of the muscles which act on them. Those joints which must be fixed in order to retain the fragments in position can only be moved after the period of immobilisation has ceased. Following removal of the plaster there will be a certain amount of residual stiffness. No forced movement is to be given. Faradism is sometimes applied while the limb is still immobilised, in order to obtain muscle contractions, without causing movement in any joint. Faradism may also be employed at a later stage to help restore muscles to full strength. If afforded to assist in the restoration of power, faradism must not be permitted to take the place of voluntary movement. Infra-red radiation may improve the circulation, decrease pain and lay the path for active movement. Ultra-violet light may be employed in cases where there is an infected wound.

Fractures in metacarpal bones

Metacarpal fractures are the most frequently encountered fractures in the greyhound. The injuries to these bones vary from single or multiple complete fractures to greenstick fractures (fracture, in which one side of a bone is broken, the other being bent; an infraction, an incomplete fracture without displacement of fragments) and on occasions haemorrhages occur under the periosteum of these bones.

Radiological examination frequently reveals the presence of greenstick fractures which have been present for some time. When the matter is discussed with the trainer, it is often found that they are the consequence of some traumatic incident. If observed at the time of occurrence, the trainer finds that a specific metacarpal bone is extremely sore but exhibits little or no swelling in the area. The dog may exhibit little or no lameness. The greenstick, or hairline, fracture in the metacarpal bone, once established, will not heal unless the foot is relieved from weight-bearing for a short period of time by means of splints or plaster casts.

The track history of greyhounds with metacarpal fractures invariably reveals a decline in performance which is generally confined to specific portions of their races, e.g., being slow from the boxes and for the first 100 metres of a run, loss of manoeuvrability, and failure to take advantage of breaks in the field to pass other dogs and, perhaps the most obvious example, awkwardness on the turns. The most commonly encountered conclusion reached by the trainer is that the dog has developed vices in running. If the trainer does notice that a particular metacarpal bone is sore, because of the fact that there is generally negligible swelling and lameness, the subsequent home treatment usually involves the application of preparations such as bone radiol and a rapid regression of pain is noted. This is the most frequent root of establishment of chronic greenstick fracture. Hence I cannot emphasise too strongly the importance of X-ray of any metacarpal bone in which pain responses are elicited by pressure.

DISLOCATIONS

A dislocation, or luxation, is a condition in which the articular surfaces of the bones forming a joint are completely displaced from each other by violence and remain so displaced. At the time of the injury there is intense pain, worse than that of a fracture. The pain is less severe later, unless the displaced bone is pressing on a nerve. There is deformity of the limb, the joint is fixed, and limb function is lost. Later, the pain is of a dull, aching nature and increases on movement. The signs of acute inflammation develop, frequently with marked swelling of the limb. Variable degrees of bruising appear after a few days. As with fractures, adhesions and disuse atrophy are prone to occur if treatment is neglected or improperly administered. Dislocation may be complicated by fracture, e.g., fracture of the neck or shaft of the humerus, with dislocation of the shoulder. There may be risk of skin damage and infection if the fracture is comminuted. There may be injury to the periosteum, when the inflammation in that membrane gives rise to an out-throwing of osteoblasts, impeding the movements of the joint

Proven sire, Prince Champion (previously Prince's Imp), by Solar Prince out of Millie Hawthorn, considered by eminent judges to be faster than his notorious brothers, Faithful Hope and Winning Hope. Unplaced six times from twenty-nine starts and retired due to injury *(Courtesy of F. Schock)*

or lodging in the nearest muscles. Certain dislocations, notably those of the shoulder joint, are liable to recur. Paralysis may be the consequence of nerve injury, e.g., the circumflex nerve may be injured in dislocation of the shoulder, or the ulnar nerve in dislocation of the elbow. Severe dislocations may be accompanied by extensive muscle damage such as rupture or partial rupture of fibres or tendons. Before movement becomes full and painless the muscles must recover, and this frequently delays ultimate recovery for a few months. Haemorrhage, ischaemia, or gangrene may be the outcome of injuries to blood vessels.

Treatment aims at reduction of the displacement so that the joint surfaces are again opposed and this necessitates an anaesthetic because muscles respond to injury by protective spasm and sufficient relaxation must be achieved to permit reduction. Unlike fractures, in which reduction must be maintained by fixation, a dislocated joint is generally stable once reduction has been achieved. The muscles usually provide adequate splintage and protection from further injury, in the majority of cases, and fixation is not required. Rest is essential to permit the inflammatory reaction to subside and damaged

structures to heal. However, there are two schools of thought on this matter. Some veterinarians feel that the only way to ensure adequate rest is by immobilisation for several weeks and they therefore immobilise the joint as for fracture cases. It should be noted, however, that this is done for the benefit of the structures around the joint rather than for the bony injury as in the case of fractures. Other veterinarians are of the opinion that since the muscles will splint the joint, early movement is to be encouraged, provided it is carefully given, as it reduces the danger of adhesions and the inevitable loss of muscle power which follows when joints are immobilised. As with fractures, the prevention of adhesions and disuse atrophy are of paramount importance and pain and swelling must be relieved. All free joints must be exercised. Following immobilisation, full mobility and strength must be regained.

Dislocation of the shoulder in the greyhound is the commonest of all dislocations and may be caused by direct or indirect violence, i.e., by a fall or a blow on the joint itself, or by a fall on the outstretched foot, causing violent abduction of the foreleg. The latter form of violence is the commoner cause. Complications include fracture of the great tuberosity or surgical neck of the humerus; rupture of the supraspinatus tendon, which is torn away from its attachment to the head of the humerus; injury to the circumflex nerve; and recurrence of the dislocation, which happens more frequently with the shoulder than any other joint. Other tendons of the short muscles of the shoulder may be torn, in addition to the supraspinatus tendon. Injury to the circumflex nerve is not uncommon. Care must be taken to ensure that the deltoid does not contract, and if there is any doubt, the sensation in the skin over the muscle should be tested and a veterinary surgeon consulted. Slight circumflex injury is frequently the cause of a belated recovery from this injury. It may not be discovered at all or by the time anyone thinks of looking for such a thing, the nerve may have partially or completely recovered. In the meantime, the deltoid has wasted and the joint has stiffened. A lesion of the circumflex nerve in a shoulder injury is much more easily missed than is a lesion of the ulnar nerve in an elbow injury. It should be noted that the dog may be able to perform weak abduction with the supraspinatus, the nerve supply of which is more than likely intact.

Dislocation of the radius and ulna from the humeral articular surfaces (true dislocation of the elbow joint) may be caused by a fall on the elbow or foot, i.e., forced extension of the elbow. Dislocation may be forward, backward, lateral, or divergent, the most common type being posterior dislocation.

Traumatic dislocation of the hip is rare because of the great stability of the joint and the strength of the iliofemoral ligament, fracture of the neck of the femur being much more common. Only extreme violence produces an injury of this nature in the greyhound. The damage may occur as a simple dislocation, with tearing of the lower part of the capsule, or of a more severe complicated lesion, with rupture of the iliofemoral ligament and fracture of the acetabulum. Displacement may be anterior or posterior, but in either instance the head of the femur passes out of the joint through the lower part of the capsule and then either forward or backward, the latter direction being more common. Complications of posterior dislocation include injury to the sciatic nerve, myositis ossificans, and fracture of the femoral neck or necrosis of the femoral head. Injury to the femoral artery is a complication of anterior dislocation of the hip.

Injuries to the knee include dislocated knee, dislocated patella, slipped semilunar cartilage, and injury to the medial ligament without displacement of the cartilage. In instances of dislocated knee there is almost invariably damage to the bones—the spine of the tibia may be broken off or one or both cruciate ligaments may be ruptured, in addition to part of the capsule. Dislocation may be anterior, posterior, or lateral and is very serious because, unless the cruciate ligaments heal properly, the knee will always be unstable. For this reason the joint is invariably immobilised and support implies virtual fixation. At least eight weeks are necessary for complete repair of the ligaments. A knee plaster or support may have to be worn by the dog for four to six months in all from the time of injury, before free movements and weight-bearing are allowed. Because of the lengthy immobilisation period, it is essential to prevent atrophy of muscles, notably the flexors and extensors of the knee.

Dislocated patella occurs without accompanying bony and muscular injury and weakness of the quadriceps is a predisposing cause. Certain dogs exhibit deficient development of the external femoral condyle, or of the knee joint, causing the patella to slip outwards easily. Dislocation is almost invariably outward and is liable to recur constantly.

A tear of the medial semilunar cartilage may occur at the junction of the anterior and posterior parts, or it may be torn longitudinally down the centre, and complete extension of the knee is not permitted. Authorities believe that a force sufficiently strong to tear the cartilage will automatically strain the coronary ligament and perhaps the medial ligament. The lateral semilunar cartilage, because of its greater breadth and more secure attachments, is less prone to injury than that on the inner side. Also, the firm pressure between tibia and femur on the outer side of the knee tends to keep it in position.

The stability of the knee is largely dependent on the cruciate ligaments and if both are injured the knee hyperextends and there is abnormal lateral mobility. The knee is rendered weak and undependable and liable to give way when weight is borne on it.

The sacro-iliac joint is that between the articular surfaces of the sacrum and ilium. The bones are connected by the anterior sacro-iliac ligament and the much stronger posterior sacro-iliac ligament. During pregnancy the ligaments become relaxed, and following whelping they tighten again. Unilateral or bilateral displacement may take place. The ilium may be displaced forwards on the sacrum, or the sacrum forward on the ilium as a result of strain or injury. There is pain over one or both sacro-iliac joints or in the lumbar region and there may be referred pain in the gluteal region or abdomen. Pain on pressure is felt over the posterior superior spines of the ilium, which lie directly behind the joint. If actually displaced, the articular surfaces are put back into correct position under anaesthetic. The veterinary surgeon fully flexes and extends the hip and lumbar spine, thereby obtaining full anteroposterior movement in the sacro-iliac joints also, abducts each hip, rotates the pelvis, and performs any special manipulations necessary to obtain perfect replacement of the articular surfaces. Strengthening of the muscles by exercise provides the necessary support for the joint following manipulation. On the evening of the same day of the manipulation, the dog should be treated by a dose of infra-red radiation and the joints then moved passively. The following day heat and gentle massage of the hips and back are given. As soon as possible, active movements are added. The joint and all the muscles in the neighbourhood (gluteal and lumbar muscles) should later be treated by vigorous massage and heat is afforded as long as pain is present.

14

THE MUSCULAR SYSTEM

DESCRIPTIVE TERMS

Abduct (ab+L. ducere = to draw). To draw away from the median line or from a neighbouring part or limb.

Adduct (L. adducere = to draw toward). To draw toward the median line of the body or toward a neighbouring part.

Anterior (L. anterior = before). The ventral or belly surface of the body, the front surface.

Distal (L. distans = distant). Farther from the trunk. Synonymous with inferior.

Extend (ex+L. tendere = to stretch). The movement by which the two ends of any part are pulled assunder. A movement which brings the members of a limb into or toward a straight condition. To stretch out or to straighten.

Flex (L. flexus = bent). To bend or put in a state of flexion. To make an angle.

Insertion (L. insertio = from in = into + serere = to join). The place of attachment of a muscle to the bone which it moves.

Lateral (L. lateralis = lateral). A structure situated farther from the midline of the body.

Medial (L. medialis = middle). A structure situated nearer to the median plane or the midline of a body or structure.

Origin (L. origo = beginning). The more fixed end or attachment of a muscle.

Plantar (L. planta = sole). Pertaining to the sole of the foot.

Posterior (L. posterus = behind). The back or dorsal surface of the body.

Proximal (L. proximus = next). Nearer the trunk. Synonymous with superior.

Retract (L. retractio = from re = back + trahere = to draw). The act of drawing back.

Rotate (L. rotare = to turn). To turn or revolve on a long axis. Movement of a body about its axis.

TABLE OF MUSCLES

MUSCLE	ORIGIN	INSERTION	INNERVATION	ACTION
Biceps brachii Biceps muscle of front leg. (2 heads)	**Caput longum** Upper border of glenoid cavity. **Caput breve**— Apex of coracoid process.	Radial tuberosity and deep fascia of foreleg.	Musculocutaneous	Flexes foreleg, supinates foot.
Biceps femoris Biceps muscle of thigh. (2 heads). Hamstring.	**Caput longum**— Ischial tuberosity. **Caput breve**— Linea aspera of femur.	Head of fibula, lateral condyle of tibia.	**Caput longum**— Tibial. **Caput breve**— Peroneal, popliteal.	Flexes leg, extends thigh.
Brachialis Brachial muscle.	Anterior surface of humerus.	Coronoid process of ulna.	Radial, musculocutaneous.	Flexes foreleg.
Coccygeus Coccygeal muscle.	Ischial spine and lesser sacrosciatic ligament.	Lateral border of lower sacrum, upper coccyx.	Third and fourth sacral.	Supports and raises coccyx.

189

MUSCLE	ORIGIN	INSERTION	INNERVATION	ACTION
Deltoideus Deltoid muscle. Monkey muscle.	Clavicle, acromion, spine of scapula.	Deltoid tuberosity of humerus.	Axillary.	Abducts, flexes, extends front leg.
Extensor digitorum brevis Short extensor muscle of toes.	Dorsal surface of os calcis.	Extensor tendons of the four toes.	Deep peroneal.	Extends toes.
Extensor digitorum longus Long extensor muscle of toes.	Anterior surface of fibula, lateral condyle of tibia, interosseous membrane.	Common extensor tendon of the four toes.	Deep peroneal.	Extends toes.
Flexor digitorum brevis Short flexor muscle of toes.	Medial tuberosity of os calcis, plantar-fascia	Middle phalanges of the four toes.	Medial plantar.	Flexes toes.
Flexor digitorum longus Long flexor muscle of toes.	Posterior surface of shaft of tibia.	Distal phalanges of the four toes.	Posterior tibial.	Flexes toes and extends foot.
Extensor digitorum Extensor muscle of front toes.	Lateral epicondyle of humerus.	Common extensor tendon of each toe.	Deep radial.	Extends wrist joint and phalanges.
Flexor digitorum profundus Deep flexor muscle of front toes.	Shaft of ulna, coronoid process.	Distal phalanges of front toes.	Ulnar and anterior interosseous.	Flexes distal phalanges.
Flexor digitorum superficialis Superficial flexor muscle of front toes. (2 heads).	**Caput humeroulnare**—Medial epicondyle of humerus, coronoid process of ulna. **Caput radiale**—Oblique line of radius, anterior border.	Middle phalanges of front toes.	Median.	Flexes middle phalanges.
Gastrocnemius Gastrocnemius muscle. (2 heads).	**Caput mediale**—Popliteal surface of femur, upper part of medial condyle, capsule of knee. **Caput laterale**—Lateral condyle, capsule of knee.	Aponeurosis unites with tendon of soleus to form the Achilles tendon.	Tibial.	Plantar flexes the hock joint, flexes the knee joint.
Gluteus maximus Greatest gluteal muscle.	Lateral surface of ilium, dorsal surface of sacrum and coccyx, sacro-tuberous ligament.	Iliotibial band of fascia lata, gluteal tuberosity of femur.	Inferior gluteal.	Extends, abducts, and rotates thigh outward.

MUSCLE	ORIGIN	INSERTION	INNERVATION	ACTION
Gluteus medius Middle gluteal muscle.	Lateral surface of ilium between anterior and posterior gluteal lines.	Greater trochanter of femur.	Superior gluteal.	Abducts thigh.
Gluteus minimus Least gluteal muscle.	Lateral surface of ilium between anterior and inferior gluteal lines.	Greater trochanter of femur.	Superior gluteal.	Abducts, medially rotates thigh.
Gracilis Gracilis muscle.	Inferior ramus of pubis.	Medial surface of body of tibia.	Obturator.	Abducts thigh, flexes knee joint.
Iliacus Iliac muscle.	Iliac fossa and base of sacrum.	Lesser trochanter of femur.	Femoral.	Flexes thigh.
Infraspinatus Infraspinous muscle.	Infraspinous fossa of scapula.	Greater tubercle of humerus.	Suprascapular.	Rotates humerus laterally.
Intercostales externi External intercostal muscles.	Inferior border of rib.	Superior border of rib below.	Intercostal.	Draws ribs together in respiration and explusive movements.
Intercostales interni Internal intercostal muscles.	Inferior border of rib and costal cartilage.	Superior border of rib and costal cartilage below.	Intercostal.	Draws ribs together in respiration and expulsive movements.
Latissimus dorsi Latissimus muscle of back. Fan muscle.	Spines of thoracic and lumbar vertebrae, lumbodorsal fascia, iliac crest, lower ribs, inferior angle of scapula.	Crest of intertubercular sulcus of humerus.	Thoracodorsal.	Abducts, extends, and medially rotates humerus.
Longissimus dorsi Longissimus thoracis. Longissimus muscle of thorax.	Transverse and articular processes of lumbar vertebrae and lumbodorsal fascia.	Transverse processes of all thoracic vertebrae, nine or ten lower ribs.	Lumbar and thoracic.	Extends thoracic vertebrae.
Masseter Masseter muscle.	**Pars superficialis** Zygomatic process of maxilla and lower border of zygomatic arch. **Pars profunda** Lower border and medial surface of zygomatic arch.	**Pars superficialis** Angle and ramus of manible. **Pars profunda** Upper half of ramus and lateral surface of coronoid process of mandible.	Mandibular division of trigeminal.	Raises mandible, closes jaws.
Obliquus externus abdominis External oblique muscle of abdomen.	Lower eight ribs at costal cartilages.	Crest of ilium, linea alba through rectus sheath.	Lower intercostal.	Flexes and rotates vertebral column, compresses abdominal viscera.

MUSCLE	ORIGIN	INSERTION	INNERVATION	ACTION
Obliquus internus abdominis Internal oblique muscle of abdomen.	Inguinal ligament, iliac crest, lumbar aponeurosis.	Lower three or four costal cartilages, linea alba, conjoined tendon to pubis.	Lower intercostal.	Flexes and rotates vertebral column, compresses abdominal viscera.
Obturatorius externus External obturator muscle.	Pubis, ischium, and superficial surface of obturator membrane.	Trochanteric fossa of femur.	Obturator.	Rotates thigh laterally.
Obturatorius internus Internal obturator muscle.	Pelvic surface of hip bone, margin of obturator foramen, ramus of ischium, inferior ramus of pubis, internal surface of obturator membrane.	Greater trochanter of femur.	First, second, and third sacral.	Rotates thigh laterally.
Pectoralis major Greater pectoral muscle.	Clavicle, sternum, six upper ribs, aponeurosis of obliquus externus abdominis. These origins are reflected in the subdivision of the muscle into clavicular, sternocostal, and abdominal parts.	Crest of intertubercular groove of humerus.	Anterior thoracis.	Adducts, flexes, medially rotates forelegs.
Pectoralis minor Smaller pectoral muscle.	Third, fourth, and fifth ribs.	Coracoid process of scapula.	Anterior thoracic.	Draws shoulder forward and downward.
Psoas major Greater psoas muscle.	Lumbar vertebrae and fascia.	Lesser trochanter of femur.	Second and third lumbar.	Flexes trunk, flexes and medially rotates thigh.
Psoas minor Smaller psoas muscle.	Last thoracic and first lumbar vertebrae.	Iliopectineal eminence.	First lumbar.	Flexes trunk on pelvis.
Pyramidalis Pyramidal muscle.	Front of pubis, anterior pubic ligament.	Linea alba.	Last thoracic.	Tenses abdominal wall.
Rectus femoris Straight muscle of thigh.	Anterior inferior iliac spine, brim of acetabulum.	Patella, tubercle of tibia.	Femoral.	Extends leg, flexes thigh.
Rhomboideus major Greater rhomboid muscle.	Spinous processes of second, third, fourth, and fifth thoracic vertebrae.	Vertebral margin of scapula.	Dorsal scapular.	Retracts, elevates scapula.

MUSCLE	ORIGIN	INSERTION	INNERVATION	ACTION
Rhomboideus minor Lesser rhomboid muscle.	Spinous processes of seventh cervical to first thoracic vertebrae, lower part of ligamentum nuchae.	Vertebral margin of scapula at root of the spine.	Dorsal scapular.	Adducts, elevates scapula.
Sartorius Sartorius muscle. Whip muscle. Pencil muscle.	Anterior superior spine of ilium.	Medial side of proximal end of tibia.	Femoral.	Flexes thigh and leg.
Semimembranosus Semimembranous muscle. Hamstring.	Tuberosity of ischium.	Medial condyle of tibia.	Tibial.	Flexes leg, extends thigh.
Semitendinosus Semitendinous muscle. Hamstring.	Tuberosity of ischium.	Upper and medial surface of tibia.	Tibial.	Flexes leg, extends thigh.
Serratus anterior Anterior serratus muscle.	First seven or eight ribs.	Vertebral border of scapula.	Long thoracic.	Draws scapula forward, rotates scapula to raise shoulder in abduction of leg.
Serratus posterior inferior Inferior posterior serratus muscle.	Spines of two lower thoracic and two or three upper lumbar vertebrae.	Inferior border of four lower ribs.	Ninth to twelfth thoracic.	Lowers ribs in expiration.
Serratus posterior superior Superior posterior serratus muscle.	Ligamentum nuchae, spinous processes of upper thoracic vertebrae.	Second, third, fourth, and fifth ribs.	Upper four inter-costal.	Raises ribs in inspiration.
Soleus Soleus muscle.	Fibula, popliteal fascia, tibia.	Os calcis by Achilles Tendon.	Tibial.	Plantar flexes hock joint.
Subscapularis Subscapular muscle.	Subscapular of scapula.	Lesser tubercle of humerus.	Subscapular.	Rotates humerus medially.
Supraspinatus Supraspinous muscle.	Supraspinous fossa of scapula.	Greater tuberosity of humerus.	Suprascapular.	Abducts humerus.
Temporalis Temporal muscle.	Temporal fossa and fascia.	Coronoid process of manible.	Mandibular divi-sion of trigeminal.	Closes jaw.
Tensor fasciae latae Tensor muscle of fascia lata.	Iliac crest.	Iliotibial band of fascia lata.	Superior gluteal.	Flexes, abducts thigh.

MUSCLE	ORIGIN	INSERTION	INNERVATION	ACTION
Trapezius Trapezius muscle.	Occipital bone, ligamentum nuchea, spinous processes of seventh cervical and all thoracic vertebrae.	Clavicle, acromion, spine of scapula.	Spinal accessory and cervical plexus.	Rotates scapula to raise shoulder in abduction of the leg, draws scapula backward.
Triceps brachii Triceps muscle. (3 heads). Egg muscle.	**Caput longum** Infraglenoid tuberosity of scapula. **Caput laterale** Posterior surface of humerus, lateral border of humerus, lateral intermuscular septum. **Caput mediale** Posterior surface of humerus below radial groove, medial border of humerus, medial intermuscular septa.	Olecranon of ulna.	Radial.	Extends foreleg, adducts and extends leg.
Vastus intermedius Intermediate great muscle. Portion of Quadriceps Femoris.	Anterior and lateral surfaces of femur.	Patella, common tendon of Quadriceps Femoris.	Femoral.	Extends leg.
Vastus lateralis Lateral great muscle. Portion of Quadriceps Femoris.	Capsule of hip joint, lateral aspect of femur.	Patella, common tendon of Quadriceps Femoris.	Femoral.	Extends leg.
Vastus medialis Medial great muscle. Portion of Quadriceps Femoris.	Medial aspect of femur.	Patella, common tendon of Quadriceps Femoris.	Femoral.	Extends leg.

MUSCLES

This tissue endows the animal kingdom with the power of movement. Applied to an inert skeletal framework, skeletal muscles cause the framework to move, as in walking, galloping, and hurdling. Supporting this activity, there is a specialised type of musculature in the heart—cardiac muscle tissue—which by its constant contraction and relaxation enables the heart to beat and to supply blood to all parts of the body. A third type of muscular tissue constitutes the viscera—the organs of the body such as the stomach, intestine, and uterus. Visceral muscle is responsible for such internal activity as churning food in the stomach and passing it through the intestine. Muscular tissue accounts for forty to fifty per cent of the body weight, the percentage being slightly greater in dogs than bitches. The muscles are named from their size, shape, structure, situation, direction, action, and attachments. The structure and mechanism of contractility, the essential virtue of muscle, are similar throughout the animal kingdom, though the amount and speed of contraction may vary widely between the classes of animals and between the muscles in the same animal.

'No more diverse array of engines, in shape, size, power, speed, and the methods by which they are coupled between bones or other tissues, can well be imagined than the numerous designs of muscle and tendon devised to execute voluntary movements. The design is all the more remarkable considering the impress of inheritance, the compromise required between power and speed, the admirable disposition whereby their bulk confined within certain regions works in harmony with closely packed neighbours and in other regions tapers to long tendons where joints must enjoy the freest movement.'

Physiological characteristics of muscle tissue

Muscular tissue is composed of specialised cells, the characteristic functions of the tissue being essentially the same as the functions of the cells comprising the tissue. Living tissue exhibits excitability, the quality of reacting to a stimulus. Muscular tissue responds to stimuli. Another characteristic of muscle tissue is its contractility.

A muscle, when stimulated, has the ability to become shorter and thicker, performing work. Muscle tissue also exhibits extensibility. Skeletal muscles are generally arranged in antagonistic pairs so that when one muscle contracts, the opposing muscle is extended. Cardiac muscle tissue exhibits extensibility when the chambers of the heart are distended as they fill with blood. Visceral muscle exhibits great extensibility, as when the stomach is distended with food or when the urinary bladder is distended by accumulated urine. The ability of muscle tissue to return to its normal length after the force applied to it has been relieved is referred to as its elasticity.

Types of muscle tissue

1. Smooth muscle

There are two types of smooth muscle tissue:

a. *Syncytial type*

This is the more common type, in which the cells form a continuous network enabling a

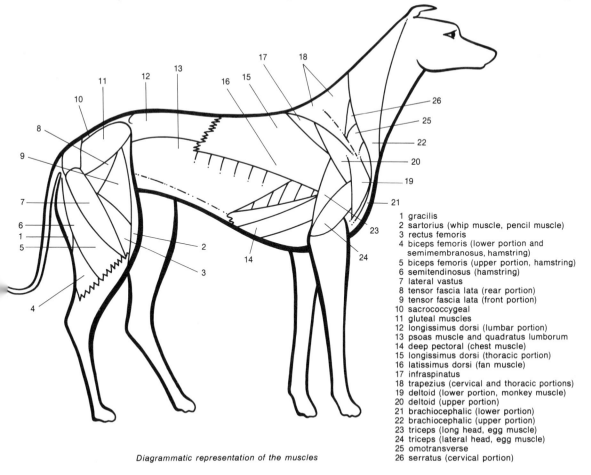

Diagrammatic representation of the muscles

1 gracilis
2 sartorius (whip muscle, pencil muscle)
3 rectus femoris
4 biceps femoris (lower portion and semimembranosus, hamstring)
5 biceps femoris (upper portion, hamstring)
6 semitendinosus (hamstring)
7 lateral vastus
8 tensor fascia lata (rear portion)
9 tensor fascia lata (front portion)
10 sacrococcygeal
11 gluteal muscles
12 longissimus dorsi (lumbar portion)
13 psoas muscle and quadratus lumborum
14 deep pectoral (chest muscle)
15 longissimus dorsi (thoracic portion)
16 latissimus dorsi (fan muscle)
17 infraspinatus
18 trapezius (cervical and thoracic portions)
19 deltoid (lower portion, monkey muscle)
20 deltoid (upper portion)
21 brachiocephalic (lower portion)
22 brachiocephalic (upper portion)
23 triceps (long head, egg muscle)
24 triceps (lateral head, egg muscle)
25 omotransverse
26 serratus (cervical portion)

contraction wave to spread over the entire muscle. These rhythmic contractions are called peristaltic waves and are typical of this type of musculature. Examples of this type of smooth muscle are found in the muscular wall of the stomach, intestine, uterus, ureters, and urinary bladder. Because this is the type of muscle found in the walls of the hollow viscera, it is frequently referred to as visceral muscle. Visceral muscle contracts and relaxes slowly and is capable of great extensibility.

b. *Multi-unit type*

This type consists of individual fibres, which often contract quickly and do not exhibit peristaltic movement, each with its own motor nerve ending. Examples of this type of smooth muscle are found in the walls of blood vessels, in the arrector muscle attached to hair follicles, in the intrinsic muscles of the eye, and in the nictitating membrane of the eye.

All smooth muscle receives its innervation from the autonomic nervous system. Since these nerves are not controlled directly from the conscious part of the brain, they, and the muscles that they control, are involuntary.

2. *Cardiac muscle*

Cardiac muscle composes most of the wall of the heart and is intermediate in structure between visceral and skeletal muscle. The tissue consists of a branching network of fibres that spreads over the atria of the heart and causes these chambers to contract as a single unit. Another similar set of muscles forms the walls of the ventricles of the heart. Cardiac muscle, like visceral muscle, is involuntary. Heart muscle posesses the outstanding ability to contract tirelessly for all the years of the animal's life.

There are some interesting features in the physiology of cardiac tissue. During ordinary contraction the muscle will not respond to an additional stimulus. Thus, its refractory period is rather long, lasting from one to five seconds. Its relaxation cannot entirely be prevented; neither is it possible for the heart muscle to maintain a state of complete contraction.

3. *Skeletal muscle*

Skeletal muscles are those muscles which are designed primarily to give movement to the skeletal framework. These muscles represent a considerable portion of the body weight and are ordinarily attached to bones by tendons. Since the gross action of skeletal muscles may be directed by higher centres of the brain, their action is voluntary and they are referred to as voluntary muscles.

Miscroscopically, skeletal muscle appears to be composed of numerous fibres extending along the length of muscle, each fibre being finely striated with alternating dark and light bands. These fibres represent the structural unit of a muscle and are cylinders of approximately the same size as human hair. They may extend the entire length of the muscle and become inserted in its tendons. The fibre is enclosed in a strong sheath called the sarcolemma which encloses the fluid protoplasm of the fibre, or sarcoplasm. Cross-striated, thread-like structures called myofibrils are found within the sarcoplasm of the fibre. The electron microscope reveals that the myofibril is composed of thick filaments about $0·01$ micron in diameter and $1·5$ microns in length and thin filaments about $0·005$ micron in diameter and about 2 microns long. (A micron is $0·001$ millimetre.) The two types of filaments slide over each other whenever there is an alteration in muscle length. The cross striated muscle shortens or lengthens in specific areas, but the filaments remain essentially of constant length.

TENDONS

Tendons are not often accorded due measure of their importance in muscular action. They act as buffers, protecting the limbs against the sudden strain and excessive speed that muscle without tendon intervention would produce. The elastic recoil of a stretched tendon adds a catapult increase to the muscular action. The passive role of tendon in its elastic and tensile qualities and its balance in length and thickness, all carefully adjusted to specific muscles, are important features in the general structure of a muscle.

Tendons are unspecialised, inelastic, nonvascular, and inexpensive in upkeep. They are designed to withstand pressure, but owing to their meager blood supply they readily die (slough) when exposed to infection. Where a muscle presses on bone, ligament, tendon, or other unyielding structure, the fleshy fibres always give place to tendon. Furthermore, if the tendon is subjected to friction, a lubricating device — a synovial bursa or a synovial sheath — is always interposed.

Observation reveals that the cross sectional area of the tendon of a muscle is much less than that of the fleshy belly. Hence, a muscle that arises by fleshy fibres and is inserted by tendon has a much more extensive origin than insertion.

Ling Bird, imported from England to Australia by F. J. Schock, has been described as the fastest dog of his day in England. Photo aged nine years *(Courtesy of F. Schock)*

Hence, the precise site of attachment of a tendon, where the force of a muscle pull is concentrated, is of greater practical importance than that of a widespread fleshy attachment where forces are dissipated and make no mark on the bone. At tendinous attachments, forces are concentrated and thus ridges are created, and also tubercles and facets, and if the attachments are large they may produce traction epiphyses.

Tendons are immensely strong: it is estimated that a tendon whose cross-sectional area is 1 square centimetre is capable of supporting a weight of from 700 to 1200 kilograms (Cronkite). The fibres of a tendon turn about each other in such a manner that fibres from any given point at the fleshy end of the tendon are represented at all points at the insertional end; thus, the pull of the entire muscle can be transmitted to any part of the insertion. The fan-shaped manner in which the majority of tendons are inserted into bone ensures that successive parts of the insertion take the full pull of the muscle as the angle of the joint alters.

The fibres of tendons, ligaments, and other fibrous structures usually pass through a pad of fibrocartilate before making their bony attachment. Concomitant with the rubber pad employed by the electrician at the junction of the free and the fixed point of a wire, the pads assist in the prevention of fraying from frequent flexing.

Synovial bursa (L. bursa = a purse)

A synovial bursa is a closed sac differentiated out of areolar tissue and interposed between surfaces which glide upon each other. It may be simple or multilocular in structure, and subcutaneous, submuscular, subfascial, or subtendinous in location. Its delicate walls are separated from each other merely by a film of slippery fluid similar to egg white. As a lubricating device, reducing friction and permitting free movement, a bursa is more effective than areolar tissue.

Synovial sheath

A synovial sheath is a tubular bursa that envelops a tendon. In fact, it is two tubes, one within the other. The visceral, or inner, tube adheres closely to the tendon and is separated from the parietal,

197

or outer, tube by the synovial cavity. The visceral and parietal tubes are united longitudinally, along the surface least subjected to pressure, by a synovial fold called the mesotendon, which transmits vessels to the tendon. If the range of movement of the tendon is considerable, the mesotendon may disappear or be represented by threads called vincula.

A synovial sheath is present only where a tendon is subjected to pressure or friction on two or more surfaces. The friction results from the presence of bone on one surface and of a retinacular ligament on the other. In order to allow sufficient play such sheaths extend approximately 2 centimetres above and below the sites of friction.

THE PHYSIOLOGY OF MUSCLE CONTRACTION

For many years scientists have worked to explain the mechanism that enables a loose, semi-fluid sarcoplasm to exert the powerful pull exhibited by the contraction of muscle. Investigators have revealed that some muscle proteins and specific organic phosphates with high energy bonds are involved. Of the various proteins present in muscle fibre, two are of interest in relation to contraction. These are myosin and actin and they may be individually extracted from muscle and purified. They combine, in solution, to form a more complex protein called actomyosin. Artificially fabricated fibres of actomyosin placed in a test tube will contract if supplied with adenosinetriphosphate, or ATP.

Myosin is the more plentiful protein and is found in the thick filaments of the A bands. Myosin may act as an enzyme in dephosphorylising ATP. It catalyses the removal of a phosphate group from ATP (ATP→ ADP), transforming chemical energy into mechanical energy. Actin is present in the thin filaments of the I bands. Under the electron micrograph striated muscle tissue exhibits broad, dense areas called A bands. The less dense area passing through the middle of the A band is the H zone. The wide, light coloured areas are the I bands. The black band passing through the I band is the Z line.

The exact nature of muscular contraction is not clear, although considerable progress has been made. It has been determined that there is electrical activity in muscle tissue because there is an alteration in surface potential as a contraction wave passes over a fibre. Each fibre is enveloped by an electrically polarised membrane.

The outside of the resting membrane is positive and the inside is approximately $0 \cdot 1$ volt negative. Upon stimulation of a motor nerve, the nerve impulse is relayed to the muscle membrane by chemical and physical changes that take place at the myoneural junction or end plate. An action potential develops and a wave of electric change moves swiftly over the muscle fibre and initiates contraction.

A number of products are formed during muscular contraction, the more significant for our consideration being lactic acid, carbon dioxide, and organic phosphates. Oxygen, glycogen, and organic phosphates are reduced in quantity during muscular activity. Initially, it was assumed that the breakdown of glycogen to lactic acid supplied energy for muscle contraction, but experimentation has proved that this is not so. Oxidation has taken place at some stage in the series of chemical reactions because of the fact that oxygen is used up and carbon dioxide is given off during muscular activity. Glucose has the chemical formula $C_6H_{12}O_6$ and is stored in the liver and muscles in a slightly altered form called glycogen. The formula for lactic acid is $C_3H_6O_3$. Hence, one molecule of glucose could form two molecules of lactic acid without the addition of oxygen. Apparently, oxidation is not required for this reaction and it has also been demonstrated that a muscle is capable of contracting for some time in an atmosphere from which oxygen has been removed.

Experimentation has proved that lactic acid is not essential to initial contraction, since treating an isolated muscle with sodium iodoacetate prevents lactic acid formation, but the muscle is capable of responding to stimuli for a considerable time. Lactic acid supplies energy required for the recovery phase but does not supply energy for immediate muscle contraction. The formation of lactic acid from glycogen is complex because there are many compounds formed by enzymatic action in the muscle prior to the production of lactic acid.

Two phosphate compounds, ATP and creatine phosphate, CP, supply the energy necessary for the initial contraction of muscle. It is supposed that the rapid breakdown of ATP into ADP and phosphoric acid supplies the energy for contraction. Resyntheseis of ATP is brought about through the transfer of phosphate to ADP from CP. The breakdown of glycogen to pyruvic and lactic acids supplies energy for the enzymatic resynthesis of CP. These reactions take place during the non-oxidative, contractile phase of muscle action.

Resynthesis of compounds broken down during contraction largely characterises the recovery phase of muscle. Glycogen plays a major role for it is here that part of the lactic acid produced is oxidised to supply energy for the resynthesis of the remainder back to glycogen. Lactic acid is the reduced form of pyruvic acid. The reversible reaction occurs readily in the tissues. The energy produced in the breakdown of these chemical compounds can be measured in calories, heat being a form of energy. Energy resulting from oxidative processes is far greater than that resulting from non-oxidative reactions. Contracting muscles exhibit two phases of heat production:

1. *Initial heat*

The initial heat of contraction and relaxation develops rapidly and because the process is non-oxidative, it supposedly comes primarily from the breakdown of organic phosphates rather than the breakdown of glycogen to lactic acid.

2. *Recovery heat*

Recovery heat develops more slowly following relaxation and is a consequence of the oxidation of lactic acid.

It has been estimated that muscles convert twenty-five to thirty per cent of the energy into movement, or work, while the remainder is given off as heat, which assists in the maintenance of body temperature. When the animal becomes cold, the muscles become tense and eventually break into uncontrolled contractions referred to as shivering. These rapid contractions produce heat and consequently aid in warming the animal. On a very hot day muscles have a tendency to be relaxed and flaccid and the animal will move about as little as possible.

The animal requires approximately 200 to 300 cubic centimetres of oxygen per minute when resting and many times this amount for vigorous exertion such as galloping. The conditioned greyhound can utilize 4 or 5 litres of oxygen per minute and the unconditioned greyhound considerably less than this amount. The oxygen requirement for vigorous exercise may be 16 to 20 litres per minute or higher, depending on the degree of exertion. It is apparent that in extreme exertion oxygen intake will be considerably less than the oxygen requirement of the muscles. Therefore, the animal must go into debt for oxygen. The greyhound breathes heavily as he rests after the race, until the oxygen debt is repaid.

Fortunately, energy necessary for the immediate contraction of muscle is supplied by non-oxidative reactions. However, the animal could not perform strenuously for more than one or two minutes if deprived of oxygen. Oxygen is essential in the recovery phase of muscle. Lactic acid accumulates following strenuous muscular activity, if sufficient oxygen is not available. Lactic acid is transported to the liver where enzyme systems convert the majority of it to glycogen. A small portion is oxidised to carbon dioxide and water, supplying energy for the resynthesis of glycogen. Oxidative energy is also essential for the rebuilding of organic phosphates. The animal can go into debt for oxygen, but the debt must be paid prior to the resumption of normal muscular activity. Moderate exercise, such as walking, may incur no oxygen debt. Physiological adjustments are such that sufficient lactic acid is oxidised as it forms to supply energy for resynthesis; this is referred to as the steady state. A greyhound in training can perform moderate exercise without additional lactic acid appearing in the bloodstream.

Muscle action

The structural unit of a muscle is a muscle fibre. The functional unit, or motor unit, consists of a nerve cell, situated in the anterior horn of the spinal cord, and all the muscle fibres controlled by the nerve fibre of that cell. When an impulse is relayed by the nerve fibre to its muscle fibres, they all contract almost simultaneously for a brief time (5 to 8 milliseconds). The result is a twitch of a small volume of the entire muscle. Where great precision is required, as with the muscles of the eye, one nerve fibre controls only about twelve muscle fibres. Movements are produced by throwing an increasing number of motor units into action and at the same time relaxing, to varying degrees, the antagonistic muscles (reflex relaxation). The majority of bodily actions call into play principal muscles and many assistants. The principal muscles, prime movers or agonists, by actively contracting produce the desired movement. The muscles so located that they would usually produce movements in the opposite direction are referred to as antagonists. When a prime mover passes over more than one joint, specific muscles are called upon to steady the intervening joints. These muscles are called synergists (Gk. syn =

together; ergon = work). When antagonists contract normally during a movement, their role is synergistic. Other muscles, fixators, are called upon to steady the more proximal parts of the limb or trunk. The same muscle may act as prime mover, antagonist, synergist, or fixator in different circumstances.

Muscle tone or tension

Muscles normally exhibit a very mild state of contraction referred to as tone. It is frequently described as an involuntary resistance to stretching and applies to all three types of muscle tissue—smooth, cardiac, and skeletal. Muscle tone in skeletal muscle is dependent, not upon the muscle fibres themselves, but upon connections with the central nervous system. Severing of these connections with the central nervous system would cause the muscles to become soft and flabby and lose tone. Tonic contraction in muscles concerned with body carriage assist the animal to stand erect for long periods. Muscles of the neck hold the head up; jaw muscles keep the jaw closed; muscles of the eyelids keep the eyes open. Muscle tone promotes coordination in muscular activity and improves the speed of contraction for there is no slack to take up before contraction. Such a muscle is certainly different from one with its nerve supply cut.

Cardiac and smooth muscle also exhibit tone. Smooth muscles in the walls of blood vessels maintain a state of tonic contraction. The heart beats and pumps blood against the resistance of muscles in the walls of arteries to maintain blood pressure. Good digestion is partially promoted by good tone in the muscles of the digestive tract. Tone in cardiac and smooth muscle is not entirely dependent upon connections with the nervous system, since both types of muscle exhibit tone even when their nerve connections are severed. Exercise and conditions associated with good health increase the tone of muscles. Lack of exercise or illness may reduce muscle tone markedly.

Muscle fatigue

Muscular fatigue occurs rapidly with strenuous exercise, and, as an air cuff then applied to stop the circulation in a limb so exhausted prevents recovery of strength until the circulation is resumed, apparently the site of fatigue is in the muscle, not in the central nervous system. As fatigue sets in there is a loss of efficiency as the muscle gradually shortens. The response is slower and the time necessary for contraction increases and the relaxation period becomes slower and slower. It is important to grasp the fact that in fatigue not only does the muscle gradually fail to contract, but that it also fails to relax. This may explain why fatigued muscles sometimes cramp. Muscle contracts more efficiently when warm. If the animal becomes chilled in very cold weather, the muscles may not perform efficiently and cramp may result.

The major cause of fatigue in muscles is the accumulation of waste products of their own activity. During exercise there may be loss of nutritive materials from the muscles, but the toxic effect of accumulating waste materials is a more important cause of fatigue. If the exercise is not too strenuous or prolonged, it may be assumed that the waste products are quickly carried away from the muscles by the blood and that nutritive materials and oxygen will be supplied. Following severe exertion or prolonged exercise, it may be necessary for the animal to rest for several hours in order to completely recover.

Power, range and speed

The greater the number of fibres in a muscle the greater is its strength, and the longer the fibres the greater is the range of movement available. Where the range of movement required is short, and power is required, then nature utilises numerous short fibres. For a wide range of movement without the necessity for strength, long but fewer fibres are employed. Weight for weight the muscle with the greatest number of fibres is the more powerful. Speed varies with individual muscles and it is an intrinsic quality of the muscle itself, depending on its biochemical and physicochemical constitution and is not entirely dependent on the nervous system. The muscles moving the eyeball contract more rapidly than the gluteus maximus moving the thigh, but relative to weight and time, use more energy, and thus, like a high-powered car, are more expensive to run. A compromise must be made between energy and speed, depending on the functions required of a specific muscle. The blink of an eyelid requires speed but little power, in contrast to the movements of the body.

The power, range, and speed produced by a muscle is concomitant with the number and length of the fibres, the intrinsic quality of speed in the muscle, the mechanics of its location relative to the joints or structures to be moved, and the loads involved.

Fasciae

Fascia is a packing medium. The superficial fascia is a complete subcutaneous covering of fibro areolar fat-containing tissue. It loosely unites the dermis to the deep fascia, allowing freer movement of the skin on the flexor than on the extensor aspects of the limbs and trunk, but binds the skin firmly to the deeper structures in the pads of the feet and the flexure lines throughout the body. It affords a soft nidus for the superficial nerves, vessels, and lymphatic nodes.

The deep fascia is a dense, tough, bluish-white, fibrous tissue devoid of fat, which surrounds each muscle in a fascial sheath continuous with that of neighbouring muscles. The deep fascia passes between muscle groups as definite septa attached to bony ridges and prominences and thus affords additional attachment for muscles. The fascial beds transmit vessels and nerves and also determine the course of effused fluids which may travel considerable distances from their sources to areas where they 'point' superficially. It facilitates the gliding of adjacent structures freely upon each other, this best being observed in the living animal.

Nerve supply

Nerves to a muscle contain both sensory and motor fibres in almost equal proportions. Bundles of these fibres divide successively until each motor nerve fibre (the axon of a nerve cell) supplies a specific group of muscle fibres, sending to each fibre a branch which terminates in a motor end plate on the surface of each muscle cell. The nerve cell, its axon, and its group of muscle cells form a motor unit, and an entire muscle is a company of these units. The muscle fibres of a unit are distributed throughout the entire muscle to ensure uniform activity of the muscle when all its units are not in action at once. Upon stimulation, each motor unit contracts fully or not at all, the unit comprising the least number of fibres that may normally be engaged in reflex or voluntary action, and the activity of the entire muscle is geared by the number, size, and power of its units stimulated. Control is more delicate and precise the fewer the number of muscle fibres to the unit, as in the case of the extrinsic muscles of the eye.

The motor unit system works in shifts and consequently provides continuous activity without fatigue during light exercise. The more vigorous the exercise the more units are engaged at the same time and for maximum effort all units are engaged. The smaller the part to be moved the smaller the unit, the smaller the muscle, and the more rapid is its action. Muscle always exhibits tone, even at rest, previously supposed due partially to the activity of the motor unit system. Electromyographic instruments do not register any activity in the muscle entirely at rest.

Special endings called muscle spindles, usually located around the muscle fibre near the tendon, give rise to sensory nerve fibres. These are afferent paths to the central nervous system for stimuli initiating the reflexes controlling and coordinating muscular activity.

Efferent nerves to striated muscle cause the muscle to contract. They do not produce relaxation which is brought about by reduction or cessation of the neuromotor stimuli. In contrast, in cardiac and non-striated muscle efferent nerves excite and inhibit.

Muscles of the head and neck

The two principal muscles involved in opening and closing the mouth are the temporal muscle and the masseter muscle.

On either side of the sagittal process and overlying the parietal bones, is a recess into which the fibres of the temporal muscle are attached. These muscles provide a slight elevation of the skin surface covering them. The powerful temporal muscle is inserted in the upper end of the coronoid process of the maxilla, but its fibres mingle here with those from the masseter muscle. The action of the temporal muscle is to raise the lower jaw and also to retract it.

The equally powerful masseter muscle underlies the skin of the cheek while the temporal muscle underlies that of the forehead and assists in shaping it. The masseter muscle arises from the lower rim of the zygoma and is inserted into the roughened surface of the coronoid process of the maxilla below the insertion of the temporal muscle, although, as previously mentioned, their fibres are somewhat interwoven. The masseter muscle plays the principal role in closing the jaws and it also permits the jaw to be carried on one side or the other by its unilateral contraction.

Both muscles are closely associated. They close the jaws by leverage upon the coronoid process, while the temporal muscle also serves to keep the jaws closed when the mouth is not functioning as a channel for admission of food.

The digastricus muscle, a smaller muscle lying immediately behind the upper part of the hinder periphery of the mandible, assists in opening the mouth.

Attached along the upper edge of the neural spine of the axis is the ligamentum nuchae, which extends the entire length of the neck as far as the dog's withers, where it is attached to the tip of the spinous process of the first dorsal vertebra, where it becomes continuous with the supraspinal ligament which extends down the spine as far as the sacrum, being attached to each of the spinous processes. The ligamentum nuchae effects a downward curvature of the cervical vertebrae and helps to support the head and neck. Assisted by the many muscles contained within the neck, a short ligamentum nuchae helps to maintain high head carriage.

The neck is supported and moved in a variety of directions by muscles passing between the transverse processes of the vertebrae and by muscles running the entire length of the neck, some of which extend into the forelimb and help to move it and bring the limb forward, particularly when the head and neck are extended at the same time as in galloping.

The brachiocephalic muscle originates from the occipital bone of the skull and the anterior end of the ligamentum nuchae and inserts into the humerus. A strong, lengthy, well-developed neck considerably enhances forward movement of the forelimb. When the forelimb is fixed and the brachiocephalic muscle on one side contracts, the head and neck are turned in that direction.

Muscles of the forelimb

The deltoid muscle is a short, thick muscle located above the articulation of the arm at the shoulder. It arises from the distal third of the clavicle, the acromion process, and spine of the scapula, and is inserted by a stout tendon into the deltoid tuberosity of the humerus. Its contraction raises the elbow in which instance the contracted muscle can be felt as a hard bunch of muscle above the shoulder joint.

The biceps brachii arises from two points of attachment. The short head arises from the coracoid process of the scapula. The long head has its origin on the supraglenoid tuberosity, a bony process of the scapula just above the articulation of the humerus at the shoulder. The

tendon of the long head passes over the head of the humerus and into the intertubercular groove; the tendon is protected by the synovial membrane of the joint. The two heads unite above the elbow joint and form the body of the biceps brachii. The action of the biceps muscle is to flex the elbow and assist in drawing the foreleg forward, being opposed in co-operative antagonism by the triceps muscle. The biceps muscle also acts to rotate the foreleg outward, a movement called supination. The movement of the muscle in supination is most evident when the foreleg is flexed.

The brachialis assists the biceps in flexing the foreleg at the elbow. The brachialis muscle arises from the anterior surface of the lower three-fifths of the humerus and is inserted into the tuberosity of the ulna. It is purely a flexor of the foreleg.

The triceps brachii is the principal extensor of the foreleg. It arises from three heads; the long head arises from the scapula just below the glenoid fossa, the lateral head from the posterior side of the shaft of the humerus, proximally, and the medial head from a fleshy attachment on the posterior side of the humerus distally from the radial groove. The three heads unite to form a large muscle on the posterior side of the leg. The insertion is by means of a strong tendon on the olecranon process of the ulna. This muscle is the antagonist of the biceps and the brachialis. When the triceps muscle contracts it forces the weight of the body to pass over the forelimb, which then becomes fixed in a state of momentary rigidity because the olecranon process of the ulna is being forced into the olecranon fossa at the lower end of the humerus. By virtue of the solidity so produced, the whole limb is converted into a rigid prop during this phase of every forward stride.

The combined action of the biceps and triceps muscles, which operate the elbow joint, are essential to the forward movement of the body.

The front of the external tuberosity of the humerus exhibits a groove through which passes the upper tendon of the biceps muscle. Between the groove and the tendon is a synovial bursa which is frequently injured and becomes a cause of lameness in the greyhound.

The scapula provides anchorage for a number of muscles which operate the forelimb and assist in neck movements. These muscles attach the forelimb to the body, the spine and the ribs without the help of any bony structure whatsoever. The thorax is thus suspended between the two scapulae with considerable freedom of movement in all parts involved. The upper ends of the scapulae are inclined slightly inwards by the pull of the muscles which unite them to the dorsal vertebrae.

The under surface of the scapula carries a flat muscle, the subscapularis, upon which it rides freely over the surface of the underlying ribs. This muscle occupies the fossa in the under surface of the scapula and is inserted into the upper end of the humerus medial to its articular head.

The pectoralis major muscle may be subdivided into clavicular, sternocostal, and abdominal origins. It is inserted into the crest of the intertubercular groove of the humerus. Pectoralis major adducts, flexes, and medially rotates the foreleg. Pectoralis minor originates from the third, fourth, and fifth ribs and is inserted into the coracoid process of the scapula. It acts to draw the shoulder forward and downward.

The trapezius muscle presents as a triangular sheet overlying the scapular region and exhibits two sections. The cervical section is attached to the ligamentum nuchae and to the spinous processes of the second to fourth dorsal vertebrae and is inserted into the spine of the scapula. The dorsal section unites with the spine of the scapula and is inserted into the tenth dorsal vertebra.

The rhomboideus muscle is inserted into the cervical angle (upper anterior angle) of the scapula and is attached to the ligamentum nuchae in the neck in addition to the spinous processes of the first two or three dorsal vertebrae.

Serratus anterior originates from the first seven or eight ribs and is inserted into the vertebral border of the scapula. It acts to draw the scapula forward and rotates the scapula to raise the shoulder in abduction of the leg. Serratus posterior inferior originates from the spines of the two lower thoracic and two or three upper lumbar vertebrae. It is inserted into the inferior border of the last four ribs. It acts to lower the ribs in expiration. Serratus posterior superior originates from the ligamentum nuchae and spinous processes of the upper thoracic vertebrae. It is inserted into the second, third, fourth, and fifth ribs. The muscle raises the ribs in inspiration.

In the foreleg are a number of muscles which are classified as flexors or extensors of the wrist and foot. They have their origin on the humerus, radius, or ulna. They are inserted by means of long tendons on the bones of the wrist, or tarsus, foot, or toes. The flexors are located on the anterior side of the leg and the extensors on the posterior side.

A large number of muscles, extensors, and flexors, with their tendons and accessory ligaments, play a part in the maintenance of stability and exert an effect on body propulsion. This intricate mechanism of muscles, tendons, and ligaments may affect the general shape of the foot or be held responsible for variations in its shape in accordance with the state of the muscular tissue, tendons, and ligaments. Muscles become thicker and stronger if they are exercised. It is important to bear in mind the nature of the ground on which the exercise is performed as this will exert an effect on the shape of the foot. Rough ground will necessitate a bunching up of the toes in order to negotiate it, while smooth, soft ground enables the dog to travel flat-footed without discomfort. Feet which are nicely arched under some conditions may become slack and splayed under others, not as a consequence of a fault in the conformation of the dog. Similarly, firm straight pasterns resulting from regular exercise, may become relaxed and yielding when the dog is confined within a small kennel for long periods.

Generally speaking, feet may be classified under two main categories:
1. 'Cat-foot'
The toes are well bunched like those of a cat. This is partly brought about by muscular contraction and partly by shortening of the ligaments.
2. 'Hare-foot'
The feet are flattened and more lengthy like those of a hare. The ligaments are slacker enabling the distal joints to extend slightly.

In some instances the forefeet may be cat-like and the hind feet of the hare type!

Muscles of the chest

The pectoralis major is the large triangular muscle covering the upper part of the chest anteriorly. It arises from attachments to the clavicle, the sternum, and the cartilages of the upper six ribs. The lower part of the muscle arises from the aponeurosis of the external oblique muscle. From this broad area of attachment the muscle fibres converge and are inserted by a short, flat tendon into the lateral margin of the intertubercular groove of the humerus. When the foreleg is raised, the pectoralis major, in co-operation with other muscles, pulls the leg down toward the chest. It also draws the leg across the chest and rotates the leg medially or inward. The pectoralis major is the principal flying muscle of birds. The pectoralis minor lies directly under the pectoralis major and receives the same nerve supply.

The intercostal muscles are located between the ribs and comprise two muscles that fill each intercostal space. The external intercostal is the thicker, outer sheet of muscle, and the internal intercostal forms the thinner, inner sheet. The external intercostal muscles pull adjacent ribs toward each other and so elevate the ribs, increasing the volume of the thoracic cavity, as in inspiration. The internal intercostal muscles depress the ribs, decreasing the volume of the thoracic cavity, as in expiration.

Muscles of the back

The right and left trapezius muscles are roughly trapezoid in shape and arise from a flat aponeurosis extending down the dorsal midline from the occipital bone; they also attach to the dorsal vertebral spines as far down as the twelfth thoracic. The upper part of the muscle is inserted into the clavicle; the median and lower parts insert on the acromion process and spine of the scapula. The trapezius is a large muscle over-lying other muscles of the shoulder. Contraction of the trapezius pulls the scapula toward the vertebral column and upward.

The splenius muscle of the head, splenius capitis, originates from the lower half of the ligamentum nuchae, the spines of the seventh cervical and three upper thoracic vertebrae. The muscle is inserted into the occipital bone and its action is to extend and rotate the head.

The splenius muscle of the neck, splenius cervicis, originates from the spinous processes of the third to sixth thoracic vertebrae and is inserted into the transverse processes of two or three upper cervical vertebrae. Splenius cervicis extends and rotates the head and neck.

The latissimus dorsi muscle has a very extensive origin from an aponeurosis attached to the spinous processes of the lower six thoracic verte-brae and all the lumbar vertebrae and from the dorsal surface of the sacrum and the posterior part of the crest of the ilium. There is also some attachment to the lower three or four ribs. From this broad area of origin the muscle tapers forward to a tendinous insertion in the inter-tubercular groove of the humerus. The action of the latissimus dorsi is to draw the foreleg down-ward and backward when the trunk is fixed. It also rotates the foreleg medially or inward. When both forelegs are fixed above the head, the contraction of the latissimus dorsi draws the trunk forward.

The trapezius and latissimus dorsi are super-ficial muscles of the back. The sacrospinalis is one of the muscles of the deeper layers. The sacrospinalis, or erector spinae, is the name afforded the fibres of the more superficial of the deep muscles of the back, originating from the sacrum, spines of the lumbar and the eleventh, twelfth, and thirteenth thoracic vertebrae, and the iliac crest, which split and insert as the iliocostalis, longissimus, and spinalis muscles. These muscles are inserted in such a manner that there is a consistent arrangement whereby one set of fibres has its origin posterior to the insertion of the adjacent set. With such a system of overlapping fibres, the sacrospinalis can exert a strong pull dorsad of the vertebral column. This is an important posture muscle, since when both sides act together it serves as an extensor for the spinal column. When acting unilaterally, it pulls the spinal column toward that side.

The diaphragm and muscles of the abdominal wall

The diaphragm is a dome-shaped muscle that forms a wall between the thoracic and abdominal cavities. It is attached around the lower cir-cumference of the thorax to the inner surfaces of the xiphoid process and the lower six costal cartilages, and also by tendinous and muscular slips to the lateral surfaces of the upper lumbar vertebrae. The muscle fibres converge and are inserted into an aponeurosis called the central tendon. As the muscles contract, the diaphragm loses some of its convexity and the capacity of the thoracic cavity is increased. Supported by other muscles which act on the ribs, inspiration is accomplished by the elevation of the ribs and the lowering of the diaphragm. To accomplish a forced expiration, as in coughing, a deep inspiration must precede the act. Muscles that depress the ribs and others that act to compress the abdomen then support a forcible expulsion. The diaphragm also aids in such acts as vomiting, defaecating, and micturating, and in birth of puppies.

The diaphragm has three large openings: the vena cava passes through one opening in the right half of the central tendon; the oesophageal opening located posterior to the central tendon on the left transmits the oesophagus and branches of the vagus nerves; and a more posterior opening permits the passage of the aorta and the thoracic duct.

The muscles that form the anterior and lateral walls of the abdomen are the external and internal oblique muscles, the transversus abdominis, the rectus abdominis, and the pyramidalis.

The external oblique is the most superficial of these muscles. It is a broad, thin sheet of muscle arising from the outer surfaces of the lower eight ribs. From these points of origin the fibres pass obliquely across the abdomen, the upper and middle portions of the muscle being inserted in a broad aponeurosis that covers the anterior part of the abdomen. The lower fibres are inserted directly into the crest of the ilium and by an aponeurosis, with the inguinal ligament. The inguinal ligament is not a true ligament; it is a tendinous band extending from the anterior superior iliac spine to the pubic tubercle. It is formed by the folded aponeurosis of the lower part of the external oblique muscle. The subcutaneous inguinal ring is an opening in the aponeurosis of the external oblique muscle. This is the external opening of the inguinal canal which transmits the spermatic cord in the dog and the round ligament of the uterus in the bitch. The opening is somewhat larger in the dog than in the bitch.

The linea alba is a narrow tendinous sheath extending anteriorly along the middle of the abdomen from the xiphoid process of the sternum to the symphysis of the two pubic bones. It is formed by the aponeurosis of the oblique and transversus muscles of both sides uniting in the midline. The umbilicus lies in the linea alba a little below the middle. The pyramidalis muscle arises from the pubis and is inserted in the linea alba. Its contraction causes a pull to be exerted on the linea alba and thereby increases its tension.

The internal oblique muscle lies directly under the external oblique muscle, but its fibres run approximately at right angles to those of the muscle overlying it. The internal oblique muscle arises from the inguinal ligament, iliac crest, and deep fascia in the lumbar region. Spreading upward, the fibres insert on the costal cartilages of the lower three ribs, into the aponeurosis of the linea alba and on to the crest of the pubis.

The transversus abdominis is the innermost of the flat muscles comprising the abdominal wall. The muscle arises from deep lumbar fasciae of the back and lower ribs, the iliac crest and the inguinal ligament. Most of the fibres transverse the abdomen horizontally and are inserted by an aponeurosis into the linea alba and on to the crest of the pubis. The abdominal wall is greatly strengthened by the three-layered arrangement of the external and internal oblique and transversus muscles.

The rectus abdominis is a long, flat, paired muscle extending along the anterior side of the body from the xiphoid process and cartilages of the fifth, sixth, and seventh ribs to the crest of the pubis. The muscle lies in a sheath formed by the aponeurosis of the oblique and transversus muscles. Each muscle is transversed by three or four tendinous bands. These rectangular divisions of the muscle may be observed in greyhounds with well-developed musculature.

The abdominal muscles act to compress the abdomen and, assisted by the descent of the diaphragm, aid in such acts as vomiting, urinating, defaecating and whelping. The muscles also support the abdominal viscera and aid in expiration.

The muscular wall of the body is incomplete as a consequence of openings which permit the passage of arteries, veins, nerves, and other structures. These areas, which must remain open, constitute weak areas in the body wall where rupture may occur. Rupture, or hernia, means the protrusion of a part of the viscera through the body wall. Abdominal hernia usually implies the protrusion of a portion of the intestine or mesentery through an opening. The inguinal canal constitutes such an opening. This canal extends from the inguinal ring, an opening in the fascia of the transversus muscle, to the subcutaneous inguinal ring which lies in the aponeurosis of the external oblique muscle just above the pubic tubercle. The inguinal canal is about 3 centimetres long and lies just above the inguinal ligament and parallel with it. Occassionally, the intestine is forced through the inguinal canal to constitute an inguinal hernia. Femoral hernia occurs at the femoral ring, the internal entrance to the femoral canal, located below the inguinal ligament and parallel with it. Occasion- the femoral artery and vein at that point where they pass from the body cavity to the hind leg. On the medial side of the femoral vein the sheath also covers the femoral canal, which may permit passage of a pouch of the peritoneum in the case of femoral hernia. Femoral hernia is not common. Umbilical hernia occurs at the umbilical ring or navel and is more common in puppies, although it can occur in older dogs. Weakening of the muscular wall and lack of muscle tone are conditions conducive to hernia. Coughing increases abdominal pressure and may cause hernia.

Muscles of the hind limb

The iliopsoas is a muscle composed of two closely related muscles—the iliacus and the psoas major. The iliacus arises from the crest of the ilium and from the iliac fossa. The fibres pass under the inguinal ligament and converge toward their insertion on the lesser trochanter of the femur. The psoas major arises from the transverse processes, the bodies and the intervertebral discs of the lumbar vertebrae. The psoas major is a much longer muscle than the iliacus, but it also passes under the inguinal ligament and the two muscles share a common tendinous attachment on the lesser trochanter of the femur. The iliacus and psoas major act together in holding the spinal vertebrae steady and flexing the spine or hip joint. The muscles flex the thigh on the pelvis when the pelvis is fixed. The iliopsoas muscle aids in flexing the trunk on the thigh. The gluteus maximus is a powerful antagonist.

The gluteus maximus is the largest and most superficial of the three gluteal muscles. The muscle fibres are coarse and covered with a layer of fat. Since this muscle is concerned with sitting and with an erect posture, it is much better developed in humans than in quadrupeds. The gluteus maximus arises from the outer surface of the ilium and sacrum and is inserted on the gluteal ridge of the femur and into a heavy sheath of connective tissue called the fascia lata. The muscles of the thigh are covered by this dense sheath which extends downward from the hip to the knee joint, where it blends with the capsular ligament around the knee. The action of the gluteus maximus is complex. It extends the thigh and is implemented in jumping and walking uphill, but plays little part in ordinary walking.

The quadriceps femoris is a very large muscle of the anterior part of the thigh. The muscle arises by four heads and differentiates into four muscles—the rectus femoris, the vastus lateralis, the vastus medialis, and the vastus intermedius.

The rectus femoris is the only muscle of the group attached to the pelvis. It arises by two tendons from the ilium, while the other three muscles arise along the femur. All four muscles have a common insertion into the tendon that passes across the knee joint and is attached to the tuberosity of the tibia. The tendon below the knee joint becomes the patellar ligament—so-called because the patella develops in it as a sesamoid bone. The quadriceps femoris is a powerful extensor of the leg at the knee and is said to be three times as powerful as the muscles that oppose it.

The sartorius (whip muscle) is a long, slender muscle running diagonally across the quadriceps femoris from its origin on the anterior superior spine of the ilium to the medial side of the knee, where it is inserted on the upper part of the tibia near the tuberosity. The sartorius is the longest muscle in the body and, although it is an anterior thigh muscle, it can, by virtue of its attachments, flex the leg at the knee. Sartorius is the only anterior thigh muscle that flexes the leg.

There are several adductor muscles on the medial side of the thigh which arise from the front of the pelvis and attach at different levels to the femur. These muscles draw the thigh inward or pull the legs toward each other. The gracilis is one of this group of muscles.

The biceps femoris, semitendinosus, and semimembranosus are three of the muscles of the posterior aspect of the thigh which are commonly referred to as the 'hamstrings'. The biceps femoris arises by two heads—the long head arises from the tuberosity of the ischium and the short head from the middle and distal portion of the femur. The muscle is inserted on the head of the fibula. The semitendinosus and semimembranosus arise, with the long head of the biceps femoris, from the ischial tuberosity. The long tendons of these muscles pass back of the knee joint and outline the popliteal space, which lies between them, the tendon of the biceps lying on the outer side. The tendons of the semitendinosus and semimembranosus muscles lie on the medial side and are inserted on the proximal part of the tibia. The action of this group of muscles is concerned with flexing the leg at the knee and extending the thigh at the hip joint. The posterior thigh muscles extend across two joints, namely, the hip and knee joints. Their antagonist, rectus femoris, also extends across these two joints but on the opposite side. It should be noted that the hip and knee joints flex in opposite directions.

While the word 'leg' commonly refers to the entire hind leg, I will employ the term to denote that portion between the knee and the foot.

The anterior muscles of the leg are the tibialis anterior and the extensor muscles concerned with extending the toes. The tibialis anterior arises from the lateral condyle and proximal half of the shaft of the tibia. Its tendon crosses to the inner side of the foot and is inserted on the base of the first metatarsal bone and on the median cuneiform bones. Tibialis anterior flexes and inverts the foot. The extensor muscle of the anterior portion of the leg is the extensor digitorum longus which arises from the lateral condyle of the tibia and upper anterior surface of the fibula. This muscle lies lateral to tibialis anterior and terminates in a tendon that divides into four slender tendons, each of which is inserted on the dorsal surface of one of the four toes. The extensor muscles extend the toes by drawing them up dorsally. They also assist in flexing the foot upon the leg.

The peroneal muscles occupy a lateral position on the leg. Peroneus longus arises from the lateral condyle of the tibia and upper part of the shaft of the fibula. The muscle terminates in a long tendon at the ankle and is enclosed in a common sheath with the tendon of the peroneus brevis. The peroneus brevis arises from the lower lateral part of the shaft of the fibula. The peroneal muscles extend and evert the foot. Peroneus longus and tibialis anterior offer strong support for the foot.

The superficial muscles of the posterior aspect of the leg are the gastrocnemius and soleus. Deeper muscles include the flexor digitorum longus and tibialis posterior. The gastrocnemius and soleus constitute the muscles of the calf. Gastrocnemius arises by two heads from areas just above the medial and lateral condyles of the femur. Soleus arises from the proximal posterior portions of both the tibia and the fibula and lies beneath the gastrocnemius. The achilles tendon is the common tendon of both muscles and is inserted on the calcaneus. These muscles are extensors of the foot. Gastrocnemius, since it is attached above the knee joint, also assists in flexing the leg at the knee.

The flexor digitorum longus has its origin along the posterior side of the shaft of the tibia and extends downward on the medial and posterior side of the leg. A strong tendon transverses the plantar aspect of the foot where it divides into four tendons, each inserted on the ventral surface of one of the toes. Contraction of this muscle flexes the toes and inverts the foot and also aids in supporting the foot.

The tibialis posterior arises from the upper part of the shaft of both the tibia and the fibula and also from an aponeurosis between the two bones. The muscle extends downward just posterior to the tibia. The muscle tendon passes obliquely to the medial side and under the medial malleolus of the tibia and forward under the foot where it is inserted on several tarsal and metatarsal bones. Tibialis posterior acts with tibialis anterior in inverting the foot. Since the medial malleolus acts as a pulley, the muscle extends the foot and thus acts as an antagonist to tibialis anterior.

Tendons of the ankle and foot are generally covered with synovial sheaths. A number of sesamoid bones develop in the tendons of the foot and there are numerous bursae for the protection of muscles and joints.

The muscles of the leg that control movements of the foot by the action of their tendons are called extrinsic muscles. Intrinsic muscles are those located within the foot proper. On the dorsum of the foot the extensor digitorum brevis assists the long tendons of extrinsic muscles in extending the toes.

The plantar aponeurosis is a heavy sheath of connective tissue on the plantar aspect of the foot which supports and strengthens the foot. The flexor digitorum brevis lies just above the plantar aponeurosis and flexes the toes and helps to strengthen the state of the foot. Other intrinsic muscles of the foot are concerned with various movements and support of the foot.

MUSCLE INJURIES

Confusion frequently arises as to the different degrees of ligamentous and muscle injury. A strain is an injury to a ligament which does not stretch it beyond the normal limits of elastic recovery and no fibres are ruptured. There is localised pain and swelling and possibly a small degree of effusion into the joint concerned. A sprain is the result of a more violent stretching which ruptures some of the ligamentous fibres within the outer sheath, rendering the ligament slightly longer, and although there is a greater amount of swelling, pain, and limitation of movement than occurs with a strain, there is little or no haemorrhage. In neither of these injuries is there displacement or joint instability,

Golden Spur (Gabriel Mist (imp.)–Leeander Lass) is out of one of the most successful litters to race in Australia. Between them they have won 127 races. Golden Spur scored twenty-six wins and twenty-four placings from fifty-nine starts and broke three track records *(Courtesy of South Australian Greyhound Trainer)*

although in a sprain the joint surfaces are parted initially but do not remain so.

The treatment of sprains is not difficult and all are dealt with on similar lines. There is no deformity and the joint can be moved, although movement causes pain. The pain is severe at the time of the injury but later consists of a dull ache which becomes sharp on movement, when the injured structures are put on the stretch.

A certain amount of rest is necessary to permit the acute inflammatory reaction around the joint to subside. There is a great risk of adhesions forming, as with any inflammatory condition, and it is important to prevent this. Treatment aims at:

1. Prevention of adhesions by preventing organisation of the highly fibrinous inflammatory exudate, i.e., minimising or reducing swelling and encouraging early movements.
2. Relief from pain as the pain precludes movement as the dog is unwilling to incur pain by using the joint.
3. Restoration of full mobility as soon as possible.
4. Maintenance, or restoration, of full muscle power is of paramount importance because if the muscles are not restored to full strength they may be incapable of preventing recurrence of the injury and the dog will have a joint that 'gives'.

Heat, massage, and exercise are employed in the treatment of sprains. Dr James Cyriax states: 'Contrary to general belief, deep massage and passive movements are the mainstay of treatment during the early stage of articular sprains. The present insistence on active movement alone greatly retards recovery at some joints.' The movements between bone and ligament are the same during a passive movement as during an active movement, but the range of passive movement is always greater in a sprained joint than that of an active movement. Furthermore, passive movements prevent formation of adhesions. Of passive movements, in which Cyriax includes deep massage and gentle forced movements, he says: 'The movements must not be so forcible as to overstretch those fibrils that are gaining longitudinal attachment within the healing breach; nor should they be so gentle as to fail to disengage those fibrils that are gaining abnormal transverse adherence. A safe rule is to push movements to the point of discomfort, but not of pain.' The value of active movements must, of course, not be discounted.

A sprained wrist may be the consequence of violent wrenching of the wrist in any direction, usually forward or backward into forced flexion or extension. Those ligaments and muscles injured depends on the direction of the causative force. Violent extension wrenches the anterior radiocarpal ligament and flexor muscles and will probably cause tenosynovitis of their sheaths, while violent flexion causes similar damage to the structures of the posterior aspect of the wrist. Occasionally, the medial or lateral radiocarpal ligaments, or some of the small ligaments between the carpal bones, are injured. A tender spot will be found over the torn ligament and, in a bad sprain, there may be swelling which extends some way up the leg. Generally, a firm bandage over cotton wool, or strapping, affords sufficient support. Occasionally, a splint with cotton wool and bandage may be necessary. Cold compresses, such as a Cryogel Cold Pack, frequently afford relief. Later, massage should be given to reduce the swelling and, if swelling is diffuse, should include the whole leg. Special attention should be directed to the toes and foot and full use of the foot encouraged. Full flexion and extension of the toes is important as this assists in dispersal of fluid. Movement should be full and painless in seven to fourteen days. Residual stiffness will require massage and passive stretching of the joint.

Injuries of muscles and their tendons includes inflammatory conditions in the muscle fibres, connective tissue, tendons, and synovial sheaths and also rupture of actual muscle fibres, tendons, and aponeuroses. Inflammatory conditions include:

1. Myositis—inflammation of actual muscle tissue.
2. Fibrositis—inflammation of connective tissue, whether between muscles or in their substance.
3. Tendinitis—inflammation of the tendon itself or at the junction of the tendon with the periosteum of the bone to which it is attached.
4. Tenosynovitis and tenovaginitis—inflammation of the synovial sheath. The tendon sheath, where present, as well as the tendon proper, may be the seat of the trouble. The surfaces of the sheath and tendon may be roughened, giving rise to pain and crepitus where they glide on one another. This condition is referred to as tenosynovitis. Tenovaginitis is the term afforded a primary lesion in the sheath itself which is inflamed and thickened. No crepitus is present in this type of injury.

Muscle fibres, tendons, or aponeuroses may be partially or completely ruptured. Repair is by white fibrous scar tissue which results in a certain degree of loss of elasticity in muscle, and this may or may not seriously incapacitate the greyhound. Complete or partial ruptures are the consequence of traumatic forces. There is pain in the affected area, which is increased by pressure or movement, aching, swelling and altered consistency. Tendons feel spongy and crepitus is present. Muscles may feel soft and inelastic, or hard and firm, nodules sometimes being palpable. There is loss of function in the limb where the inflammation is present because of the loss of power in the inflamed muscles and the pain which restricts movement. A common complication is pressure on the nerves in the vicinity, resulting in cramp or neuralgia.

In the acute stage of muscle and tendon injuries rest is needed to allow the inflammatory reaction to subside. The highly fibrinous inflammatory exudate must be absorbed in order to prevent the formation of adhesions and full function must be restored. This implies the maintenance or restoration of mobility and strength, and for this to be achieved the initial aim is to relieve pain. Heat and massage will assist the absorption of fluid and the relief of pain. Movement will restore function.

In the chronic stage of muscle and tendon injuries adhesions and scarring will have formed, with resultant loss of function. Mobility must be regained and muscle power increased. The most important treatment consists of deep massage to soften and stretch adhesions and scar tissue, followed by exercise. Ultrasound treatment is invaluable during the later stages of these injuries because of its thermal and mechanical qualities. Ultrasound will raise the temperature of the injured tissues, increase the blood flow in the area, and so assist healing. The micro-massage effect of the ultrasound will reduce the formation of adhesions and soften scar tissue. I must stress, at this juncture, the danger of employing ultrasonic therapy too soon following muscle injury. Ultrasound may, by virtue of its vibratory massaging effect, loosen the cells responsible for sealing ruptured blood vessels and so give rise to unwanted and prolonged haemorrhage. Following shrinkage and sealing of the ruptured blood vessels, by means of a Cryogel Cold Pack or ice packs, during the initial 5 to 10 hours following injury, the blood supply to the area can be increased effectively by ultrasonic therapy. Ultrasound will explode the dead cells, thus facilitating their removal by the blood stream, reduce swelling, and aid repair processes.

Rupture of the gastrocnemius muscle may be encountered by the trainer. Sudden, strong contraction of the muscles of the calf while the dog is balanced on the toes of that leg will cause this injury, or it may merely be the result of a false step, the dog having contracted his muscles over strongly in order to avoid a fall. There is severe pain at the moment of the injury, followed by weakness in the action of plantar flexion. There is pain on dorsiflexion of the hock. A great deal of difference of opinion exists with regard to the best way of treating this injury, but the principles are generally the same as in other muscle and tendon injuries. It is probably best for the dog to use the leg rather than rest it, or to rest it only for a couple of days if the injury is not too severe. Whether the dog is to rest in more severe injuries and for what length of time depends entirely on the severity of the injury and the views of the person handling the dog. In some cases a few days will suffice, in other cases the dog must be rested for about a week. It is of paramount importance to check effusion both in this and all cases of ruptured muscle fibres, otherwise it will organise and result in the formation of thickening and adhesions in the muscle. Consequently, heat and massage should be employed daily. When all inflammation has subsided, vigorous massage and exercise are indicated.

15

THE URINARY SYSTEM

THE KIDNEYS

The kidneys lie in the dorsal part of the abdominal cavity, covered by peritoneum and embedded in fat. They are somewhat bean-shaped and reddish brown in colour and the right kidney is usually lower than the left. The depression near the middle of the concave border is the hilus. Blood vessels and nerves make contact with the kidney at the hilus, and the ureter passes downward to the bladder from this region.

A longitudinal section of a fresh kidney exhibits the outer portion, or cortex, which contains renal corpuscles, convoluted tubules, and blood vessels. Masses of cortical tissue fill in between the pyramids of medullary tissue. The renal pyramids are wedge-shaped structures containing collecting tubules. The broad base of the pyramid is toward the cortex and the narrow apex forms a soft, red papilla which projects into a small collecting area called the calyx. Each papilla contains openings through which the urine passes into the calyx, which empties into the renal pelvis. The ureter drains the renal pelvis.

The functional unit of the kidney, the nephron, consists of a capsule, a capillary network within the capsule, and the renal tubules. The glomerulus is a microscopic mass of coiled capillaries within the capsule (Bowman's capsule). The afferent arteriole leading blood into the glomerulus is of slightly greater diameter than the efferent arteriole which leads the blood away. Renal corpuscles are located in the cortical portion of the kidney. Bowman's capsule may be regarded as the greatly enlarged end of the proximal convoluted tubule. There is an inner membrane continuous with the outer membrane of the capsule, the thin inner membrane immediately surrounding the glomerulus.

After following an irregular course the proximal convoluted tubule becomes straight and forms the loop of Henle which lies deeper in the kidney tissue than Bowman's capsule. Beyond the loop of Henle the ascending tubule follows a tortuous path again and is designated as the distal convoluted tubule. It then enters a collecting duct, which receives many such tubules. Approximately twenty collecting ducts are found at the apex of each pyramid, and their contents pass through corresponding openings in the renal papillae and then into the calyxes, the renal pelvis, and the ureter.

The kidneys receive an abundant blood supply through the large, short renal arteries which carry blood at high pressure from the aorta. Branching readily into smaller arteries, the blood is carried by afferent arterioles to the glomeruli. Since the diameter of the afferent arteriole is greater than that of the efferent arteriole, the pressure within the glomerulus remains high. The blood circulates at a much lower pressure in the capillary network around the tubules after it has passed through the glomerulus. The blood is collected by a number of smaller veins and leaves the kidneys via the renal veins which empty into the inferior vena cava.

The kidneys receive an abundant nerve supply from the autonomic nervous system. The sympathetic nerves reach the kidneys from some of the great plexuses of the abdomen and via the splanchnic nerves. Parasympathetic fibres are carried by the vagus nerve. The nerves are primarily vasomotor and are concerned with regulation of blood flow and blood pressure within the kidney.

Each kidney contains approximately 1 million nephrons. The capillary surface available for filtration in 2 million glomeruli is extremely great. Many substances in solution in the blood are filtered through the glomerulus and the capsule. The blood proteins are large and do not normally pass into the glomerular filtrate; but other substances, such as salts and sugars, pass through readily. Glomerular filtrate is very similar to protein-free blood plasma or extracellular fluid. There is very extensive reabsorption into the capillary network surrounding the tubules. As the fluid passes through the tubule, sugar is normally completely reabsorbed, as is the majority of the sodium and chloride. Some of the urea is reabsorbed, as well as other substances, in varying amounts. Such extensive reabsorption tends to concentrate excretory products into the urine, which is a different substance from glomerular filtrate.

Renal clearance refers to the removal of a substance by the kidneys from a specific volume of blood passing through the glomeruli in one minute. The rate of clearance is expressed in terms of the least volume of blood containing a given substance, in relation to the amount of this substance appearing in one minute's urine. Clearance varies with the concentration of a given substance in the blood; there will also be a corresponding change of concentration in the kidney. Renal clearance becomes most valuable when the rate of clearance of several filterable substances is compared. The clearance value of glucose is zero, because all the glucose that is filtered through the glomeruli is reabsorbed through the tubules and returned to the bloodstream. Glucose, therefore, is not normally present in the urine.

Blood cells are much too large to be filtered through the glomerulus and even the large molecules of the plasma proteins do not ordinarily pass through. The presence of any considerable amount of protein in the urine (proteinuria) is generally considered to be an indication of renal damage. Temporary proteinuria is fairly common following severe exercise. Plasma protein in minute amounts, however, is known to pass through the glomerulus but most of it is reabsorbed through the wall of the tubule in the normal kidney. Glucose filters readily through the glomerulus, and normally all of it is reabsorbed in the tubules. If the blood sugar rises to such a level that all of the glucose filtered by the glomerulus cannot be reabsorbed, then sugar appears in the urine, a condition known as glycosuria. In diabetes mellitus there is an abundant flow of urine containing glucose, and increased thirst. The fact that the filtrate contains an abnormal amount of sugar in solution tends to raise its osmotic pressure and to lower the rate of water reabsorption. That is to say more water is used in washing out the increased amount of sugar in the filtrate.

Salty food increases thirst and a greater pro-

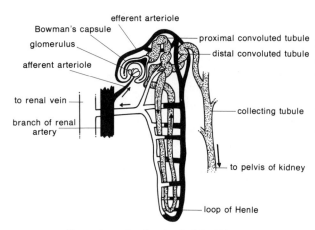

The nephron—functional unit of the kidney

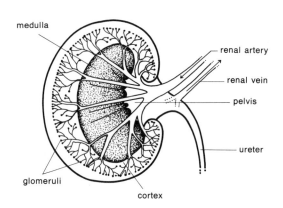

Diagrammatic longitudinal section of the kidney, to show distribution of glomeruli

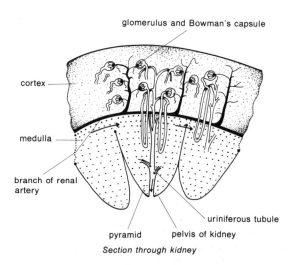

Section through kidney

portion of water is used by the kidneys in the excretion of the excess salt. Drinking large amounts of water produces an abundant flow of urine of low concentration. Low intake of water, or excessive loss by panting and sweating through the pads of the feet or from haemorrhage, results in the production of a small amount of urine of much higher concentration. The reabsorption of water is achieved in several ways. Considerable water is reabsorbed as the solvent for substances reabsorbed, for example, glucose is very actively reabsorbed as a solute in water. Conversely, a considerable increase of dissolved solids in the tubules raises the osmotic pressure and decreases water reabsorption. To a certain extent this mechanism enables the kidney to adjust automatically to perform its work, for a greater accumulation of dissolved waste tends to produce a greater flow of urine. This is the mechanism in diabetes mellitus that produces the diuresis (increased secretion of urine) associated with glycosuria; an abnormal amount of sugar that cannot be reabsorbed prevents the normal reabsorption of water.

The yellow colour of urine is due to a pigment called urochrome. This is formed from urobilin, which, in turn, is formed from bile pigment. Urine is about ninety-five per cent water and contains inorganic salts and organic wastes. Sodium chloride is by far the most abundant of the inorganic salts, which include chlorides, sulphates, and phosphates of sodium, potassium, calcium, and magnesium. Some of the sulphates and phosphates may be in combination with organic substances. Organic wastes include urea, uric acid, and creatinine. The amount of urea, a product of the deamination of amino acids, varies with the amount of protein in the diet. Uric acid is a breakdown product of nucleoproteins, which are compound proteins found notably in the nuclei but also in the cytoplasm of cells. Creatine is present in various tissues but especially in muscle, where it is formed from phosphocreatine during muscle metabolism. It is resynthesised and the amount excreted as creatinine in the urine remains fairly constant. A rise in the amount of creatinine excreted is called creatinuria and may be the consequence of fevers, prolonged starvation, diabetes, or other disturbances of carbohydrate metabolism.

Each kidney is drained by a tube that extends from the kidney to the urinary bladder. These tubes are the ureters, the walls of which are composed of three coats—an outer connective tissue layer, a muscular coat, and an inner mucous membrane. The smooth muscular layer propels urine into the bladder by peristaltic movements. The urinary bladder is a muscular bladder that varies in size in accordance with the amount of urine contained. When full, it is nearly spherical in shape and projects into the abdominal cavity. The muscular coat of the urinary bladder is composed of three layers and makes up the greater portion of the wall of the bladder. There is an inner and outer layer of longitudinal muscles separated by a median layer of circular muscles. The internal mucous membrane is a soft, reddish lining which is folded when the bladder is empty. The ureters enter the urinary bladder through narrow slits that remain closed except when peristaltic muscular movement forces urine through the openings. The urethra is the duct that leads from the urinary bladder to the exterior. It is considerably longer in the dog, since it traverses the penis. The internal orifice at the urinary bladder is surrounded by circular smooth muscle fibres forming the internal vesicle sphincter. The external urethral orifice is a slit at the distal end of the penis. The urethra of the bitch extends from the internal orifice in the urinary bladder along the wall of the vagina to the external orifice located between the clitoris and the vaginal opening.

The act of voiding urine, micturition, is a highly reflex act upon which voluntary control is superimposed. The puppy voids urine reflexly whenever the pressure of accumulating urine in the bladder becomes sufficiently great to provide an adequate nerve stimulus. Gradually the young pup learns to control these impulses.

The kidneys are the main regulator of the internal environment of the body, since they are largely responsible for the maintenance of the composition of the blood. These regulatory functions of the kidneys may be summarised as follows:

1. The kidneys aid in regulating the acid-base balance of the blood, and indirectly that of the tissues, by excreting excess acid or alkaline substances.
2. The kidneys help to maintain the water balance of the tissues by excreting excess water or by conserving water as the situation demands. They conserve water and many other substances by reducing excretion if there is a reduced intake of liquid or unusual

loss as in profuse panting or sweating through the pads of the feet.

3. The kidneys regulate osmotic equilibrium and ionic balance in the blood and tissues by controlling the excretion of various inorganic substances such as the salts of sodium, potassium, calcium, and magnesium.

4. The kidneys play an important role in eliminating the by-products of catabolism, some of the products of which are toxic and would become extremely injurious if permitted to accumulate. Waste products arise in every cell but, through absorption into the bloodstream and continuous excretion by the kidneys, they fail to attain injurious concentrations. The constancy of the internal environment of the body is primarily the consequence of this continuous exchange of materials between the blood and the tissues. It is dependent upon a balance between the processes of anabolism and catabolism and is frequently acknowledged to result in a dynamic equilibrium, the kidneys playing a very important role in helping to maintain such an equilibrium.

The urine

Examination of the urine is one of the most important routine examinations made, not only in renal diseases but in all diseases. It must never be omitted. Urine which is left standing is liable to contamination with bacteria, hence the importance of fresh samples is obvious. Examination of the urine includes the following tests:

1. *Specific gravity*

The specific gravity of urine (which is measured by a urinometer) varies principally with the amount passed. The larger the amount the lower the specific gravity and vice versa. Certain substances in the urine exert a profound effect on the specific gravity, especially sugar, which raises the specific gravity markedly.

2. *Tests for proteins (albumin)*

Normal healthy glomeruli of the kidney do not allow the protein in the blood to filter through into the tubules. One of the first and most constant signs of damage to the kidneys (whatever the cause) is the presence of protein (albumin) in the urine, and, conversely, if no albumin is present, it is a good indication in most cases of the absence of a serious kidney lesion. Testing for albumin is therefore of great importance in establishing whether or not kidney damage is present. The causes of albuminuria

are many and varied, the most important causes include congestive heart failure; prolonged coma; all stages of nephritis, pyelitis, and cystitis; toxaemias of pregnancy; tumours of the kidney; and any acute febrile disease (pertaining to or characterised by fever).

Protein lost into the urine, when it occurs as a kidney loss, involves the dual loss of protein from the greyhound's serum and the loss of protein passed into the urine is an obvious loss to the body. This creates a greater demand on the body to synthesise protein and this, in turn, causes an additional energy drain that may be reflected in the performance of the greyhound.

3. *Volume and reaction*

The amount of urine passed varies with many factors, especially the amount of fluid drunk and also the amount lost in panting and sweating. An increased output of urine is usually referred to as polyuria, a diminished output as oliguria and a complete supression as anuria. If there is any reason to suspect that the dog is not passing an adequate amount, a check on the output must be made. A severe reduction in the amount of urine passed is always a serious matter and calls for prompt attention, especially in the acutely ill and in old dogs. It must be ascertained that the dog is drinking sufficient. At this juncture it is perhaps opportune to mention that, in my opinion, fresh drinking water should be available to greyhounds at all times.

The reaction of the urine is normally slightly acid so that it turns blue litmus paper red; alkaline urine turns red litmus paper blue. Strongly alkaline urine frequently indicates the presence of bacteria involved in bladder infections. These bacteria have the ability to break down urea with a resultant increase in the alkalinity of the urine caused by a strong ammonia content, hence the increased smell of ammonia in the urine sample.

4. *Tests for sugar*

The presence of any appreciable amount of sugar in the urine is in most cases due to the disease, diabetes mellitus. In the early stages of diabetes, however, the symptoms may not be characteristic and suggestive of the disease, although sugar is usually present in the urine.

5. *Normal deposits*

a. Urates may form a sediment in the urine in cold weather, but they dissolve on heating. They are generally a brownish or salmon-pink colour.

b. Phosphates generally appear when the urine

214

During 1981, $25 000 was refused for top South Australian stayer Canadian King (Toronto King–Bristol Chant) *(Courtesy of South Australian Greyhound Trainer)*

is neutral or alkaline in reaction. They are white in colour and dissolve when acetic acid is added.

c. Mucus is often present as a transparent, fluffy deposit, easily recognised.

6. *Tests for blood (haematuria)*

If blood is present in any quantity, it is obvious to the naked eye as it colours the urine red. Lesser amounts of blood produce a typical smoky appearance. If only small amounts of blood are present, the colour of the urine, while dark, may not be diagnostic. The most reliable test for blood is therefore by microscopic examination, when the actual red cells may be observed. Causes of haematuria include bleeding into the urinary tract; calculi (stones) in the kidney, ureter, or bladder; acute nephritis (where the urine is generally smoky); tumours of the renal tract; infection; bacterial endocarditis (when the haematuria is the result of emboli in the kidneys); sulphonamide crystals; overdosage with anti-coagulant drugs; trauma; scurvy; certain poisons, such as Ratsak; and in some instances it is indicative of problems in areas of the body other than the urinary tract. Seasonal bitches will obviously afford a positive result.

7. *Test for pus*

The only satisfactory examination for the presence of pus in the urine is examination under the microscope, when the pus cells can be observed. Pus is generally present in the urine in cases of inflammation of the renal tract, especially pyelitis, cystitis, and urethritis.

8. *Tests for bile*

a. Bile pigments. Bilirubin is present in the urine in cases of obstructive jaundice. Urine containing bile is dark with a yellow or greenish colour. One of the simplest methods of detecting bilirubin is to shake the urine in a test tube, and, if the froth is yellow, bilirubin is present. Normally, in the absence of bile, the froth is white. Another bile pigment, urobilin, is found in the urine in cases of haemolytic jaundice in addition to bilirubin. The detection of urobilin is a more complicated procedure.

b. Bile salts. Bile salts are usually present in the urine, together with bilirubin, in obstructive jaundice.

9. *Tests for ketone bodies (ketosis or acidosis)*

Ketone bodies (acetone and diacetic acid) generally occur in the urine in diabetes mellitus (and

215

are always present in diabetic coma), excessive vomiting, acute febrile states in pups, starvation, and in severe destruction of muscle cells. Severe destruction of muscle cells may occur in the greyhound and the fact that the kidneys need to pass large amounts of muscle pigments can result in kidney damage. The damaging effects of these pigments to the kidneys can primarily be attributed to their tendency to precipitate into solid masses in the tubules of the kidneys and consequently block the kidneys. In moderate to severe cases of acidosis, the excessively dark-brown colour of the urine is evidence of the muscle cell destruction. The reader is referred to the section on nutrition for further information concerning metabolic acidosis.

Nephritis

Nephritis, or Bright's disease, is a very common disease of the kidneys. It is an inflammatory disease of which the exact cause is unknown, but it generally follows a streptococcal infection, so that usually there is a history of acute tonsil-litis or other streptococcal infection prior to the onset of acute nephritis. Nephritis may be classified into three groups:

1. *Acute nephritis*

This generally occurs in young dogs and frequently the dog has had a sore throat about seven to ten days before. The onset is fairly sudden, with fever, pain in the back, headache, and vomiting. The presence of oedema is typical, particularly around the dog's eyes and in the wrists and hocks. It tends to be worse in the morning and better in the evening. The dog exhibits a characteristic bloated appearance. In severe cases fluid may accumulate in the pleural cavity (pleural effusion) or the peritoneal cavity (ascites). Urinary changes are fairly constant and are most significant as they denote the degree and severity of the kidney damage. There is diminished output of urine (oliguria), albumin is always present (usually in very heavy amounts), the urine is dark, concentrated, and often smoky in colour from the presence of blood (haematuria), and casts are present. Red blood cells and granular casts are the types of cast most frequently present in the acute stage of nephritis. Casts, when present in any number, are always evidence of severe kidney disease, notably nephritis. The blood pressure is usually elevated, and in severe cases may be extremely high, with severe headaches, vomiting, and perhaps convulsions. Most dogs with acute nephritis

recover completely, but a small percentage become chronic.

The dog must have complete rest in a warm, well-ventilated kennel. Complete rest is indicated until all symptoms have gone and the urine is free from red blood cells and albumin. However, in some dogs the albumin persists indefinitely in the urine (the acute nephritis progressing to the chronic stage) and it may not be possible to keep the dog completely rested until the urine is normal. Because of the necessity to rest the diseased kidneys as much as possible, perhaps the most important factor in the treatment of acute nephritis is the diet. As most of the work of the kidneys consists of excreting the waste products of protein, as little protein as possible is given in the vital early days. In addition, owing to the presence of oedema, fluids and salt are restricted. To carry out these principals of diet an initial period of starvation is necessary, when only one pint a day of barley water is given. Nothing else is given until the kidneys begin to recover, the signs of this being an increased output of urine and the lessening or disappearance of blood from the urine. In most cases a diuresis sets in after a few days and the diet can then be increased by the addition of bread, cereal, and milk. Eggs, fish, cheese, and meat are gradually added later with the continued improvement of the dog. It is of paramount importance to realise that an initial starvation period followed by a very limited protein diet is of the utmost value in resting the kidneys. However, if there is no improvement in the urinary findings after two or three weeks, this low protein diet must be increased in order to supply sufficient protein to build up the dog's general nutritional state. A check of urine output and fluid intake must be made and the urine examined frequently for albumin, red cells, and casts. Penicillin may be given to treat any infection present.

2. *Chronic nephritis*

The minority of cases of acute nephritis which do not completely clear up pass into the chronic stage of nephritis, wherein permanent renal damage is present. Many cases of chronic nephritis have no history of a previous acute attack. The presence of chronic nephritis may be discovered by a routine examination of the urine, which reveals the presence of albumin and casts. There may be no symptoms or the dog may simply appear lethargic. Anaemia is a fairly constant feature and the blood pressure is often elevated. Many cases of chronic nephritis exhibit oedema at some stage. Very heavy albuminuria is a constant finding in the oedematous stage and it is this continuous loss of protein from the blood that mainly accounts for the oedema. Chronic nephritis may reach the stage of renal failure, in which the symptoms are weakness, vomiting, lethargy, and eventually coma. The blood urea is extremely high as is the blood pressure.

In the latent stage of chronic nephritis the dog may continue with his normal exercise program as far as possible, although excessive fatigue must be avoided. A normal, well-balanced diet is given, with perhaps a slight restriction in the amount of protein. The anaemia must be treated with iron. In the oedematous stage, if severe, the dog is best confined to his kennel and rested until the oedema has subsided. The diet in this stage is very important. Salt is restricted as it tends to retain water in the body and thus increase the oedema. Since there is a continued loss of protein in the urine in this stage, a moderately high protein diet is often given. If the oedema fails to respond to a low salt and high protein diet, diuretics are given. Chronic nephritis generally runs a prolonged course. The most significant factors in the treatment are provision of a suitable diet, varying in accordance with the stage of the nephritis present, avoidance, as far as possible, of infections which may exacerbate the nephritis, and modification of the dog's daily work program to suit his state of health.

3. *The nephrotic syndrome*
This condition is characterised by generalised oedema and by heavy albuminuria. So much albumin is lost in the urine that the plasma protein is seriously depleted. Often the cause of the nephrotic syndrome is unknown. Cortisone and its allies are often successful in reducing the oedema and albuminuria. Salt is restricted and diuretics may be used, as in chronic nephritis.

16

THE
NERVOUS SYSTEM

The nervous system is of great complexity and functionally has developed two outstanding characteristics—excitability (reaction to stimuli) and conductivity (transmission of nerve impulses along a nervous pathway). As the departments of a central telephone exchange are interlinked by complex receivers, transmitters, diffusers, and amplifiers, so the activity of every part of the central nervous system is coordinated with the rest, and from it, like telephone wires, radiate the fibres of the peripheral nervous system to every structure of the body. For descriptive purposes the nervous system is often divided into a central nervous system and a peripheral nervous system, but structurally and functionally these divisions are artificial. The basic unity of the nervous system must never be overlooked, especially since its study is simplified by analysis of different systems and regions separately, for example, part of the nervous system is concerned with maintenance within the body of conditions suitable for life, such as breathing and digestion, and part is concerned with the reactions of the animal to cope with its environmental conditons. These systems are described separately yet the separations are by no means clear and the systems react extensively upon each other. As humans, it is important to remember not to measure a dog's intelligence in accordance with how it adapts itself to the human way of living.

The neuron, or nerve cell, is the structural and functional unit of the nervous tissue. A functional classification of neurons includes:

1. Motor neurons, motoneurons, or efferent neurons, which convey impulses to muscles.
2. Sensory or afferent neurons, which transmit stimuli inward from various receptors.
3. Association neurons, which are found between sensory and motor units and convey impulses from sensory to motor neurons. Such connecting neurons are also referred to as intercalary, internuncial, or central neurons.

The cell body, or soma, of a neuron contains protoplasm with a well-defined nucleus and nucleolus. Within the cytoplasm are small areas of deep-staining material called Nissl bodies, this substance being a nucleoprotein and having some relation to the physiological activity of the cell. Cell bodies vary markedly in size and shape and are a vital part of the neuron. If, as a consequence of mechanical injury or disease, the cell body is unable to survive, then the processes also die and are unable to carry nervous impulses. Paralysis of muscles occurs if injury to neurons prevents nervous impulses from reaching the muscles. Groups of nerve cell bodies appear grey and predominantly comprise the grey matter of the brain and spinal cord. Nerve cells in the adult dog are not capable of mitotic division and are consequently unable to increase in numbers. The cell bodies of motor neurons are situated near the end of the neuron, but in sensory neurons the cell body may be located some distance from the end. Dendrons or dendrites (Gk. *dendron* = tree) are branches of a neuron that conduct the nervous impulse toward the cell body. The dendron of a sensory neuron may be long and exhibit little branching while in motor neurons there are, generally speaking, several short dendrons with tree-like branches. The axon is the process that conducts the impulse away from the cell body and usually there is only one axon. The axon of a motor neuron may be very short or it may be 60 to 90 centimetres long, as are those extending from the spinal cord to the muscles of the toes. The difference in function differentiates the axon and the dendron, rather than any contrast in structure. The nervous impulse passing over a group of neurons flows from the axon of one to the dendrons and cell body of another. Nerve fibres generally terminate in fine branches referred to as terminal filaments.

A layer of fatty tissue frequently covers the nerve fibres and is thought to be protective in

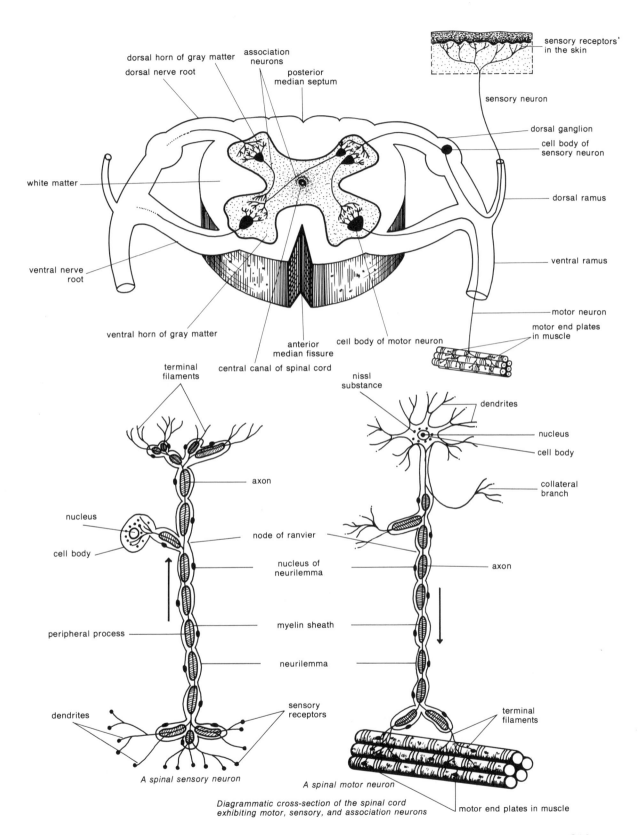

sensory receptors in the skin

dorsal horn of gray matter

association neurons

dorsal nerve root

posterior median septum

sensory neuron

dorsal ganglion

cell body of sensory neuron

white matter

dorsal ramus

ventral ramus

ventral nerve root

motor neuron

motor end plates in muscle

ventral horn of gray matter

anterior median fissure

cell body of motor neuron

central canal of spinal cord

terminal filaments

nissl substance

dendrites

nucleus

cell body

collateral branch

axon

nucleus

cell body

node of ranvier

nucleus of neurilemma

axon

peripheral process

myelin sheath

neurilemma

dendrites

sensory receptors

terminal filaments

A spinal sensory neuron

A spinal motor neuron

motor end plates in muscle

Diagrammatic cross-section of the spinal cord exhibiting motor, sensory, and association neurons

219

function. Such fibres are referred to as medullated or myelinated fibres, but not all possess this covering. Thin areas of myelin are spaced at regular intervals and are known as the nodes of Ranvier. The neurilemma, a delicate nucleated membrane, covers the myelin sheath and follows the surface of the sheath down into the nodes of Ranvier, thus permitting the fibres to be nourished by tissue fluids at these points. The nodes are thought to represent relay stations for the propagation of the nerve impulse. The terminal branches of dendrons and axons are neither medullated nor covered by neurilemma. However, there are fibres which are nonmedullated but covered with neurilemma, for example the fibres of the olfactory nerves and the non-medullated fibres of the autonomic system. White matter exists where there is a predominance of fibres rather than cell bodies, rendering the nervous tissue light-coloured rather than grey. The white matter of the brain and spinal cord is comprised largely of medullated fibres with no neurilemma. The nuclei of the neurilemma apparently play an important role in nerve regeneration and this probably accounts for the fact that nerves of the brain and spinal cord are incapable of regeneration. The typical nerve fibre of cranial and spinal nerves is medullated and covered with neurilemma, the olfactory, optic and auditory nerves being exceptions.

The terminal filaments of the motor neuron branch and penetrate the sarcolemma of a muscle fibre. The myelin sheath disappears, while the neurilemma is assumed to fuse with the sarcolemma. Enlargements, known as motor end plates, occur on the surface of the muscle fibres where the distal ends of the terminal filaments of motor neurons are applied to muscle fibres. This intimate contact between nerve and muscle is referred to as the neuromuscular junction. The nerve impulse is believed to release acetylcholine, which acts as a transmitter between nerve and muscle, on arrival at the end plate. The release of this substance gives rise to an electronegative charge—the end plate potential— and a wave of depolarisation and a change of potential then sweeps over the membrane of the muscle fibre, resulting in its contraction. Cholinesterase, an enzyme, hydrolises acetylcholine and destroys its effectiveness in approximately 1/500 of a second, in which time the acetylcholine effect would be destroyed prior to the muscle fibre membrane becoming repolarised.

The transmission of nervous impulses from one neuron to another is effected by minute terminal-thickened areas called synaptic knobs, that are thought to create a state of activity on the cell surface comparable to the local excitatory state in nerve. Since the local excitatory state is below the threshold level, it is capable of summation with excitatory states set up by other synaptic knobs in the immediate neighbourhood. There appears to be sound evidence that, in the central nervous system, acetylcholine is the chemical released at the ends of terminal filaments and that it acts as a chemical mediator, providing for transmission of the impulse across the synaptic junction. The motor end plate is similar to the synaptic junction and it is supposed that the two function in the same manner. Transmission of the nerve impulse across the synaptic junction differs from conduction along a fibre. A nerve fibre will conduct an impulse in either direction, but the impulse passes across the synapse in one direction only—from the axon of one neuron to the dendrons and cell body of another. The synapses are more susceptible to fatigue and to the action of anaesthetics than the nerve fibres themselves.

Many of the nerves are large, complicated structures, consisting of bundles of fibres separated and secured in place by connective tissue containing fat cells and capillaries. When a nerve branches this implies that the axis fibres of certain neurons are directed into the branch of the nerve. While some nerves contain only motor neurons or exclusively sensory neurons, the majority of nerves are composed of both motor and sensory neurons and are called mixed nerves. Sections of neurons cannot survive if severed from their cell bodies and the axis fibres that are separated from the cell body degenerate and the neurilemma surrounding the severed fibres undergoes extensive degeneration. If regeneration does take place, the developing axis fibre grows from the cell body into the old neurilemma of the severed portion. The neurilemma is an essential factor in regeneration of nerve fibres since regeneration does not occur in neurons without a neurilemma, such as those in brain tracts or in the spinal cord.

The conduction rate of the nerve impulse varies with the temperature, the type of animal, the diameter of the fibre, and the nature of the fibre covering (i.e., whether or not the fibre is myelinated). Generally speaking, the largest fibres record the highest conduction rates and the greatest potential and vice versa. Conduction in a myelinated fibre is about ten times as rapid as in a non-myelinated fibre of the same diameter. Even within a single nerve the rate of conduction varies with the size of the fibre. Extensive research has revealed that there is an electrical change associated with the conduction of the nerve impulse. This change is referred to as an action potential and is brought about by the rapid depolarisation of the membrane as the impulse moves along the axon. It is assumed that the membrane covering a neuron is electrically polarised. There is an excess of positively charged ions on the outside of the membrane and an excess of negatively charged ions on the inside. Under resting conditions the membrane is impermeable to these charges, but at the point of stimulus the membrane loses its polarisation and becomes permeable to the electrically charged ions. An action potential is formed and the ions move through the membrane and, as the alteration of potential affects adjacent regions, the nerve impulse moves away from the point of stimulation. The fluid on the outside of the membrane is composed mainly of sodium and chloride ions, while the ions on the inside of the fibre are largely potassium ions, together with various negatively charged organic ions. The membrane is selectively permeable and allows the movement of sodium and potassium ions even in the resting fibre; but, for reasons unknown, the sodium ions that enter appear to be forced out and the potassium ions retained. 'As the nerve impulse passes, sodium ions rush inside the fibre until they are in excess there; potassium ions move outside the membrane. For about 1/1000 second the inside of the nerve fibre becomes positive and the outside negative as the nerve impulse passes.'

It is important to comprehend the concept of the motor unit. A motor unit consists of a motor neuron and its terminal filaments which innervate individual muscle fibres. The fibres of skeletal muscle are innervated in groups of about a hundred by the branches of a single motor neuron; with such a common innervation these fibres will thus respond as a unit.

In contrast to a current of electricity, the nerve impulse does not become progressively weaker as it moves away from the point of stimulation. The nerve impulse is self-propagating and its energy does not diminish. A strong stimulus increases the frequency of the impulses passing along a nerve fibre and more fibres may be involved. A strong sensory stimulus may cause pain and a strong motor stimulus may cause gross contractions of muscles. The passage of the nerve impulse uses up the energy of the nerve fibre and for a fraction of a second the nerve is unable to conduct another impulse, this being referred to as the absolute refractory period. The nerve fibre potential is restored during a relative refractory period when the response of the nerve fibre is sub-normal. The relative refractory period has been estimated by authorities to be in the vicinity of $0 \cdot 001$ seconds in the neurons of large nerves of mammals.

Nervous tissue uses oxygen and gives off carbon dioxide, as do all other body tissues, and minute amounts of heat even though the nerve is resting. The amount of heat given off is increased over fifty per cent when the nerves activate, but the amount of heat is so minor that it is barely significant to contribute toward body heat. It has been estimated by authorities that 'the initial heat of muscular contraction, based on a single contraction of frog muscle, is 30 000 times as great as the initial heat of nerve'. Energy for conduction of nerve impulses is thought to be obtained from the rapid breakdown of creatine phosphate. This phase of metabolism is concomitant with that occurring in muscle, but the recovery phase in nerve differs in some respects. Glycogen remains relatively unchanged. Experimentally, nerves will respond to stimulation for some time in the absence of oxygen. The development of electric potential across the nerve membrane will necessitate an outlay of energy which is most probably derived from the adenosinetriphosphate system. Since nerve tissue exhibits a very rapid recovery following the passage of a nerve impulse, it has been difficult to demonstrate fatigue in nerve fibres. Continued activity lowers the irritability of the nerve fibre, lowers metabolic activity, and has the effect of lengthening the refractory period. Fatigue of nerve fibres has been demonstrated experimentally, but should not be confused with general body fatigue in the greyhound that may arise from overworking the muscles or from other causes.

Sensory receptors can initiate sensory impulses, which travel in toward the central nervous system over many individual neurons. Motor impulses can arise from various parts of the brain. When these impulses are directed toward a muscle, they must converge and travel over ventral root neurons to cause contraction of muscles. The spinal motor neuron represents the final common pathway over which all impulses must pass to reach the muscle effector. While motor stimuli are ordinarily directed into a final common path, the number of connections that can be made are almost infinite. A certain degree of resistance to the passage of the nerve impulse at the point of synapse may assist to channel impulses into relatively few restricted pathways. Habit formation can induce them to follow a definite course. Under certain circumstances widespread diffusion of nerve impulses to muscles may occur, giving rise to convulsions or uncontrolled contractions of numerous muscles. Diffusion of nerve impulses takes place much more readily in pups than in adult dogs; convulsions are commoner in pups. It is assumed that in pups there is less resistance to the diffusion of nerve impulses, so that a strong pain stimulus, for example, may result in convulsions. Caffeine is believed to facilitate the flow of impulses across synapses, thus rendering the animal more wide awake than usual. All greyhounds operate under some degree of nervous inhibition or resistance. Generally speaking, greyhounds in good health display better resistance to disturbing elements that frequently play a large part in the attitude of the dog to his daily routine.

A cross section of the spinal cord reveals an interior portion of grey matter shaped like the letter H, surrounded by white matter. The white matter is composed of the axis fibres of neurons which are nearly all medullated but have no neurilemma. They are grouped into great columns concerned with the transmission of nerve impulses either up or down the spinal cord. Some columns represent ascending pathways and others, descending pathways. While the grey matter of the cord is generally portrayed in cross section, it is important to realise that it consists of several columns composed primarily of the cell bodies of neurons and unmedullated fibres. The slender dorsal columns contain numerous fibres of the dorsal spinal nerves and the cell bodies of some of the afferent ascending neurons whose fibres traverse the white matter of the cord. The cell bodies of the neurons forming the anterior roots of spinal nerves lie in the larger ventral columns. Descending neurons in the white matter make synaptic connections with these cell bodies, establishing a pathway by which motor impulses from the brain are transmitted to muscles. Between the dorsal and ventral columns in the pars intermedia there is an intermediolateral column which contains the cell bodies of motor neurons of the sympathetic system. The grey matter also contains association neurons which form synaptic connections between the dorsal and ventral roots or between the right and left sides of the cord. Many of these neurons make connections vertically between different levels of the cord.

The central canal is a minute tube extending the length of the cord and opening anteriorly into the fourth ventricle of the brain and terminating posteriorly in the filum terminale of the cord. It contains cerebrospinal fluid.

The spinal nerve has two roots close to the cord, a dorsal afferent (sensory) root and a ventral efferent (motor) root. The dorsal afferent root is composed of sensory neurons which bring impulses in toward the central nervous system. The cell bodies of these neurons are situated outside the cord in the ganglion of the dorsal root. A ganglion is a group of nerve cells outside the brain or spinal cord. The cell bodies arise as bipolar nerve cells in the embryo; one fibre grows outward to a sensory receptor located, for example, in the skin or in a muscle, and the other fibre grows inward toward the cord through the dorsal root of the spinal nerve. The fibre entering the cord may not make immediate connection with an association or motor neuron as certain of these fibres may extend to upper or lower levels of the cord prior to making these connections. The neurons comprising the ventral root have their cell bodies situated in the ventral columns of grey matter of the cord and their fibres extend outward and generally terminate in a muscle or gland. The sensory and motor roots merge as they pass outward through openings between the vertebrae, forming a mixed nerve. All spinal nerves are mixed nerves. Spinal nerves divide into two large branches just outside the vertebral column, the dorsal branches innervating the muscles and skin of the posterior portions of the neck and trunk and the ventral branches being distributed to the ventral part of the body wall and to the extremities.

The spinal nerves and the cord form a pathway for nerve stimuli, permitting reflex movements. The sudden retraction of the foot as the consequence of a pain stimulus, the protective closure of the eyelids when an object comes close to the eye, or the coordinated muscular movements that enable the dog to maintain his balance are common examples of reflex movements. Other reflexes, involving smooth muscles, are not as obvious. Sensory stimuli may affect the heart, stomach, blood vessels, or any other organ reflexly so that automatic adjustments to varying conditions may be made constantly.

The sensory receptor, the sensory neuron, usually association neurons within the spinal cord, and the motor neuron are the structural elements of a reflex arc. Specialised structures called receptors receive sensory stimuli. These peripheral receptors are of various types and incorporate structures in the skin for the reception of stimuli arising from change in temperature, touch, pressure, and pain, in addition to receptors for the higher senses situated in the eye, ear, nose, and on the tongue. The fine nerve endings themselves act as receptors for the sense of pain. The sensory neuron carries the nerve impulses inward toward the brain or cord. Association neurons can connect directly with motor neurons on the same side of the cord, or they can make multiple connections, some crossing over to the other side. The motor neurons carry impulses to muscles. There are always a number of neurons participating in a reflex act, although reflex acts are frequently described as though only one sensory neuron and one motor neuron were involved. Simple reflexes are those that do not involve centres in the brain and are generally simple nervous circuits through the cord. Reflexes involving the brain are extremely complicated. Many activities can be carried on below the level of consciousness. The respiratory, cardiac, and vasoconstrictor centres are situated in the medulla. The cerebellum functions as a coordinator of muscular activity and helps to maintain balance. Midbrain, thalamus, and cerebral cortex function to maintain posture and coordinate movements. Many reflexes are conditioned by experience. The Russian physiologist, Pavlov, demonstrated that the salivary response in dogs can be conditioned in various ways, such as by the ringing of a bell, the flash of a light, or by the sight of objects of different sizes and shapes. If a bell is rung as the dog is fed, the animal soon associates the ringing of the bell with the presence of food and since salivation is a normal reaction associated with hunger and anticipation of eating, the dog can be conditioned so that its saliva will flow merely at the sound of a bell. The conditioned reflex may be the basis of habit formation. The voiding of urine by puppies is probably controlled as a spinal reflex act as when the urinary bladder becomes distended to a certain degree, a passage of nerve impulses develops that results in the emptying of the bladder. As the pup develops, however, he learns to control this act; cerebral control is superimposed over the simple reflex and it becomes a conditioned reflex. Investigation reveals that simple reflexes may be conditioned by experience; these experiences, good or bad, may be made the basis of habit formation.

THE AUTONOMIC NERVOUS SYSTEM

Extensive bodily changes support emotional states. A state of fear in the dog may induce the desire to run, but the dog will not run far unless physiological adjustments support the effort. Anger may mean that the dog is prepared to fight, but it will not be an efficient battle unless the dog's circulatory system makes necessary adjustments to provide strength and endurance for the contest. The situation need not be a highly emotional one as work and exercise are supported by the same physical adjustments. Regulation of the internal environment of the body with respect to temperature and body fluids is a normal function of the autonomic nervous system. A good example of its operation is the adjustment of the body to a marked temperature change in the surrounding medium. As the temperature rises, the sweat glands are stimulated and, if the humidity of the air is sufficiently low, evaporation produces a cooling effect. At the same time peripheral vasodilation of the arterioles and capillaries of the skin permits a greater volume of blood to be brought to the surface. When the body is subjected to high temperatures skeletal muscles tend to relax. When the body is exposed to cold, the surface arterioles constrict to keep more of the blood away from the cool surface and consequently conserve heat. Skeletal muscles increase their tone, and shivering may be induced to produce more heat from the contraction of muscles.

Physical adjustments to an emergency are primarily controlled by the autonomic system. Preparations to strengthen the animal's body for a critical situation include acceleration and strengthening of the heart beat, elevation of blood pressure, release of glucose from the liver, and secretion of a small amount of epinephrine by the adrenal glands. Breathing is facilitated by relaxation of the muscles in the bronchial tubes. During an emergency, digestion can be delayed and the activity of the digestive system

White Panther, a 33-kg dog by White Superoo out of Simply Super. 1980 South Australian Greyhound of the Year, winner of thirty-eight races, and current joint Angle Park track record holder over 512 metres (30·18 seconds) with Lively Sheen *(Courtesy of South Australian Greyhound Trainer)*

is altered and depressed and the blood supply is largely diverted from the digestive system to aid skeletal muscles. These effects are obtained primarily by the stimulation of the sympathetic (thoracolumbar) division of the autonomic nervous system.

The autonomic nervous system may be artificially divided into a sympathetic (thoracolumbar) and a parasympathetic (craniosacral) section. The sympathetic division is composed of a chain of ganglia and nerves on either side of the spinal cord, extending from the cervical region through the thoracic and lumbar regions. Each ganglion is connected to a spinal nerve by a communicating branch in the thoracic and lumbar regions. Fibres extend upward to the head from the superior cervical ganglion and downward from sacral ganglia, thus increasing the distribution of sympathetic fibres. Motor impulses from the spinal cord to smooth muscles are conveyed over two sets of visceral efferent fibres instead of one as in somatic (pertaining to the body, as distinguished from the mind) motor nerves. A synaptic connection normally is made in a ganglion of the sympathetic chain, although this is not always so. There is a preganglionic neuron, with its cell body situated in the intermediolateral column of grey matter of the cord and with its fibre normally extending from the cell body to the autonomic ganglion outside the cord, and a postganglionic neuron with its cell body situated in a ganglion and its fibre extending to visceral muscle. The preganglionic fibre can extend through the autonomic ganglion to a collateral ganglion, in which instance there will be a short postganglionic fibre to the organ supplied. This arrangement is significant as it provides for the rapid, widespread response characteristic of the sympathetic system. There appears to be no doubt that the hypothalamus functions as a centre for many activities of the sympathetic system. Experimentally it has been demonstrated that stimulation of the hypothalamus in anaesthetised animals results in dilation of the pupils, increase in blood pressure, and stimulation of respiration.

The parasympathetic division of the autonomic nervous system is associated with specific cranial and sacral nerves in which autonomic fibres are incorporated. Typically, the parasympathetic preganglionic fibre extends from its nucleus in the brain or sacral region of the cord to the organ supplied. The postganglionic fibre is frequently a very short fibre situated within the organ itself. The preganglionic fibre can end in a collateral ganglion, as in the case of preganglionic fibres extending out to the ciliary ganglion of the eye. The postganglionic fibres in this instance are longer than those incorporated within certain organs. The parasympathetic system functions as an antagonist of the sympathetic system if an organ is supplied by both systems. If the sympathetic system is the accelerator system (as in the heart), then the parasympathetic system is the inhibitor, its function in this instance being to slow the accelerated heart and restore normal heart rate. Even though it acts as an inhibitor, it does not normally depress the heart rate below normal unless unduly stimulated, as from the action of drugs or pressure on a nerve.

Autonomic effects are generally conditioned by other factors such as the presence of hormones in the blood stream or by circulatory effects. The secretion of a gland can be depressed by the stimulation of an inhibitor nerve or by vasoconstriction of blood vessels supplying the gland, thus limiting its blood supply. While the sympathetic system acts as an accelerator to the heart, the situation is reversed in the case of the digestive tract, where the action of sympathetic nerves depresses peristalsis and the secretion of digestive glands during emotional excitement, while the parasympathetic system, as an accelerator, effects a return to normal. The sympathetic and parasympathetic nerves are antagonistic in the same sense as when two muscles oppose each other to facilitate flexion and extension of a part. The nerves from the two systems can produce opposite effects, but they provide a correlated adjustment to meet many physiological conditions. Autonomic effects are not always clearly antagonistic.

Investigation by authorities has revealed that nervous impulses conducted by efferent neurons of the autonomic system do not produce their effect on muscle tissue directly, but release a chemical substance at the nerve endings which combines with another substance in the tissue to produce the effect. Generally, the postganglionic fibres of the sympathetic system release a substance called sympathin, or norepinephrine, at their terminal endings and such fibres are referred to as adrenergic. There are two types of receptive substances in the tissues — one, upon combination with norepinephrine, causes contraction of visceral muscle; the other, after combining, causes relaxation. Parasympathetic fibres also produce a chemical mediating substance called acetylcholine, which is rapidly converted to choline and acetic acid by the action of an enzyme called cholinesterase. Since acetylcholine does not remain in its most active state for any great length of time, it is probable that its effects are entirely local. Unlike norepinephrine, it is probably not carried by the bloodstream. All preganglionic fibres, whether sympathetic or parasympathetic, have been proved to liberate a cholinergic substance, probably identical with acetylcholine, which means that the transmission of the nervous impulse across the point of synapse between the preganglionic and postganglionic fibre is accomplished by the production of acetylcholine.

There are afferent fibres arising in the viscera and associated with the autonomic nervous system. These fibres do not give rise to sensation in the ordinary sense. The viscera are relatively insensitive to pain in the way that pain is generally recognised from a cut or burn on the skin or the crushing of a toe. The receptors of visceral afferent neurons are located in the viscera. From cell bodies located in the ganglia of dorsal spinal nerve roots, processes enter the dorsal horn of grey matter of the cord together with the processes of sensory spinal nerves. The exact way in which visceral pain arises is not well understood although it is thought to be caused by certain kinds of muscular contraction in visceral muscle or by pressure within a hollow organ. Internal pain is not readily localised and may be referred to some surface area.

THE BRAIN

The three primary divisions of the brain and their secondary divisions are as follows:

1. *Forebrain*
a. Telencephalon (anterior part).
b. Diencephalon (posterior part).
2. *Midbrain (mesencephalon)*
Becomes part of the brain stem.
3. *Hindbrain*
a. Metencephalon (anterior part).
b. Myelencephalon (posterior part).

The brain and spinal cord are protected by the meningeal membranes. These are three in number and consist of a tough, fibrous outer layer — the dura mater; a delicate, serous intermediate membrane — the arachnoid; and an inner vascular layer — the pia mater. The dura mater within the cranium consists of two layers, the outer layer being fused with the cranial bones and the inner layer extending down over the spinal cord, forming a protective covering. The delicate arachnoid membrane lines the dura mater and extends down over the cord. It does not normally follow the sulci closely, as does the pia mater, consequently there is a subarachnoid space at each depression between the convolutions of the brain. The subarachnoid spaces are filled with cerebrospinal fluid which protects the brain and spinal cord from mechanical injuries. Diseases that attack the central nervous system or the meninges can alter the composition or increase the amount of cerebrospinal fluid. Diagnosis and treatment of such diseases can be greatly assisted by analysis of the fluid. A sample is obtained by a procedure called lumbar puncture. Since the spinal cord ends at the first or second lumbar vertebra and since the dura mater and arachnoid membranes extend below this point, it is possible to insert a needle between the vertebrae and into the subarachnoid space of this region and obtain cerebrospinal fluid. Spinal anaesthetics are introduced into the subarachnoid space in the same region by lumbar puncture. The pia mater contains a dense network of blood vessels and is closely applied to the brain surface, following down into the sulci and fissures. It is closely applied to the spinal cord also.

The neuroglia may be regarded as the connective tissue of the brain and spinal cord. It is assumed that the function of the neuroglia is to afford structural support for the cell bodies and fibres within the brain and spinal cord, but it may also aid in the nutrition and insulation of neurons.

The cavities of the brain communicate with each other and are continuous with the central canal of the spinal cord. The ventricles are filled with the same fluid that fills the subarachnoid space, the cerebrospinal fluid. The largest cavities are the lateral ventricles of the telencephalon. Located one in each hemisphere of the cerebrum, they are connected with the third ventricle of the diencephalon by the foramina of Monro. The third ventricle communicates with the fourth through the aqueduct of the cerebrum which traverses the midbrain. The fourth ventricle is continuous with the central canal of the spinal cord and has openings in its roof that lead into the subarachnoid space.

Fissures are deep depressions on the brain surface, the numerous lesser depressions of the surface being referred to as sulci, which separate the elevations, or convolutions. The surface of the brain has a covering, or cortex, of gray matter composed of millions of unmedullated nerve cell bodies and fibres. Beneath the cortex the inside of the brain appears white because it is composed largely of medullated nerve fibres. These fibres usually lie in tracts and may connect the cortex with the spinal cord, or they may extend between different parts of the brain itself. Fissures divide the cerebrum into anatomical sections called lobes. These are the frontal, parietal, temporal, and occipital lobes and the insula, formerly referred to as the island of Reil. The central sulcus separates the frontal and parietal lobes. The lateral cerebral fissure demarcates the temporal lobe. The occipital lobe lies posterior to the parieto-occipital fissure. The lobes, with the exception of the insula, lie under cranial bones of the same name. The insula is a lobe of grey matter located below the lateral cerebral fissure and may be observed only when the adjacent portions of the frontal and temporal lobes are raised.

It is impossible to localise many of the functions of the cerebrum, but a number of cerebral functions originate in localised areas. The motor area lies just anterior to the central sulcus and it is in the neurons of this area that motor impulses arise. These are voluntary impulses that cause contractions of voluntary muscles. Experimentally, it can be demonstrated that when particular parts of the motor area are stimulated certain groups of muscles or individual muscles will respond. Not only is the motor area inverted with respect to the position of the body it controls but the motor area of the right cerebral hemisphere governs the movement of the muscles of the left side of the body and vice versa. The reason for this lies in the fact that the nerve tracts from the motor area cross over either at the base of the medulla or at various levels in the spinal cord. A knowledge of the location and function of the motor area has been invaluable in the diagnosis of many types of brain injuries.

Posterior to the central sulcus lies a sensory area for the interpretation of sensations such as touch, pain, temperature, pressure, and muscle sense and this area may be referred to as the cutaneous sensory area. It is thought that the subdivisions of this area correspond approximately to those of the motor area just anterior to the central sulcus. The right sensory area interprets sensations received from the left side of the body and vice versa.

The visual interpreting area is located at the back of the brain in the occipital lobes. Nervous impulses arising in the retina are conveyed back to the interpreting area by nerve tracts. This sensory area enables the dog to interpret and understand what he sees.

The auditory areas are concerned with the interpretation of the sense of hearing and are located in the temporal lobes. Each area receives nervous impulses from both ears.

Interpreting areas for the sense of taste and

smell have not been definitely located, but a cortical area associated with the sense of taste is located near the Sylvian fissure and at the base of the central sulcus. Located ventrally below the frontal lobes of the cerebrum are the two olfactory bulbs. The interpreting area for the sense of smell is assumed to be along the olfactory tracts which extend inward from the olfactory bulbs.

Experimentation by authorities suggests that probably all areas of the cortex are actually sensorimotor, i.e., they are not exclusively sensory or exclusively motor. It is true that the area directly anterior to the central sulcus is predominantly motor, whereas the region posterior to the central sulcus is predominantly sensory, or afferent; but even areas such as the visual cortex contain motor fibres. Motor fibres in localised sensory areas produce a motor response in muscles associated with the activity of the sense organ involved, for example, stimulation of the visual area may evoke eye and head movements. Only the precentral motor area governs movements of the body as an entity.

The thalamus is the largest of a number of areas of grey matter deep within the brain called the basal ganglia and is an important relay centre for both motor and sensory impulses and possesses extensive cortical connections. It has been likened to a telephone switchboard where messages are received and relayed.

The hypothalamus is composed of structures located in the basal section of the diencephalon. Various autonomic functions are governed from centres in the hypothalamus. The heat regulatory centre and the centre concerned with water metabolism are located here. It is a regulatory centre for both the sympathetic and parasympathetic divisions of the autonomic nervous system. 'Sham' rage in animals, a reaction of fury and savageness, has long been associated with stimulation at the hypothalamic level. Functionally, the hypothalamus is closely allied with various endocrine activities of the pituitary gland (the hypophysis).

The midbrain, pons, and medulla comprise the brain stem. Great nerve tracts connecting the spinal cord with higher synaptic levels in the cerebrum pass through the brain stem. The greater part of the midbrain, the upper portion of the brain stem, consists of nerve tracts that carry impulses between the cerebrum and the cerebellum, medulla, and spinal cord.

The metencephalon lies just below the mid-brain, its most apparent structures being the cerebellum, which lies posterior to the brain stem, and a bridge of nerve tracts, the pons, extending across the anterior part of the brain stem. The fourth ventricle is the cavity of this region. All ventricles contain choroid plexuses, in which cerebrospinal fluid is formed, which are highly vascular folds and elaborations of the pia mater.

There are two cerebellar lobes located below the occipital lobes of the cerebrum. The cerebellum has a cortex of grey matter which differs from that of the cerebrum in several ways. It is not convoluted in the same manner, but appears as a series of layers. Within the cortex are the large cells of Purkinje, which are found exclusively in the cortex of the cerebellum. The interior of the cerebellum is largely composed of white matter although the grey matter of the cortex descends deeply into the white matter and elaborates into an inverted tree-like pattern of branching. Great nerve tracts, the cerebellar peduncles, connect the cerebellum with the cerebrum, the pons, and the medulla. The pons consists of horizontal nerve tracts that connect the two hemispheres of cerebellum anteriorly and vertical tracts that connect the cerebrum with the medulla.

The cerebellum has been referred to as the 'secretary' to the cerebrum as it does not initiate motor responses but functions to coordinate muscular movements so that the action is smooth and efficient instead of being jerky and unco-ordinated. In addition, the cerebellum is concerned with equilibrium and is connected by nerve fibres with the semicircular canals of the inner ear, which are likewise concerned with equilibrium. The cerebellum is able to direct the muscular coordination that keeps the body balanced in particular attitudes. The cerebellum assists in the maintenance of muscle tone. Each cerebellar hemisphere governs largely the muscles on the same side of the body. Normally, an injury in the right cerebellar hemisphere will affect muscular coordination in the right side of the body. Equilibrium appears to be controlled from two centres, one in an anterior and one in a posterior cortical region.

The medulla is the base of the brain stem, or myelencephalon, and is continuous with the spinal cord but does not exhibit the same internal structure. While the nerve tracts are continuous, some are larger and more defined in the medulla and some of the fibres cross to the opposite side. The continuous grey matter of the cord is divided into groups of nuclei in the medulla. The central canal of the cord is continuous anteriorly through the medulla, where it opens into the lower section of the fourth ventricle. The medulla contains vital reflex centres, such as the cardiac inhibitory centre which, via the vagus nerve, acts in slowing the heart rate; the vasoconstrictor centre, responsible for the constriction of peripheral blood vessels and consequent rise in arterial pressure; and a respiratory centre, which provides the nervous stimulus for regular respiratory movements. In addition, the medulla controls several common reflex activities, such as coughing and sneezing, and many of the activities of the digestive tract.

A diffuse mixture of grey matter throughout the white matter of the brain stem is referred to as the reticular formation. Investigation has revealed that this formation receives fibres from the cortex, the hypothalamus, and from the nuclei of cranial nerves associated with the brain stem region. In addition, it receives collateral branches from ascending sensory tracts and acts as a reflex centre. Nerve impulses are relayed or projected to specific cranial nerves and to descending tracts of the spinal cord. Some of the nerve cells in the reticular formation exhibit an inhibitory function as they project to descending spinal neurons and they elevate the threshold of motor neurons receiving impulses and inhibit muscular activity. Other nerve cells are excitatory and facilitate muscular contraction. Stimulation of the reticular formation causes the unanaesthetised dog to be aroused from sleep. Ascending spinal sensory tracts give off collateral branches to the reticular system. An interpretation of arousal is that sensory impulses excite the reticular system and then slowly diffuse through the subcortical areas and when they arrive at the cerebral cortex, wakening or return to consciousness takes place. Unconsciousness can be brought about by injury or destruction of the midbrain reticular formation.

The cranial nerves arise in pairs from the brain within the spinal cavity and are essentially like spinal nerves but more highly specialised.

The spinal cord is that section of the central nervous system within the vertebral canal and is continuous with the base of the brain anteriorly and posteriorly tapers to a thread-like strand below the second lumbar vertebra. There are cervical and lumbar enlargements in the regions where large nerves to the appendages are given off. The cord is suspended loosely in the spinal canal and since its diameter is considerably less than that of the canal, the vertebral column can be moved freely without injury to the cord. Ascending tracts in the spinal cord carry impulses concerned with touch, pressure, pain, temperature, and muscle sense, while descending tracts, such as the pyramidal tracts, are motor to muscles of the trunk and the appendages. The cord functions as a pathway for impulses between the body and the brain. The large tracts in the dorsal part of the cord are ascending pathways. Injury to these tracts results in lack of coordination since spinal reflexes are disturbed; walking becomes uncoordinated, movements are jerky, and the dog may find it difficult to maintain his balance. The nerve fibres of the cord are incapable of regeneration following injury, probably because the neurilemma is absent or inadequate. Degeneration of fibres proceeds upward away from the cell bodies in ascending tracts and downward in descending motor tracts. Severing a motor pathway results in muscular paralysis.

Pairs of spinal nerves arise from the cord and are grouped as cervical, thoracic, lumbar, sacral, and coccygeal. Nerves leaving the spinal cord form complex interlacing networks called plexuses in the cervical, brachial and lumbosacral regions. The lumbosacral plexus is a very large network with nerves extending to the lower extremities, included among which are the femoral nerve and the very large sciatic nerve. Inflammation and injury to the sciatic nerve may cause a neuralgic condition referred to as sciatica.

17

INTERNAL PARASITES

WORMS

The aim of this chapter is to discuss the range of the worm parasites commonly encountered in Australia. Other parasites which cause disease in dogs are encountered from time to time, and these are generally treated by veterinarians whose training equips them with specialised knowledge. This chapter describes the worm parasites which greyhound owners may sometimes observe, the symptoms of worm infestation commonly observed, the manner in which worm parasites are spread from animal to animal, some of the drugs in common use by greyhound owners in the treatment of worm parasites, and the hygiene which owners should employ to minimise risk of infestation.

In recent years medical and veterinary research has lead to a greater understanding of the importance of worm parasites in dogs. This knowledge is increased each year as more and more effort is devoted to research. Emphasis has been afforded to the ways in which dogs in close contract with humans and our farm livestock may unwittingly be responsible for the spread of disease. One should be aware of the hazard of such disease both to the humans and to the livestock whose well-being is essential to the well being of the Australian economy. Awareness of parasitic disease and knowledge of treatment and control methods is vital as our environment becomes increasingly heavily populated by humans and their domestic animals. It is of interest to note that for some inexplicable reason greyhounds fed a clove of garlic on a daily basis do not have major worm infestations. Dogs kept in the same kennels but not fed garlic, do develop helminth infestations. These are findings from centrifuged faecal flotation samples.

The majority of greyhound owners now appreciate that from time to time worming is necessary. Many appreciate that dogs may have both roundworm and tapeworm parasites, but few are aware of the different roundworms and tapeworms which commonly infest dogs in Australia.

Large roundworm (Toxocara canis)

Adult roundworms 7 to 15 centimetres long, pointed at each end, white or semi-transparent, may be observed in dog's droppings.

Pups and young dogs are most heavily infected. The parasite may cause serious disease. Infested animals exhibit unthriftiness, decreased appetite, pot belly, harsh coat, and vomiting and/or diarrhoea.

Adult female worms may lay up to 200 000 eggs per day and these are passed in the dog's stools. After a period of about two weeks a baby worm, or 'lava', develops in the egg, which is then infective if swallowed by a suitable host. The eggs hatch in the intestine, and the larvae bore through the intestinal wall and are transported via the bloodstream through the liver to the lungs. Larvae are coughed up, swallowed, and when they reach the small intestine develop into mature worms which produce eggs six to eight weeks following infestation.

In a bitch, larvae may be arrested in the muscles instead of returning to the intestine. During pregnancy not only do larvae complete their journey through the lungs to the small intestine, but roundworms enter the unborn pups, passing into their lungs. As soon as the pups are whelped they cough up larvae which are then swallowed and may commence to lay eggs within three weeks. Larvae may migrate to the mammary glands of the bitch and infest pups with their first sucks of colostrum.

Rodents, insects, or earthworms may swallow fertile eggs and become infested with larvae. Any dog which then eats such a transport host may thus become infested with roundworms. Children may also be infested by swallowing fertile eggs. Larvae migrate through the intestinal wall to be carried via the bloodstream to wander in the liver and the lungs or they may reach the eye, brain, or spinal cord. In such situations unusual symptoms may arise; these are difficult to diagnose and may lead to serious illness.

Puppies should be routinely treated with a reputable preparation, such as Canex (Pfizer Agricare Pty Ltd) used as directed. Generally speaking, puppies should be dosed at two, three, four, six, eight, ten, and twelve weeks of age. From then onwards in most normal circumstances where hygiene is adequate, and/or climatic conditions do not favour survival of infective stages of parasites (i.e., hot, dry, or very cold), dog population is low. Routine dosing is recommended every three months. In situations where adult dogs are confined to restricted areas, a sudden massive increase in infection rate may occur when either warm weather, high humidity, adequate shade, or damp surfaces favour development and survival of roundworm eggs and hookworm larvae. Although these conditions may occur in the southern regions of Australia, sudden dangerous infections, especially of hookworms, most frequently occur in the summer rainfall regions from coastal New South Wales northwards. At certain times of the year repeated dosing at short intervals may be necessary in these circumstances. In severe cases, treatment may be indicated every one to two weeks and guidance as to appropriate intervals of treatment should be obtained from a veterinarian.

It is of paramount importance to ensure a high standard of hygiene during a bitch's pregnancy to prevent entry into the bitch of fresh larvae and eggs which could then enter the milk and also the unborn pups. Nevertheless, despite all hygiene precautions, the bitch may contain in her tissues some larvae which can enter the gut, mature, commence egg laying, and re-contaminate a clean environment, giving rise to further sources of infection for the unborn or new-born pups. Therefore, as a preventative measure, it is recommended that all pregnant bitches be wormed every three weeks during pregnancy and while feeding pups.

Experimentation by authorities has proven that in order to ensure adequate protection of dogs against the harmful effects of hookworm and roundworm in all situations one must adhere strictly to the dosage regime set out by reputable manufacturers.

Hookworms (Uncinaria and Ancylostoma)

Two types of hookworm commonly infest dogs of all ages in Australia, Uncinaria in the south of the continent and Ancylostoma species from Sydney northwards. They are small worms, up to 1 centimetre long, and are generally diagnosed by the symptoms caused.

Hookworms cause symptoms in dogs of all ages, but are most severe in puppies. Hookworms are voracious blood suckers, causing unthriftiness, lack of stamina in racing dogs, and anaemia, which may progress to death. Stools are dark, soft, and foul-smelling due to the presence of blood. Penetration of the larvae invading from contaminated ground may give rise to eczema of the feet.

Female hookworms lay thousands of eggs which are passed into the stools. In approximately one week eggs hatch and minute larvae exist for months in the soil, lawns, and gardens. Larvae infest dogs either by being swallowed with soil or by penetrating the pads of the feet or skin of the lower parts of the body. Swallowed larvae may develop into adult worms in the intestine or, like the roundworms, larvae migrate through the body tissues to the lungs and thence to the intestine. Larvae which penetrate skin migrate to the lungs prior to reaching the intestine where they mature and commence egg laying within three or four weeks. In the pregnant bitch hookworm larvae migrate to the mammary glands, and pups may become infested as soon as suckling commences and may become severely anaemic to the point of death within weeks of whelping.

The dosage regime recommended for treatment of roundworm is concomitant for treatment of hookworm if preparations such as Canex are administered — Canex being effective in the treatment of both of these worm parasites. Since hookworm larvae may persist in a contaminated environment for a year, treatment at monthly intervals is necessary in such situations to prevent recontamination.

Hookworm and other worm larvae can only be reduced by rigid hygiene measures. Stools must be collected daily and rendered innocuous by burning or burial a metre or so deep. Such precautions are of the utmost importance in breeding kennels where risk of worm infestation is high. Dog runs should be constructed of easily cleaned concrete floors with chain wire fences.

Whipworm (Trichuris)

Whipworms are a common parasite in older dogs, but do not usually endanger pups under twelve weeks of age. Whipworm is often diagnosed in Australia when veterinarians carry out microscopic examination of stools of dogs with chronic diarrhoea. Heavily infested dogs are generally thin with voracious appetites. The stools are usually soft and pink-tinged.

Female whipworms lay eggs which are passed in the stools. After two weeks larvae develop within the eggs which are then infective if swallowed by dogs. This parasite lays extremely resistant eggs which can survive for many years and accumulate on the ground in ever increasing numbers if dogs are permitted to go untreated. Infective eggs hatch in the intestine and the larvae burrow into the wall of the large intestine, both damaging and thickening it. Larvae return to the large bowel and attain egg-laying maturity in two months.

Diagnosis is usually carried out by a veterinarian. Canex Plus (pyrantel pamoate + oxantel pamoate) is highly efficient against hookworm and roundworm, and in addition contains oxantel, which is highly effective in eliminating whipworm infections. As whipworms are not a problem in pups under twelve weeks of age, Canex is the drug of choice against hookworm and roundworm — the major puppy parasites. Canex Plus is quite safe to use in pregnant bitches and can be substituted for the three-weekly treatments instead of Canex.

Strict attention to hygiene is necessary to ensure control of whipworm infestation. Concrete runs and impervious floors, which may be easily scrubbed clean, are thus desirable.

Heartworm (Dirofilaria)

Heartworm infestation is common in sub-tropical and tropical regions of northern Australia and has spread southward to irrigation areas which are favourable to mosquitoes.

Adult heartworms may cause severe lung damage in addition to reduction in the efficiency of the heart. Symptoms include chronic cough, lack of stamina, breathlessness, unthriftiness, dropsy, and death in adult dogs. Adult heartworms exist in the heart and pulmonary artery. Female heartworms release live larvae into the blood and these circulate in the body. They must be ingested by a feeding mosquito and undergo development within the mosquito for approximately three weeks. Upon completion of development, the larvae escape from the mosquito as it feeds on another dog, penetrate the skin, circulate in the blood stream, and attain maturity in the heart. Heartworm can only be distributed from dog to dog by a suitable mosquito.

Treatment should be executed only by a veterinarian as death of adult heartworms may give rise to severe lung complications. 'Dirocide', diethylcarbamazine citrate, (Burroughs Wellcome & Co. Ltd) kills larval heartworms in the bloodstream before they are able to reach the heart and mature. Daily administration of Dirocide throughout the mosquito season is a preventative measure against infection of dogs. Dogs suspected of carrying heartworm should be examined by a veterinarian prior to treatment.

Tapeworm

Different species of tapeworms may be found in dogs throughout Australia, the worms varying in length from about 0.5 centimetre (hydatid) to 4.5 metres long (bladder tapeworm). The head of the tapeworm is attached to the wall of the small intestine and gives rise to a chain of segments which serially increase in size. The oldest and largest segments of the tapeworm's tail contain thousands of tapeworm eggs and are shed from time to time. These mature segments, up to 1 centimetre in length, are creamy white when fresh, or brown when dry, and may be observed in the stools or attached to, or in the vicinity of, the anus of the dog. A dog may carry light tapeworm infestation without exhibiting ill health. Heavy tapeworm infestations produce unthriftiness, capricious appetite, intermittent diarrhoea and constipation, and a harsh, dry coat. Tapeworm segments may be mobile and cause anal irritation as they make their way out and may thus be a cause of the dog displaying anal discomfort by dragging his bottom along the ground.

Of greater importance than the harm done to the dog is that larval tapeworms may infest humans and or meat-producing animals. Human infestation by hydatid larvae may lead to death or demand major surgery. Massive economic loss to primary industry and export trade may be the consequence of sheep and cattle infestation. Dog tapeworms are therefore a human problem.

The primary host of the adult egg-producing tapeworms is the dog. When eggs are passed in the stools they are dispersed and must then be swallowed by another intermediate host in order to sustain life. The intermediate host differs in accordance with the species of tapeworm and may include man, sheep, cattle, pigs, kangaroos, rodents, fish, and dog fleas. When swallowed by an intermediate host the eggs hatch and tapeworm larvae migrate to a particular organ within the body of the host where they form a cyst and then wait until the intermediate host is eaten by the dog (primary host). Once swallowed by the dog the larval tapeworm cyst ruptures and each tapeworm larva attaches its head to the wall of the small intestine. After approximately three weeks of growth the oldest segments become filled with eggs and are shed from the tapeworm to sustain the life cycle.

Hydatid tapeworm

Hydatid tapeworm is widely distributed but concentrated in higher-rainfall areas in southern Australia. Segments are rarely observed in a dog's stools because they are very small. Diagnosis is generally made by a veterinarian purging the dog and examining the purge. Children fondling an infected dog may be infested with eggs. Eggs may contaminate herbage eaten by cattle and sheep. Once swallowed, eggs form hydatid cysts in the liver, lungs, brain, or spinal cord and such cysts grow and produce daughter larvae. Cysts damage organs of the body and may lead to the death of humans. Many sheep and cattle organs are condemned each year. Dogs become infested by eating hydatid cysts present in sheep or cattle offal or by scavenging from carcasses.

Sheep measles tapeworm

Sheep measles tapeworm is found throughout southern Australia. The larval stage forms cysts, which are very hard to detect, within the muscles of the sheep. The discovery of these cysts in meat exported to the United States of America has resulted in the banning of mutton and lamb export trade.

Sheep bladder tapeworm

Sheep bladder tapeworm is common throughout Australia. When eggs are swallowed by sheep, cattle, pigs, or goats the larvae hatch and migrate through the liver to the body cavity. Resultant liver damage leads to condemnation of vast quantities of liver.

Dog flea tapeworm

Dog flea tapeworm infests dogs throughout Australia. The egg must be swallowed by larval fleas to develop within the flea (intermediate host). The flea is then eaten by the dog, which then becomes infested with the adult tapeworm. The dog flea tapeworm is the most common tapeworm of domesticated dogs. It may infest children, but does not cause serious harm. In addition to the obliteration of tapeworms it is obvious that one must control flea populations with appropriate insecticides and rigid hygiene to prevent re-infestation.

Other dog tapeworms require hares, rabbits, rats, mice, fowls, and fish as their intermediate host.

All dog tapeworms may be removed efficiently with reputable products such as Scolaban, Bunamidine hydrochloride, equivalent to 200 mg Bunamidine (Burroughs Wellcome & Co. Ltd). Scolaban tablets are administered orally on an empty stomach without crushing the tablet. It is preferable to feed a normal evening meal and dose the next morning. A light feed may follow 3 hours later. Treated dogs should be rested for 24 hours and not subjected to strenuous exercise or excitement. Animals suffering from heart disease or severe debilitation should be given two-thirds of the recommended dose under veterinary supervision.

Dosage:

Under 2 kg	¼ tablet
2–5 kg	½ tablet
5–9 kg	1 tablet
9–18 kg	2 tablets
18–27 kg	3 tablets
27–36 kg	4 tablets
Over 36 kg	5 tablets

Scolaban eliminates tapeworms without purging. Both the head and body of tapeworms are killed within the intestine, and tapeworm segments are not usually observed in the stools following treatment. The stools may be loose after Scolaban treatment. Some dogs may vomit, but if not within one hour of treatment, efficiency is not reduced. Scolaban may be administered during pregnancy.

When hydatid infestation is diagnosed or suspected, treatment should be repeated in 48 hours and dogs should be treated regularly at monthly intervals to prevent re-infestation.

Bunamidine is an irritant to the eyes. Avoid transferring any particles to the eye.

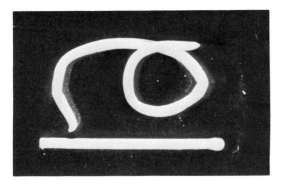

The adult *Toxocara canis*, or roundworm, is a very large worm

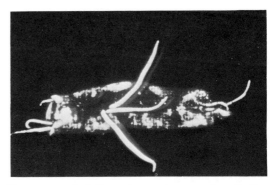

The presence of adult roundworms has caused penetration and rupture of the wall of the small intestine, causing infection of the abdomen and death. Infections of roundworms should be controlled *before* adults reach this size

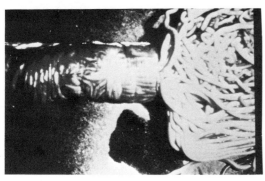

Fully-grown adult roundworms in an infection which has got out of control. The adults have completely blocked the small intestine, killing the pup

In the small intestine of an infected pup there is usually a mixture of adult roundworms laying fresh eggs alongside hatching larvae from in-coming infective eggs which the dog picks up daily by mouth

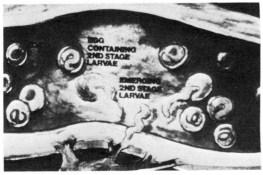

Once swallowed, the eggs hatch and roundworm larvae quickly pass through the wall of the intestine to enter a vein, where they are rapidly transported to the liver by the portal vein system

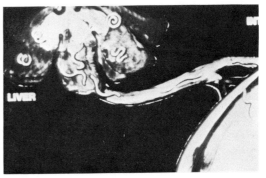

Roundworm larvae migrate within the liver for a few days causing some damage before re-entering the veins which drain blood from the liver to the heart. They are now third-stage larvae, shown here as plump red worms

233

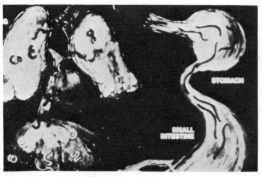

This photograph shows the whole process from the egg hatching to the re-entry of the young worms into the intestine from the lungs. The tissue migration takes about two to three weeks to complete

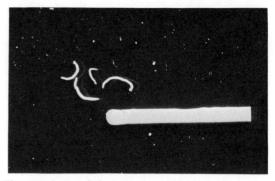

The actual size of the hookworm. Although this is the smallest of the important dog worms, it is definitely the most dangerous

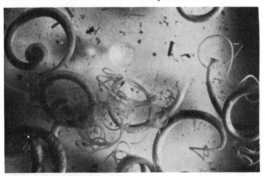

This shows how the adult whipworms appear when taken fresh from the dog

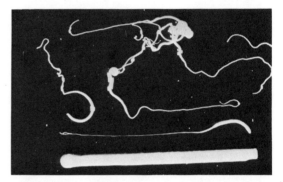

This photograph clearly shows the characteristic whip-like appearance of this parasite. The head is at the thin end and the thicker 'whip handle' contains the reproductive organs. The head is found attached to the deep layers of the lining of the caecum and causes inflammation. The caecum is part of the large bowel of the dog

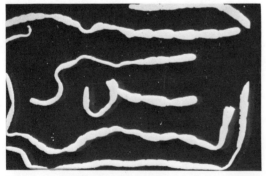

Tapeworm is not often a problem in terms of health. The common Dipilidium tapeworm of dogs uses a flea to complete its development, hence rigid flea control will assist in controlling this parasite

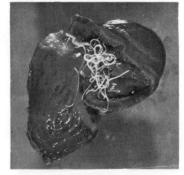

Heartworm, *Dirofilaria immititis*

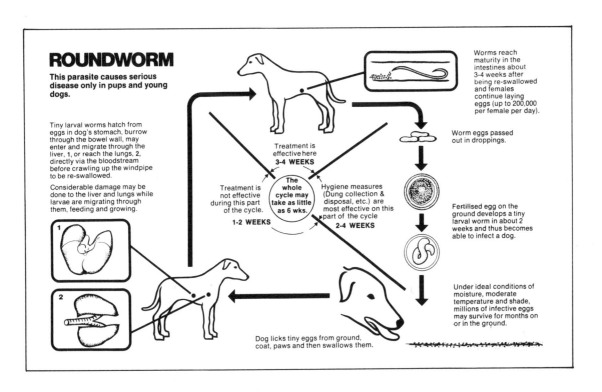

ROUNDWORM

This parasite causes serious disease only in pups and young dogs.

Tiny larval worms hatch from eggs in dog's stomach, burrow through the bowel wall, may enter and migrate through the liver, 1, or reach the lungs, 2, directly via the bloodstream before crawling up the windpipe to be re-swallowed.

Considerable damage may be done to the liver and lungs while larvae are migrating through them, feeding and growing.

Treatment is effective here **3-4 WEEKS**

Treatment is not effective during this part of the cycle. **1-2 WEEKS**

The whole cycle may take as little as 6 wks.

Hygiene measures (Dung collection & disposal, etc.) are most effective on this part of the cycle **2-4 WEEKS**

Worms reach maturity in the intestines about 3-4 weeks after being re-swallowed and females continue laying eggs (up to 200,000 per female per day).

Worm eggs passed out in droppings.

Fertilised egg on the ground develops a tiny larval worm in about 2 weeks and thus becomes able to infect a dog.

Under ideal conditions of moisture, moderate temperature and shade, millions of infective eggs may survive for months on or in the ground.

Dog licks tiny eggs from ground, coat, paws and then swallows them.

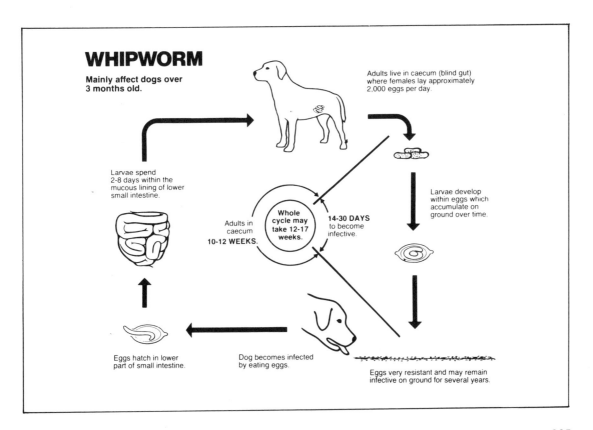

WHIPWORM

Mainly affect dogs over 3 months old.

Adults live in caecum (blind gut) where females lay approximately 2,000 eggs per day.

Larvae spend 2-8 days within the mucous lining of lower small intestine.

Adults in caecum **10-12 WEEKS.**

Whole cycle may take 12-17 weeks.

14-30 DAYS to become infective.

Larvae develop within eggs which accumulate on ground over time.

Eggs hatch in lower part of small intestine.

Dog becomes infected by eating eggs.

Eggs very resistant and may remain infective on ground for several years.

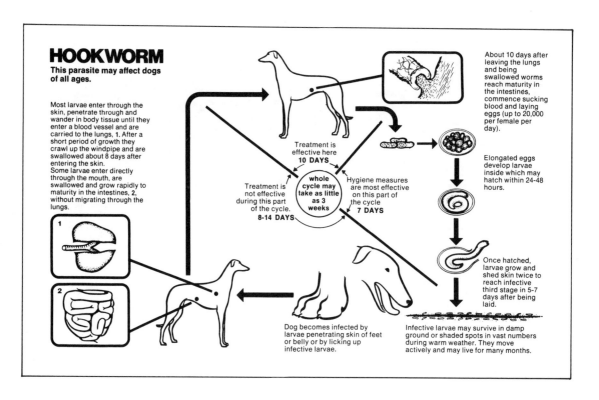

HOOKWORM

This parasite may affect dogs of all ages.

Most larvae enter through the skin, penetrate through and wander in body tissue until they enter a blood vessel and are carried to the lungs, 1. After a short period of growth they crawl up the windpipe and are swallowed about 8 days after entering the skin.
Some larvae enter directly through the mouth, are swallowed and grow rapidly to maturity in the intestines, 2, without migrating through the lungs.

About 10 days after leaving the lungs and being swallowed worms reach maturity in the intestines, commence sucking blood and laying eggs (up to 20,000 per female per day).

Treatment is effective here
10 DAYS

Treatment is not effective during this part of the cycle.
8-14 DAYS

whole cycle may take as little as 3 weeks

Hygiene measures are most effective on this part of the cycle
7 DAYS

Elongated eggs develop larvae inside which may hatch within 24-48 hours.

Once hatched, larvae grow and shed skin twice to reach infective third stage in 5-7 days after being laid.

Dog becomes infected by larvae penetrating skin of feet or belly or by licking up infective larvae.

Infective larvae may survive in damp ground or shaded spots in vast numbers during warm weather. They move actively and may live for many months.

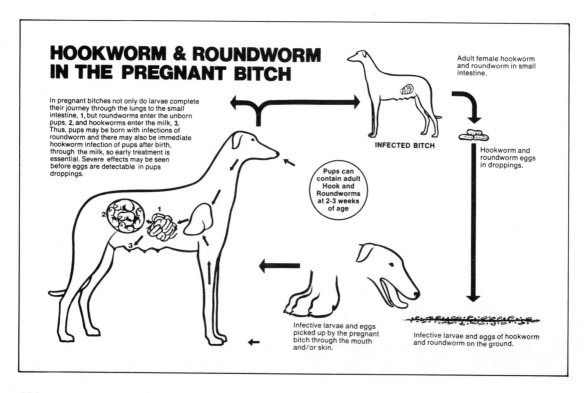

HOOKWORM & ROUNDWORM IN THE PREGNANT BITCH

In pregnant bitches not only do larvae complete their journey through the lungs to the small intestine, 1, but roundworms enter the unborn pups, 2, and hookworms enter the milk, 3. Thus, pups may be born with infections of roundworm and there may also be immediate hookworm infection of pups after birth, through the milk, so early treatment is essential. Severe effects may be seen before eggs are detectable in pups droppings.

Adult female hookworm and roundworm in small intestine.

INFECTED BITCH

Pups can contain adult Hook and Roundworms at 2-3 weeks of age

Hookworm and roundworm eggs in droppings.

Infective larvae and eggs picked up by the pregnant bitch through the mouth and/or skin.

Infective larvae and eggs of hookworm and roundworm on the ground.

18

TRAINING

Learning what a trainer does,
does not make a trainer.

The effort that could be spent on training a racing greyhound is almost limitless, the only effective brake being the cost and the time available to the trainer. From the stand-point of expense, it would be unwise to spend more than the value of the expected benefits.

It is a requirement that owners, owner-trainers, trainers, and handlers of greyhounds be appropriately registered with the relevant State body and that licences be annually renewed. A person registered as an owner cannot train the greyhound himself. A handler is a person who is given permission to handle greyhounds on the racetrack on behalf of a registered owner or trainer. A person to become registered as a handler must be at least sixteen years of age or seek special permission from the appropriate authority.

There are numerous and varied ideas and approaches to greyhound racing both in this country and in other countries throughout the world. Nevertheless, the goal is unvaried—to develop and maintain the greyhound's ability to the fullest possible extent and to achieve the best results possible on the racetrack—not on the trial track!

In formulating a training programme, certain factors must come under consideration: purpose, past experience in training, the nature and general condition of the dog, and the attitude of the trainer. The purpose of training should be the creation of the opportunity to develop both the skill of the dog and of the trainer. They are acquired through study and through practical experience and the application of learning to experience in solving problems. Clarity of training method is served by a specific exposition of the basic facts or assumptions on which a programme rests. There is no generally accepted theory of learning and some authorities feel that learning occurs through emotional experience, such as fear. For example, many of us may remember our refusal to learn to swim, but, on being thrown into the water, we learned because of our fear of drowning. Similarly, the trainer, like the animal, learns through instinct, observation, and chance. Clarity and brilliance in teaching won't necessarily make a man or a dog learn; you can lead them to class, but you can't make them think. Greyhound training is two-sided, one side of which is theory, the other, the actual practice and proficiency in training when theory is applied and the goal attained.

Some of the characteristics of a sound training programme include:
1. A clear, determined objective.
2. The careful, graduated training and guidance of the dog.
3. Constant review of results achieved.
4. Correction of unsatisfactory results by locating, analysing, and correcting problems.
5. Utilisation of the resources of the trainer and of the dog to the best possible advantage and to the best balance.
6. Evaluation of over-all performance.

Plans may misfire through lack of experience. Good judgement marks the trainer who intelligently applies knowledge and common sense. If the cause of error is poor judgement, whether due to inadequate education or experience, or failure to use appropriate information in decision making, correction can generally be made. The trainer may improve his education, acquire broader experience, or learn to take better stock of the situation before making a decision. In training a greyhound it is vital that mistakes be discovered in time and corrective steps be taken. The ability of the trainer to develop the dog to its fullest potential, the effectiveness of that which the trainer has learned both theoretically and practically, foresight, and sound decision making can be measured in the performance of his dog. However, in some instances, the trainer is not necessarily responsible for poor results as the dog may lack the ability to be a good performer for reasons unconnected with the trainer. Whether the trainer undertakes to inquire into the dog's performance or assigns the animal to another trainer, time must be spent in ferreting out causes of poor results. Because the passage of time may make the recall of facts quite difficult, it is necessary to record the daily work programme and performance of the dog and to make a note of any medication or treatment administered to the animal. Discovery of mistakes may come too late for effective action but such information should be interpreted in terms of implications for the future. No trainer is really completely successful unless he can correct mistakes and the best way to correct mistakes is to avoid them.

The trainer needs to be willing to learn and to take advantage of new knowledge and techniques. This necessitates a humble approach to his success and limitations. The intelligent digesting of articles and books affords a great contribution to the trainer. It is possible that in the future there might be special greyhound training establishments in which trainers at all levels would be able to spend time on being brought up to date on a specific area of new knowledge and technique. More and better techniques in greyhound training must be found if the widening gap between knowledge and practice is to be narrowed.

Another important point for the trainer to grasp is the necessity to obtain the right information in the right form and at the right time. Tailoring information requires much intelligence. Trainers themselves must become involved in tailoring the information they require and they should realise that information gathering and summarising is of great importance. The trainer must often settle for small advances so that cumulatively, and over a period of time, larger advances may be made.

The main aim of the greyhound trainer is to develop and maintain a high level of fitness in his dog. Attention should be directed toward improving the strength, stamina, speed, suppleness, and skill of the animal. Two more requirements are time and effort. Stamina or endurance implies not only the ability to carry out a vigorous exertion, but also the ability to recover at a sufficiently rapid rate to repeat the exertion. This is particularly important in training greyhounds for coursing. One method of increasing

stamina is by the interspersion of fast and slow walking. Another method is by the use of a set programme of exercises which become progressively harder, but the time allowed for their performance becomes gradually shorter.

Sleep and rest are as important in maintaining the health and fitness of the dog as is proper nutrition and exercise. Sleep offers the only sure means of recuperation for the nervous system and it is during sleep that most of the tissue building and repair takes place. The sleep needed depends on the age, activity, and mental development of the animal, and it must be remembered that a shorter period of sound, uninterrupted, restful sleep is more beneficial than a longer period of semi-conscious tossing about. Sleep patterns differ widely with individual dogs. The positive physical well-being of the dog is closely allied with his mental fitness, which is essential in the discharge of his daily work performance.

It is inadvisable to subject a dog to fast, vigorous exercise without first gradually developing and maintaining an adequate level of fitness in the animal. It is important to develop the dog's fitness at a rate that suits him without him becoming sore and stiff. Galloping a dog into condition is a malpractice; there must be preparatory walking. Muscle injury is frequently the result of galloping dogs before they have been conditioned to perform such exercise. The training programme should aim at:
1. Increasing the strength of important muscle groups needed for galloping.
2. Increasing the ability of muscles employed in essential body movements so that they may function efficiently.
3. Increasing the speed of response of the important body muscles.
4. Maintenance of joint mobility and muscular suppleness.
5. Improving the efficiency and capacity of the heart, lungs, and other organs.
6. Increasing the dog's capacity for physical exertion.
7. Improving the dog's rate of recovery from vigorous exertion.

Unless adequately exercised, muscles will become weak and inefficient. A bulging, sagging belly resulting from weakened abdominal muscles is detrimental to good conformation. Muscle efficiency will develop through regular, vigorous exercise. It has been estimated that fit muscles will use forty per cent less energy to do the same work. A fit dog is less susceptible to injury, and, if injured, recovers more rapidly. Regular, vigorous exercise plays a prominent role in controlling the dog's weight.

All greyhounds should have some body fat. However, excess fat storage, particularly around vital organs, impairs physical efficiency and health by making, e.g., the heart work harder. A high level of fitness cannot be reached when a dog is overweight. The accumulation of fat can be prevented or reduced either by reducing the carbohydrate intake or by increasing the physical activity of the dog. It is perhaps best to employ a combination of the two. It is essential that the trainer realises the importance of finding out his dog's best racing weight and the necessity for constantly checking its weight. The trainer who is able to maintain his dog at a constant, best racing weight is to be admired, while those who allow their dog's weight to fluctuate at almost every start indicate that the trainer has still a lot to learn. If the dog performs well at his first important race start then this is a guideline as to his correct weight. Correct racing weight is the weight at which the dog wins or produces his best. Allowance must be made for alteration in the dog's weight as he matures.

The weight of a greyhound presented to race shall not vary more than 1 kilogram either way from its declared weight nor 1 kilogram from the greyhound's weight at the previous start at the track concerned. Such weight shall be recorded by a weighing official of the club when the greyhound is first presented for racing and the trainer must acknowledge in writing the weight recorded. This weight must remain in force for three months unless the greyhound changes trainer. No variation in weight shall be allowed for a minimum period of fourteen days.

The capacity and efficiency with which the greyhound can function depends on the degree of development of both muscular and organic power through a regular training programme. The level to which these powers can be developed is influenced by such factors as conformation, the diet, presence or absence of disease or injury, rest, and sleep. The greyhound is physically fit only when his muscular and organic power is sufficiently developed to perform with the highest possible efficiency. Heredity and health are determining factors which affect the development of the dog's potential physical capacity. This capacity varies with individual dogs, e.g., some dogs could undergo adequate training for their lifetime and never come close to being good per-

formers simply because they weren't 'built' for it. The top level at which the dog can perform physically at the moment prior to undergoing a training programme is known as his acquired capacity because it has been acquired or developed through physical activity in his daily routine. A pup reared in a large run may have developed quite a high acquired capacity because he has had sufficient opportunity and space to exercise. The greyhound's body, like a car, functions most efficiently well below its acquired capacity. A car driven at a top speed of 150 kilometres per hour uses more petrol per kilometre than when it is driven at 60 kilometres per hour, which is well below its capacity. The dog's body functions in the same manner in that the ratio of work performed to energy expended is better when it functions well below acquired capacity. Wastage of energy can be avoided by training the animal to a level of physical capacity well above the level required to perform a particular exertion. This is achieved by the combination of a balanced, regularly performed exercise programme. The capacity of the dog increases as he progressively increases the load on the muscular and organic systems. Exercise increases the stamina of the animal and consequently provides a greater energy reserve.

Similarly, as a balanced diet must be composed of sufficient quantities of the proper types of food to ensure adequate nutritional requirements, so should a balanced training programme be composed of an adequate amount of the proper type of physical activity in order to sufficiently exercise the important parts of the animal such as the muscles of the shoulders, abdomen, back, and hind quarters, as well as the heart, lungs, and blood vessels. It is important to realise that no single activity provides a truly balanced development for all parts of the animal's body as this can only be attained by regular exercise of varying types. A combination of slow and fast walking, trotting, galloping, and swimming is most beneficial. Many greyhound trainers incorporate swimming as part of their over-all training programme, particularly in the summer months. This form of exercise is very valuable in maintaining fitness in greyhounds with chronic wrist or metacarpal problems as there is no jarring of bone or joint in the water. Swimming twice weekly is generally sufficient, commencing at three minutes for the initial swim and increasing by one minute each successive swim up to a maximum of eight to ten minutes. Following a swim in salt water the coat should be rinsed thoroughly with fresh water to avoid itching and drying of the skin. Care must be taken to ensure that the dog's ears do not collect and retain water and so lead to serious ailments.

It is of paramount importance that any training programme commence at a low level of activity and progressively work upwards. It is also essential that the animal be warmed up sufficiently, e.g., a short walk or perhaps a short, straight handslip, before strenuous activity such as galloping. The older the dog, the more necessary proper warming up becomes in order to avoid strained muscles. I have frequently observed handlers standing or crouching down with their dog in the parade ring prior to the race instead of walking the dog to warm it up.

No greyhound should be subjected to any sort of training programme without first ensuring that the animal is in good health. The dog should undergo a general examination carried out by a veterinarian, and a sample of the dog's faeces should be taken for testing and the dog should then be wormed with the appropriate anthelmintic. The dog must be clean inside and out prior to the commencement of training. The importance of ridding the dog of worms cannot be emphasised too strongly as a dog harbouring worms cannot be expected to perform well. The dog's vitality is sapped and good food and work are wasted. Training a greyhound infested with worms is very much like trying to build a house with no foundations. The dog must be free from fleas and lice as these parasites are a continual source of annoyance to the animal. It is also advisable to have the dog checked by a reputable muscle man who is educated and experienced in the knowledge of the structure of the greyhound and the cause and effect of injury to these structures. He should possess the ability to remedy such damage or refer the trainer to a veterinarian if necessary.

Greyhounds differ widely in temperament and habits and to train greyhounds successfully it is necessary to understand each one thoroughly. The trainer should recognise the likes and dislikes of his dog and arrange the training programme accordingly. Many problems may confront the trainer which will require his utmost vigilance. The trainer who trains all dogs the same and feeds all the same should devote his time to some other occupation for this will never bring about worthwhile results.

Experience is a distinct advantage in greyhound training because the experienced trainer is more apt to notice changes in the conditions of his dogs than is the novice. Most experienced trainers are pleased to advise the newcomer, but it should be borne in mind also that many will give advice who are totally unqualified to do so.

The sooner a pup learns to chase the better, and this stage of training may commence quite early. The use of a squeaker toy or a rabbit skin may prompt the pup to chase with keen interest and enthusiasm. Activities which serve to excite the pup's interest in moving objects are of paramount importance. Never chastise a pup for chasing and biting at moving objects as this may cause confusion with regard to the right and the wrong thing to do. One cannot deter the pup from chasing some objects and then expect him to chase others. Prompting the pup to chase generally pays off when he is introduced to the racetrack where he will become very enthusiastic when he sights the mechanical lure and the older dogs in pursuit.

Preliminary education, such as handling and teaching the pup to lead, may commence at about four months of age. The young pup must become accustomed to noise, traffic, bright lights, crowds, travelling, and other dogs. It is advisable to take the pup for a ride to the trial track occasionally and allow him to observe other dogs and to become accustomed to the racetrack atmosphere. Some dogs become quite timid and others very vicious when in the track atmosphere. Fear of the starting boxes, noises, and other dogs and their handlers may be detrimental to a potential winner during his racing career.

Generally speaking, dogs should not be introduced to serious training routines before they are sixteen months old and bitches before they are fifteen months old. This allows time for them to mature and while some pups come to hand much earlier and win races, eighteen months is a reasonable age for a pup to make his debut on the racetrack. Investigation has revealed that the majority of greyhounds which have raced at a young age either break down or have very short racing careers. The pup's education should not be forced and the dog should not appear on the racetrack until such time as he has been correctly educated. Top performance appears to be at the age of approximately three years. A greyhound generally races from the age of eighteeen months for about four years,

The Neil Rolins trained Anne's Record 'ran her rivals off their feet in the 1974 Ladies Bracelet over 512 metres at Angle Park, Adelaide. Setting a solid pace in front—the best they could do was chase her home' *(By permission of W. Atkins)*

depending on the care and attention that he has been afforded, upon the number of race starts and upon the gameness, enthusiasm, and general condition of the animal.

The reason for graduation of the exercise programme is so that the animal adapts without undue strain and with substantial improvement in general health and appearance. It is false to assume that big dogs require more walking than smaller ones. The amount of walking an animal requires is dependent upon such factors as weight, sex, age, and constitution. Some animals cannot cope with long walks and it is up to the trainer to decide the correct amount of exercise for his particular dog. It is essential to avoid overwork. It is generally conceded that the bulk of the exercise be given in the cool of the evening during the summer months or very early in the morning. A dog should not be subjected to physical exertion in the heat of the day.

During the preliminary phase of approximately six to ten weeks walking, depending on the dog's acquired capacity, patience is essential. Within three to four weeks there should be noticable improvement in the dog's muscular and general condition. The dog should be walked morning and evening when training commences approximately 3 kilometres in the morning and 1·5 kilometres at night for the initial two or three weeks. There should be a gradual increase in the pace of the walk over a given distance. Many trainers prefer to walk their dogs at a constant pace for a specific time rather than walk a set distance. Walking should be performed on firm surfaces where possible in order to toughen the dog's pads and keep the toenails short. It is detrimental to walk the dog on bitumen if he has soft pads or if the bitumen is hot, as this can cause serious damage to the

dog's pads. On returning from each walk, the dog's feet must be thoroughly inspected to ensure that there are no cuts or foreign matter of any kind lodged between the toes or in the pads. Toenails should also be checked. Foreign bodies may penetrate the pads and unless the dog's feet are thoroughly inspected and cleansed following exercise these particles may pass unnoticed and lead to injuries and infection which will hinder training considerably. The toenails require constant attention and must never be permitted to grow too long. With the greyhound in the normal standing position, one should easily be able to slide a piece of thin cardboard between the toenails and the ground. The dog must also be groomed and massaged on returning from his work and then be confined to his kennel. The principal meal should be given in the evening when the dog has cooled down following exercise. Under no circumstances should food be given until all signs of exertion have disappeared as indigestion and other disorders can often be traced to the practice of feeding animals before they have cooled down. The dog should not be permitted to drink excessively while he is still hot after exercise. A small drink is sufficient. After the dog has cooled down he may drink his fill. Ample, regular opportunity for elimination of waste, in addition to the time taken while out walking, must be allowed. An animal should be allowed to empty out every four hours.

When the dog has become conditioned by walking he is ready for a combination of walking and straight hand-slips over distances of 200 to 300 metres once a week. Once the dog has become accustomed to being hand-slipped alone, a competitive element may be introduced. The use of a squeaker toy and/or rabbit skin generally

241

prompts the dogs to run from the assistant to the trainer with enthusiasm.

It is an offence to exercise greyhounds without muzzles and off the lead, and it is well that the trainer considers the harm that incidents involving greyhounds without muzzles do to the sport. Greyhounds should not be released on the beach or public reserves, etc., where they may attack other dogs, the reporting of which is to the detriment of other trainers and the sport generally. Greyhounds are not to be led or exercised in public parks without the permission of the respective councils, and when permitted to be led or exercised in public parks must afford full respect to any conditions made by the local governing bodies. All greyhounds led on public streets or highways must be properly muzzled and not more than four greyhounds may be led at any one time by one person. Also, no person under the age of sixteen (unless accompanied by an adult) may lead or exercise greyhounds in public places.

Following two or three weeks of walking combined with hand-slipping and free galloping perhaps twice a week, a dog should be ready for track practice. Trialling should commence in daylight and when the dog is doing well, he may be trialled under lights.

Various establishments throughout Australia specialise in educating and breaking-in greyhounds and all have the necessary equipment for training. Four to six weeks is the usual period of time taken to educate a greyhound to mechanical lure racing. Each stage of education must follow in correct sequence. If a fault is not corrected immediately it occurs, then it generally becomes extremely difficult—sometimes impossible—to remedy.

Owners and trainers are warned that any person trialling a greyhound on an unlicenced trial track is liable to penalty. Furthermore, persons who have been issued private trial track licences must not allow other owners and trainers to make use of the same licence.

It is advisable to begin the pup's education on a straight track, so that he may learn to balance himself, with the lure starting from a position in front of the boxes so that the dog can be hand-slipped from in front of the boxes and allowed to chase the lure when it commences to move. The lure is gradually slowed down and the dog encouraged to tug and bite at it. Pat the dog and perhaps reward him with a small piece of biscuit for his effort. The pup should be given straight

hand-slips behind the lure over 100 metres, gradually increasing at each run to a distance of 300 metres.

When the pup has become accustomed to hand-slipping and is chasing keenly he may be introduced to the starting boxes:

1. The dog is placed in the box, backwards from the front, with the rear door of the box closed so that he fails to realise that there is a back door and thinks that there is only one way out—from the front—and he will not turn in the box. When the front lid is raised the dog is allowed to jump out and grab a rabbit skin with a squeaker toy hidden inside it.

2. Both the front lid and back door of the box are left open. The trainer puts the dog in the box and crouches behind the dog, holding on to him around his neck and chest. If the dog is held in this manner he is unable to somersault or turn in the boxes and he is able to see the lure in front of him. The lure driver starts the lure from a position just in front of the boxes. When the lure moves away, allow the dog to chase it.

3. During this stage of box training the front lid is closed and the back door remains open. The dog is placed in the box and held as in phase 2. An assistant teases the dog in front of the boxes with a rabbit skin so that he is encouraged to 'get down'. The dog is allowed to jump out and grab the lure. Another method of teaching a dog to get down in the boxes is to cover the front of the box with a bag, leaving a 25-centimetre gap at the bottom of the lid so that the dog learns to box keeping his head down and tilted toward the rail side from which position the lure will first be sighted. Once again he is teased from in front of the boxes with a skin tied to the front rail side corner of the lid. The lure is started, the skin disappears above the dog's head as the lid opens and he jumps out and chases the lure. The trainer should give the dog a firm push from behind as the lid goes up, to push him out of the box.

4. The lure is then brought from a position behind the boxes and each day it is advanced faster so that the dog learns that he must jump quickly in order to catch it.

5. Both doors of the box are closed and the trainer stands aside and observes the dog. If the dog turns in the box, quickly tap the front of the box and call or tease him so that

he faces the correct way. If he continues to turn in the boxes, go back to the previous stage and start again from there. Once a dog has entered the box never take him out through the back door. Under no circumstances should anyone bang on the back door of the box, as the dog may turn around to investigate. Care must likewise be exercised to avoid shutting the dog's tail in the door.

When the dog is boxing well and chasing keenly on the straight, he may be introduced to the circular track. Do not spend unnecessary time on the straight track as the dog may find difficulty in changing from the straight to the circle. The first thing is to hand-slip the dog behind the lure on a curve, not on a straight section, because when the lure disappears momentarily round a curve the dog may pull up because he cannot see the lure. It is wise to hand-slip the dog on the circular track with the lure kept close to him so that he does not lose sight of it and so that he is enduced to rail. The first time, the dog may be hand-slipped over about 200 metres. The initial run from the boxes should be carried out with the front lid and back door open because the lure now appears from behind the boxes and the dog cannot sight it until it is in front of the boxes and going away. Much care is required during this phase of training. The next phase is executed with the front lid closed and the back door open, the dog being given a firm push from behind when the lid opens. The next stage is carried out with both doors closed. Each phase must be repeated until the dog is familiar with, the procedure before commencing the next phase. The run up to the lure should be the same as at the track so that the dog does not become impatient and stand up.

If the dog is doing everything right but is a little tardy from the boxes it may prove beneficial to starve him for a day to make him hungry and to tease him from in front of the boxes with a piece of meat on a string. As the lid goes up let him jump out and grab the meat. It would be appropriate at this stage to mention that it has been my experience that greyhounds are either good or bad box dogs; it appears to be an inbuilt quality. However, correct breaking-in has a great bearing on the dog's ability to box well. I am inclined to think that brilliant box dogs use their ears to assist them, as I have watched them cock their ears and listen for the first mechanical click intimating that the lid is about to spring.

The value of fast boxing is that it ensures a clear run into and around the first bend and from then on it is a solo trial. If the dog has boxed brilliantly and cannot win, then it has been beaten by a better dog for there can be no complaints that it could not get through or that it was checked. There are those who trap brilliantly and possess superior early pace but cannot sustain the gallop. There is no sight more common than to observe a dog hugging the rails all the way but unable to get through because several others have gone over to the rail by virtue of quicker boxing or superior early pace. A slow boxing railer is an expensive combination. Fast boxing and early pace are more valuable assets than railing ability.

When the dog is chasing keenly by himself he may be permitted to trial in the company of other dogs. It is advisable to trial with an old dog initially, perhaps an old brood bitch that has been maintained in good condition by regular exercise and good feeding, and allow the young dog to win and so gain confidence. It is unwise to trial pups that have been reared together because they may play and not keep their mind on the task at hand. Under no circumstances should any pup be broken in by allowing him to follow another dog around the track because he may become content always to do so. A young dog requires plenty of field practice and should be gradually permitted to run with an increasing number of dogs until he is able to run in a field with seven other dogs. Some dogs learn to work a field easily; others require a great deal of practice. It is unwise to trial continually with the same dogs because the pup may think that he can always beat opponents easily or vice versa. Always use a different starting box and trial over varying distances. Never trial a dog over a constant distance, say 400 metres, because he may become accustomed to this and when he competes in races he may pull up when he has run 400 metres. Don't trial a dog over long distances if it only serves to exhaust him; only when he is trialling well over shorter distances should he be subjected to the longer journey. The secret of training is to determine exactly how much exercise a specific dog requires. An over-worked dog is just as bad as an under-worked one.

If a dog fights or fails to chase keenly in the company of other dogs, then he must be trialled alone and later returned to the company of others. Dogs which refuse to chase or exhibit

243

Upsandowns, owned and trained by Neil Rolins, demonstrates the decided advantage of superior early pace in getting a dog out of trouble *(By permission of W. Atkins)*

fighting tendencies when competing with other dogs are useless for track racing under N.C.A. rules. Fighting tendencies may be the result of lack of condition, climate, ill-health, injury, diet, boredom, or a particular track. A run on live game may brighten the dog's ideas, but too much training on live game may cause the dog to become disinterested in the mechanical lure. Generally speaking, fighting is not attributable to any pugnacious streak. The fact that there is no fighting on the coursing field where the dogs are utterly engrossed in their efforts to take the quarry suggests that boredom behind the lure may be one of the basic factors. It is interesting to note that the incidence of interference is lower in the United States of America where the hare is driven much closer to the dogs—almost under their noses—and not infrequently two hares are mounted on an extended arm to intensify and maintain interest and also to allow dogs at the rear of the field to sight the hare.

Some trainers prefer to spell their pups for four to eight weeks after breaking-in so as to allow them to develop both physically and psychologically. Other trainers continue with conditioning and racing while the pup's mind is still fresh and on the job.

Once the dog is doing well and not making any mistakes, he may be taken to different tracks so that he may become accustomed to a variety of conditions. Many trainers permit their dogs to become specialists at one particular track. Greyhound tracks vary in shape, degree of banking, contour of the surface, and type of surface, and all exert an important influence on the dog's performance. The position of the starting boxes in relation to the first bend, and the position of the finishing line in relation to the last bend, are factors which determine the speed with which a dog can negotiate a certain track. The longer the distance from the boxes to the first turn the better the chance for fast box dogs with early pace to negotiate the first bend clear of their rivals. If the distance from the starting boxes to the first turn is relatively short then the dogs have only limited time to place themselves before the bend comes up and consequently more bumping and interference occurs. Another important consideration is the distance from the last bend to the finishing line. A strong finisher has little opportunity of overtaking his rivals when the winning post is only a short distance from the last bend. Strong finishers generally do better on larger tracks with longer distances between the starting boxes and the first bend, and between the last bend and the finishing line, as they can then exhibit their ability to overtake on the long straight run.

Very few greyhounds win first up on a race-track and it is wise to trial a dog several times on the special trial nights provided, so that he can familiarise with the track before being nominated for a race at that track. Greyhounds should not be trialled excessively as this is a swift, sure way of turning a dog sour. It is unnecessary to excessively trial a mature, experienced dog. Many a good dog has left its best on the trial track. Never expect a pup to beat an older more experienced dog until such time as the pup has gained sufficient experience. Running young dogs with top-class performers before they have gained adequate experience is frequently the cause for the pup 'turning it in'. It is very foolish malpractice to give dogs more than one run at the trial track at any one visit to the track. There are those who believe that if the dog does poorly at his first trial he should be trialled until he does well. This practice only serves to exhaust the dog and to make him irritable and may convert an honest dog into a non-chaser or a fighter.

Experienced dogs which have proven their ability to handle fields and are performing well in races should not be run with other dogs at trials as there is a distinct risk of injury when the dog runs solo, let alone in a field. Once a dog is having his share of galloping on the racetrack and is performing well it is unnecessary to trial him. Many dogs racing once a week do not require a mid-week gallop and a straight handslip is all that is necessary. Handslips are preferable to trials once the dog is broken-in as there is less risk of injury. Experience will dictate the frequency with which dogs should be trialled. If a dog exhibits the tendency to become hard and drawn muscularly, trialling should be reduced and the dog fed on soft food, such as stew, for several days. A greyhound which races over 450 to 500 metres generally requires approximately 6 kilometres walking per day with straight hand-slips over 200 to 300 metres about twice a week. Once the dog is 'muscled up' and well conditioned, walking may be reduced to a minimum. It is imperative to keep the dog fresh.

Many good dogs have been ruined, both physically and mentally, by being savaged by other dogs in the catching pen at the conclusion of the race and are often reluctant to race again. The handler should waste no time in taking charge of his dog immediately all dogs have entered the pen. When trialling or racing a dog a handler must always be present at the catching pen to catch the dog, preferably someone with whom the dog is familiar. The handler should deter his, or any other dogs, from fighting in the pen and must make a mental note of any bumps received by his dog so that the trainer may attend to these areas. If a dog is leading and chasing too hard into the pen and looks as though he will crash into the catching pen gate, make some sort of noise or wave your hands to deter him and distract him.

The majority of those who observe greyhound racing only watch the dog that they are interested in, largely because it is impossible to watch all runners at all points of the race and at the same time concentrate on a specific dog. A good method of observing a race is to pick out the first four dogs at the start of the race and follow them to the first bend, then, as they negotiate the turn, run your eye back to the last four dogs and watch them run into the back straight. A quick look up front will reveal how the leaders are progressing, and when they approach the last bend take another look at the last four. By this time the leaders will have straightened up for the run to the finishing line and your interest will then swing again to the leaders. A look back at the second division at this point will enable you to observe fast-finishing moves, although these should not be over-estimated as all greyhounds must exhibit something in order to have been included in the race. Some are fast box dogs, others work the field well and exhibit superb track sense, and others are strong finishers. Investigations of records has revealed that the majority of winners come from the first four dogs at the first turn, proving the theory that early speed gets a dog out of trouble which may occur in a closely packed field, and is a decided advantage.

If the race does not always go to the swift, or to the one that takes the shortest route home, or to the fast beginner, then there must clearly be some quality or compound of qualities that comprise the star greyhound. Versatility—therein lies the clue to the really first-class greyhound and certainly to the great greyhound. To be capable of winning consistently on all shapes and sizes of tracks, in all conditions of going and from all boxes, requires something more than speed and the ability to negotiate a curve. Versatility is the one quality common to nearly all top-class performers. At one time or other they have occupied all eight boxes. Just as certainly they were not always clear at the first bend and inevitably in some of their races they were checked and did not gain a clear run—but they still managed to win. The factor of paramount importance in greyhound racing is the dog's ability to place itself; to adapt his tactics according to the circumstances of each race, to pick a path through and round his converging rivals, instinctively to avoid coming on the inside or outside of a dog that he senses is going to veer. Versatility and superb track sense mark the truly great greyhounds who adorn the Hall of Fame. 'The keynote of consistency is a versatile technique.'

Although the race is won when the dogs reach the finishing line, one must not forget to observe where one's dog runs over the last section from the finishing line to the catching pen because, although the race is over for the spectators, it is not over for the majority of the dogs as they are still excited by the pursuit of the hare until it disappears. The dog that finishes on well and runs strongly over the line may do well over the longer distance. Generally speaking, a sprinter is a shorter-coupled dog than a long-distance performer and possesses a bigger back and is more heavily muscled. The sprinter expends energy at a higher rate and accumulates the waste products of rapidly expended energy at a faster rate than the stayer and consequently covers a shorter distance in so doing than the stayer before he has completed his run.

One must recognise the particular talent of one's dog and exploit this gift. If greyhound racing were conducted solely on straight tracks the fastest dog would invariably win. The interest and excitement of the sport is derived from the fact that a race is conducted, for the most part, on an oval track. A dog's ability to negotiate a bend faster than his rivals is largely dependent on balance, muscular control, coordination, and mental urges. The railer takes the shortest route by hugging the rails, whereas the wide runner takes the longer route but by virtue of this width has more scope to stretch out freely and thereby compensate a little for adopting the longer route. Few wide runners are beaten by more than their 'excess trip'.

It is a very common view that boxes 4 and 5 are bad boxes which handicap the dog to a large extent, but I feel that this depends on the type of dog which occupies these boxes. The importance of the box draw is very largely dependent on the characteristic manner of running of the particular dog. It would be foolish to claim that the box draw has no significance, but I am of the impression that the character and capabilities of the dog occupying the box far outweigh the allocation of the box. It is well to bear in mind that a good dog is capable of winning from any box.

The physical attributes of two litter brothers may be identical to the naked eye and they may be trained by the same trainer and also have been reared under the same conditions; however, one may be a champion and the other unable to run out of sight on a dark night or win a low-grade race. Since the answer to this is not a physical one it must therefore be the result of mental or nervous factors. In the company of other dogs some greyhounds are totally overcome by their will to beat their rivals and to capture the lure first, while others are satisfied to go along for the gallop and may even reach the lead and then ease and wait for the other dogs. Perhaps the most apt definition of this inbuilt quality is 'the will to win'. Careful rearing and schooling are important factors without which no greyhound is likely to develop the inherent potential that has been bred into it.

The trainer who is consistently successful in greyhound racing possesses critical and analytical judgement. He is able to assess the characteristics of the greyhound; to read a race and so identify and analyse the occurrences in the race that may hinder a particular dog; to assess the effect of the track on the performance of the dog; and to evaluate the dog's performances and predict whether or not he will win a specific race. The trainer must analyse the cause and effect of the trouble that occurs and understand why it occurs. Some greyhounds cause trouble in a field because they cut the bends or veer out as they approach a bend or they may be keen railers who happen to have drawn an outside box or they may break considerably and shorten their stride as they approach a bend. These 'faults' may be the consequence of inexperience, previous trouble and injury to the dog, soreness, or lack of courage. Trouble can also be caused by fast box dogs with little early pace. Others lead most of the way, railing keenly, then suddenly fade, causing the field to bunch up behind them, often presenting the race to a wide runner who misses the trouble by virtue of his position on the track. Wide runners appear less likely to run into trouble than the railers, unless the railer is a fast box dog with good early pace. Some greyhounds are just unlucky and happen to be in the wrong place at the wrong time, while others are totally lacking in track sense. Others don't have the courage to go through the pack unless there is a very wide gap.

A feature of the greyhound in top condition is his inability to remain still, moving incessantly from one foot to the other with its head moving attentively in various directions. This does not infer that hard pulling on the lead is an indication of fitness. The fit dog may often be observed kicking up the ground when it has emptied out, physically bouncing and exhibiting every sign of mental alertness. It has a bright, glistening coat and a crisp walk. The greyhound's spine is virtually a spring operated by the dorsal muscles and these muscles, when well-conditioned, possess a firmness that extends down to the tail, causing it to jut out a little in contrast to being flat on the buttocks. Bear in mind that the tail is an extension of the spine. Masturbation often occurs with healthy, fit, male dogs and this may seriously detract from their performance.

It is imperative that all traces of sand and/or dirt be removed from the dog's feet, especially from the area around the toenails. Wash the dog's feet in warm, soapy water, using a soft toothbrush to brush dirt away from the quicks. If necessary, medications should be employed on the pads, interdigitally or around the quicks. It is wise to carry a container of disinfectant in the car which should be used to wash the dog's feet following trialling or racing. A container of water and a sponge is also useful for sponging out the dog's mouth and wiping sand from his face.

It is inadvisable to trial dogs on tracks, both straight and circular, which are not equipped with a proper catching pen. Very often the dog will sustain neck and/or spinal injury as a consequence of being pulled up quickly and grabbing on to the lure, running into the lure, or being dragged around the track, or being permitted to tug at the lure while the lure driver runs the lure slowly around the track. This violent tugging and pulling against the lure results in serious injury to the dog, which may not be readily observed. If these injuries pass undetected, permanent damage may result. These injuries are frequently overlooked and the trainer sees a decline in the dog's keenness and alterations in his performances over a period of time. The dog may have once been a fast box dog and then slowly or suddenly, depending on the extent of his injury, loses that ability. Trainers are advised to trial only on well-equipped trial tracks. A leading greyhound authority has stated, in regard to those injuries which are not obvious: 'These injuries are only observed during a neurological

(of the nervous system) examination of the dog, and it is then found that many of the so-labelled "sookie" dogs that squeal with each touch actually have reason to do so.'

The trainer must be able to evaluate and establish the quality of his greyhound while his veterinarian must be able to maintain the physical quality of the greyhound. It is of paramount importance that one comprehends the meaning of these two difficult tasks. The majority of manipulative techniques required for the correction of spinal faults are of an extremely difficult nature and, if performed by unqualified persons, can result in extreme harm to the greyhound. The task of muscle manipulation is an extremely difficult one requiring great skill and there are very few experts.

The practice of rolling the fan or shoulder is a process of over-extending the fan musculature; this serves to relieve the spasmed fan muscle, thus allowing the greyhound to continue to function. In this instance it is pointed out that 'a ligament that runs over the shoulder blade and down the back aspect of the whole shoulder is twisted, or out of place'. No such ligament is to be encountered in this area. What is present is a spasmed fan muscle which may be likened to spasm of the calf in the human subject. Just as this calf spasm can be relieved with stretching of the calf muscle by over-extension of the foot, so the spasmed fan muscle can be relieved by over-extending the fan in drawing it upwards towards the shoulder blade. Many greyhounds have performed following procedures of this nature, but one must bear in mind that nothing has been done to correct the spinal problems in the saddle which have caused the fan to spasm initially, and which are also responsible for other symptoms in the greyhound.

Needling of muscles in the greyhound is a tremendously abused practice, which in the majority of cases only serves to add insult to injury. There are instances where needling of a muscle is indicated, but this does not condone the haphazard puncturing of greyhounds. The majority of injuries which arise in a greyhound which has been needled are, in reality, referred pain; the sciatica pain of low back injuries and the abdominal wall pain of appendicitis in the human subject serve as good examples of the phenomenon of referred pain. Needless to say, unqualified, inexperienced, and unskilful needling of greyhounds is to be avoided.

19

ELECTRO–MEDICAL APPARATUS

ULTRA-SOUND

The therapeutic application of ultrasonic energy began in Europe approximately thirty years ago following the discovery of the physical and biological effects of high-frequency sound by the American biophysicists, Loomis and Wood. Although the ultrasonic therapy unit was designed for use by the medical profession for the treatment of physical conditions pertaining to humans, it is now in common use by the greyhound fraternity throughout the world. Ultrasonic therapy is a recognised, well-proven, medical means of treating injuries to greyhounds and has become an extremely valuable form of therapy in many conditions.

The production of ultra-sound

The human ear cannot hear sound waves with a frequency of more than 20 000 vibrations per second. Vibrations of higher frequencies are termed ultrasonic waves, and the frequencies found most suitable for ultrasonic therapy range between 700 000 and 1·1 million vibrations per second.

The equipment employed for the therapeutic application of ultrasonic energy consists of a generator of high-frequency current and an applicator, sometimes referred to as a 'sound head'. The generator produces electric oscillations of the desired frequency which cause the transducer in the applicator to vibrate and generate ultrasonic waves. The ultrasonic waves are emitted from the diaphragm in front of an oscillating quartz crystal, the diaphragm being the face of the sound head. This ultrasonic energy is transmitted to the tissue by contact with the applicator face, but since air is a poor conductor of ultrasonic energy, an air-free contact must be established between the applicator and the tissue. This is accomplished by providing a coupling medium between the applicator and the skin. Paraffin oil is commonly used for coupling to relatively smooth areas. Better coupling for treatment of irregular surfaces is obtained by immersion of the part and the applicator in water.

The effects of ultra-sound on body tissues

Ultrasonic energy can penetrate body tissues to a depth of 5 centimetres or more and there affects the tissues in three ways simultaneously:

1. *Thermally*

The ultrasonic energy is transformed into heat and appears as a raising of the temperature of the tissues through which it is passing. Heat is produced at a depth of approximately 5 centimetres. The blood flow is increased, which in turn stimulates the healing process.

2. *Mechanically*

The sound waves cause a vibratory massage effect on the tissues. The mechanical effects described as 'micro-massage' or 'intra-cellular massage' have been likened to a stirring action within the tissues.

3. *Chemically*

Chemically the ultrasonic energy increases cellular permeability and therefore the diffusion of ions into and out of the cells.

The blood supply and lymph drainage of the tissue are considerably improved—more than through the application of heat alone. (Lymph is a tissue fluid which acts as a medium of exchange between the blood and the tissues). A combination of these effects cannot be obtained by other means.

Types of output

The output is measured in watts per square centimetre of the treatment head and most machines are calibrated for outputs from 0·25 to 3·0 W/cm².

Ultrasonic therapy is available with two basic types of output:

1. *Pulsed wave*

When the output is interrupted it is known as pulsed ultra-sound. Generally speaking, pulsed ultra-sound is preferred to continuous ultra-sound in those conditions where it is believed that the beneficial effects are produced by the mechanical action of ultra-sound. Pulsed operation enhances the micro-massage effect on the tissues while greatly reducing the heat effect, compared to continuous operation.

Most machines enable a pulsed beam to be used. In a pulse ratio of one to five the energy is emitted for 2 milliseconds in every 10. In treating areas in which underlying bone is covered by a relatively thin layer of soft tissue, it is desirable to employ the pulsed ultra-sound in order to avoid periosteal pain. Its use appears to be preferred in application to nerve root areas. Pulsed ultra-sound will not replace the use of continuous ultra-sound, but its use has a definite advantage in some cases.

Authorities have reported the value of pulsed ultra-sound in treating soft tissue disorders soon after injury. It is extremely efficient in getting rid of oedema and improving function of the joint. Investigations have revealed that pulsed ultrasonic therapy produces relief in cases of sciatica which proved resistant to other forms of therapy, including continuous ultra-sound. Pulsed ultra-sound is also advantageous in the treatment of neuritis, where the application of heat ordinarily increases the pain.

2. *Continuous wave*
When the ultrasonic beam is uninterrupted it is referred to as continuous ultra-sound. Generally speaking, the use of the continuous wave is restricted to conditions in which the major aim is to deliver heat to the affected tissues, for example, in the treatment of myalgia.

The waves pass into the tissue in a direct beam. The intensity is greatest opposite the centre of the sound head and decreases as the distance from the head increases. The frequency of the waves controls the depth of penetration.

Operation
1. Liberally coat the area to be treated with paraffin oil.
2. Plug the machine into the main, making certain that the output control is at zero.
3. Select the treatment time, which should range from four to eight minutes per muscle area, with the equipment timer—this also automatically switches on the machine.
4. Place the sound head against the area to be treated and increase the output control to 1·5 or 2·0.

5. If treating a fleshy area (no prominent bones), continuous output may be employed. If the area is bony, select pulsed output by changing the switch from continuous output.
6. Move the sound head over the area to be treated, which should not exceed 20 to 25 square centimetres, in a slow, rhythmical manner in the same direction as the dog's hair. It is essential that the sound head remain in perfect contact with the tissue being treated throughout the treatment time. The sound head must be held in such a position that the beam enters the tissues at right angles to the surface.

Precautions
The machine must never be switched on without the sound head being in contact with the tissues being treated, otherwise damage may result to the crystal, which is located in the sound head.

At all times a liberal quantity of oil should be applied to the treatment area—otherwise burning may occur. It is recommended that a maximum of 2 watts be used, unless treating a very deep-seated sore area.

Application techniques
Since ultrasonic energy cannot pass through air, a suitable medium must be provided to conduct the ultrasonic waves from the face of the applicator into the tissues. The use of paraffin oil is recommended as a coupling agent when application is to be made to a relatively smooth area. In the case of an irregular area, such as the foot, where it would be difficult to maintain good contact by direct application, it is recommended that the area to be treated and the applicator be immersed in water in order that the transmission of the ultra-sound to the part will be efficient.

1. *Direct application*
In employing the direct or contact application method, it is necessary to maintain an adequate film of coupling agent over the entire area to be treated. Apply sufficient coupling agent to cover the area and spread by moving the face of the applicator over the skin. The face of the applicator should also be coated with oil. Proceed with treatment. This method generally ensures application of sufficient oil for efficient conduction of ultra-sound during the entire treatment. However, it may be necessary to add more coupling agent if it becomes apparent that a good contact is not being effected.

The applicator is moved with moderate pressure over the skin in a slow, rhythmical manner with a pattern of movement which may require some variation in accordance with the area being treated. The applicator may be moved in small over-lapping circles at the rate of approximately one circle per second. An alternative method is stroking, with one stroke over-lapping by half the width of the applicator. The stroke length is about 5 centimetres. The applicator is moved gradually in the direction perpendicular to the stroke in a field of about 5 to 13 centimetres at any one time. Both methods of application allow for relatively uniform distribution of the ultra-sound. When treating a relatively large area, rather than attempting to cover the entire area during the treatment time, it is recommended that one small section of the area be treated at a time until the entire area has been covered.

2. *Underwater application*

Warm water, which may be de-gassed by boiling, or distilled water, is placed in a suitable container such as a large, plastic bucket. The water is warmed both for the comfort of the dog and maximum penetration of energy. The part to be treated and the applicator are immersed in the water and the face of the applicator is moved slowly over the area with a spacing of 1 to 3 centimetres being maintained between the face of the applicator and the area being treated. The entire sound head may be immersed in the water. Movement of the applicator may be similar to that employed in the direct application method with the coupling agent.

Air bubbles may collect on the face of the applicator or on the skin during treatment. These should be brushed away with a finger as they will interfere with efficient conduction of the ultra-sound.

Make sure that the unit is properly grounded if treatment is given using a grounded container such as a wash bowl. If the unit is not grounded, it would be possible for the dog or the operator to receive a low voltage shock from the applicator and this may alarm the dog and render him very reluctant to undergo further treatment.

The output should be increased 0·5 watts per square centimetre for the underwater application technique in order to compensate for absorption in water.

Disinfection of the applicator

The treatment surface of the applicator may be disinfected by the use of alcohol or other cold disinfectant.

Position of the dog and the operator during treatment

The position assumed by the dog during treatment will naturally be dependent upon the area to be treated. However, the position should be such that the dog will be comfortable and relaxed throughout the treatment and such that the applicator may be easily manipulated and good contact maintained with the tissues without placing the operator in a position that will induce strain or fatigue.

Ultrasonic dosage

Investigation has revealed that the following general principles are quite well established and agreed upon by most authorities.

1. Pain is an indication of over-dosage.
2. Ultrasonic therapy is a safe procedure if the dosage is kept below the threshold of pain and if the operator is completely familiar with the unit.
3. A 5-to-10-minute treatment time over a given area is sufficient.
4. Therapeutic intensities of 0·5 to 3·0 watts per square centimetre have been employed with good results. The lower intensities are recommended for the treatment of acute conditions and the higher intensities for the treatment of chronic conditions.
5. When ultra-sound is applied to the nerve root area in addition to the affected area, the intensity over the nerve root should not exceed 0·5 watts per square centimetre, and application should be made with a circular or stroking motion.

Damage to tissue may occur from an excessive dose of ultra-sound. Periosteal pain is an indication of excess intensity and, if this occurs, the applicator should be moved at a faster rate and/or bony prominences avoided and the power should be reduced. Over-dosage may exaggerate symptoms.

Factors determining ultrasonic dosage

1. *The nature of the condition*
a. Acute
b. Chronic

As might be expected, acute conditions respond more rapidly and with fewer applications than chronic conditions which may necessitate long series of treatments. Occasionally, very dramatic results occur.

Johnny Wood (Discretions−Pincano), a great tracker and a proven sire who won top-class races in the United Kingdom before importation to Australia where he won on numerous tracks over varying distances *(Courtesy of South Australian Greyhound Trainer)*

2. *The nature of the tissue*
a. Fleshy, such as found in the biceps.
b. Thin, such as found in the wrist, where the periosteum is close to the surface of the skin.

3. *The method of treatment*
a. Direct application using a coupling agent such as paraffin oil.
b. Underwater application is generally employed where irregularities of the treatment surface prevent efficient coupling with oil − as on the wrist, foot, etc., − or when the pressure of the sound head causes discomfort.

4. *Treatment time*
The treatment time may vary from 4 to 15 minutes, depending on the extent of the area being treated.

5. *Dosage figures*
Dosage figures in watts per square centimetre. For direct application using paraffin oil suggested dosage figures are:

Acute conditions	
Thin tissue	Thick tissue
0·5 to 1·0 W/cm^2	1·0 to 1·5 W/cm^2

Chronic conditions	
Thin tissue	Thick tissue
1·5 to 2·0 W/cm^2	2·0 to 2·5 W/cm^2

Indications for use of ultrasonic therapy
While a great many conditions have been treated using ultrasonic therapy, most authorities are in general agreement that ultrasonic therapy has definite value in the following conditions:
1. Musculo-skeletal dysfunctions such as:
Myositis − inflammation of a voluntary muscle.
Periarthritis − inflammation of the tissues around a joint.

251

Osteoarthritis—chronic multiple degenerative joint disease.

Rheumatoid Arthritis—a chronic disease of the joints, usually polyarticular, marked by inflammatory changes in the synovial membranes and articular structures and by atrophy and rarefaction of the bones. In late stages deformity and ankylosis develop.

Fibrositis—inflammatory hyperplasia of the white fibrous tissue of the body, especially of the muscle sheaths and fascial layers of the locomotor system. It is marked by pain and stiffness.

Bursitis—inflammation of a bursa (a sac or saclike cavity filled with a viscid fluid and situated at places in the tissues at which friction would otherwise develop).

Tendinitis—inflammation of tendons and of tendon—muscle attachments.

2. Conditions where vasodilation (dilation of a vessel; especially dilation of arterioles leading to increased blood flow to a part) is desirale. Ultrasonic therapy should not be employed too soon after muscle injury as it may, by virtue of its vibratory effect, loosen the cells which are responsible for sealing ruptured blood vessels and so cause unwanted and prolonged bleeding. Treatment should involve shrinkage and sealing of ruptured blood vessels, using ice packs, during the first 5 to 10 hours following damage; after this the blood supply to the area can be increased very effectively using ultrasonic therapy. The ultrasonic energy explodes dead cells into smaller fragments, thus facilitating their removal via the bloodstream; it also reduces oedema and aids repair processes.

3. Reduction of oedema (the pressure of abnormally large amounts of fluid in the intercellular tissue spaces of the body; usually applied to demonstrable accumulation of excess fluid in the subcutaneous tissues).

4. Induration (the process of hardening or quality of being hard) following haematoma (a tumor or swelling containing effused blood).

5. Inflammatory conditions.

6. Traumatic disorders. (trauma—a wound or injury).

7. Reduction of adhesion formation. Ultrasound is capable of separating collagen fibres from each other and of changing the tensile strength of tendons to permit greater extensibility. (Collagen—an albuminoid, the main supportive protein of skin, tendon, bone, cartilage, and connective tissue).

Contra-indications

1. Operators are warned against the use of ultra-sound in the following cases:
2. Near the heart and specialised tissues such as the eye, ear, and nose.
3. In the vicinity of the reproductive organs.
4. In cases of pregnancy.
5. Over areas of malignancy.
6. Areas of impaired blood supply.
7. Areas of reduced sensory perception, i.e., areas where there is loss of feeling or sensation.
8. Over growing bone ends in puppies.
9. Directly over the spinal cord, visceral plexi (any large interior organ in any one of the three great cavities of the body, especially the abdomen) and large autonomic ganglia (functionally independent or self-controlling groups of nerve cell bodies located outside of the central nervous system).

Cavitation

Cavitation results from excessive ultrasonic energy disrupting the tissues. This should not occur, provided that the dosages do not exceed the recommended levels. Cavitation produces a remarkable phenomenon of erosion of surfaces and is used in ultrasonic soldering to remove surface film. It is also one method of measuring ultrasonic power.

MUSCLE STIMULATION (FARADISM)

The principle of muscle stimulation has been known and used for many years. In the past the apparatus required was cumbersome and unreliable and although worthwhile results were achieved, many trainers lost interest. Today, with the development of transistors, miniature electrical parts, and printed circuits, faradic pulse stimulation has returned as an efficient and easily used precision instrument.

In 1831, Michael Faraday, an English physicist, discovered the principle of induction of electric current, that is, the production of electrical properties in one object by another without contact between them. Prior to the electronics era, current for muscle stimulation was obtained from induction coils and was known as 'faradism'. Today, a similar current is obtained from an entirely different source but is still referred to as a 'faradic' current or pulse. This

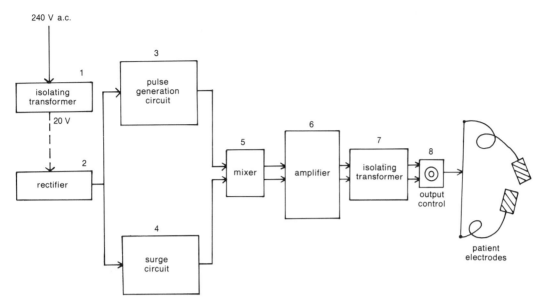

240 V a.c.

1 isolating transformer

20 V

2 rectifier

3 pulse generation circuit

4 surge circuit

5 mixer

6 amplifier

7 isolating transformer

8 output control

patient electrodes

Main circuit components

pulse is actually a series of short-duration electrical impulses, continually repeating themselves. The frequency and duration of the pulses have been carefully devised to safely stimulate muscle and nerve tissue. The equipment is called a faradic pulse generator or stimulator.

Production of faradic pulses

The generator works from the mains power. The output current is produced entirely from electronic circuits. The following diagram shows in simple form the flow of electrical energy through the main components of a typical generator.

The mains isolating transformer (1) is a most important safety factor. Besides reducing the voltage, it isolates the remainder of the circuit from the high-voltage supply. Thus there is no direct electrical connection between the faradic pulse circuit and the mains.

The rectifier (2) converts the now low-voltage current into a specially modulated direct current (d.c.). This provides precision sources of low voltages to the various sections.

The generator circuit (3) produces very short pulses (about 2 milliseconds) of faradic current repeated fifty times per second (50 hz). Control is entirely automatic.

The surge circuit (4) regulates the flow of faradic pulses to a pattern pre-set by the operator. Thus 'on' periods of stimulation and 'off' periods

of rest can be varied to suit individual muscle requirements. Most machines have an 'on' period which adjusts from 300 milliseconds to 3 seconds, while 'off' periods range from 100 milliseconds to 3 seconds.

The electronic mixer (5) combines pulse and surge energy.

The amplifier (6) increases the strength of the currents to provide ample supply for multiple electrodes or water-bath operation.

A final safety precaution is another isolating transformer (7) to ensure that there is no direct electrical connection between the instrument circuit and the patient. The resultant output is termed 'earth free'.

Amplitude or volume control (8) sets the strength of the pulse received by the patient via two electrodes.

Method of use

Faradic impulses are applied to muscle groups through soft metal plates or electrodes. These may be strapped directly on to the skin, over a thick moist pad of paper or cloth; or immersed in a foot bath. Individual muscle stimulation and testing is best carried out with a pencil electrode—a small insulated handle with a metal tip which is hand-held over the nerve or muscle. At the conclusion of treatment time *always gradually reduce amplitude to 0*, then switch off.

Electro-diagnosis is a delicate and relatively

painless procedure which elicits a well-localised muscular response with a minimum amount of current. Every nerve and every muscle, unless deeply covered by other muscles, possesses a small area where it is most easily excited and where a visible contraction can be elicited with a minimal amount of stimulation. This area is called a 'motor point'. The motor point of a normal muscle is usually located near the origin of the muscle belly, where the motor nerve enters the muscle. In a nerve trunk the motor point can be found where the position of the nerve is nearest to the skin. There may be several points of maximal irritability in the course of a long nerve.

The topography of motor points was first studied by Erb and a set of diagrams based upon his studies has been fabricated for the human body. Those doing electrical testing should frequently practise the finding of motor points. There are variations from the normal locations in different dogs and also individual differences in sensitivity to electrical stimulation. The amount of current required to induce contraction will indicate the state of the muscles and nerves. It is of paramount importance to compare contractions of the same muscle on both sides of the body and to note any difference. In this way, reactions of denervation or degeneration can be detected. Muscles to be tested should be relaxed and the dog must be in a comfortable position. When a limb is oedematous, a stronger current will be required to cause contraction and reactions of incomplete denervation may appear to be complete.

Physiological effects

A nerve impulse can be initiated by an electrical stimulus. The intensity of the current used must abruptly rise and fall in a pattern or wave form which will give maximum stimulation to motor nerve fibres. When a motor nerve trunk is so stimulated, a nerve impulse is transmitted to all connecting muscles below the point of stimulation. These muscles then contract in the same way as when receiving nerve impulses from the brain. The degree of contraction depends on the strength and frequency of the current in relation to the size and tone of the muscle group. Thus a suitable electric current, applied to a selected nerve trunk via an electrode strapped to the leg, will cause involuntary contraction of specific muscles in the leg or foot. Even when a nerve trunk has been severed the resultant denervated muscle will respond to direct application of a faradic impulse. Unfortunately, an electric current also stimulates sensory nerve fibres which send an impulse to the brain. Thus an otherwise successful muscle contraction could be accompanied by sudden and severe pain. Such discomfort may be minimised if each electrical stimulus is of very short duration, i.e., the current must 'make' and 'break' in rapid succession.

An important consideration in the physiology of artificial muscle stimulation is that of fatigue. If a muscle is continuously stimulated and kept in a state of full contraction, the individual fibres do not have a chance to relax and recover. Prolonged contraction may lead to duration tetany. To avoid such a dangerous situation, modern faradic circuits incorporate an electronic surger. This surger automatically regulates the duration of each stimulus, and hence the duration of each muscle contraction. The device also controls the intervals between stimuli to ensure adequate rest periods.

In many cases vital muscles may be exercised back to almost full function if they can be 'educated' to work again. Regular faradic treatment can restore muscle tissue to normal function. Electro-therapy may be used to strengthen or re-educate any major muscle group, following injury. Individual muscles may also be stimulated. Even when a nerve supply has been severed, direct faradic stimulation will contract a muscle and help maintain the tissue. Artificial exercise, having the effects of joint and muscle activation, may be given by the use of the faradic current and may be used to prevent disuse atrophy.

Faradic pulse technique

Any lesions must be sealed. The amplitude control should be turned to 0 (off). Set up the electrodes, wrapping the plate in towel or paper to a thickness of about 3 millimetres. Position the electrodes with the active black lead (negative or cathode) connecting to the plate over the motor point, or the origin, of the muscle; or over the main nerve supply. The other electrode (clipped to the red anode lead) goes over the muscle insertion. Always maintain a moist pad between each electrode and the skin. The anode is the return path for current back to the instrument. It is positive and coloured red. The cathode is the electrode which most affects the muscle motor point, or main nerve supply. It has negative

Encanto (Temlee–Chase Of Fame) winning the 1979 Adelaide Cup (South Australia) *(Courtesy of South Australian Greyhound Trainer)*

polarity and is coloured black. This is the 'working' electrode. In cases where individual muscle stimulation or testing is being carried out with a pencil electrode, the anode is the plate electrode and the cathode is the pencil electrode. A small piece of moist towelling is secured over the pencil electrode in this case.

Set each period control to mid-position. Set for surged output. Switch on. Gradually increase amplitude until slight contraction is observed. Adjust the period controls for adequate contraction and rest periods. Sometimes a long 'on' period and a long 'off' period is more effective than just increasing amplitude. The sounder, or buzzer, which gives an audible indication when current is flowing to the patient, will indicate the length of these periods. The electrodes may need to be moved a little to find the best position. Slowly increase amplitude within the level of patient tolerance. Treat for 15 to 20 minutes, or less if the muscles tire in cases of muscle re-education following injury. Maximum treatment time is 30 minutes. Keep the electrodes moist and firmly applied to the skin. At the conclusion of the treatment time gradually reduce the amplitude to 0, then switch the machine off. The initial treatment time should be kept short and gradually increased.

The locomotion of the racing greyhound is dependent upon the correct and coordinated operation of muscles in the manner for which they were designed. If any one muscle is not operating correctly it will tend to throw all the lines of force of other muscles out of balance and there will be a consequent alteration in the gait of the dog. It is therefore of paramount importance that all muscles function correctly to enable the greyhound to perform to its maximum ability.

ELECTROCARDIOGRAPH (HEART SCORE)

The use of the electrocardiograph is one means of achieving a measurement of the racing quality of the greyhound. The electrocardiograph is an instrument that amplifies and records the small voltages produced by the beating heart. It is essentially a string galvanometer with a recording device. The electrocardiogram (ECG) is a record of differences in electric potential initiated by the fibres of heart muscle as they contract. Electric currents spread over the heart and into the tissues around the heart. Some of these currents will spread over the surface of the body and can be recorded from electrodes placed on the right and left wrists and the right foreleg and the left hind leg or the left foreleg and the left hind leg. These are standard positions, but other leads may be used. When first using the machine on the dog it is important to establish which lead configuration works best for that dog. It may be found that the lead combination used on one dog will not work for another. Once a satisfactory combination has been found, this should be noted so that in future it is readily available.

The typical ECG records P, QRS, and T waves. The P wave represents excitation of the atria, QRS waves indicate excitation of the ventricles, and the T wave indicates repolarisation of the ventricles. The P, QRS, and T waves represent one heart cycle. Irregularities in these waves can indicate an abnormal heart condition.

So many factors influence the heart rate that statements concerning rate are only relative to various conditions. Investigation has revealed that a heart rate of 65 beats per minute is a satisfactory level. It is important to note that this is a resting rate, i.e., taken when the dog awakes in the morning and before any exercise has been undertaken. This rate is only a rough guide and may vary markedly. The digestion of a meal increases the strength and rate, partly as a consequence of the activity of the muscles of the stomach and intestine. Muscular exercise increases the heart rate. Emotional excitement affects the heart, e.g., the pounding of the heart as a result of being afraid or the depressing effect from overwhelming fear. Age and size also influence the heart rate. As a pup becomes older and larger, the heart rate becomes slower.

The heart rate is affected by the secretions of endocrine glands. The secretions of the thyroid and adrenal glands exert a marked effect. Thyroxine, the secretion of the thyroid gland, increases the heart rate and epinephrine, the secretion of the adrenal glands, increases both the rate and the strength of the heart beat. The heart is also under the control of nerves from the sympathetic and parasympathetic systems. Sympathetic fibres reach the heart via the cardiac nerves from the cervical ganglia and the first four or five thoracic ganglia of the sympathetic chain. The adrenergic substance released at the nerve endings increases the firing rate at the sinoatrial node and increases the heart rate accordingly. It also decreases the refractory period of the atrioventricular node and neuro-muscular bundle, thus increasing the rate of conduction. Fibres of the parasympathetic system reach the heart via the vagus nerves. Acetylcholine released at the nerve endings slows the heart rate and depresses the firing rate in the sinoatrial node and increases the refractory period for conduction along the neuromuscular bundle of His. (The bundle of His conducts impulses to the muscles of the right and left ventricles, respectively.)

Heart scoring forms a large part of the selection of pups for racing by many trainers. The heart score is a measure of potential ability and this potential is modified by the quality of the environment in which the pup is reared. If the rearing has been poor, then it is frequently found that a pup recording an above-average score may not fulfil this potential. If potential ability is not reflected by real ability, one must take a close look at the quality of the rearing. At the present there appears to be widespread sub-standard dietary management and husbandry techniques employed in the rearing of pups and for this reason the evaluation of a pup's potential by the use of heart scoring tends to be inadequate.

It is of paramount importance that greyhound trainers be totally aware of the fact that safety of operation of electro-medical machines is basically in their hands and not completely in the hands of the manufacturer. It is certainly the responsibility of the seller of such equipment to provide adequate instruction and ensure that the user is not lulled into a false sense of security in the belief that certain machines remove the necessity for close observance of the limits of the application of electro-therapy. Ultra-sound is a very valuable therapeutic device in certain conditions and an aid to maintaining a greyhound's performance *only if used correctly and with a clear understanding of the results to be expected.* Electro-medical apparatus has been a great boon to the greyhound industry but I strongly recommend that any trainer contemplating the purchase of such equipment be guided by proper advice as to what he may expect from the equipment.

GLOSSARY

Acidosis: A pathologic condition resulting from accumulation of acid or loss of base in the body.

Acute: Having a short and relatively severe course.

Adrenal: Situated near the kidney.

Afferent: Conveying toward a centre.

Agglutination: A phenomenon consisting of the collection into clumps of the cells distributed in a fluid.

Anabolism: Constructive metabolism.

Anaemia: A reduction below normal in the number of erythrocytes per mm³, the quantity of haemoglobin, or the volume of packed red cells per 100 mL blood.

Analgesic: An agent that alleviates pain without causing loss of consciousness.

Antagonist: An opponent. A muscle that acts in opposition to the action of another muscle; its antagonist.

Anthelmintic: An agent that is destructive to worms.

Apathy: Indifference.

Aponeurosis: A white, flattened or ribbon like tendinous expansion, serving mainly as an investment for muscle or connecting a muscle with the parts that it moves.

Areolar: Containing minute interspaces.

Articulate: Divided into or united by joints.

Astringent: Causing contraction and arresting discharges.

Atrophy: A defect or failure of nutrition manifested as a wasting away or diminution in size of cell, tissue, organ, or part.

Autoinoculable: Susceptible of being inoculated with virus from one's own body.

Autonomic: Self-controlling; functionally independent.

Bactericidal: Capable of destroying bacteria.

Bolus: A mass of food ready to be swallowed or a mass passing along the intestines.

Bronchiole: One of the finer subdivisions of the branched bronchial tree.

Bursa: A sac or saclike cavity filled with a viscid fluid and situated at places in the tissues where friction would otherwise develop.

Callosity: A circumscribed thickening of skin.

Callus: 1. A callosity. 2. An unorganised meshwork of woven bone developed on the pattern of the original fibrin clot, which is formed following fracture of a bone and is normally ultimately replaced by hard adult bone.

Capillary: Resembling a hair. Any one of the minute vessels that connect the arterioles and venules, forming a network in nearly all parts of the body.

Carcinoma: A malignant new growth made up of epithelial cells tending to infiltrate the surrounding tissues and give rise to metastases.

Cartilaginous: Consisting of or of the nature of cartilage, a specialised fibrous connective tissue forming most of the temporary skeleton of the embryo, providing a model in which most of the bones develop, and constituting an important part of the growth mechanism.

Catabolism: Destructive metabolism.

Catalyst: A substance which causes change in the velocity of a reaction but does not form part of the final product.

Cautery: The application of a caustic substance, a hot iron, an electric current, or other means of killing tissue.

Cavitation: The formation of cavities.

Cellulose: A carbohydrate forming the skeleton of most plant structures and of plant cells.

Chronic: Persisting over a long period of time.

Cilia: Plural of cilium. A minute vibratile, hairlike process attached to a free surface of a cell.

Cirrhosis: A disease of the liver, marked by progressive destruction of the liver cells accompanied by regeneration of the liver substance and increase of connective tissue.

Coagulate: To become clotted.

Collagen: An albuminoid, the main supportive protein of skin, tendon, bone, cartilage, and connective tissue.

Collateral: Secondary or accessory.

Colostrum: A mammal's first milk after whelping.

Condyle: A rounded projection of bone.

Contra-indication: Any condition, especially any condition of disease, which renders some particular line of treatment improper or undesirable.

Copulation: Sexual congress; sexual union between individuals of the opposite sex.

Corpus luteum: A yellow glandular mass in the ovary formed by an ovarian follicle that has matured and discharged its ovum.

Counter irritant: Producing a counterirritation; an irritation which is intended to relieve some other irritation.

Cryotherapy: The therapeutic use of cold.

Crypt: A minute, tubelike depression opening on a free surface.

Deamination: Removal of the amino group, $-NH_2$, from an amino body.

Defecation: The evacuation of fecal material from the rectum.

Dehydration: A condition that results from undue loss of water.

Demarcation: The marking off or ascertainment of boundaries.

Denervation: Resection of or removal of the nerves to an organ or part.

Dermatitis: Inflammation of the skin.

Dermis: The skin, sometimes used with special reference to the corium, or true skin.

Diabetes: A deficiency condition marked by habitual discharge of an excessive quantity of urine, particularly diabetes mellitus.

Dilatation: The condition of being stretched beyond the normal dimensions.

Diuretic: Increasing the secretion of urine.

Dominant: Exerting a ruling or controlling influence.

Eczema: An inflammatory skin disease characterised by varying lesions, with vesiculation, infiltration, watery discharge, and the development of scales and crusts frequently attended by constitutional disturbances as well as local itching and burning.

Efferent: Conveying away from a centre.

Effleurage: Stroking movement in massage.

Ejaculation: A sudden act of expulsion, as of the semen.

Emollient: An agent which softens or soothes the skin, or soothes an irritated internal surface.

Emulsion: A preparation of one liquid distributed in small globules throughout the body of a second liquid.

Endemic: A disease of low morbidity that is constantly present in a human community.

Endocrine: Secreting internally; applied to organs whose function is to secrete into the blood or lymph a substance that has a specified effect on another organ or part.

Enzyme: An organic compound capable of accelerating or producing some change in substance for which it is often specific.

Epidermis: The outermost and non vascular layer of the skin, made up of five layers.

Epiphysis: The end of a long bone, usually wider than the shaft, and either entirely cartilaginous or separated from the shaft by a cartilaginous disc. During the growth period epiphyses are separated from the main portion of the bone by cartilage.

Epithelium: The covering of internal and external surfaces of the body, including the lining of vessels and other small cavities.

Etymologist: One versed in the investigation of the origins and meanings of words and word-forms, tracing their history and growth through various languages, ancient and modern.

Evert: To turn out.

Exfoliation: The falling off in scales or layers.

Extravasation: A discharge or escape, as of blood from a vessel into the tissues.

Extrinsic: Coming from or originating outside.

Exudate: The escape of fuild, cells, and cellular debris from blood vessels and their deposition in or on the tissues, usually as a result of inflammation.

Faradism: Induced electricity. A faradic current of gradually increasing and decreasing amplitude.

Fascia: A sheet or band of fibrous tissue such as lies deep to the skin or forms an investment for muscles and various organs of the body.

Fibrin: A whitish insoluble protein formed from fibrinogen by the action of thrombin (fibrin ferment), as in the clotting of blood.

Fibrinogen: A plasma protein of high molecular weight that is converted to fibrin through the action of thrombin.

Fibrosis: The formation of fibrous tissue; fibroid degeneration.

Fissure: Any cleft or groove.

Fistula: An abnormal passage or communication, between two internal organs, or leading from an internal organ to the surface of the body.

Flora: The bacteria normally residing within the lumen of the intestine.

Follicle: A very small excretory or secretory sac or gland.

Fulguration: Destruction of animal tissue by electric sparks whose action is controlled by a movable electrode.

Fungus: A growth on the body resembling a fungus; a spongy mass of morbid granulation tissue.

Ganglion: A knot or knotlike mass. A group of nerve cell bodies located outside the central nervous system.

Gangrene: An eating sore which ends in mortification. Death of tissue, usually in considerable mass and generally associated with loss of vascular supply and followed by bacterial invasion and putrefaction.

Genitalia: The reproductive organs.

Gestation: The period of development of the young in viviparous (animals bearing live young) animals, from time of fertilisation of the ovum.

Gram negative: Losing the stain or decolorisation by alcohol in Gram's method of staining.

Gram positive: Retaining the stain or resisting decolourisation by alcohol in Gram's method of staining.

Granulation: The formation in wounds of small, rounded fleshy masses.

Haematoma: A tumor containing effused blood.

Haemolysis: Liberation of haemoglobin.

Haemorrhoid: Dilation of a vein about the anus.

Herbivorous: Subsisting upon grasses and herbs.

Histamine: An amine occurring in all animal and vegetable tissues. It is a powerful dilator of the capillaries and a stimulator of gastric secretion.

Histology: That department of anatomy which deals with the minute structure, composition and function of the tissues.

Homogeneous: Of a uniform quality throughout.

Homologous: Corresponding in structure, position and origin.

Hydrous: Containing water.

Hyperaemia: An excess of blood in a part.

Hyperchromic: Highly or excessively stained or coloured.

Hypertrophy: Enlargement of an organ or part due to an increase in size of its constituent cells.

Hypostatic: Abnormally static.

Idiopathic: Self-originated; of unknown causation.

Incubation: 1. The development of the embryo in the eggs of oviparous (producing eggs from which the young are hatched outside the body of the maternal organism) animals. 2. The induction of development, as the development of disease producing micro-organisms in an intermediate or in the ultimate host, or the development of micro-organisms or other cells in appropriate media.

Inferior: Situated below, or directed downward. Used in reference to the lower surface of an organ or other structure.

Inflammation: The condition into which tissues enter as a reaction to injury, the classical signs being pain, heat, redness, swelling, and sometimes added loss of function.

Inherent: Implanted by nature; intrinsic; innate.

Innervation: 1. The distribution or supply of nerves to a part. 2. The supply of nervous energy or of nerve stimulus sent to a part.

Integument: A covering or investment.

Intercellular: Situated between the cells of any structure.

Intercostal: Situated between the ribs.

Interosseous: Between bones.

Intertubercular: Between tubercles.

Intervertebral: Situated between two contiguous vertebrae.

Intramuscular: Within the substance of a muscle.

Invagination: The infolding of one part within another, specifically a process of gastrulation in which one region infolds to form a double-layered cup.

Invert: To turn in.

Ischaemia: Deficiency of blood in a part, due to functional constriction or actual obstruction of a blood vessel.

Keratin: A scleroprotein which is the principal constituent of epidermis, hair, nails, horny tissues, and the organic matrix of the enamel of the teeth.

Keratinisation: Development of or conversion into keratin. The process of becoming horny.

Keratolytic: An agent that promotes separation of the horny layer of the epidermis.

Lesion: Any pathological or traumatic discontinuity of tissue or loss of function of a part.

Lumen: The cavity or channel within a tube or tubular organ.

Lymph: A transparent, slightly yellow fluid of alkaline reaction, found in lymphatic vessels.

Macroscopic: Visible with the unaided eye or without the microscope.

Malleolus: A rounded process.

Matrix: The basic material from which a thing develops; the groundwork on which anything is cast.

Mesentery: A membranous fold attaching various organs to the body wall.

Metabolism: The sum of all the physical and chemical processes by which living organized substance is produced and maintained, and also the transformation by which energy is made available for the uses of the organism.

Mite: Minute animals, related to spiders, which are parasitic on man and domestic animals, producing various irritations of the skin.

Mitosis: A method of indirect division of a cell consisting of a complex of various processes.

Molecule: A very small mass of matter; an aggregation of atoms.

Morphology: The science of the forms and structure of organised beings.

Motor: A muscle, nerve, or centre that effects or produces movement. Producing or subserving motion.

Mucoid: Resembling mucus.

Multilocular: Having many cells or compartments.

Myelin: The fatlike substance forming a sheath around certain nerve fibres.

Myeloid: Pertaining to, derived from, or resembling bone marrow.

Necrosis: Death of tissue, usually as individual cells, groups of cells, or in small localised areas.

Neuritis: Inflammation of a nerve.

Neuron: A nerve cell with its processes, collaterals, and terminations regarded as a structural unit of the nervous system.

Nucleus: A spheroid body within a cell.

Oedema: The presence of abnormally large amounts of fluid in the intercellular tissue spaces of the body.

Orifice: The entrance or outlet of any body cavity.

Oscillation: A backward and forward motion; also vibration, fluctuation, or variation.

Ossification: The formation of bone or of a bony substance.

Osteogenic: Derived from or composed of any tissue which is concerned in the growth or repair of bone.

Palpation: The act of feeling with the hand. The application of the fingers with light pressure to the body surface to determine the consistence of the parts beneath in a physical diagnosis.

Papilla: A small nipple-shape projection or elevation.

Parasite: A plant or animal which lives upon or within another living organism at whose expense it obtains some advantage without compensation.

Pathogen: Any disease-producing microorganism or material.

Pathological: Pertaining to pathology. That part of medicine which treats of the essential nature of disease, especially of the structural and functional changes in tissues and organs of the body which cause or are caused by disease.

Peptide: One of a class of compounds of low molecular weight, yielding two or more amino acids on hydrolysis.

Pericardium: The fibroserous sac that surrounds the heart.

Peripheral: Pertaining to the outward part or surface.

Peristalsis: A wave-like contraction passing along a tube. The movement by which the alimentary canal propels its contents.

Peritoneum: The serous membrane lining the abdominopelvic walls and investing the viscera.

Phagocyte: Any cell that ingests microorganisms or other cells and foreign particles.

Physiological: Pertaining to physiology (the science which treats of the functions of the living organism and its parts).

Plasma: The fluid portion of the blood in which the corpuscles are suspended.

Pleura: The serous membrane investing the lungs and lining the thoracic cavity, completely enclosing a potential space known as the pleural cavity.

Plexus: A network or tangle.

Portal: An entrance or opening; especially the site of entrance to an organ of the blood vessels and other structures supplying or draining it.

Protoplasm: The only known form of matter in which life is manifested.

Pruritis: Itching.

Pulmonary: Pertaining to the lungs.

Putrefaction: Enzymic decomposition, with the production of foul smelling compounds.

Recessive: Not exerting a ruling or controlling influence.

Refract: To cause to deviate.

Reticulo endothelial: Pertaining to tissues having both reticular (netlike) and endothelial attributes.

Ruminant: One of the order of animals which have a stomach with four complete cavities through which the food passes in digestion. The division includes oxen, sheep, goats, and deer.

Sarcolemma: The delicate elastic sheath which invests every striated muscle fibre.

Sebaceous: 1. Pertaining to sebum. 2. Secreting a greasy lubricating substance.

Sebum: The secretion of the sebaceous glands; a thick, semi-fluid substance composed of fat and epithelial debris from the cells of the malpighian layer.

Sensory: Pertaining to or subserving sensation.

Serofibrinous: Both serous and fibrinous.

Sesamoid: Resembling a grain of sesame. A type of short bone occurring mainly in the feet and found embedded in tendons or joint capsules.

Spermatogenesis: The process of formation of spermatozoa.

Spermatozoa: Plural of spermatozoon. A mature male germ cell, the specific output of the testes.

Sphincter: A ringlike band of muscle fibres that constricts a passage or closes a natural orifice.

Spinous: Pertaining to the spine or to a spinelike process.

Sporadic: Occurring only occasionally; not widely diffused.

Squame: A scale or scalelike substance.

Stasis: A stoppage of the flow of blood or other body fluid in any part.

Stria: A narrow bandlike structure.

Stricture: The abnormal narrowing of a canal, duct, or passage.

Subcutaneous: Occurring beneath the skin.

Subfascial: Situated beneath a fascia or band of fibrous tissue.

Submucosal: Situated beneath the mucous membrane.

Subtendinous: Situated beneath a tendon.

Superficial: Pertaining to or situated near the surface.

Superior: Situated above, or directed upward. Used in reference to the upper surface of an organ or other structure, or to a structure occupying a higher position.

Sympathetic: The sympathetic nerve or system of nerves.

Symptom: Any functional evidence of disease or of a patient's condition.

Synapse: The anatomical relation of one nerve cell to another; the region of contact between processes of two adjacent neurons, forming the place where a nervous impulse is transmitted from one neuron to another.

Synovia: A transparent alkaline, viscid fluid, resembling the white of an egg, secreted by the synovial membrane, and contained in joint cavities, bursae, and tendon sheaths. Also called synovial fluid.

Synthesise: The artificial building up of a chemical compound by the union of its elements.

Tachycardia: Excessive rapidity in the action of the heart. The term is usually applied to a pulse rate above 100 per minute.

Therapeutic: 1. Pertaining to therapeutics, or to the art of healing. 2. Curative.

Thrombin: The enzyme derived from prothrombin which converts fibrinogen to fibrin.

Thromboplastin: A factor essential to the production of thrombin and proper hemostasis.

Tubercle: A nodule, especially a solid elevation of the skin, larger in size than a papule or a small eminence, such as a rough, rounded eminence on a bone.

Ultrasonic: Pertaining to mechanical radiant energy having a frequency beyond the upper limit of perception by the human ear, that is, beyond about 20 000 cycles per second.

Vasoconstriction: The diminution of the calibre of vessels, especially constriction of arterioles leading to decreased blood flow to a part.

Vasodilation: A state of increased calibre of the blood vessels.

Vertebra: Any one of the bones of the spinal column.

Villus: A small vascular process, especially such a protrusion from the free surface of a membrane.

Vincula: (Plural of vinculum)—a band or bandlike structure.

Viscera: (Plural of viscus). Any large interior organ in any one of the three great cavities of the body, especially in the abdomen.

INDEX